100% Perfect Girl

Vol. 3

WANN

NETCOMICS

100% Perfect Girl Vol. 3
Story and Art by Wann

English translation rights in USA, Canada,
UK, NZ, Australia arranged by
Ecomix Media Company
395-21 Seogyo-dong, Mapo-gu, Seoul, Korea 121-840
info@ecomixmedia.com

- Produced by Ecomix Media Company

- Translator Soyoung Jung

- Graphic Designers Hyekyoung Choi, Minchul Shin

- Cover Designer purj

- Editor Jim Scaife

- Managing Editor Soyoung Jung

- President & Publisher Heewoon Chung

NETCOMICS

P.O. Box 3036, Jersey City, NJ 07303-3036
info@netcomics.com
www.NETCOMICS.com

ISBN: 978-1-60009-218-3

First printing: July 2007
10 9 8 7 6 5 4 3 2 1
Printed in Korea

100% Perfect Girl

Vol. 3

WANN

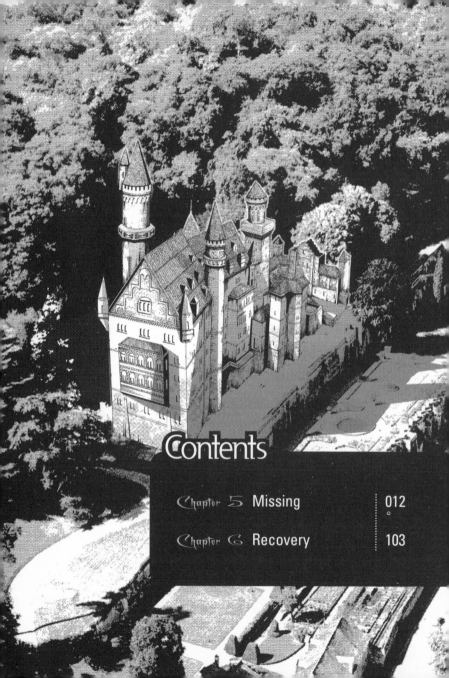

Contents

Chapter 5 Missing — 012

Chapter 6 Recovery — 103

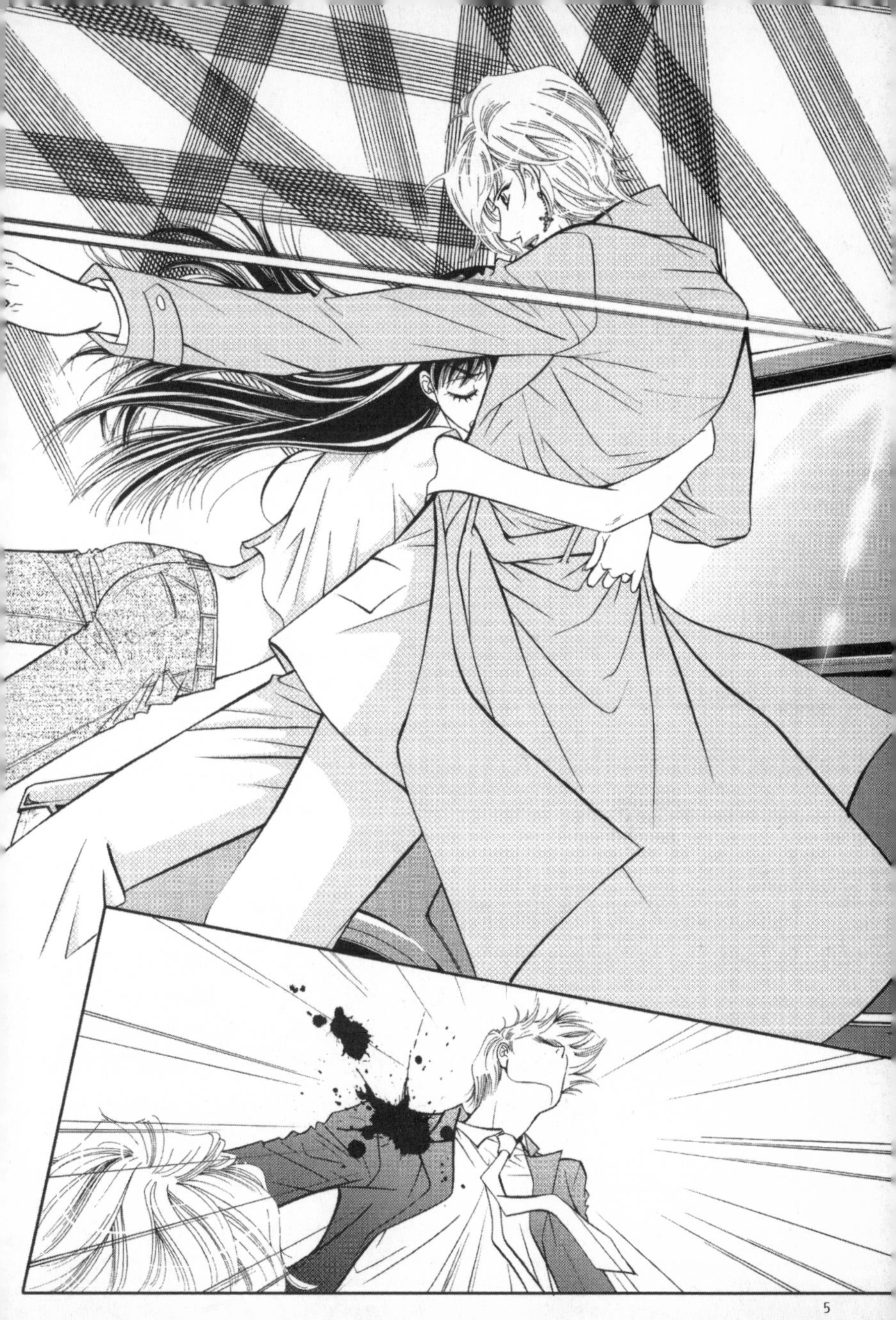

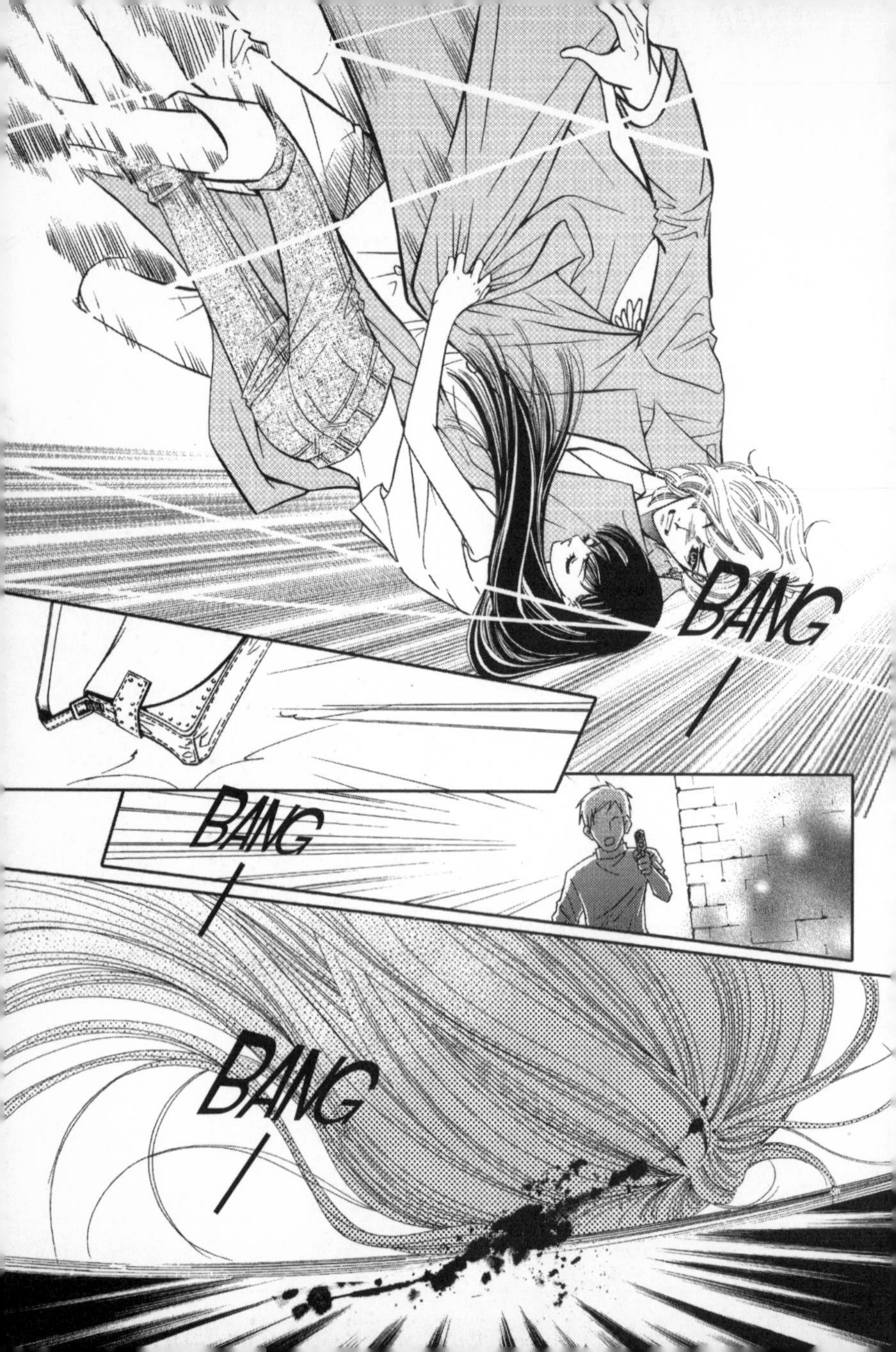
BANG
BANG
BANG

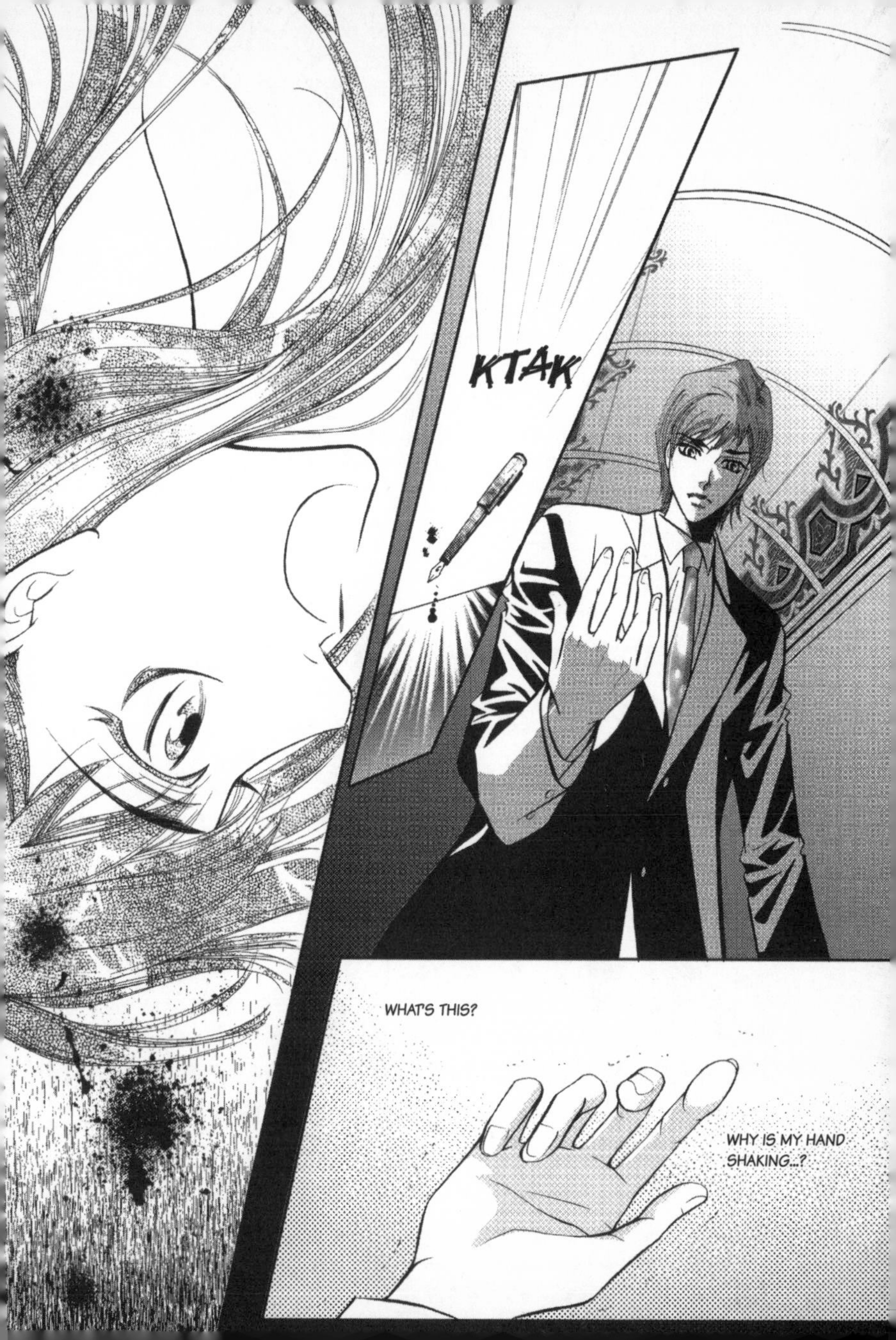
KTAK
WHAT'S THIS?
WHY IS MY HAND
SHAKING...?

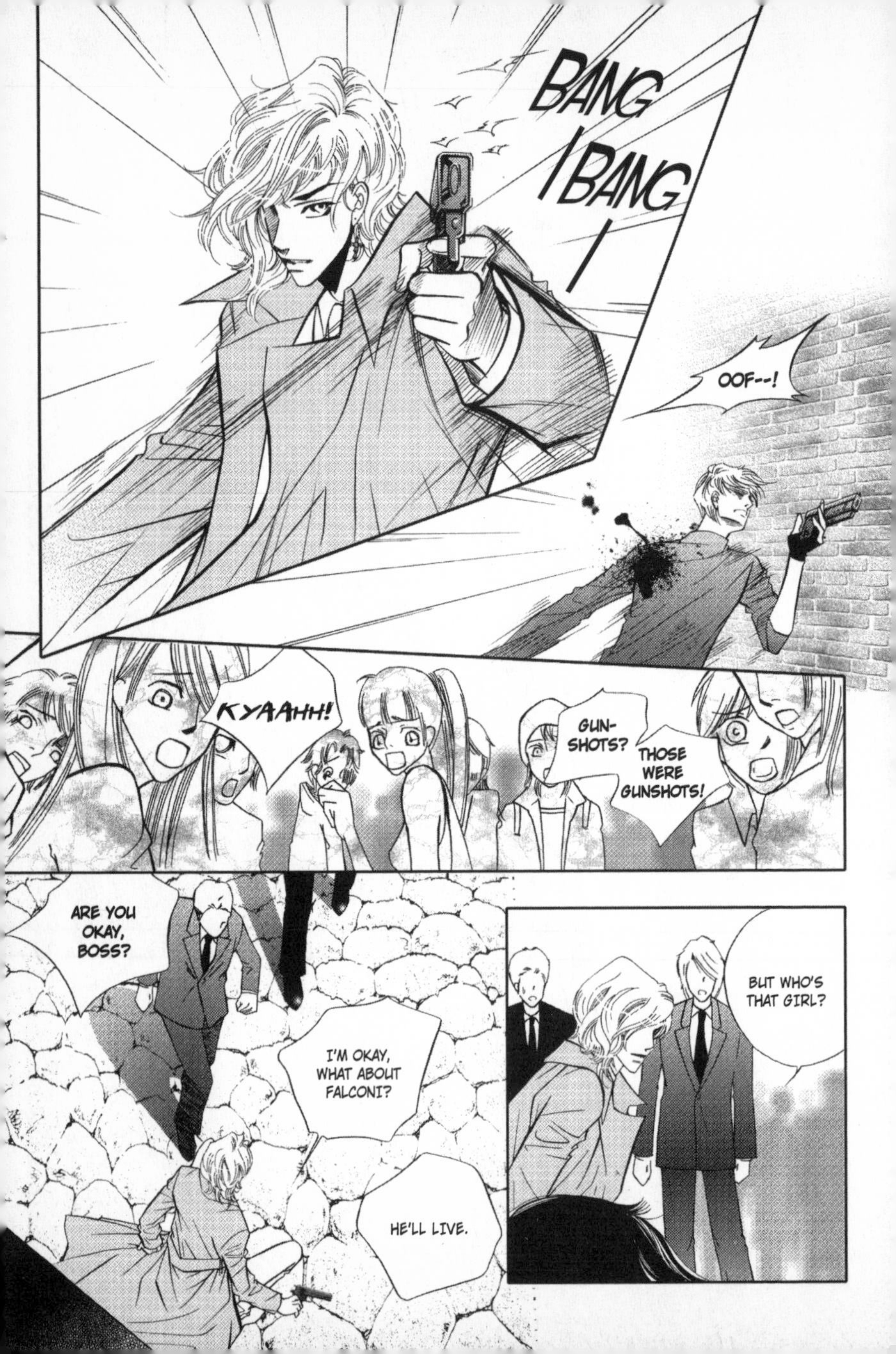
BANG
BANG
OOF--!
KYAAHH!
GUN-SHOTS?
THOSE WERE GUNSHOTS!
ARE YOU OKAY, BOSS?
I'M OKAY, WHAT ABOUT FALCONI?
HE'LL LIVE.
BUT WHO'S THAT GIRL?

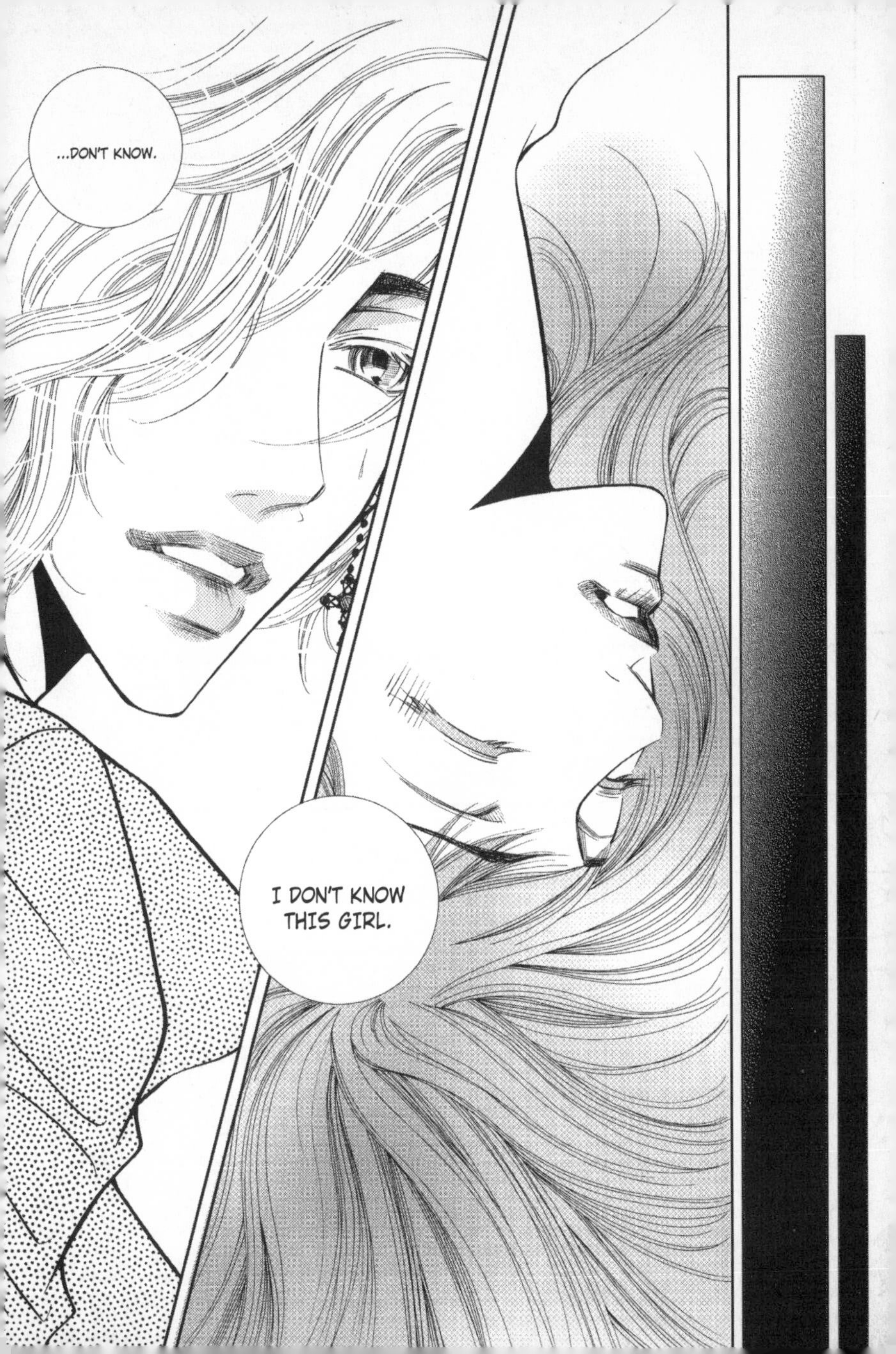
...DON'T KNOW.
I DON'T KNOW THIS GIRL.

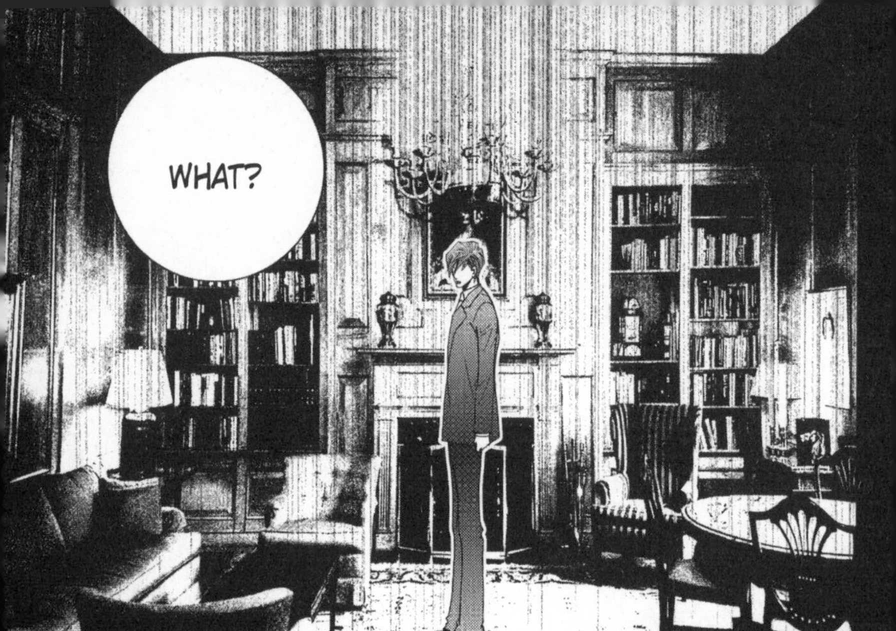
WHAT?

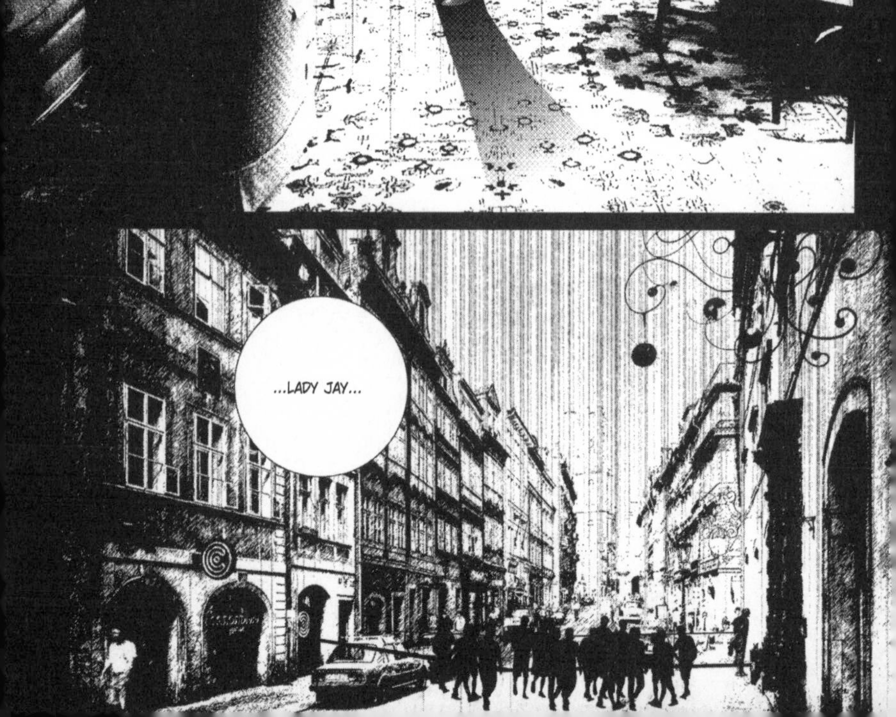
...LADY JAY...

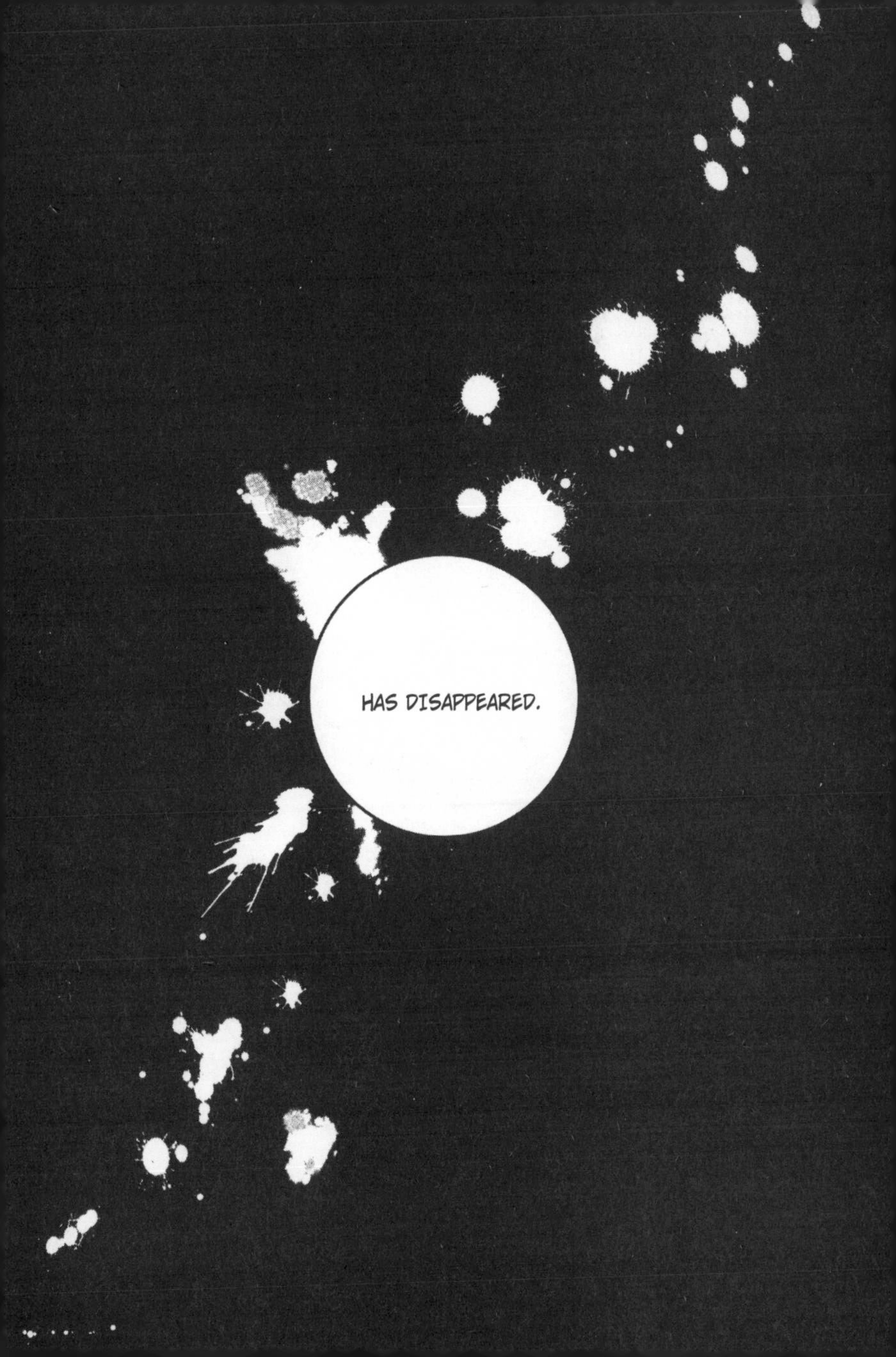
HAS DISAPPEARED.

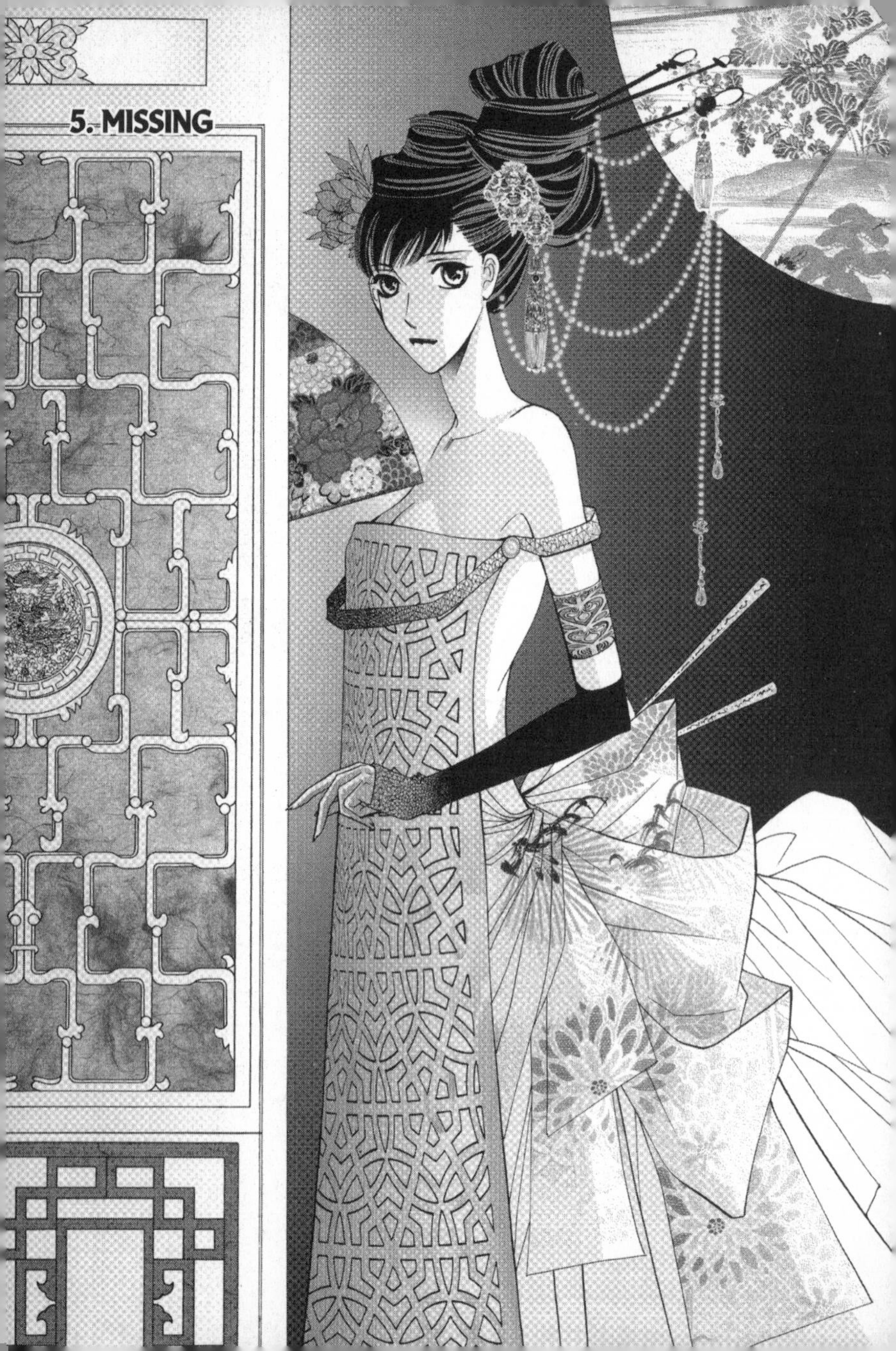
5. MISSING

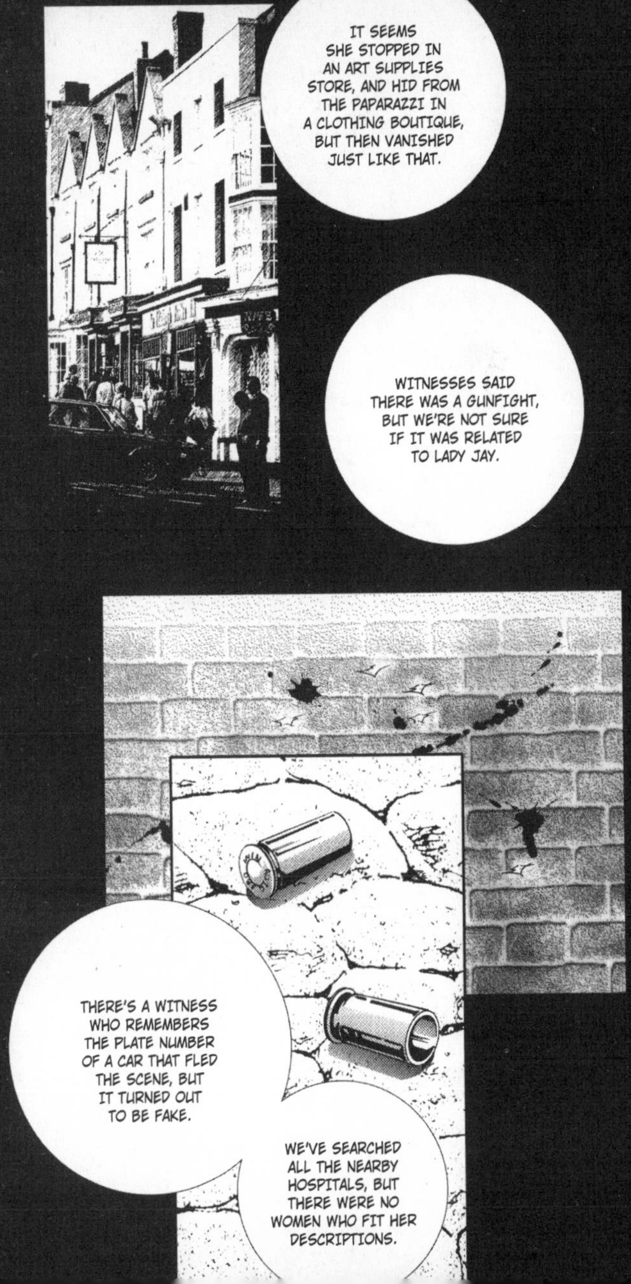
IT SEEMS SHE STOPPED IN AN ART SUPPLIES STORE, AND HID FROM THE PAPARAZZI IN A CLOTHING BOUTIQUE, BUT THEN VANISHED JUST LIKE THAT.
WITNESSES SAID THERE WAS A GUNFIGHT, BUT WE'RE NOT SURE IF IT WAS RELATED TO LADY JAY.
THERE'S A WITNESS WHO REMEMBERS THE PLATE NUMBER OF A CAR THAT FLED THE SCENE, BUT IT TURNED OUT TO BE FAKE.
WE'VE SEARCHED ALL THE NEARBY HOSPITALS, BUT THERE WERE NO WOMEN WHO FIT HER DESCRIPTIONS.

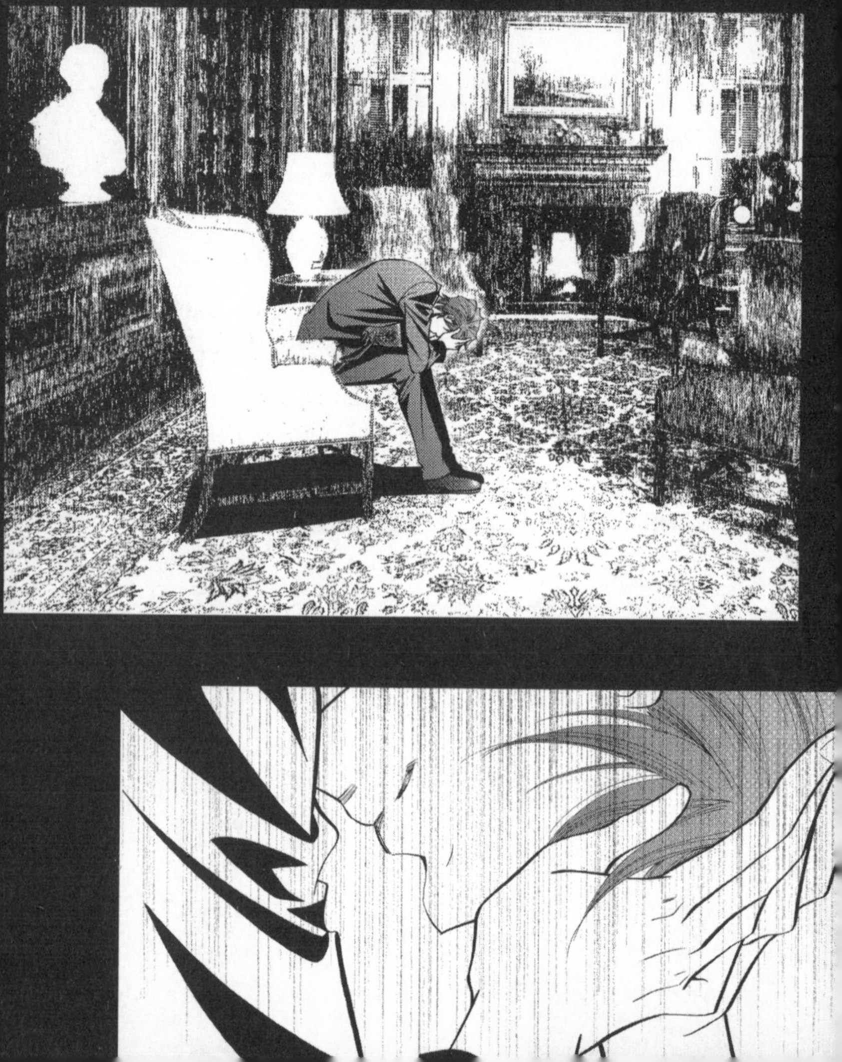

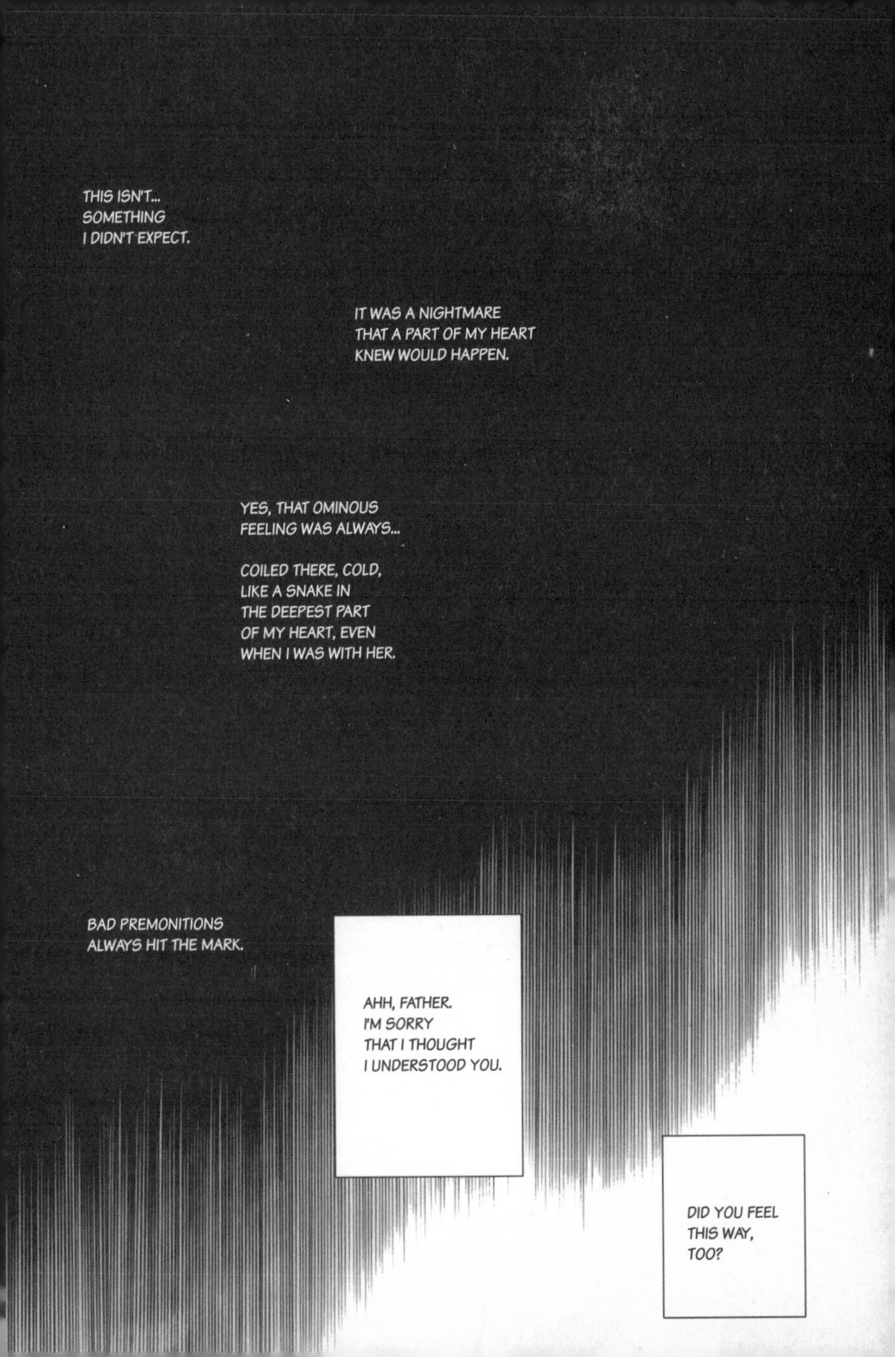
THIS ISN'T... SOMETHING I DIDN'T EXPECT.
IT WAS A NIGHTMARE THAT A PART OF MY HEART KNEW WOULD HAPPEN.
YES, THAT OMINOUS FEELING WAS ALWAYS...
COILED THERE, COLD, LIKE A SNAKE IN THE DEEPEST PART OF MY HEART, EVEN WHEN I WAS WITH HER.
BAD PREMONITIONS ALWAYS HIT THE MARK.
AHH, FATHER. I'M SORRY THAT I THOUGHT I UNDERSTOOD YOU.
DID YOU FEEL THIS WAY, TOO?

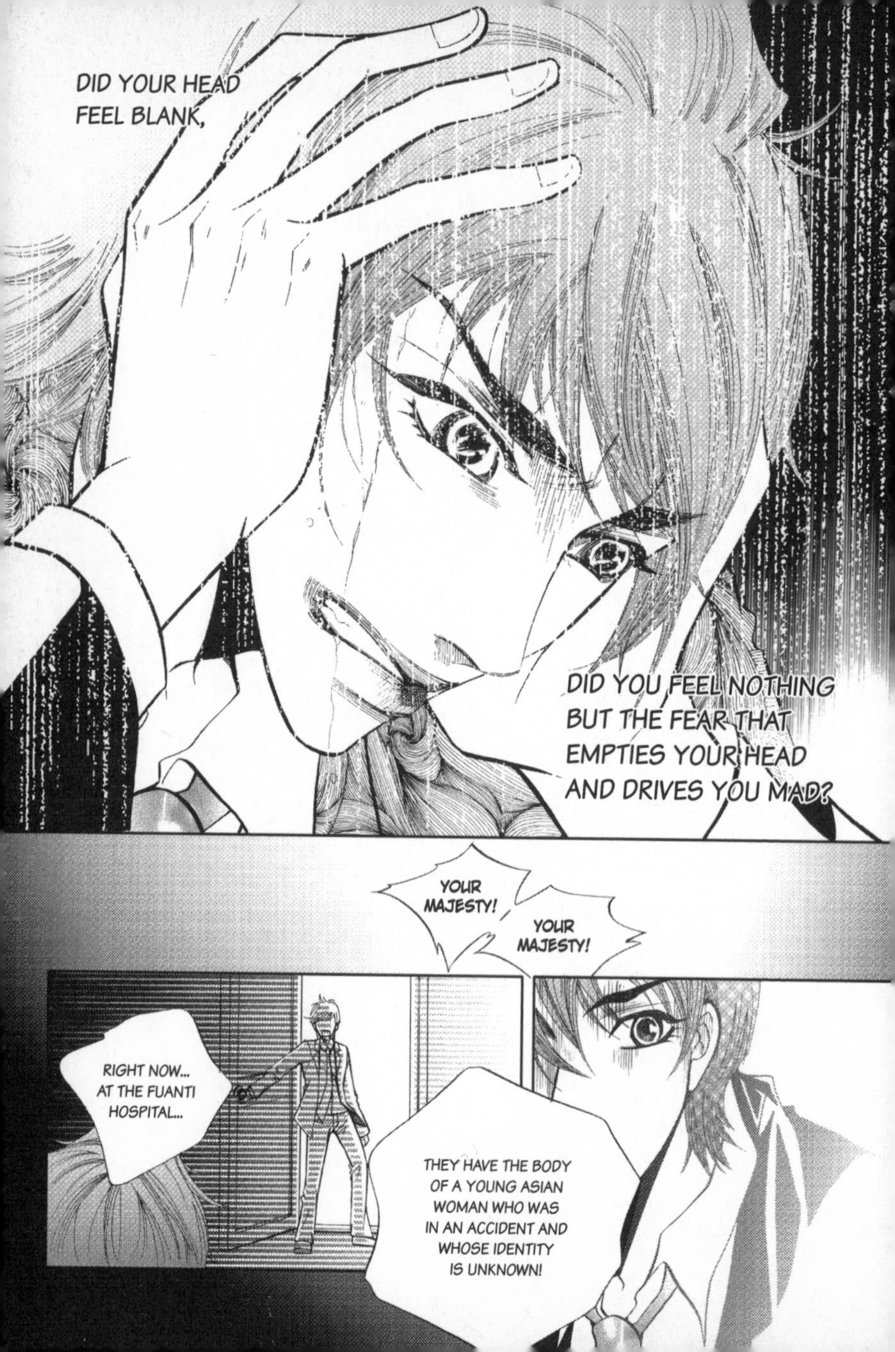
DID YOUR HEAD FEEL BLANK,
DID YOU FEEL NOTHING BUT THE FEAR THAT EMPTIES YOUR HEAD AND DRIVES YOU MAD?
YOUR MAJESTY!
YOUR MAJESTY!
RIGHT NOW... AT THE FUANTI HOSPITAL...
THEY HAVE THE BODY OF A YOUNG ASIAN WOMAN WHO WAS IN AN ACCIDENT AND WHOSE IDENTITY IS UNKNOWN!

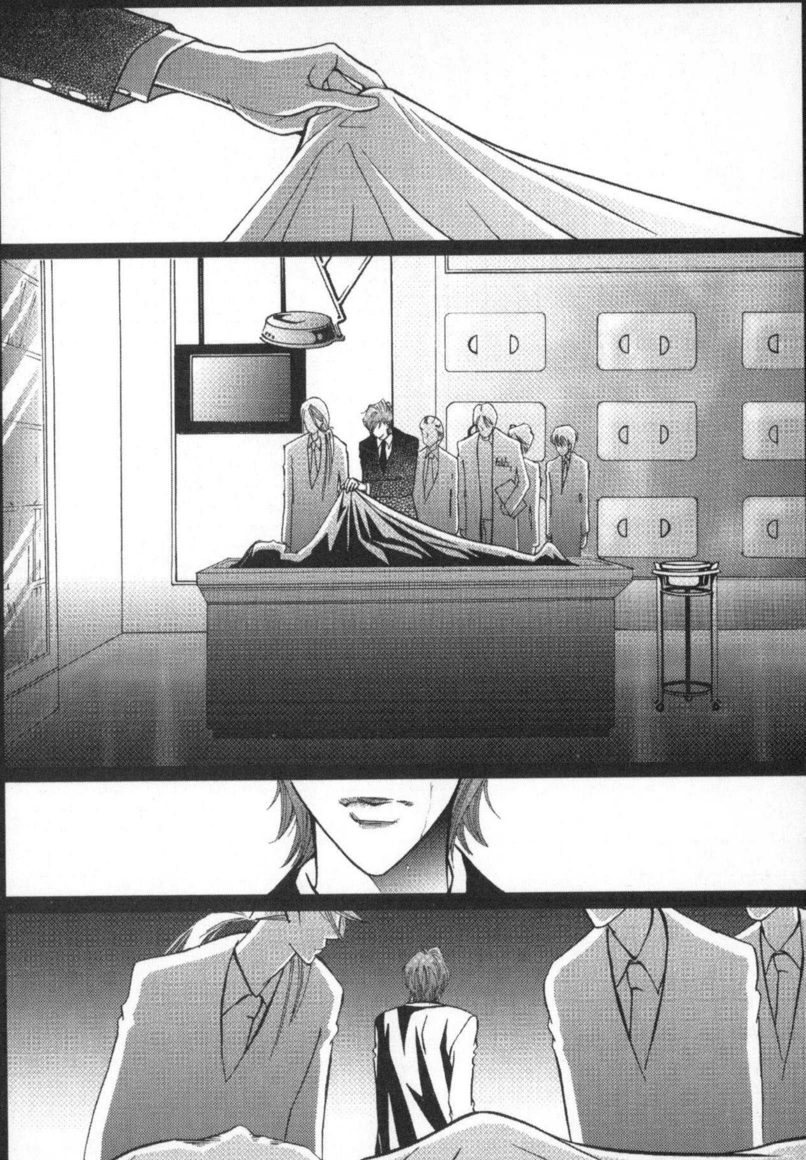

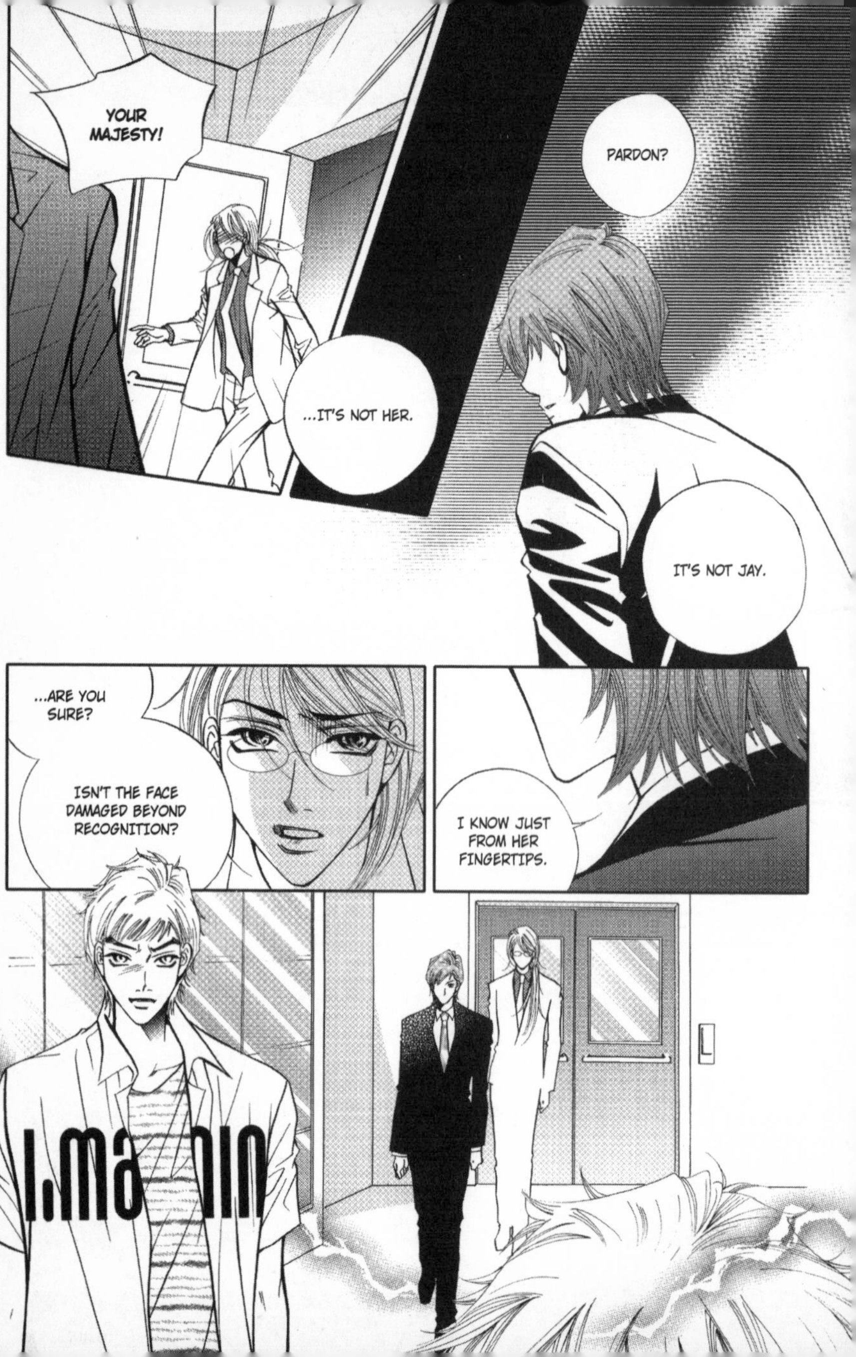
YOUR MAJESTY!
...IT'S NOT HER.
PARDON?
IT'S NOT JAY.
...ARE YOU SURE?
ISN'T THE FACE DAMAGED BEYOND RECOGNITION?
I KNOW JUST FROM HER FINGERTIPS.

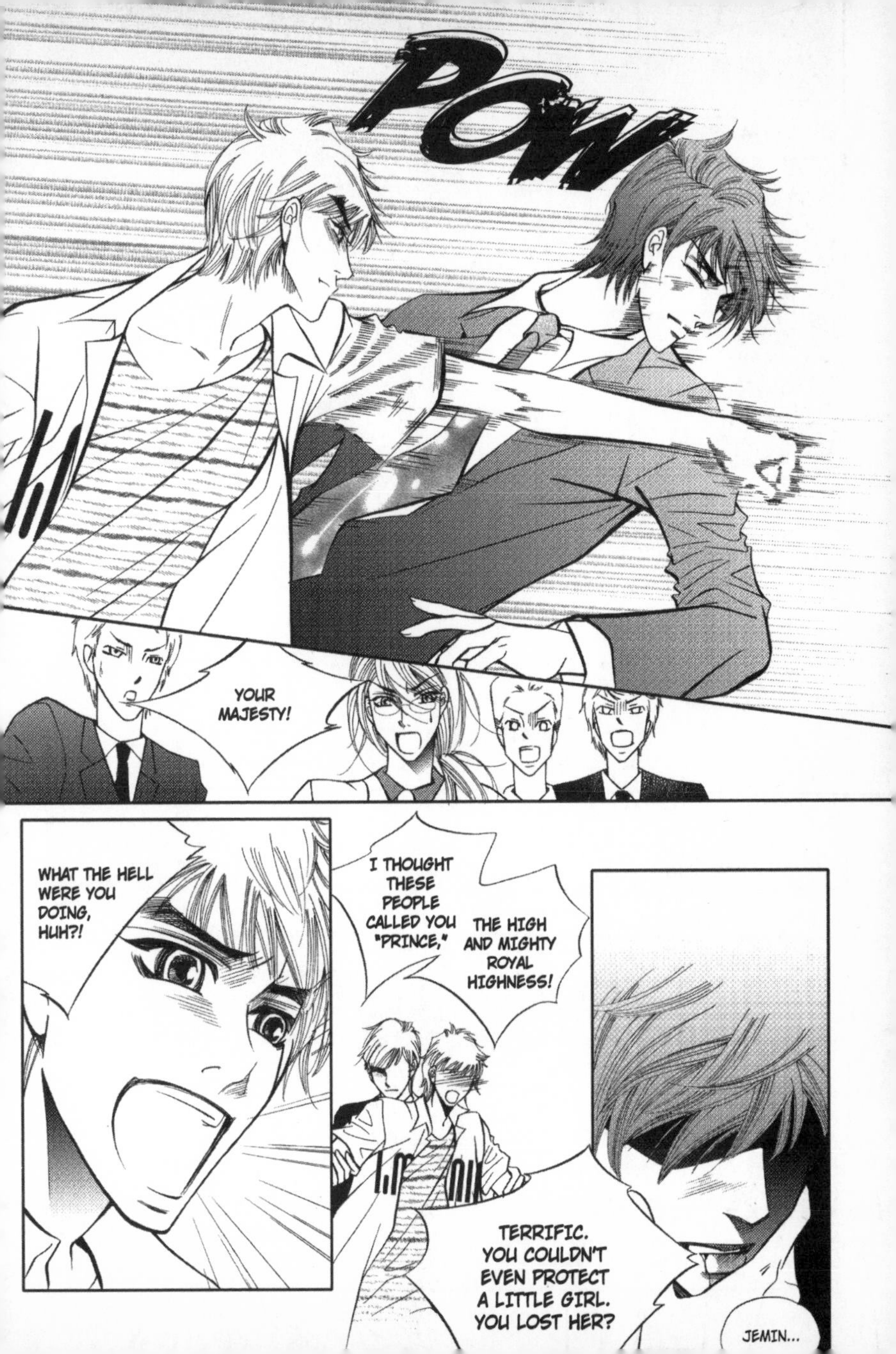
POW
YOUR MAJESTY!
WHAT THE HELL WERE YOU DOING, HUH?!
I THOUGHT THESE PEOPLE CALLED YOU "PRINCE,"
THE HIGH AND MIGHTY ROYAL HIGHNESS!
TERRIFIC. YOU COULDN'T EVEN PROTECT A LITTLE GIRL. YOU LOST HER?
JEMIN...

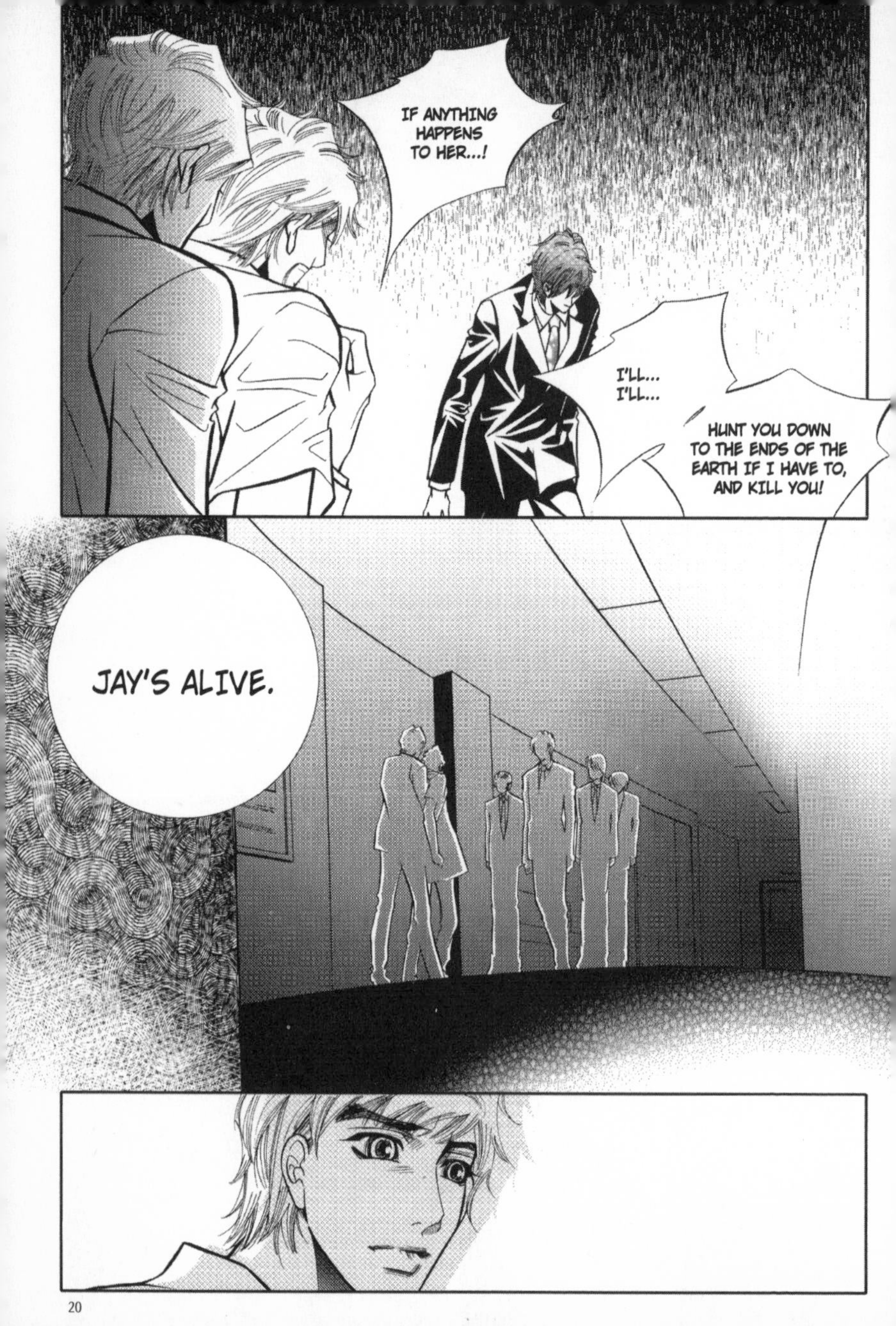
IF ANYTHING HAPPENS TO HER...!
I'LL... I'LL...
HUNT YOU DOWN TO THE ENDS OF THE EARTH IF I HAVE TO, AND KILL YOU!
JAY'S ALIVE.

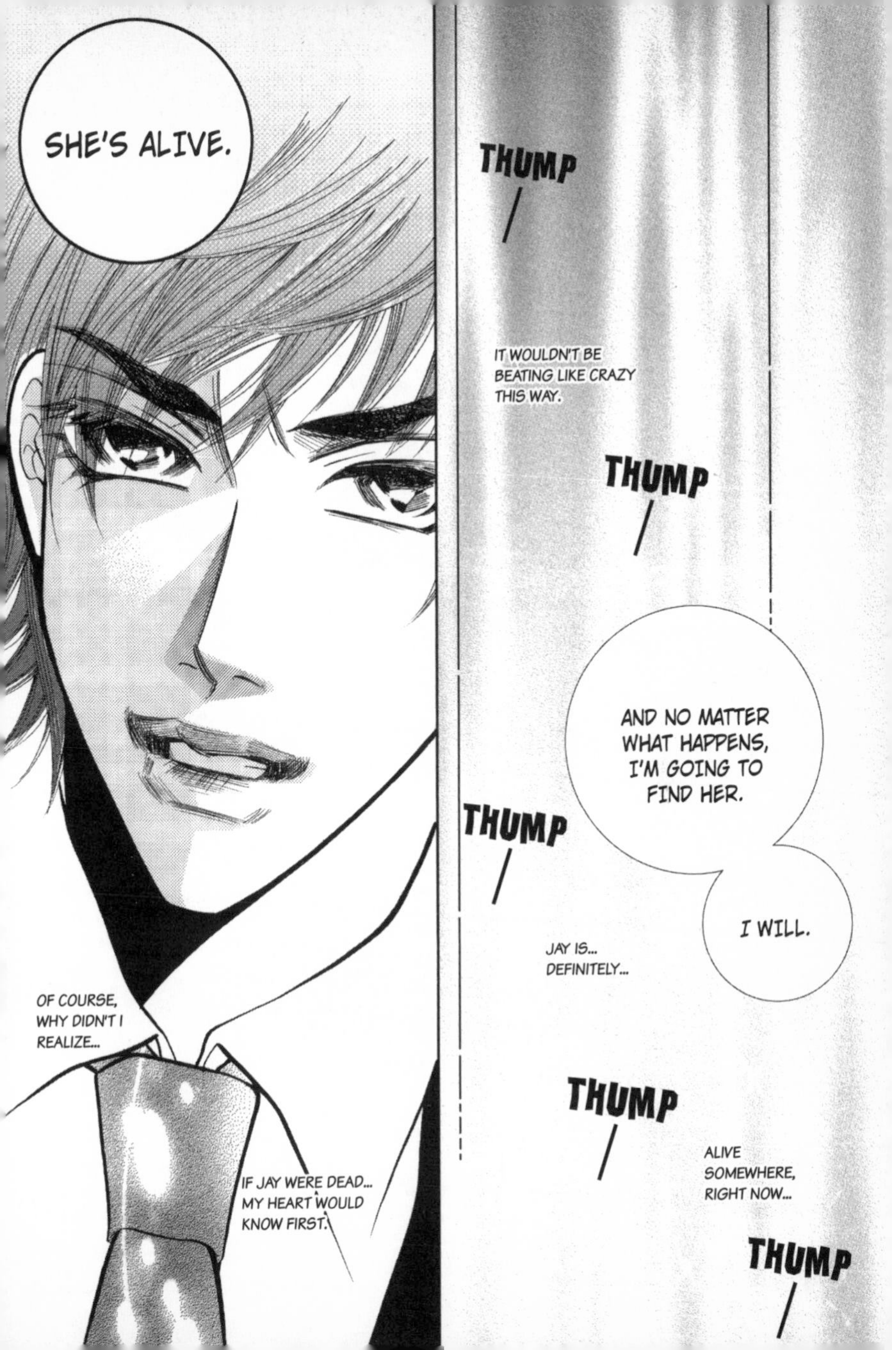
SHE'S ALIVE.
OF COURSE, WHY DIDN'T I REALIZE...
IF JAY WERE DEAD... MY HEART WOULD KNOW FIRST.
THUMP
IT WOULDN'T BE BEATING LIKE CRAZY THIS WAY.
THUMP
AND NO MATTER WHAT HAPPENS, I'M GOING TO FIND HER.
THUMP
I WILL.
JAY IS... DEFINITELY...
THUMP
ALIVE SOMEWHERE, RIGHT NOW...
THUMP

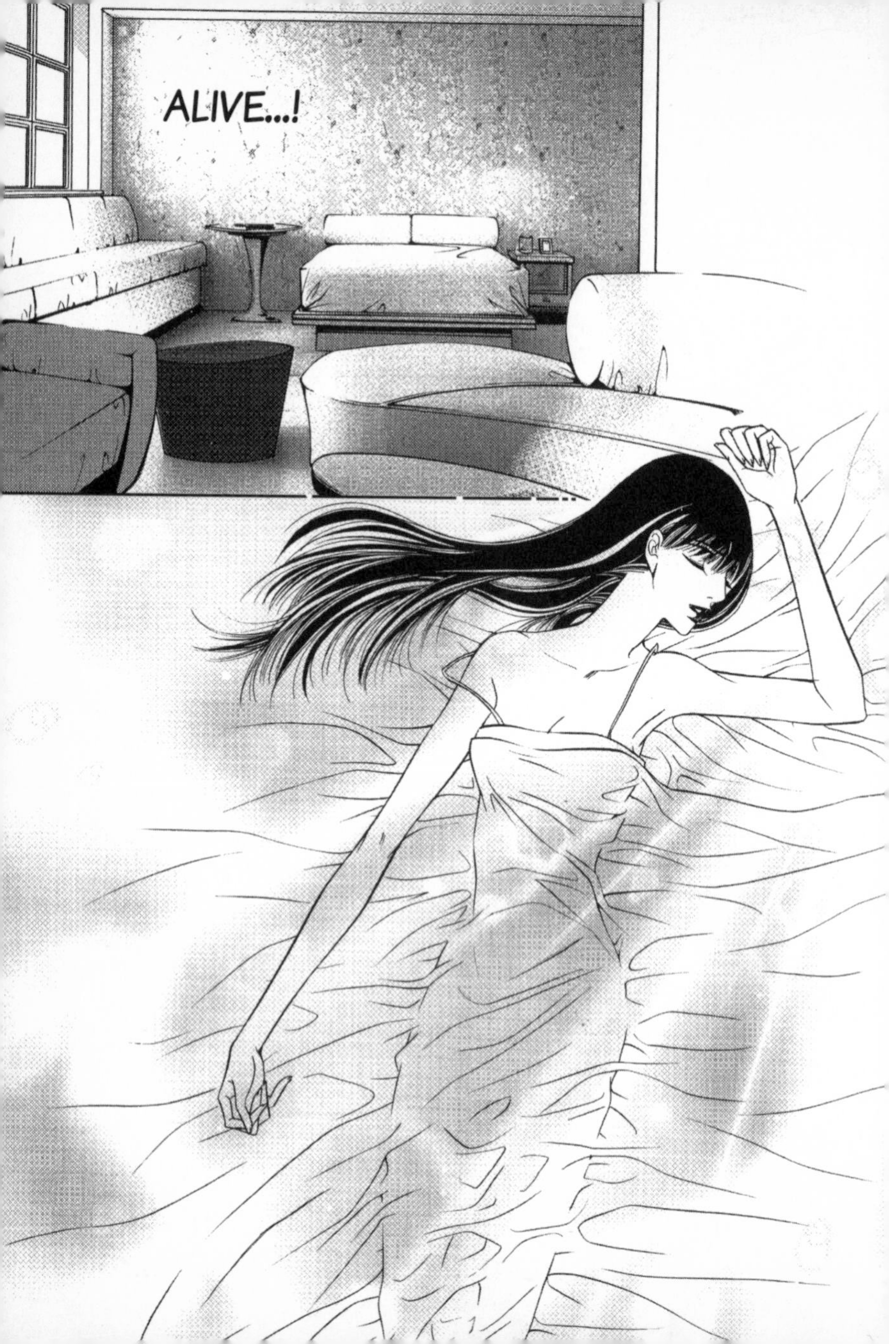
ALIVE...!

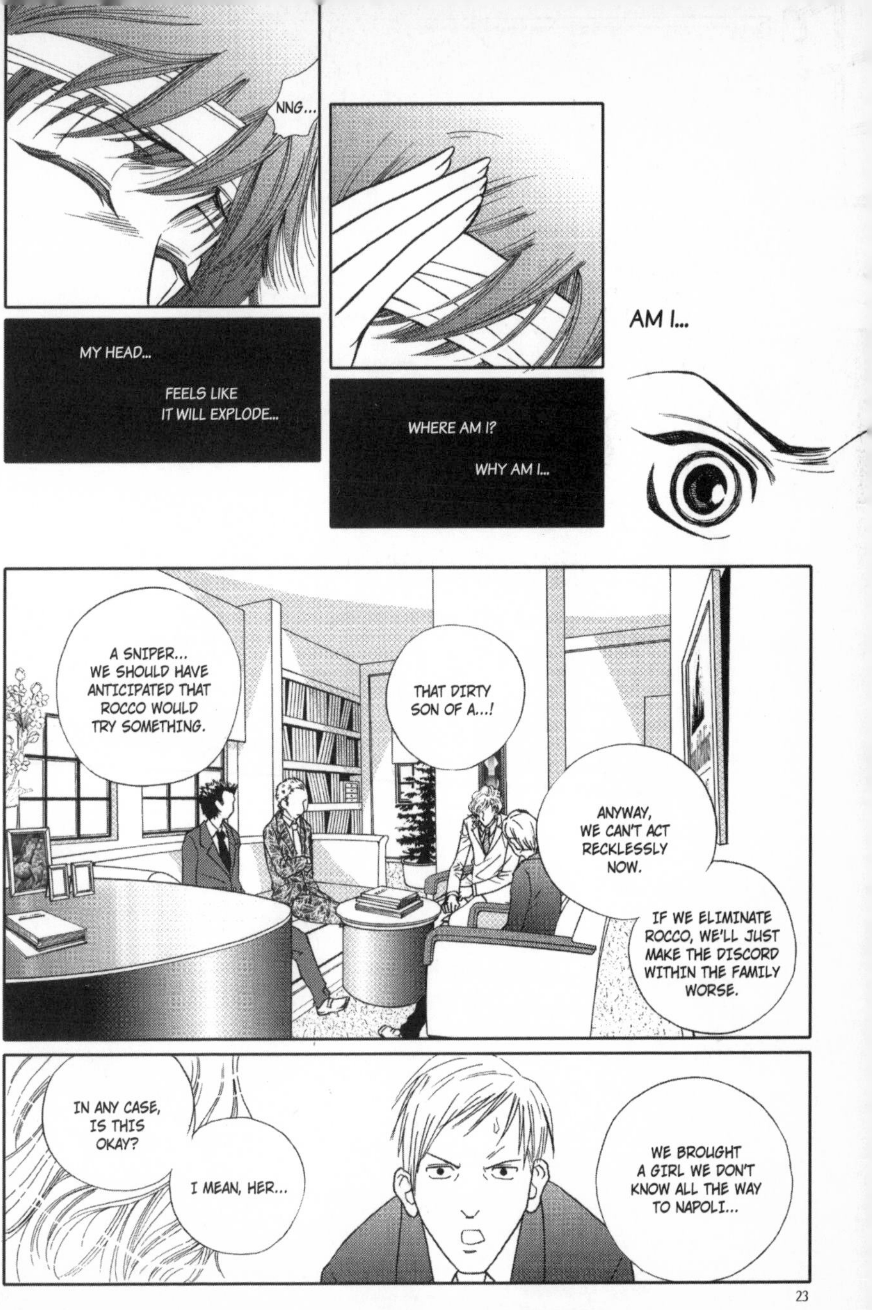
NNG...
MY HEAD...
FEELS LIKE IT WILL EXPLODE...
WHERE AM I?
WHY AM I...
AM I...
A SNIPER... WE SHOULD HAVE ANTICIPATED THAT ROCCO WOULD TRY SOMETHING.
THAT DIRTY SON OF A...!
ANYWAY, WE CAN'T ACT RECKLESSLY NOW.
IF WE ELIMINATE ROCCO, WE'LL JUST MAKE THE DISCORD WITHIN THE FAMILY WORSE.
IN ANY CASE, IS THIS OKAY?
I MEAN, HER...
WE BROUGHT A GIRL WE DON'T KNOW ALL THE WAY TO NAPOLI...

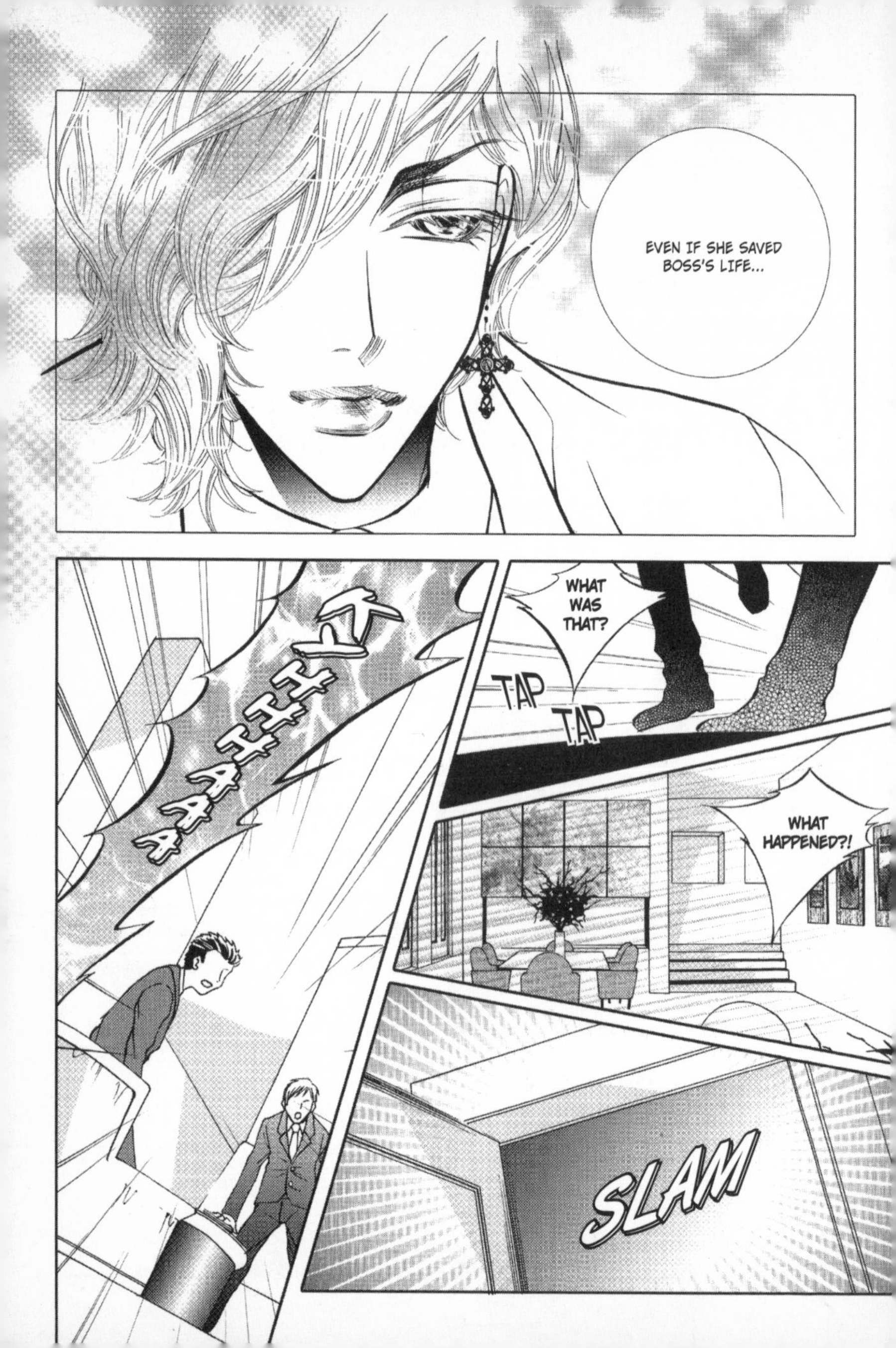
EVEN IF SHE SAVED BOSS'S LIFE...
WHAT WAS THAT?
TAP
TAP
WHAT HAPPENED?!
SLAM

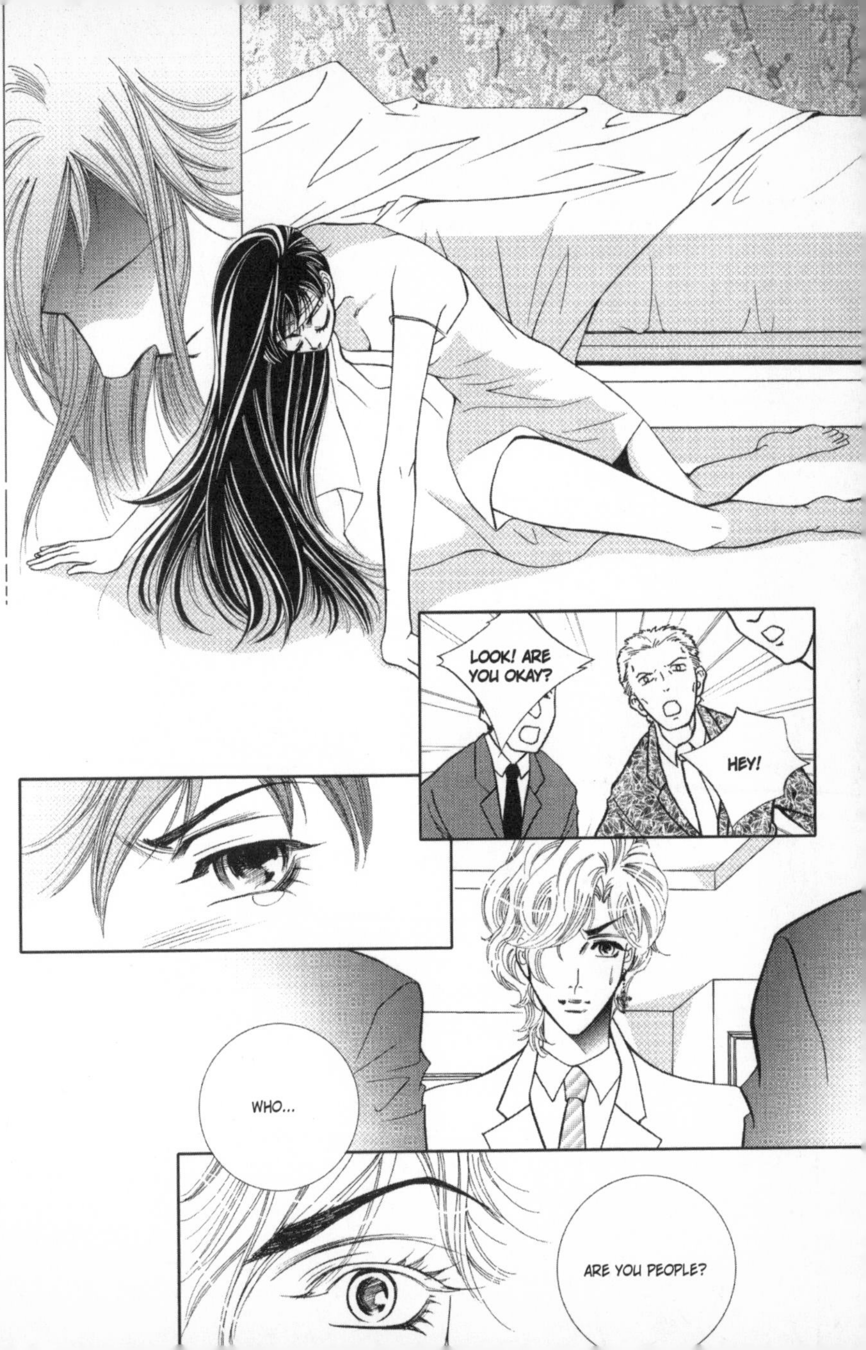
LOOK! ARE YOU OKAY?
HEY!
WHO...
ARE YOU PEOPLE?

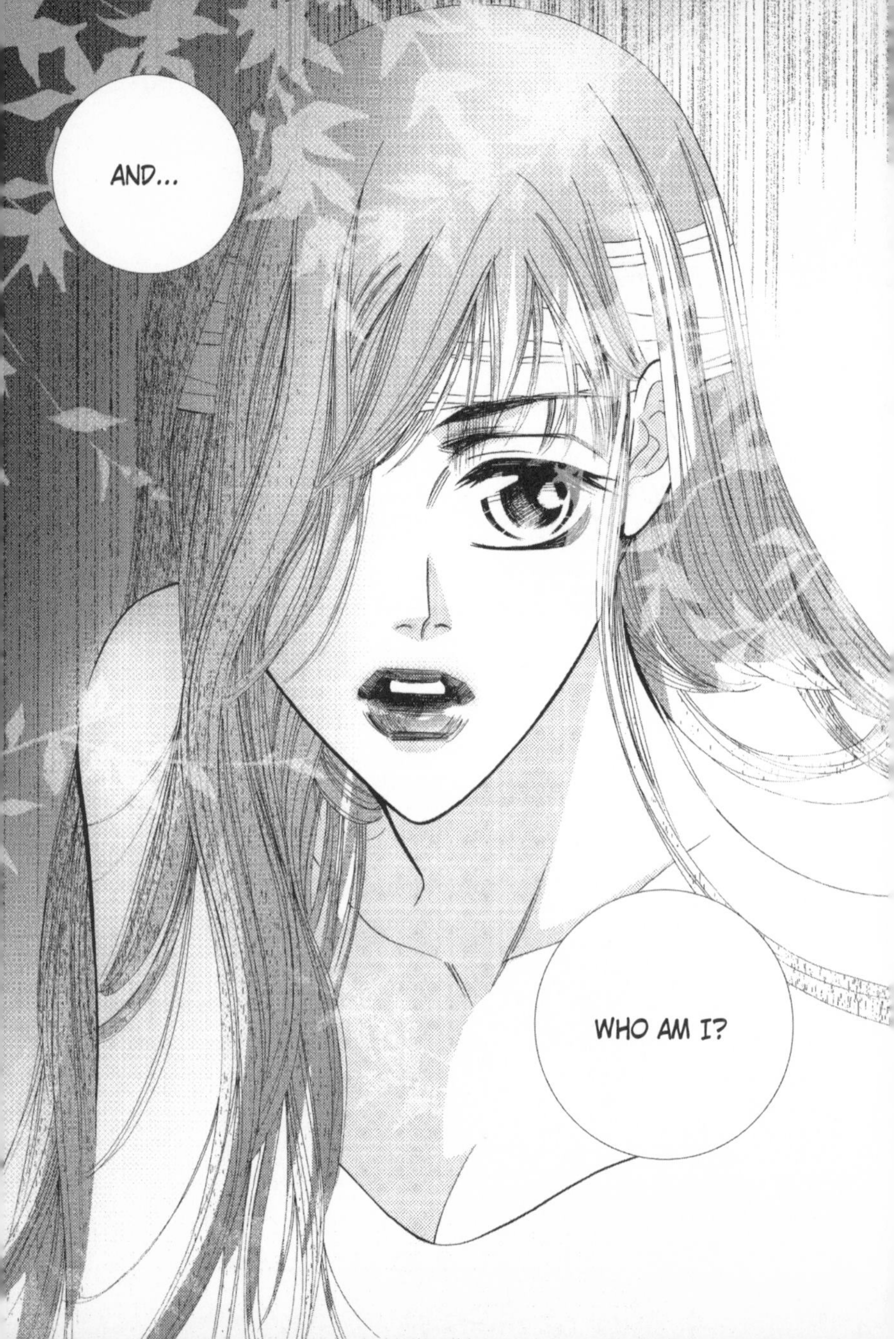
AND...
WHO AM I?

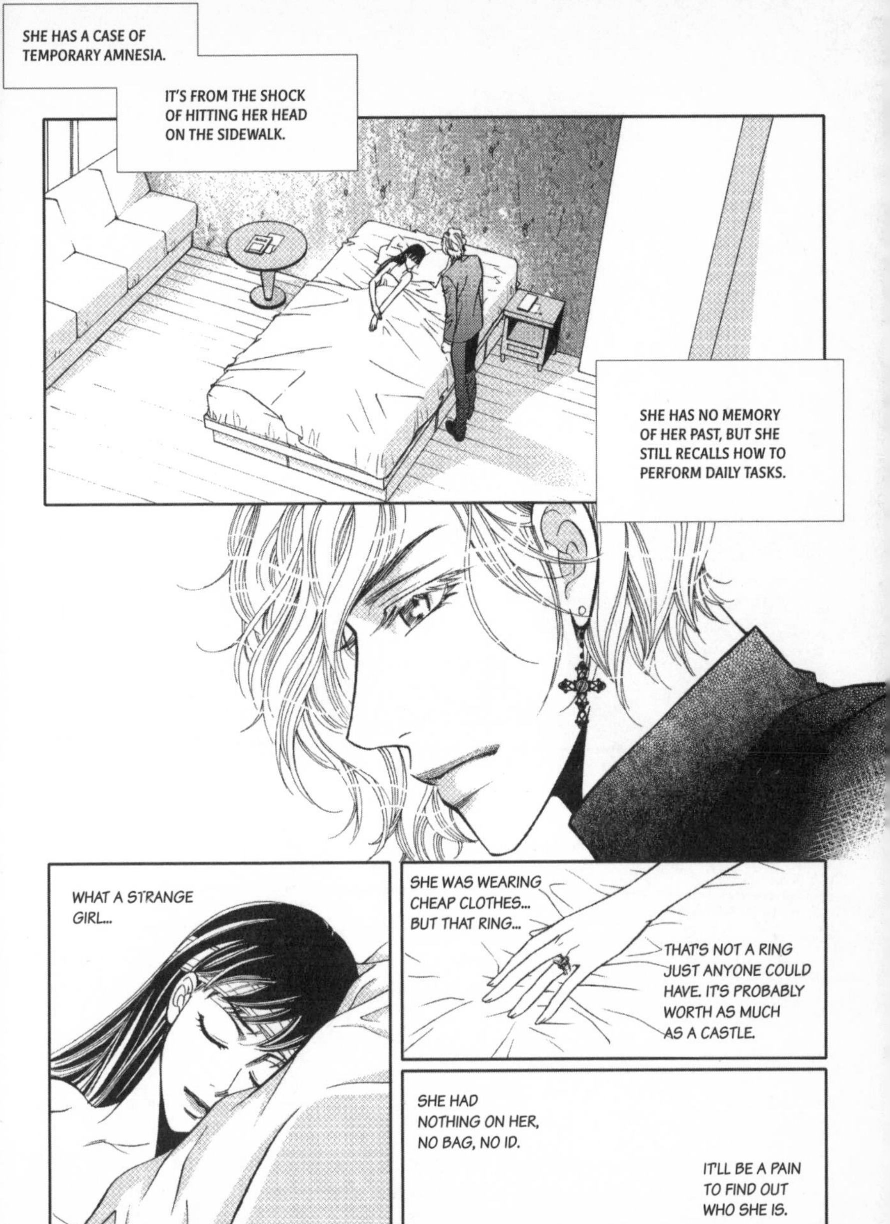
SHE HAS A CASE OF TEMPORARY AMNESIA.
IT'S FROM THE SHOCK OF HITTING HER HEAD ON THE SIDEWALK.
SHE HAS NO MEMORY OF HER PAST, BUT SHE STILL RECALLS HOW TO PERFORM DAILY TASKS.
WHAT A STRANGE GIRL...
SHE WAS WEARING CHEAP CLOTHES... BUT THAT RING...
THAT'S NOT A RING JUST ANYONE COULD HAVE. IT'S PROBABLY WORTH AS MUCH AS A CASTLE.
SHE HAD NOTHING ON HER, NO BAG, NO ID.
IT'LL BE A PAIN TO FIND OUT WHO SHE IS.

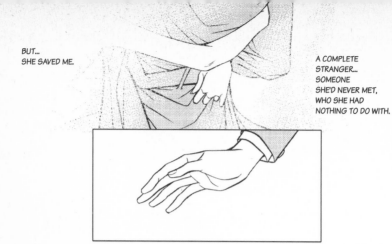

BUT...
SHE SAVED ME.

A COMPLETE
STRANGER...
SOMEONE
SHE'D NEVER MET,
WHO SHE HAD
NOTHING TO DO WITH.

RISKING HER LIFE... SHE JUMPED IN.

FOR A *STRANGER*.

HALT-

WHO WOULD BE SO...
HOW STUPID
CAN SHE BE?

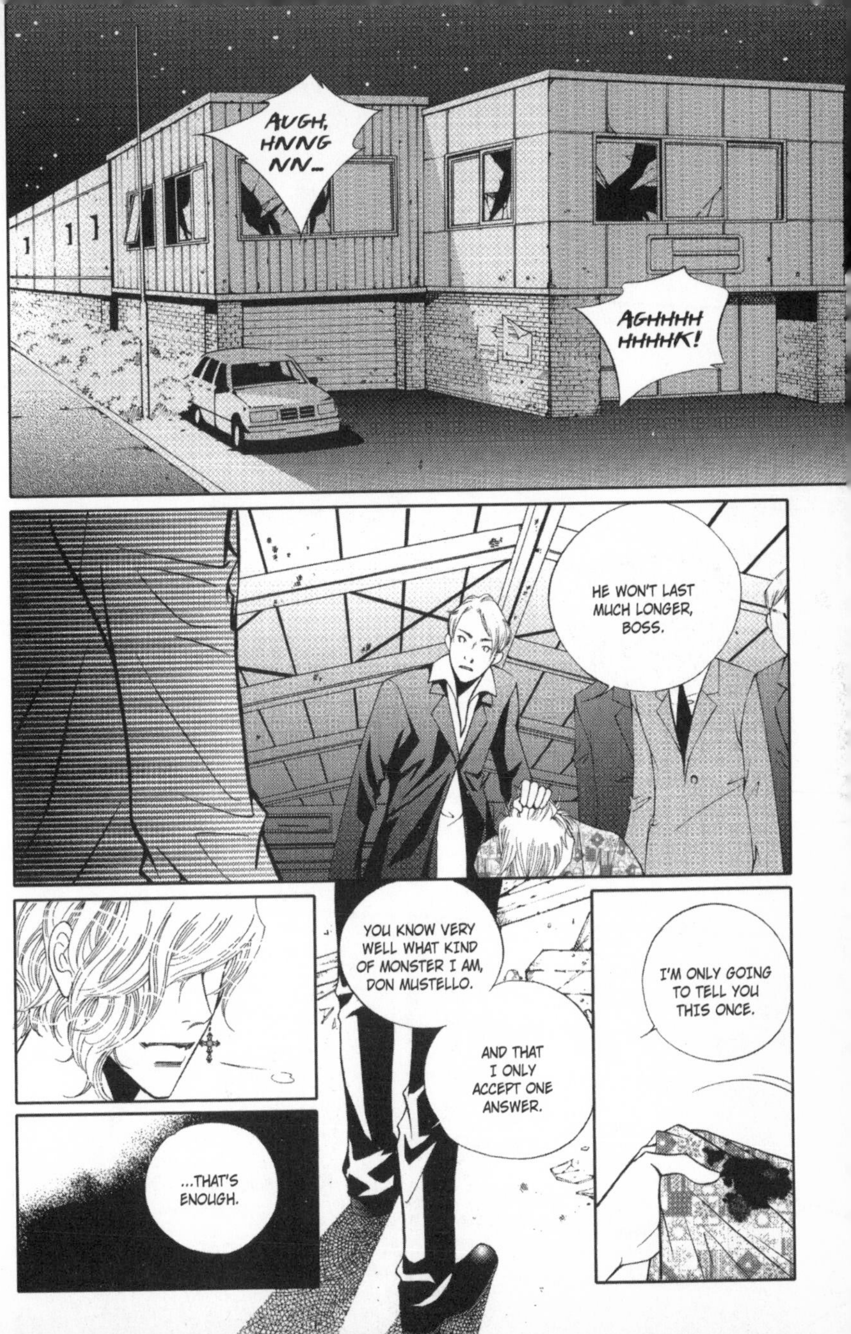
AUGH, HNNG NN...
AGHHHH HHHHK!
HE WON'T LAST MUCH LONGER, BOSS.
...THAT'S ENOUGH.
YOU KNOW VERY WELL WHAT KIND OF MONSTER I AM, DON MUSTELLO.
AND THAT I ONLY ACCEPT ONE ANSWER.
I'M ONLY GOING TO TELL YOU THIS ONCE.

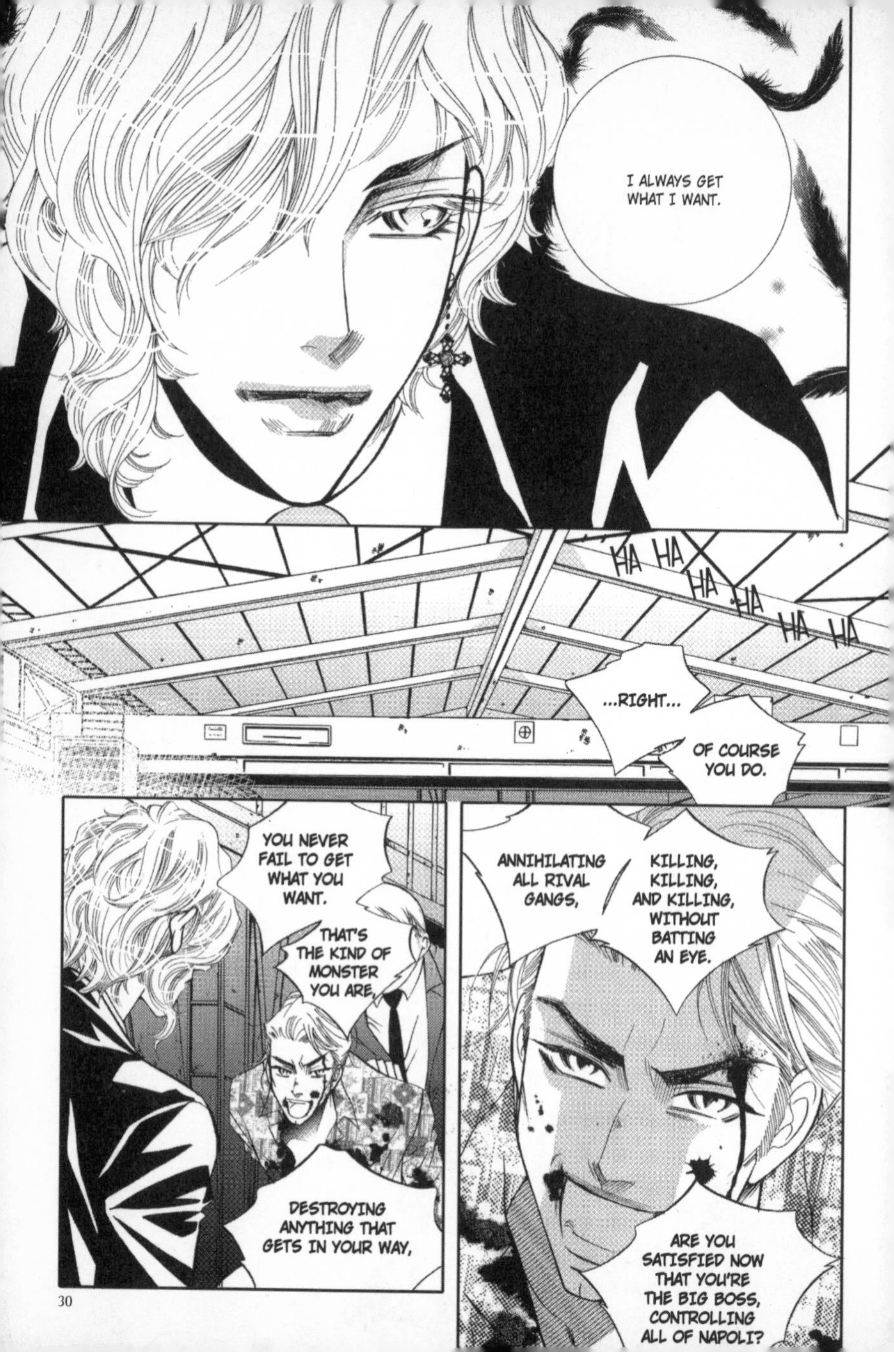

I ALWAYS GET WHAT I WANT.
HA HA HA HA HA HA
...RIGHT...
OF COURSE YOU DO.
YOU NEVER FAIL TO GET WHAT YOU WANT.
THAT'S THE KIND OF MONSTER YOU ARE,
DESTROYING ANYTHING THAT GETS IN YOUR WAY,
ANNIHILATING ALL RIVAL GANGS,
KILLING, KILLING, AND KILLING, WITHOUT BATTING AN EYE.
ARE YOU SATISFIED NOW THAT YOU'RE THE BIG BOSS, CONTROLLING ALL OF NAPOLI?

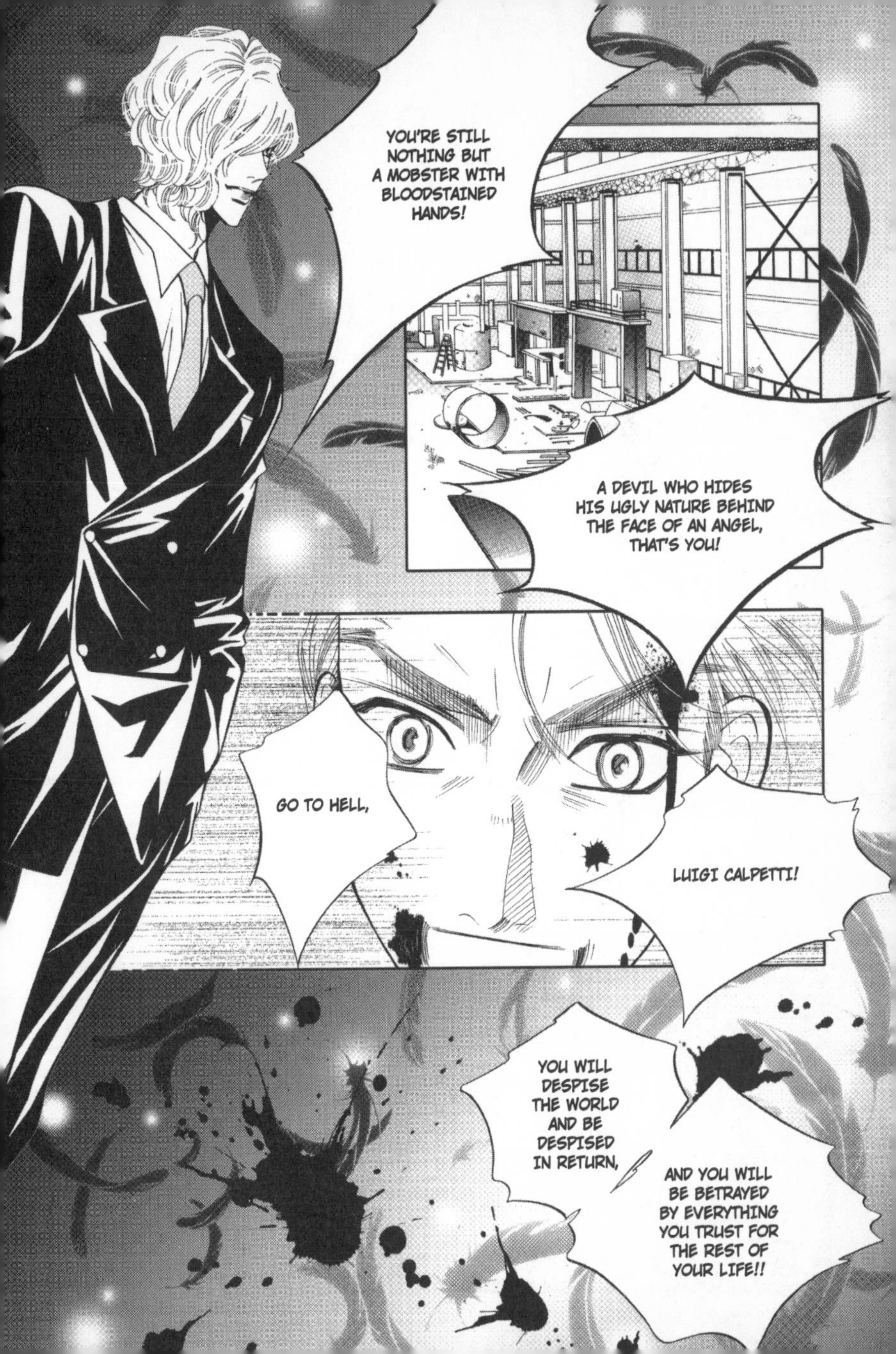
YOU'RE STILL NOTHING BUT A MOBSTER WITH BLOODSTAINED HANDS!
A DEVIL WHO HIDES HIS UGLY NATURE BEHIND THE FACE OF AN ANGEL, THAT'S YOU!
GO TO HELL,
LUIGI CALPETTI!
YOU WILL DESPISE THE WORLD AND BE DESPISED IN RETURN,
AND YOU WILL BE BETRAYED BY EVERYTHING YOU TRUST FOR THE REST OF YOUR LIFE!!

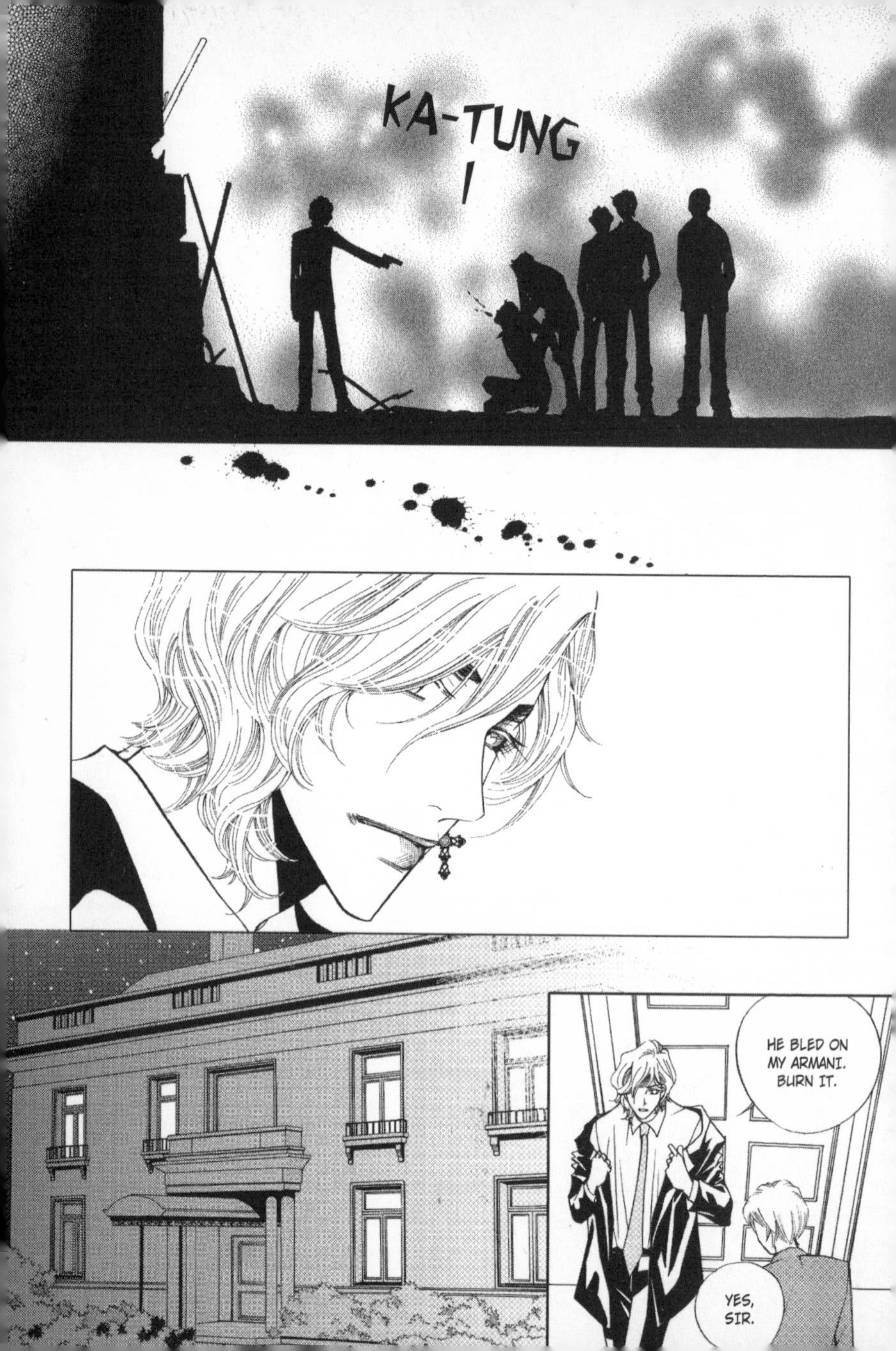
KA-TUNG
!
HE BLED ON MY ARMANI. BURN IT.
YES, SIR.

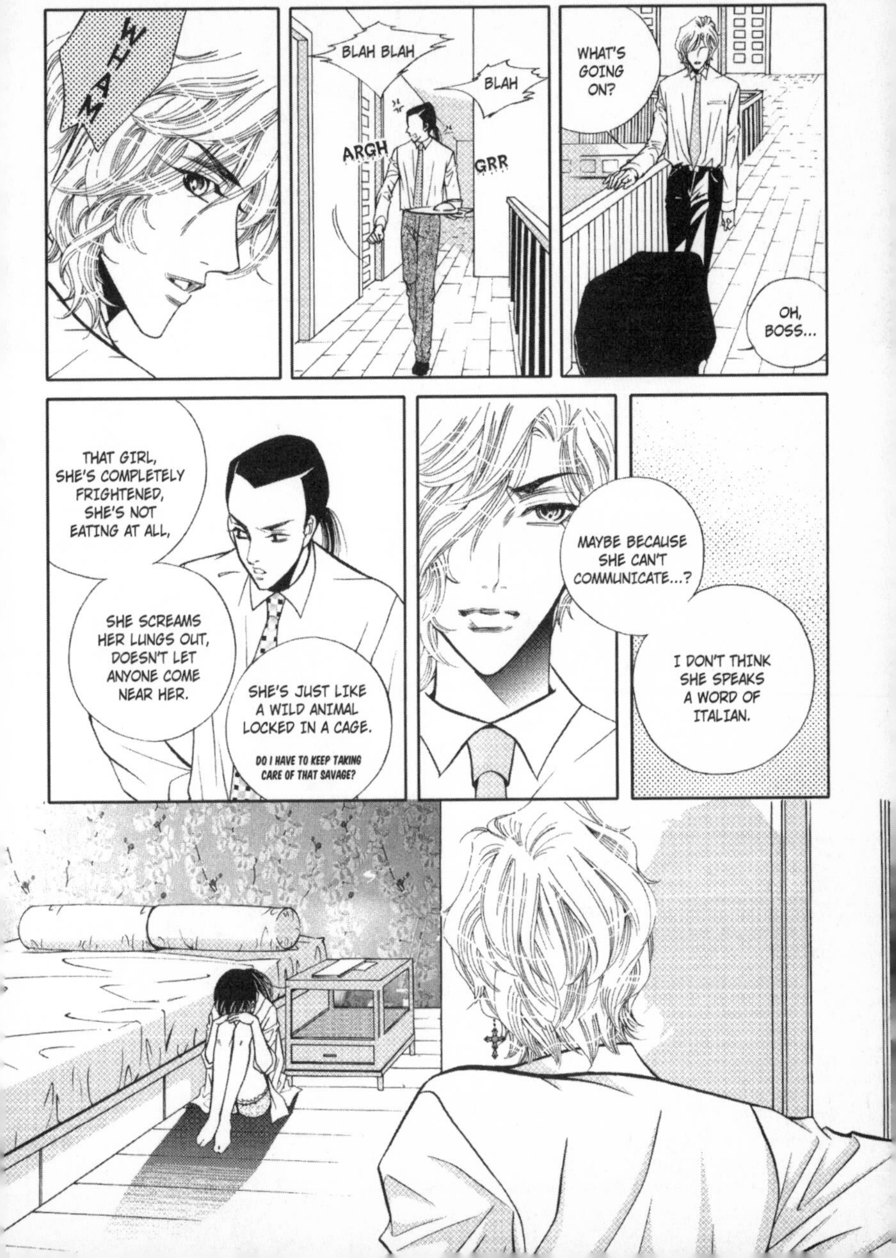
WHAM
BLAH BLAH
BLAH
ARGH
GRR
WHAT'S GOING ON?
OH, BOSS...
THAT GIRL, SHE'S COMPLETELY FRIGHTENED, SHE'S NOT EATING AT ALL,
SHE SCREAMS HER LUNGS OUT, DOESN'T LET ANYONE COME NEAR HER.
SHE'S JUST LIKE A WILD ANIMAL LOCKED IN A CAGE.
DO I HAVE TO KEEP TAKING CARE OF THAT SAVAGE?
MAYBE BECAUSE SHE CAN'T COMMUNICATE...?
I DON'T THINK SHE SPEAKS A WORD OF ITALIAN.

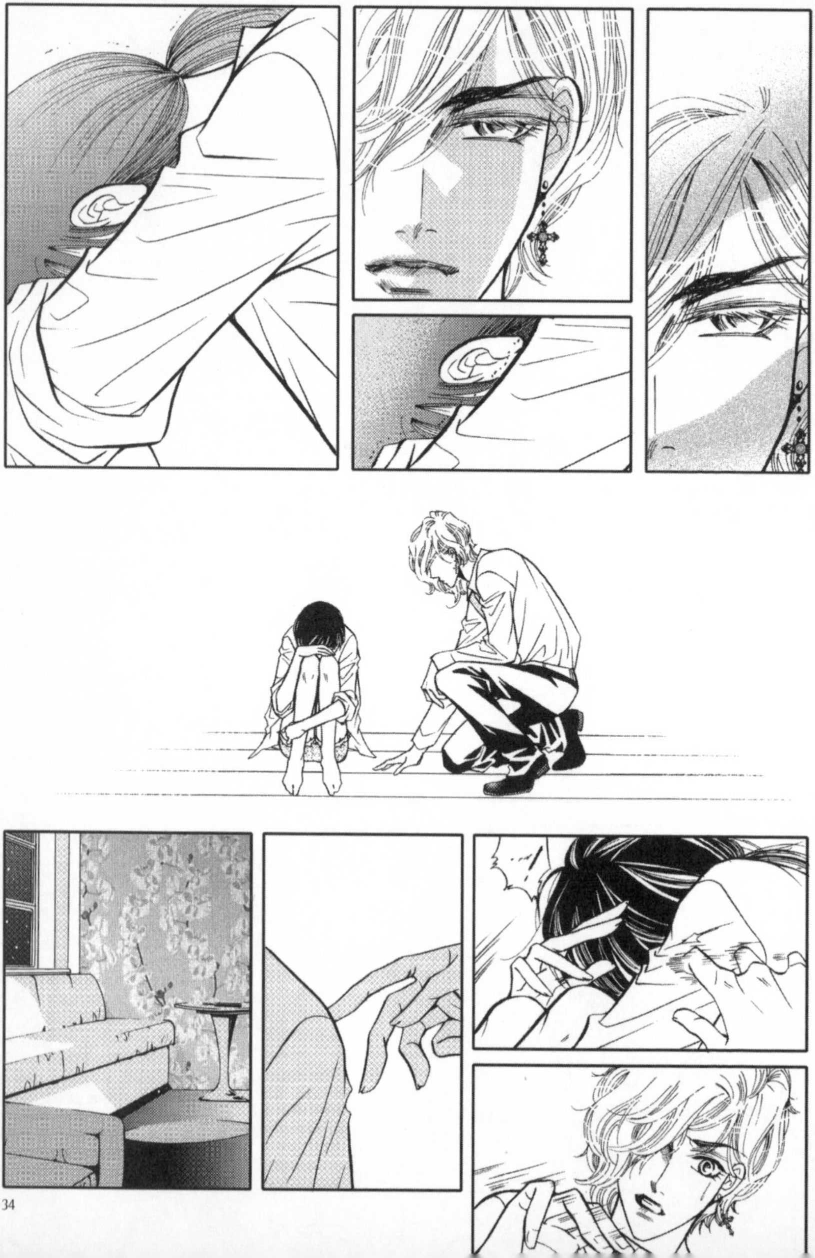

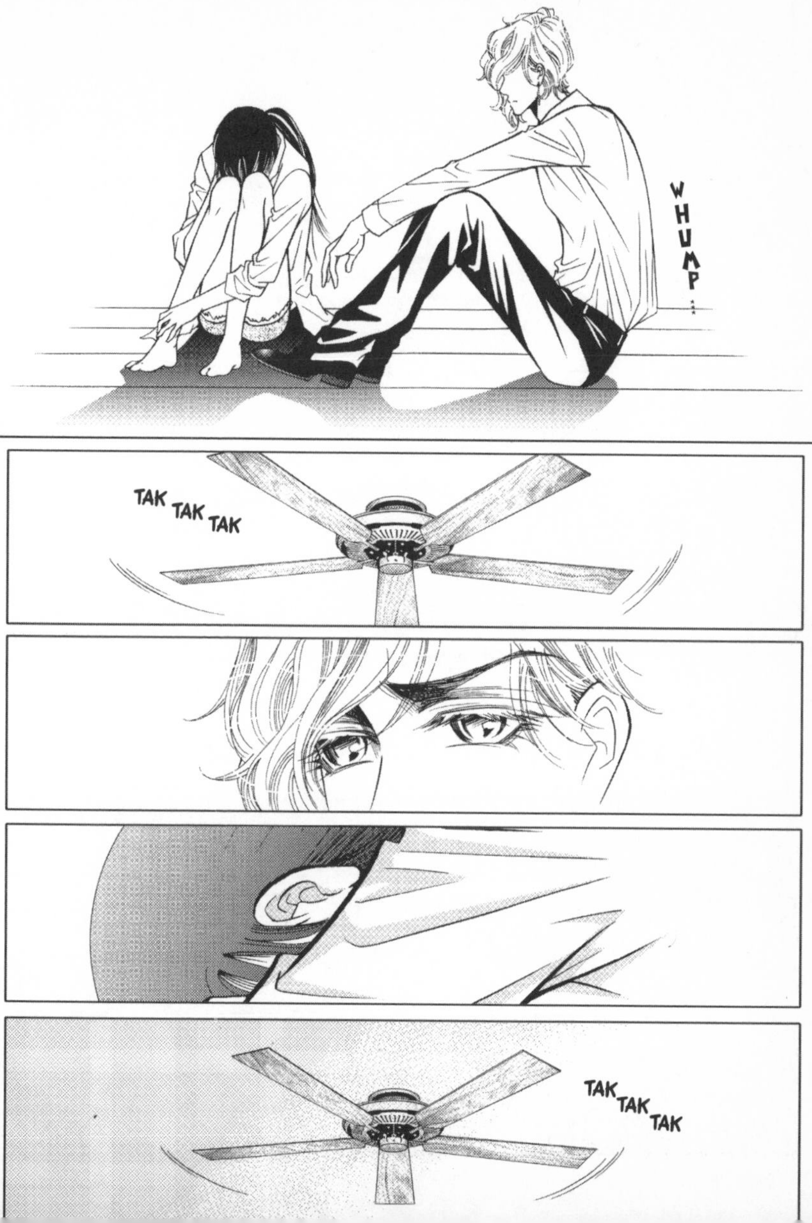
WHUMP...
TAK TAK TAK
TAK TAK TAK

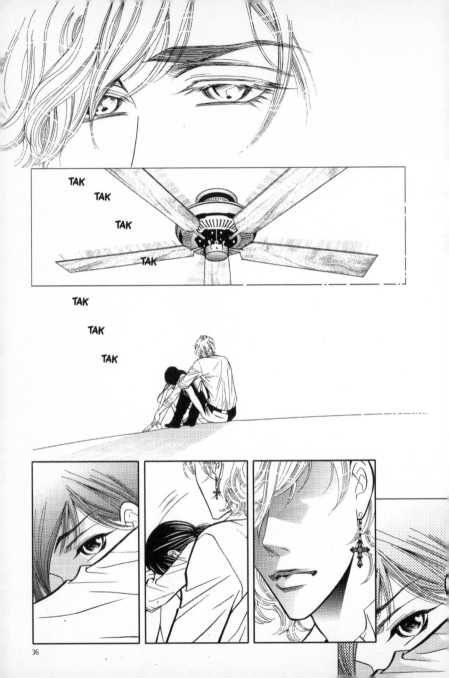

TAK
TAK
TAK
TAK
TAK
TAK
TAK

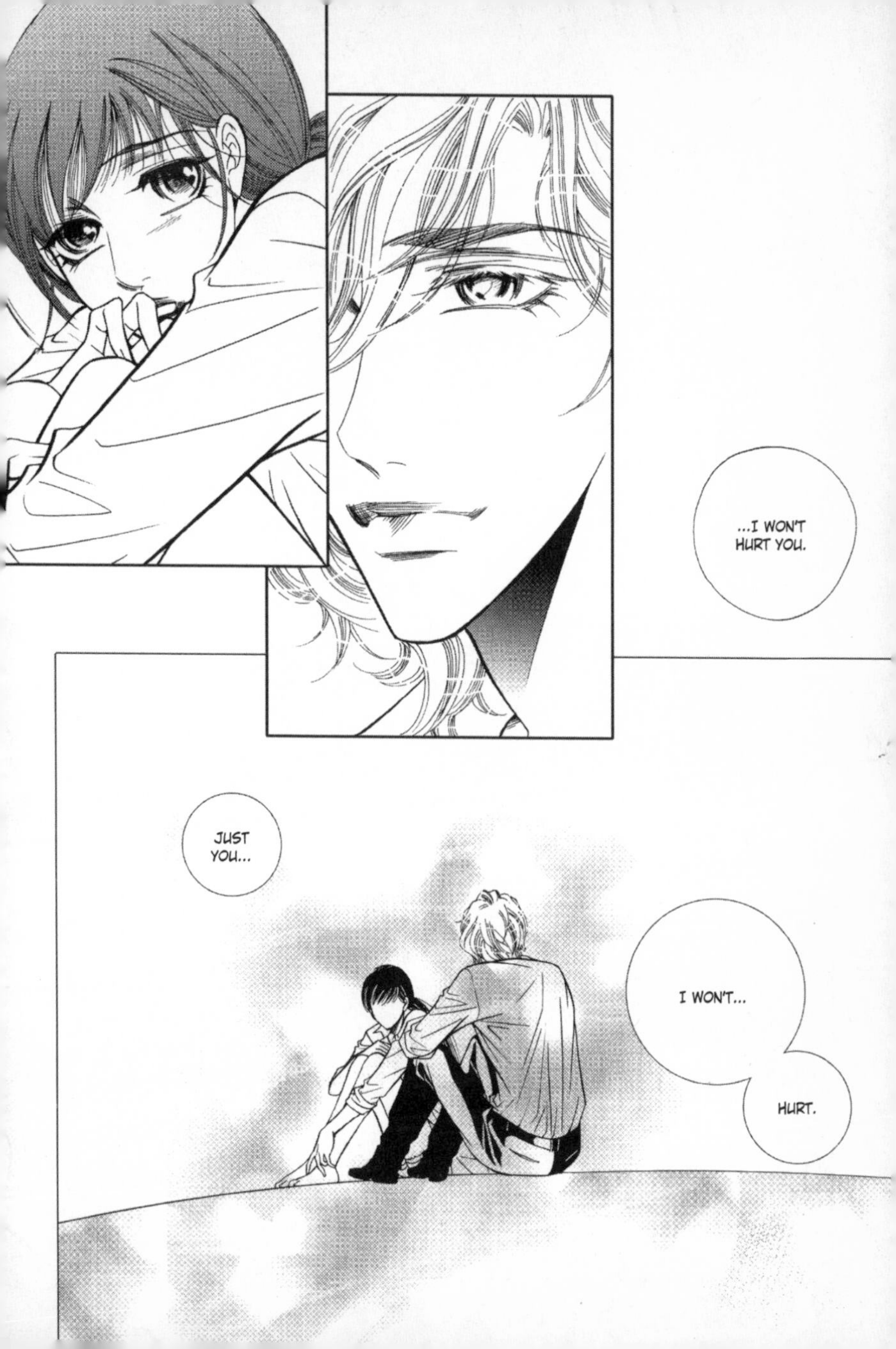
...I WON'T HURT YOU.
JUST YOU...
I WON'T...
HURT.

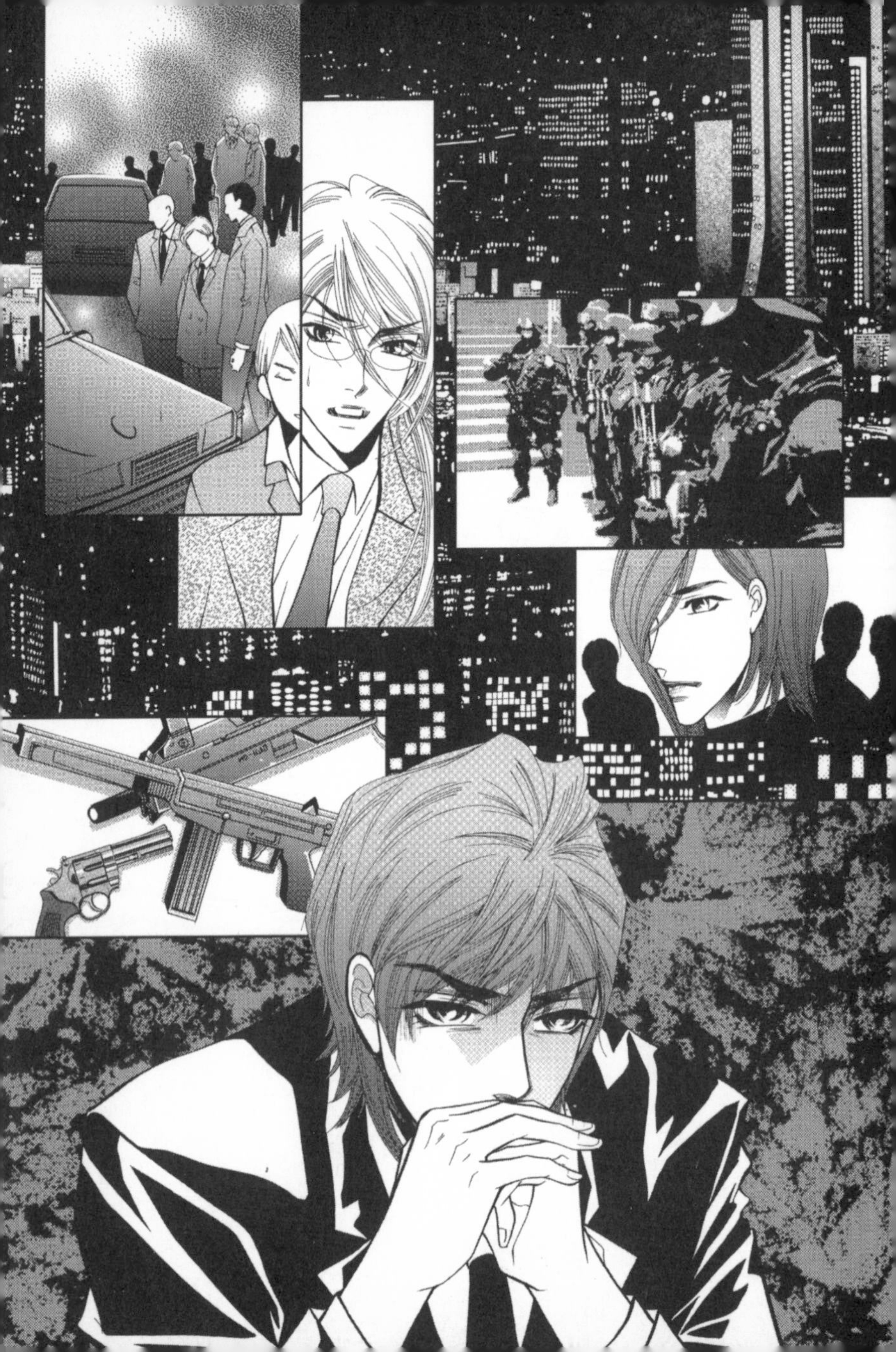

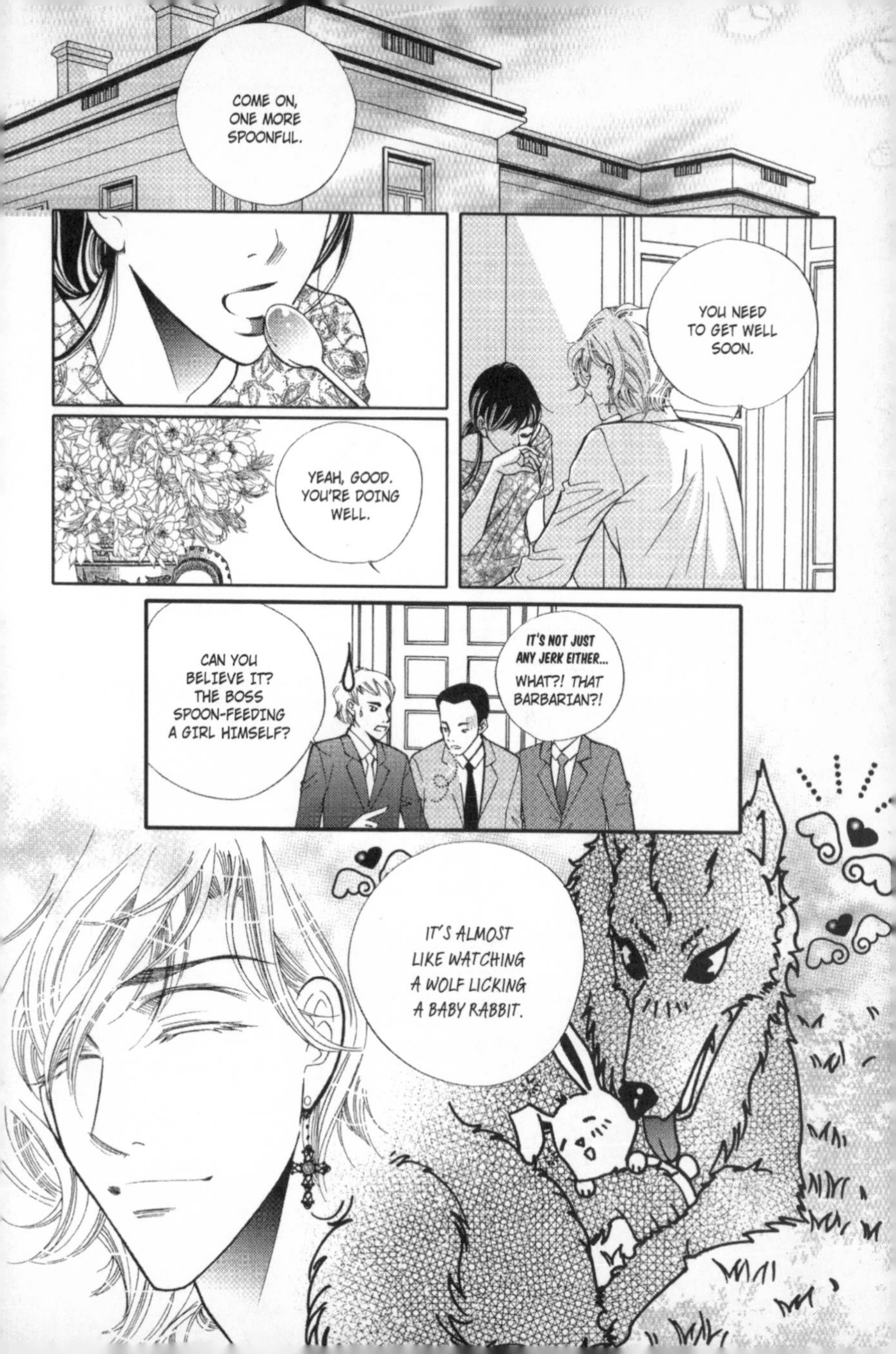
COME ON, ONE MORE SPOONFUL.
YOU NEED TO GET WELL SOON.
YEAH, GOOD. YOU'RE DOING WELL.
CAN YOU BELIEVE IT? THE BOSS SPOON-FEEDING A GIRL HIMSELF?
IT'S NOT JUST ANY JERK EITHER...
WHAT?! THAT BARBARIAN?!
IT'S ALMOST LIKE WATCHING A WOLF LICKING A BABY RABBIT.

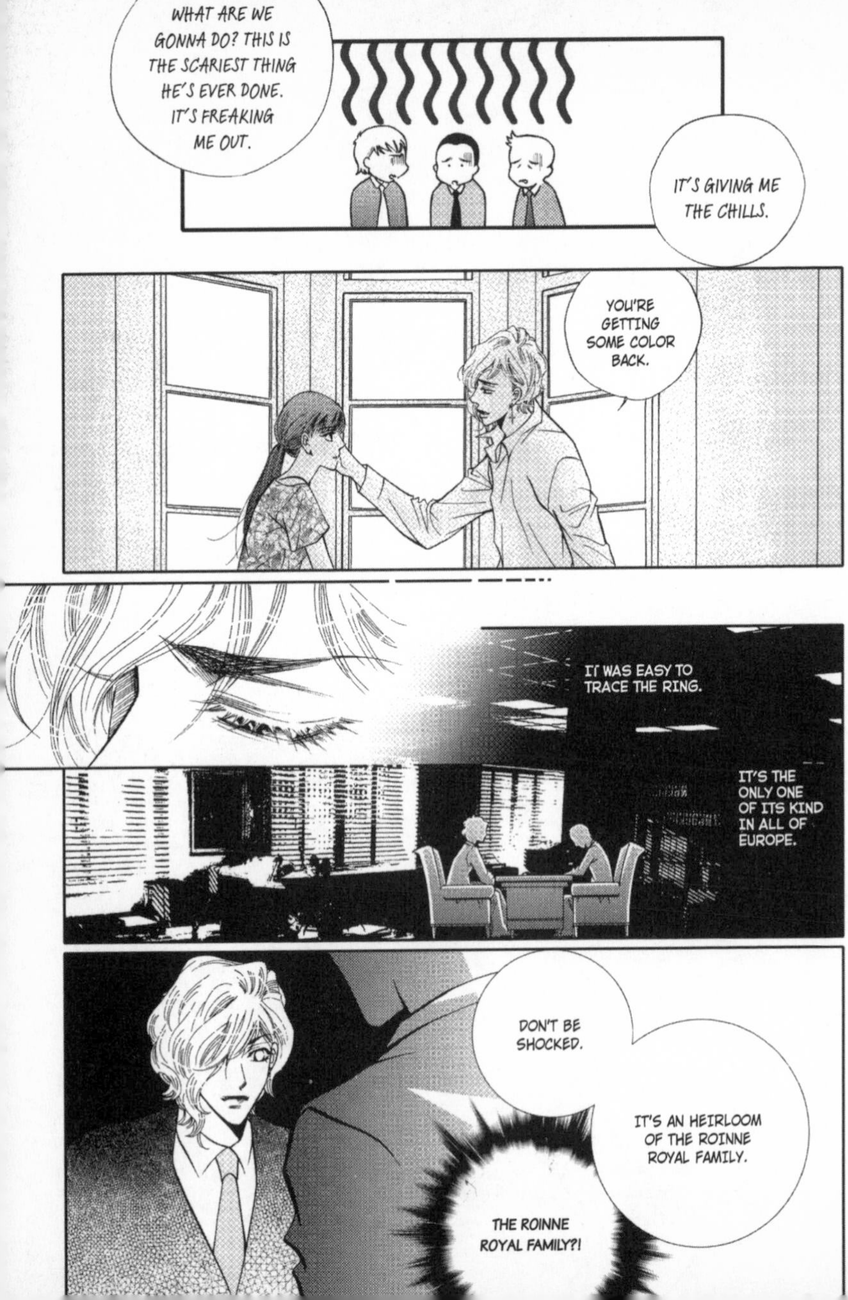
WHAT ARE WE GONNA DO? THIS IS THE SCARIEST THING HE'S EVER DONE. IT'S FREAKING ME OUT.
IT'S GIVING ME THE CHILLS.
YOU'RE GETTING SOME COLOR BACK.
IT WAS EASY TO TRACE THE RING.
IT'S THE ONLY ONE OF ITS KIND IN ALL OF EUROPE.
DON'T BE SHOCKED.
IT'S AN HEIRLOOM OF THE ROINNE ROYAL FAMILY.
THE ROINNE ROYAL FAMILY?!

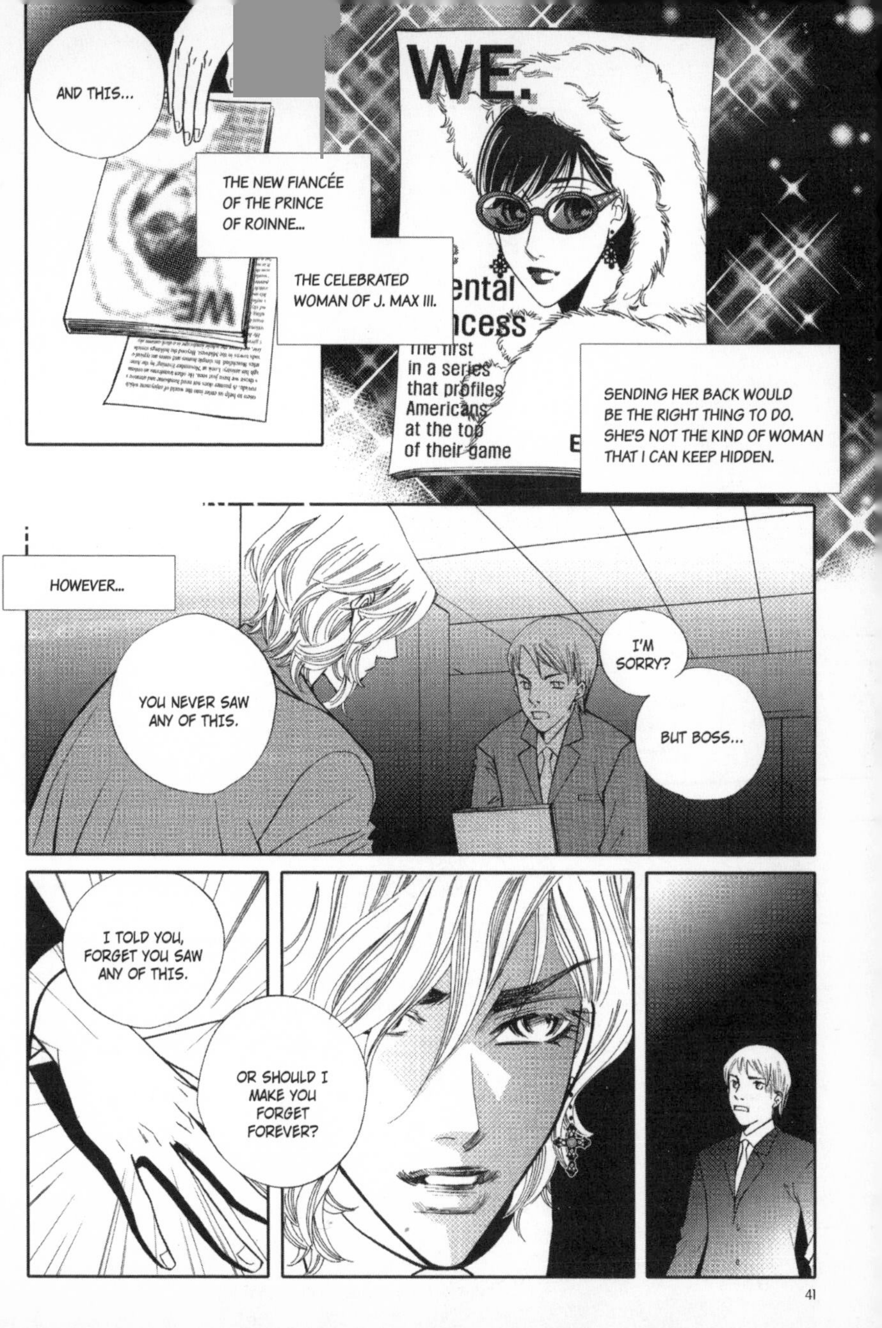
AND THIS...
THE NEW FIANCÉE OF THE PRINCE OF ROINNE...
THE CELEBRATED WOMAN OF J. MAX III.
WE.
The first in a series that profiles Americans at the top of their game
SENDING HER BACK WOULD BE THE RIGHT THING TO DO. SHE'S NOT THE KIND OF WOMAN THAT I CAN KEEP HIDDEN.
HOWEVER...
YOU NEVER SAW ANY OF THIS.
I'M SORRY?
BUT BOSS...
I TOLD YOU, FORGET YOU SAW ANY OF THIS.
OR SHOULD I MAKE YOU FORGET FOREVER?

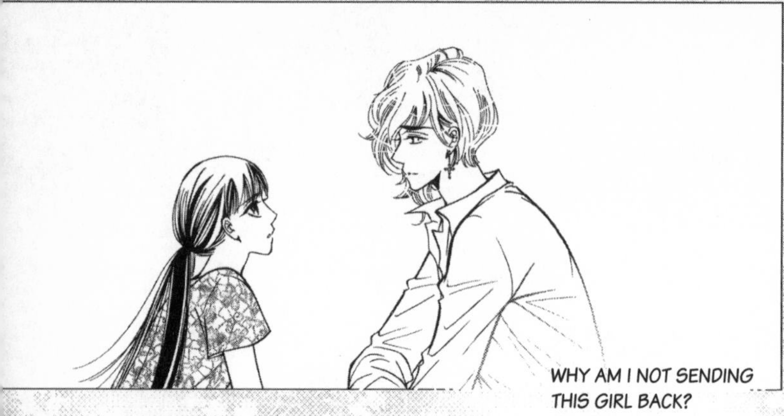
WHY AM I NOT SENDING
THIS GIRL BACK?

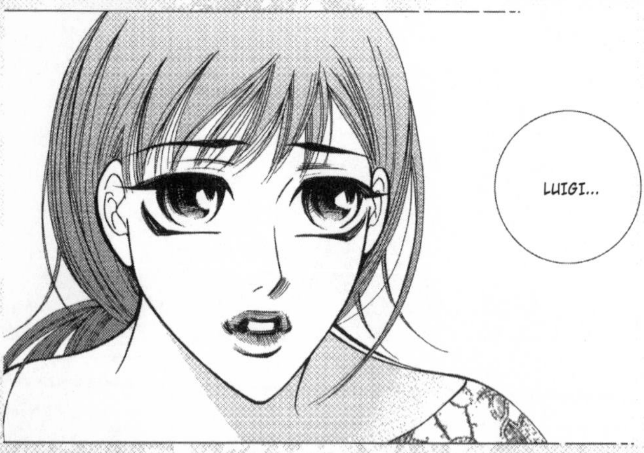
LUIGI...

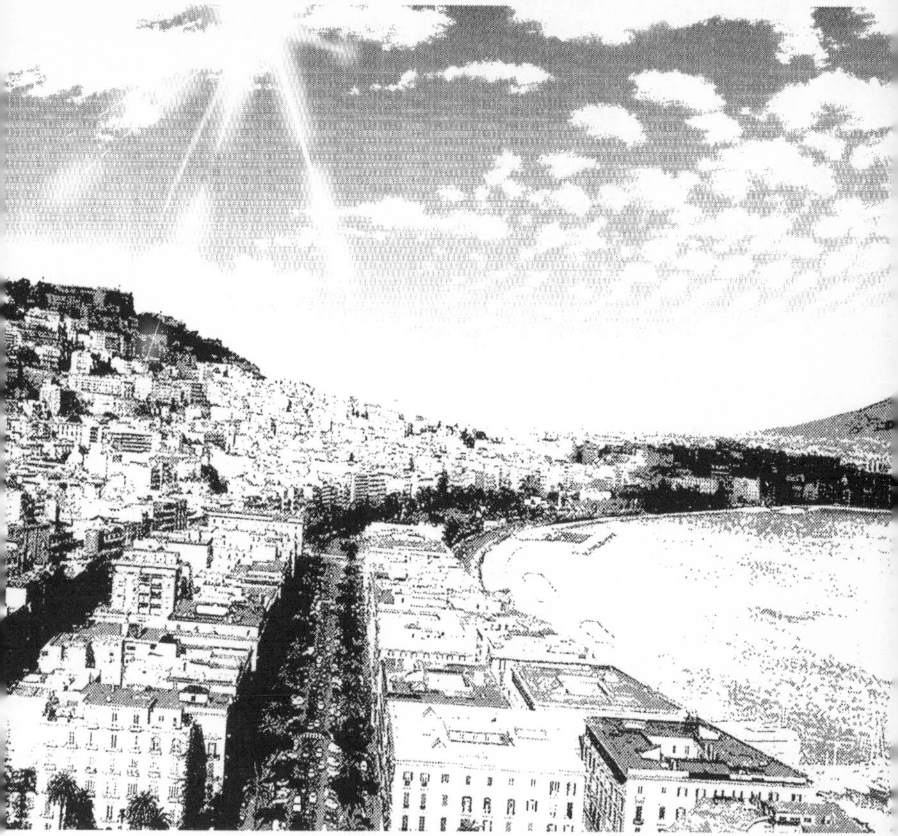
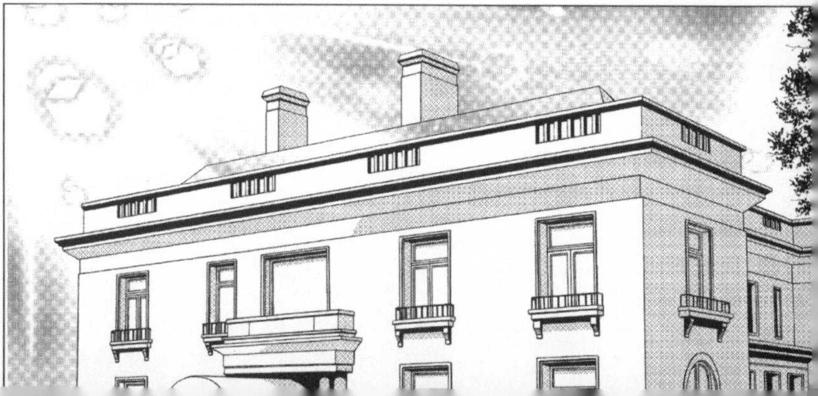

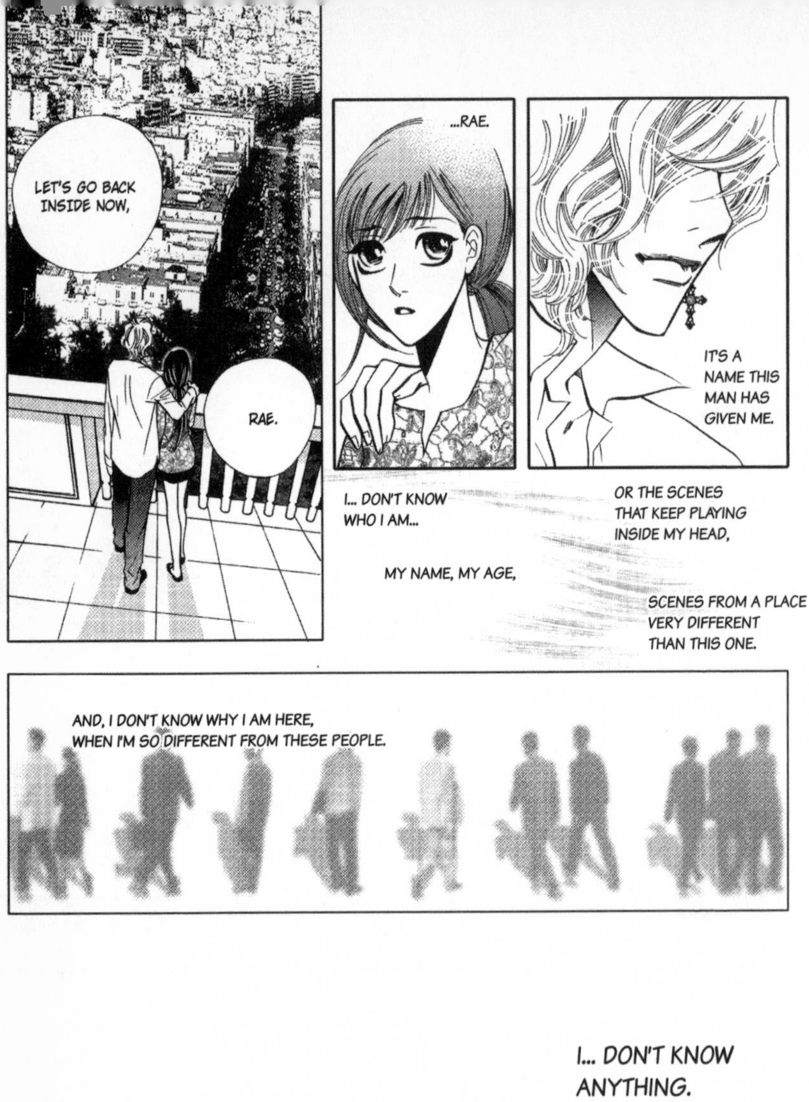
LET'S GO BACK INSIDE NOW,
RAE.
...RAE.
IT'S A NAME THIS MAN HAS GIVEN ME.
I... DON'T KNOW WHO I AM...
MY NAME, MY AGE,
OR THE SCENES THAT KEEP PLAYING INSIDE MY HEAD,
SCENES FROM A PLACE VERY DIFFERENT THAN THIS ONE.
AND, I DON'T KNOW WHY I AM HERE, WHEN I'M SO DIFFERENT FROM THESE PEOPLE.
I... DON'T KNOW ANYTHING.

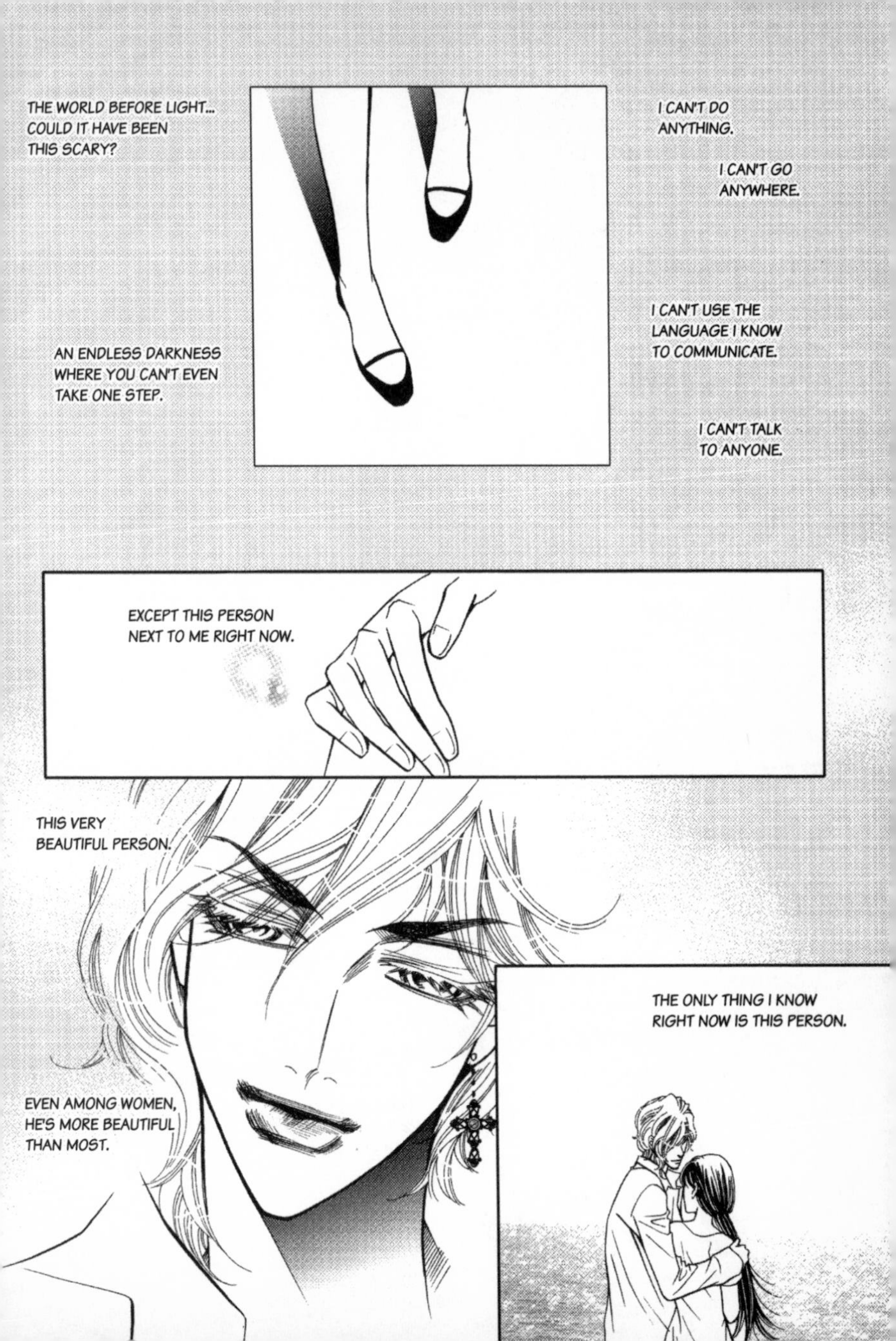
THE WORLD BEFORE LIGHT... COULD IT HAVE BEEN THIS SCARY?
AN ENDLESS DARKNESS WHERE YOU CAN'T EVEN TAKE ONE STEP.
I CAN'T DO ANYTHING.
I CAN'T GO ANYWHERE.
I CAN'T USE THE LANGUAGE I KNOW TO COMMUNICATE.
I CAN'T TALK TO ANYONE.
EXCEPT THIS PERSON NEXT TO ME RIGHT NOW.
THIS VERY BEAUTIFUL PERSON.
EVEN AMONG WOMEN, HE'S MORE BEAUTIFUL THAN MOST.
THE ONLY THING I KNOW RIGHT NOW IS THIS PERSON.

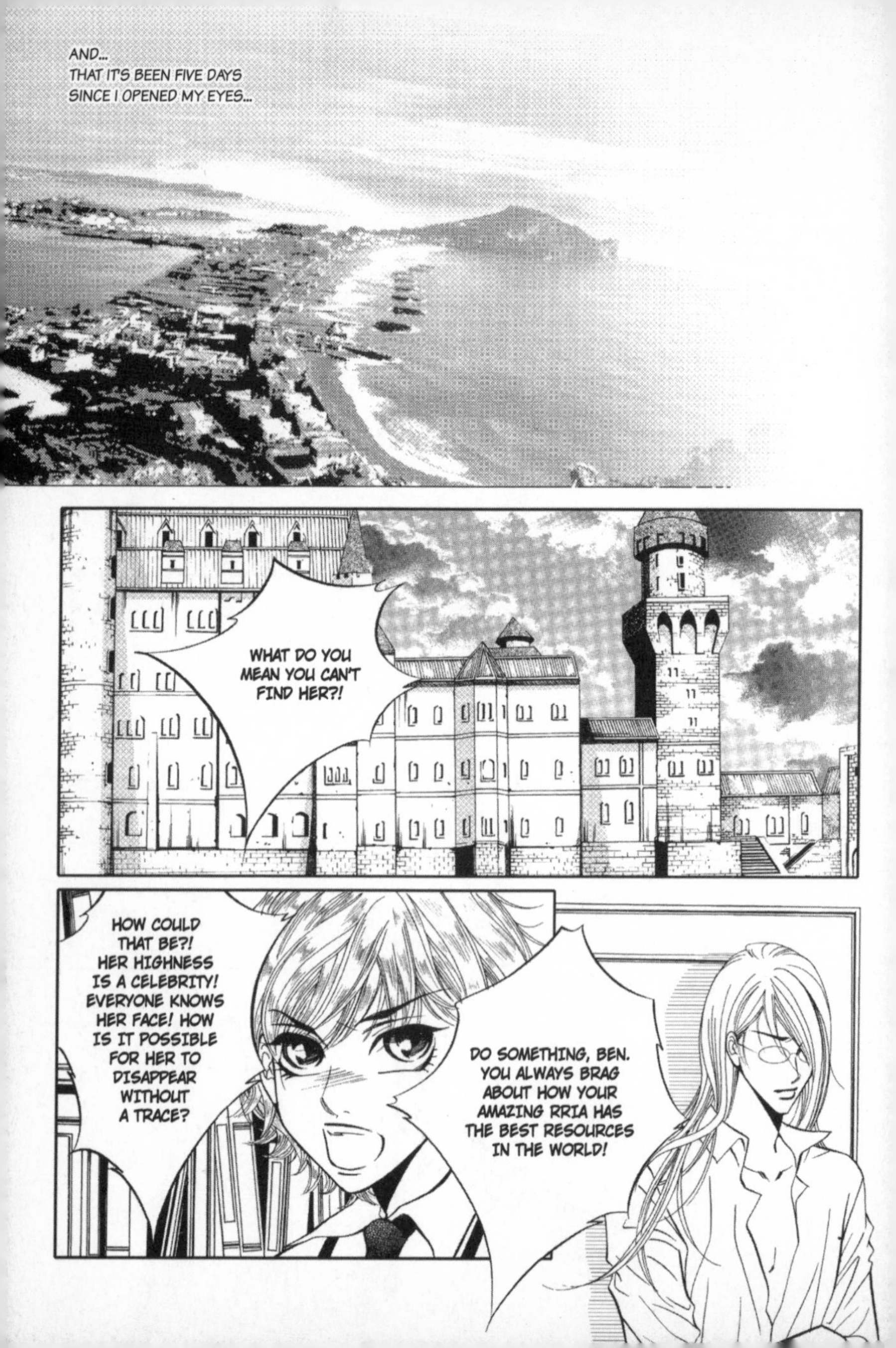
AND...
THAT IT'S BEEN FIVE DAYS
SINCE I OPENED MY EYES...
WHAT DO YOU MEAN YOU CAN'T FIND HER?!
HOW COULD THAT BE?! HER HIGHNESS IS A CELEBRITY! EVERYONE KNOWS HER FACE! HOW IS IT POSSIBLE FOR HER TO DISAPPEAR WITHOUT A TRACE?
DO SOMETHING, BEN. YOU ALWAYS BRAG ABOUT HOW YOUR AMAZING RRIA HAS THE BEST RESOURCES IN THE WORLD!

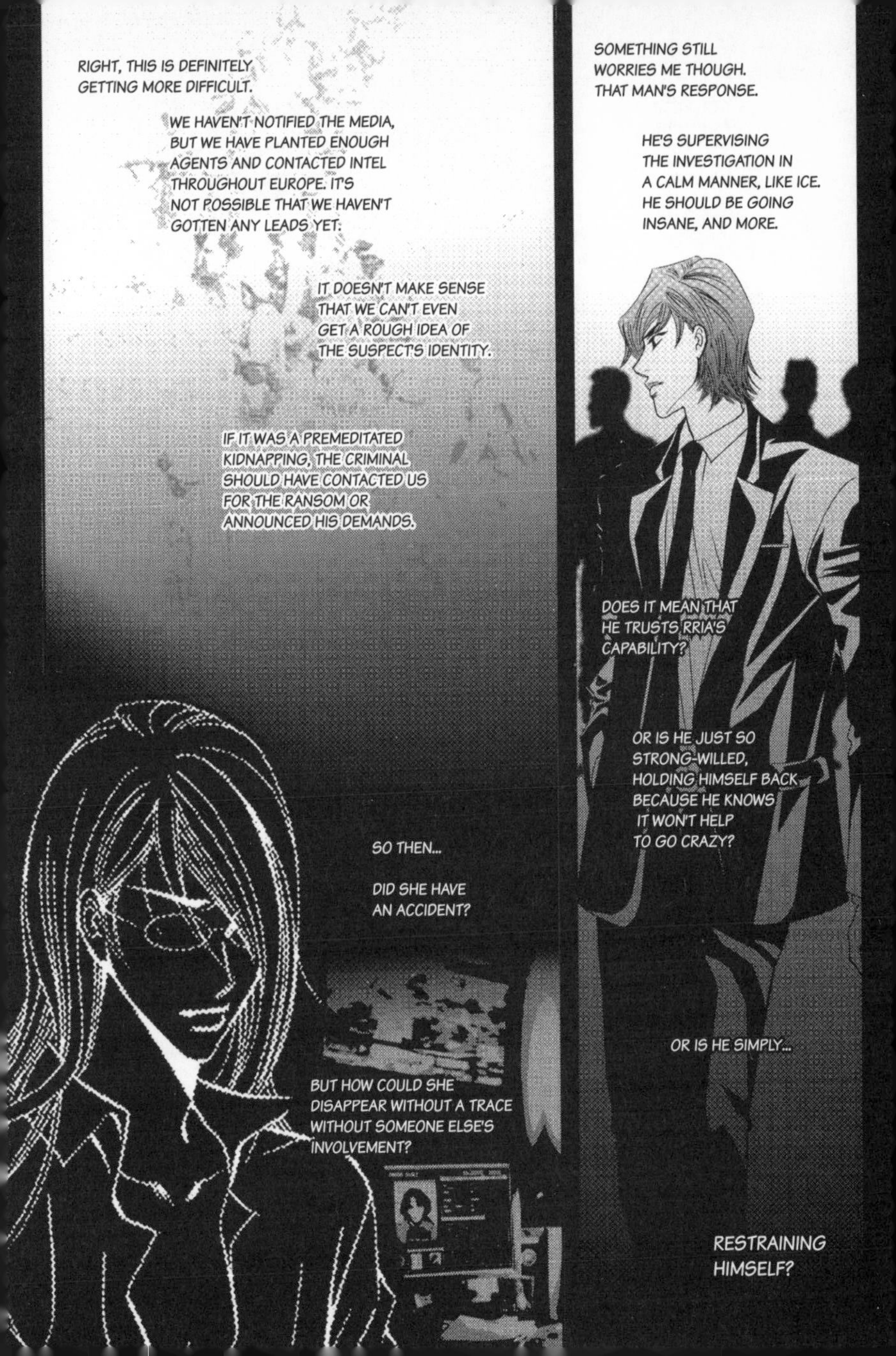

RIGHT, THIS IS DEFINITELY GETTING MORE DIFFICULT.
WE HAVEN'T NOTIFIED THE MEDIA, BUT WE HAVE PLANTED ENOUGH AGENTS AND CONTACTED INTEL THROUGHOUT EUROPE. IT'S NOT POSSIBLE THAT WE HAVEN'T GOTTEN ANY LEADS YET.
IT DOESN'T MAKE SENSE THAT WE CAN'T EVEN GET A ROUGH IDEA OF THE SUSPECT'S IDENTITY.
IF IT WAS A PREMEDITATED KIDNAPPING, THE CRIMINAL SHOULD HAVE CONTACTED US FOR THE RANSOM OR ANNOUNCED HIS DEMANDS.
SO THEN...
DID SHE HAVE AN ACCIDENT?
BUT HOW COULD SHE DISAPPEAR WITHOUT A TRACE WITHOUT SOMEONE ELSE'S INVOLVEMENT?
SOMETHING STILL WORRIES ME THOUGH. THAT MAN'S RESPONSE.
HE'S SUPERVISING THE INVESTIGATION IN A CALM MANNER, LIKE ICE. HE SHOULD BE GOING INSANE, AND MORE.
DOES IT MEAN THAT HE TRUSTS RRIA'S CAPABILITY?
OR IS HE JUST SO STRONG-WILLED, HOLDING HIMSELF BACK BECAUSE HE KNOWS IT WON'T HELP TO GO CRAZY?
OR IS HE SIMPLY...
RESTRAINING HIMSELF?

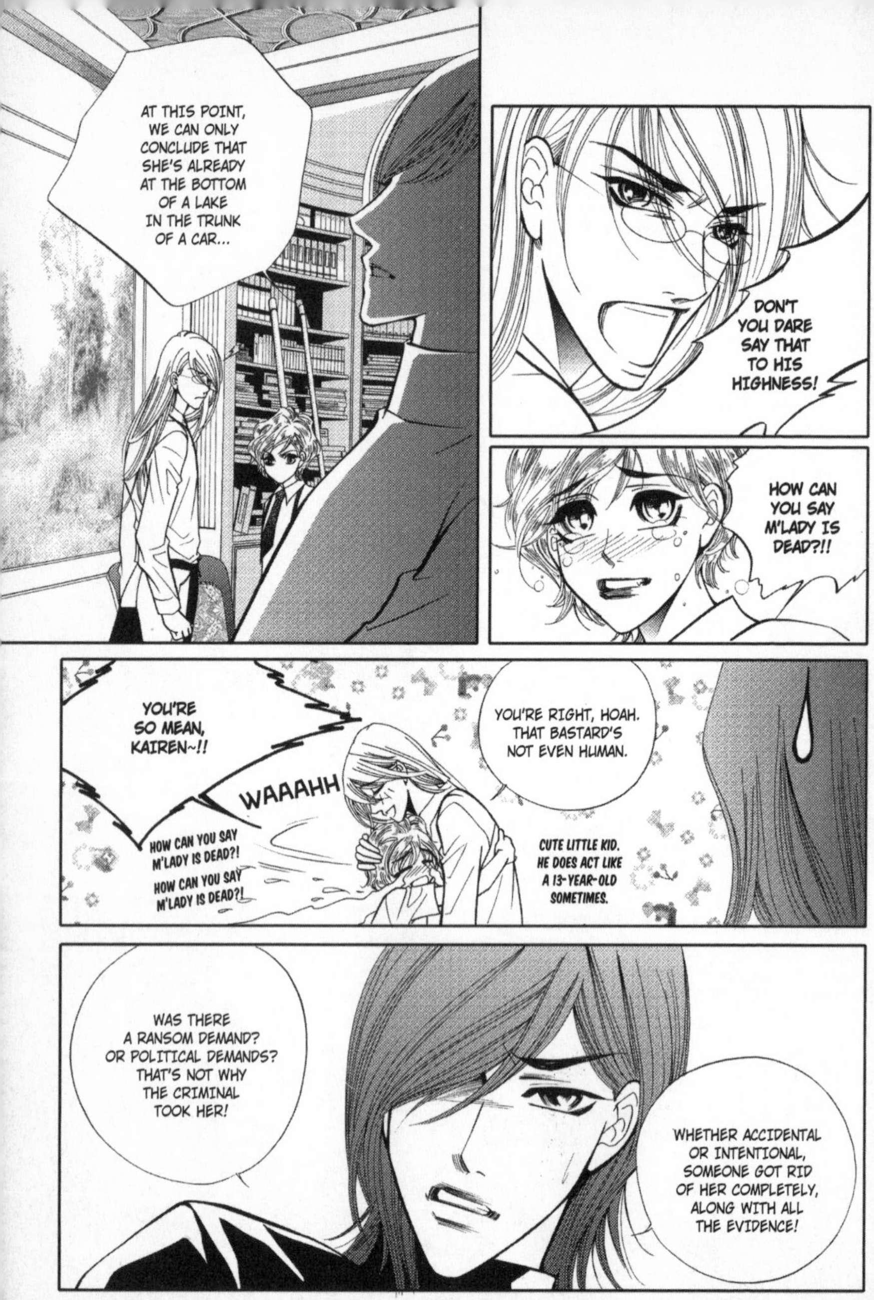
AT THIS POINT, WE CAN ONLY CONCLUDE THAT SHE'S ALREADY AT THE BOTTOM OF A LAKE IN THE TRUNK OF A CAR...
DON'T YOU DARE SAY THAT TO HIS HIGHNESS!
HOW CAN YOU SAY M'LADY IS DEAD?!!
YOU'RE SO MEAN, KAIREN~!!
WAAAHH
HOW CAN YOU SAY M'LADY IS DEAD?!
HOW CAN YOU SAY M'LADY IS DEAD?!
YOU'RE RIGHT, HOAH. THAT BASTARD'S NOT EVEN HUMAN.
CUTE LITTLE KID. HE DOES ACT LIKE A 13-YEAR-OLD SOMETIMES.
WAS THERE A RANSOM DEMAND? OR POLITICAL DEMANDS? THAT'S NOT WHY THE CRIMINAL TOOK HER!
WHETHER ACCIDENTAL OR INTENTIONAL, SOMEONE GOT RID OF HER COMPLETELY, ALONG WITH ALL THE EVIDENCE!

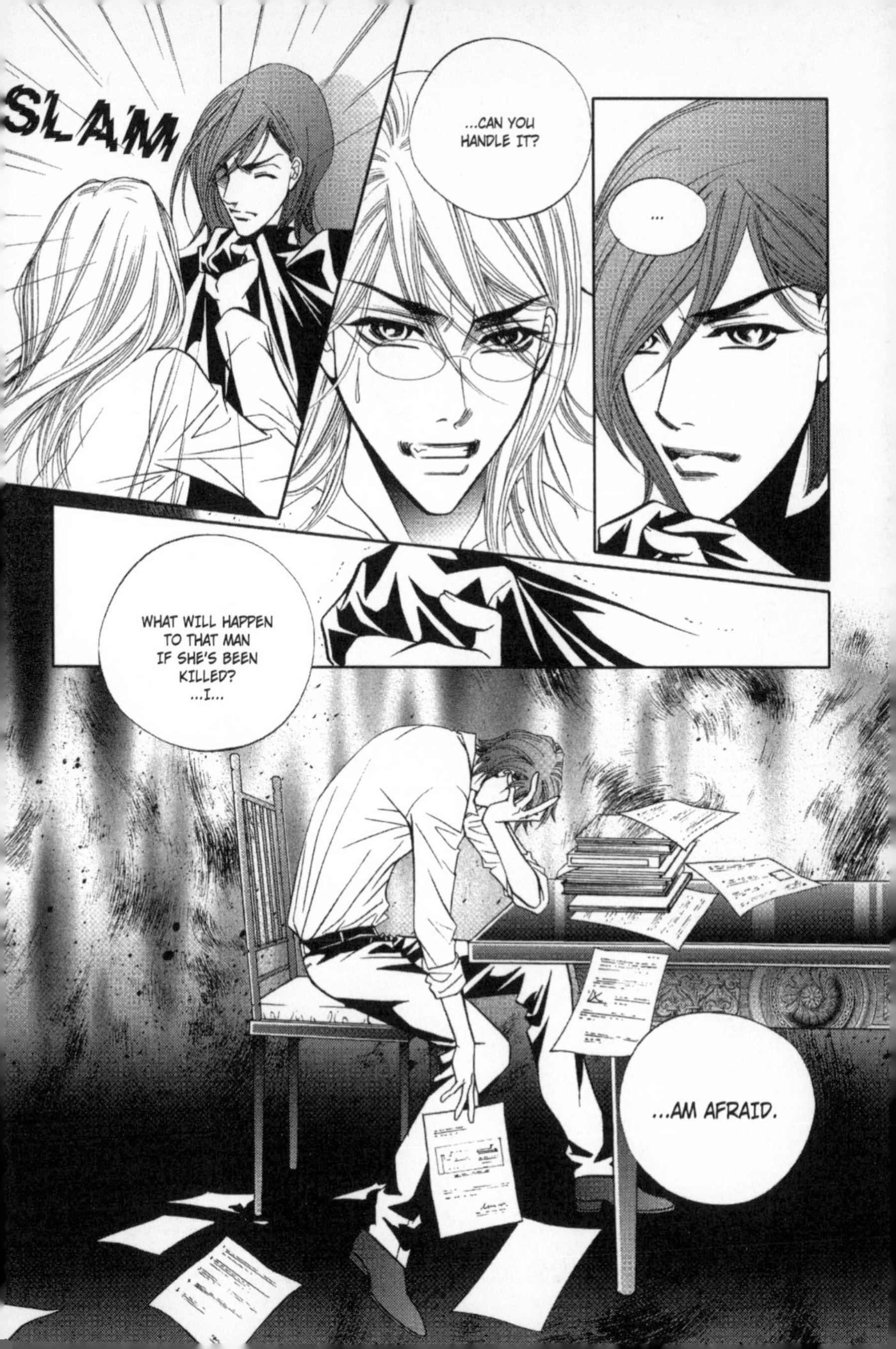
SLAM
...CAN YOU HANDLE IT?
...
WHAT WILL HAPPEN TO THAT MAN IF SHE'S BEEN KILLED? ...I...
...AM AFRAID.

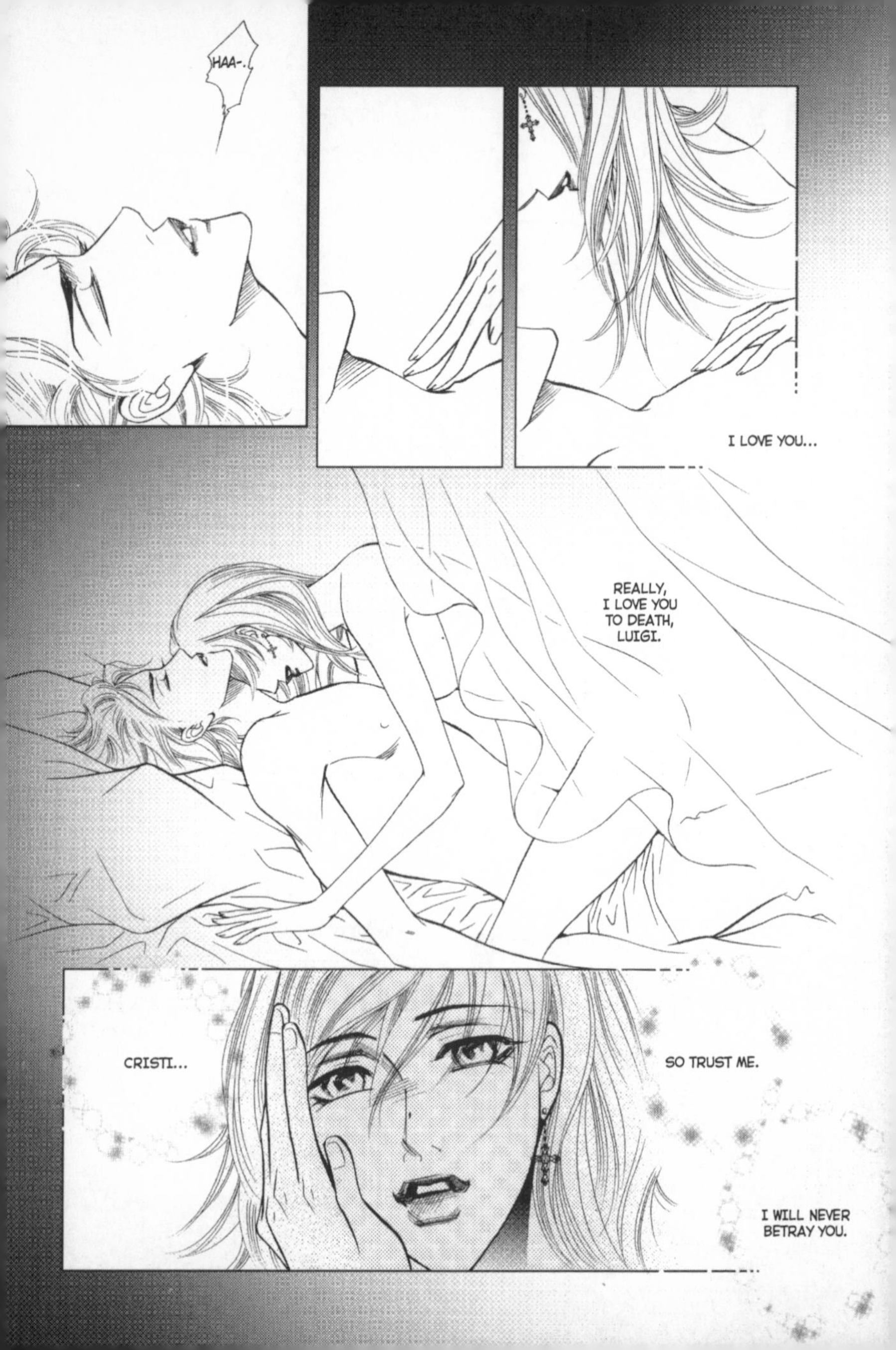
HAA-.
I LOVE YOU...
REALLY, I LOVE YOU TO DEATH, LUIGI.
CRISTI...
SO TRUST ME.
I WILL NEVER BETRAY YOU.

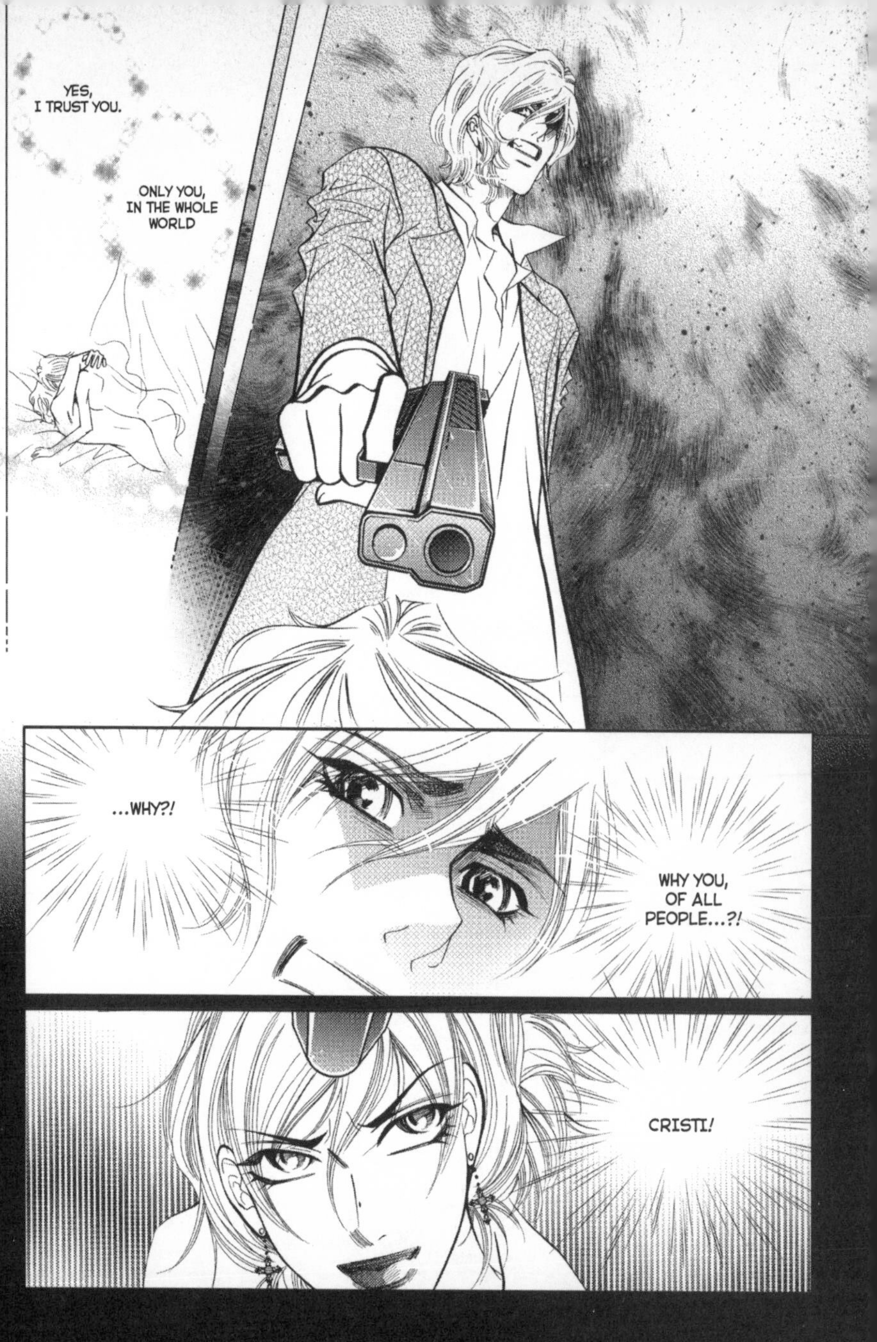
YES, I TRUST YOU.
ONLY YOU, IN THE WHOLE WORLD
...WHY?!
WHY YOU, OF ALL PEOPLE...?!
CRISTI!

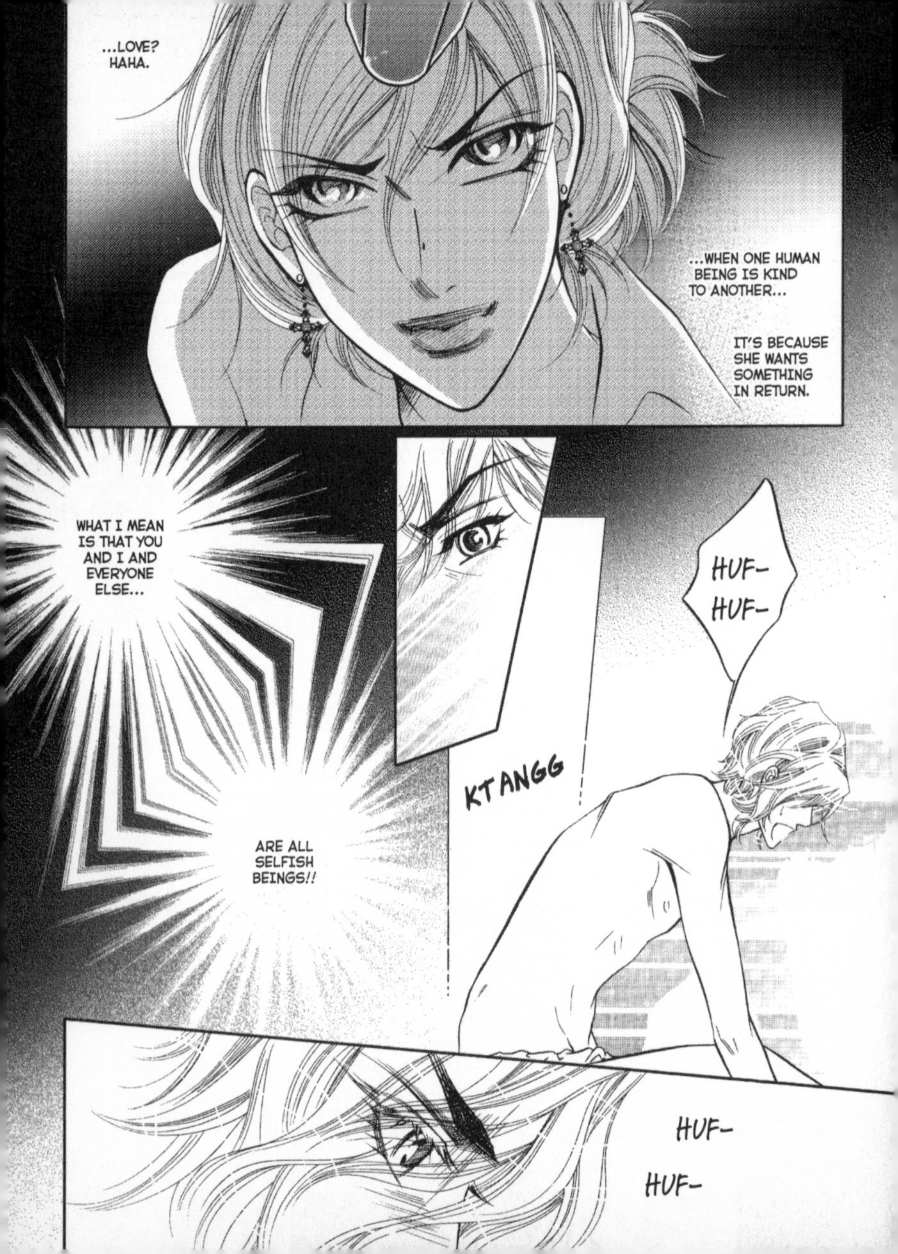
...LOVE? HAHA.
...WHEN ONE HUMAN BEING IS KIND TO ANOTHER...
IT'S BECAUSE SHE WANTS SOMETHING IN RETURN.
WHAT I MEAN IS THAT YOU AND I AND EVERYONE ELSE...
ARE ALL SELFISH BEINGS!!
HUF- HUF-
KTANGG
HUF-
HUF-

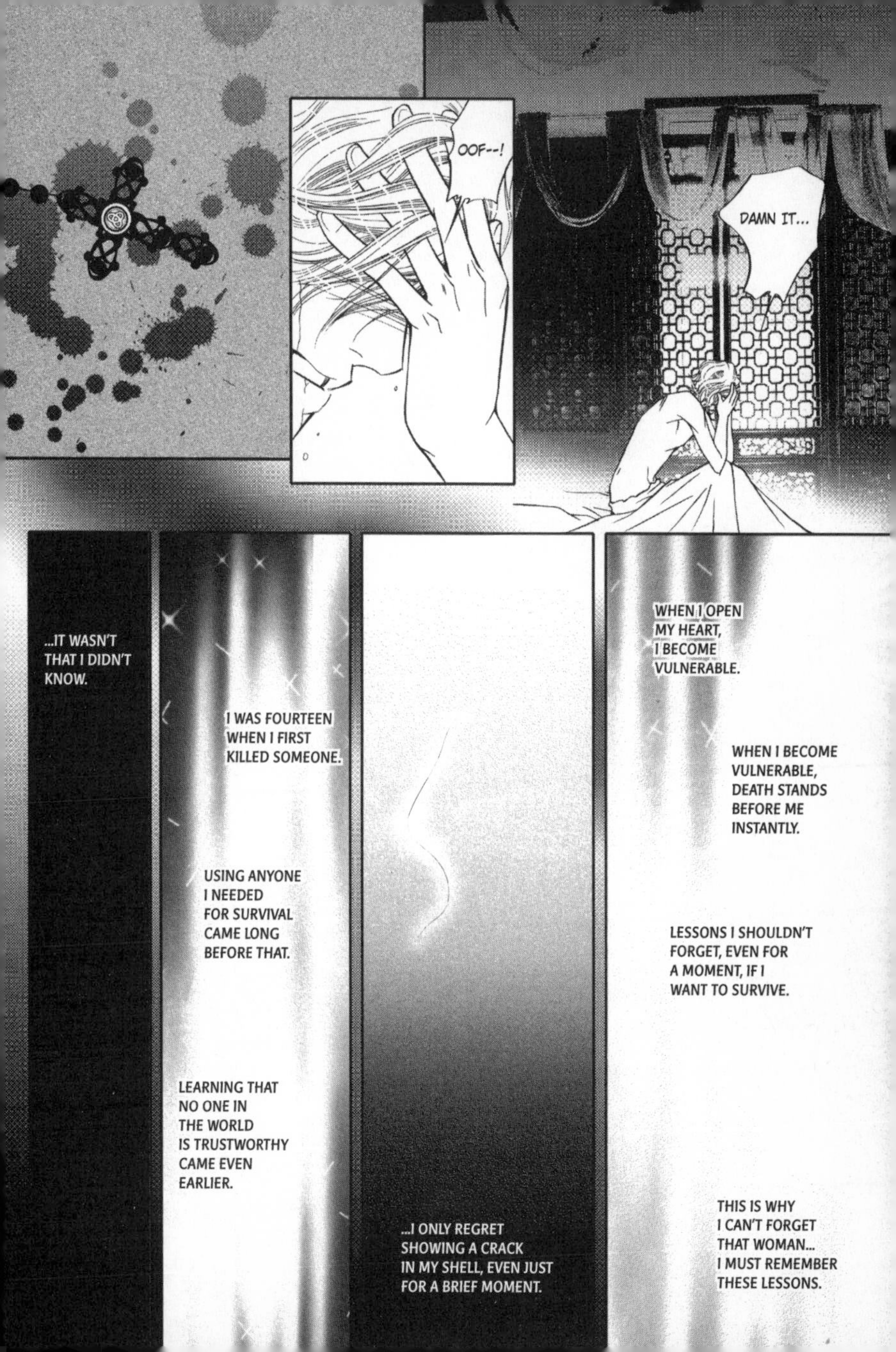
OOF--!
DAMN IT...
...IT WASN'T THAT I DIDN'T KNOW.
I WAS FOURTEEN WHEN I FIRST KILLED SOMEONE.
USING ANYONE I NEEDED FOR SURVIVAL CAME LONG BEFORE THAT.
LEARNING THAT NO ONE IN THE WORLD IS TRUSTWORTHY CAME EVEN EARLIER.
...I ONLY REGRET SHOWING A CRACK IN MY SHELL, EVEN JUST FOR A BRIEF MOMENT.
WHEN I OPEN MY HEART, I BECOME VULNERABLE.
WHEN I BECOME VULNERABLE, DEATH STANDS BEFORE ME INSTANTLY.
LESSONS I SHOULDN'T FORGET, EVEN FOR A MOMENT, IF I WANT TO SURVIVE.
THIS IS WHY I CAN'T FORGET THAT WOMAN... I MUST REMEMBER THESE LESSONS.

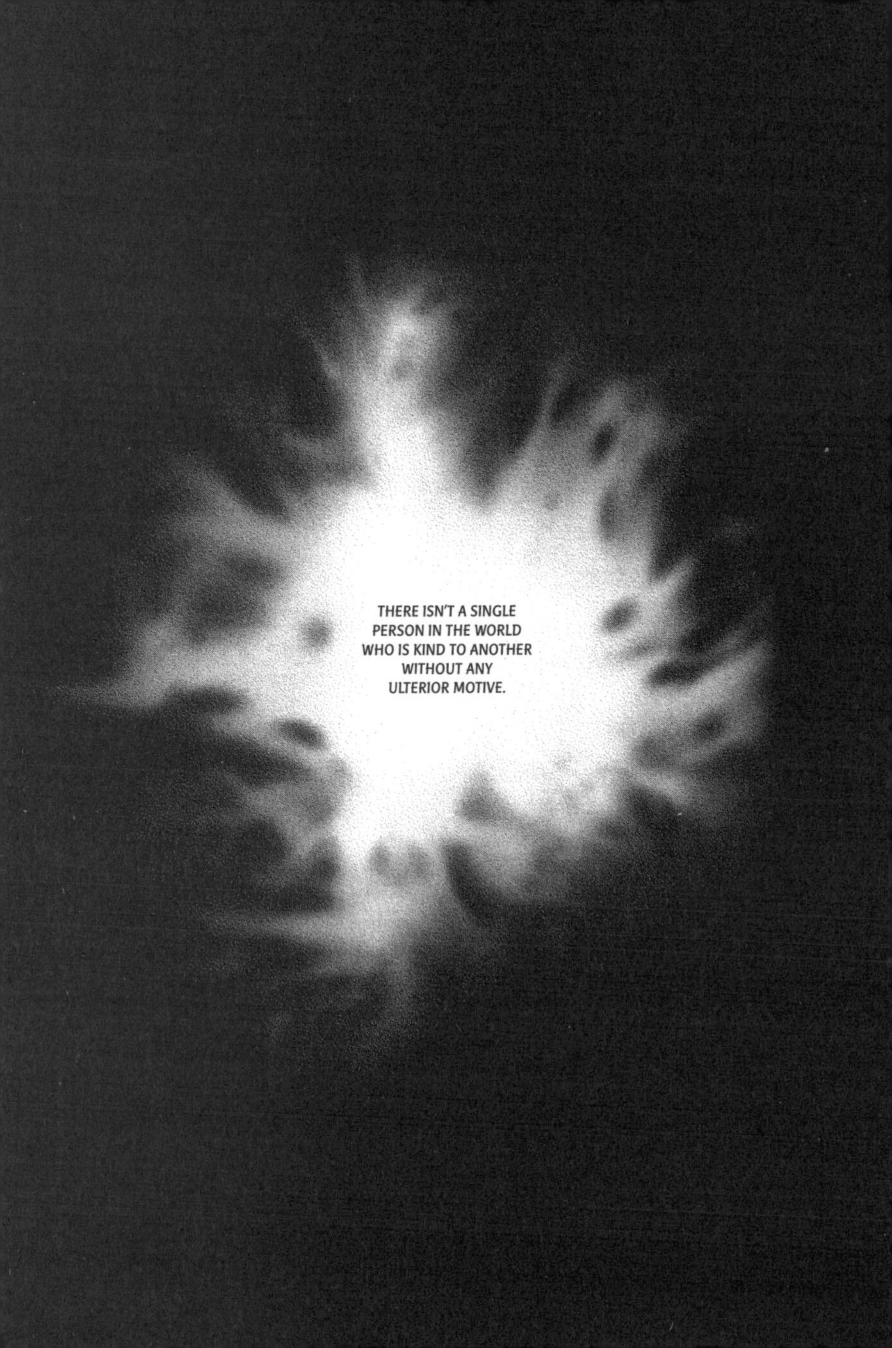
THERE ISN'T A SINGLE PERSON IN THE WORLD WHO IS KIND TO ANOTHER WITHOUT ANY ULTERIOR MOTIVE.

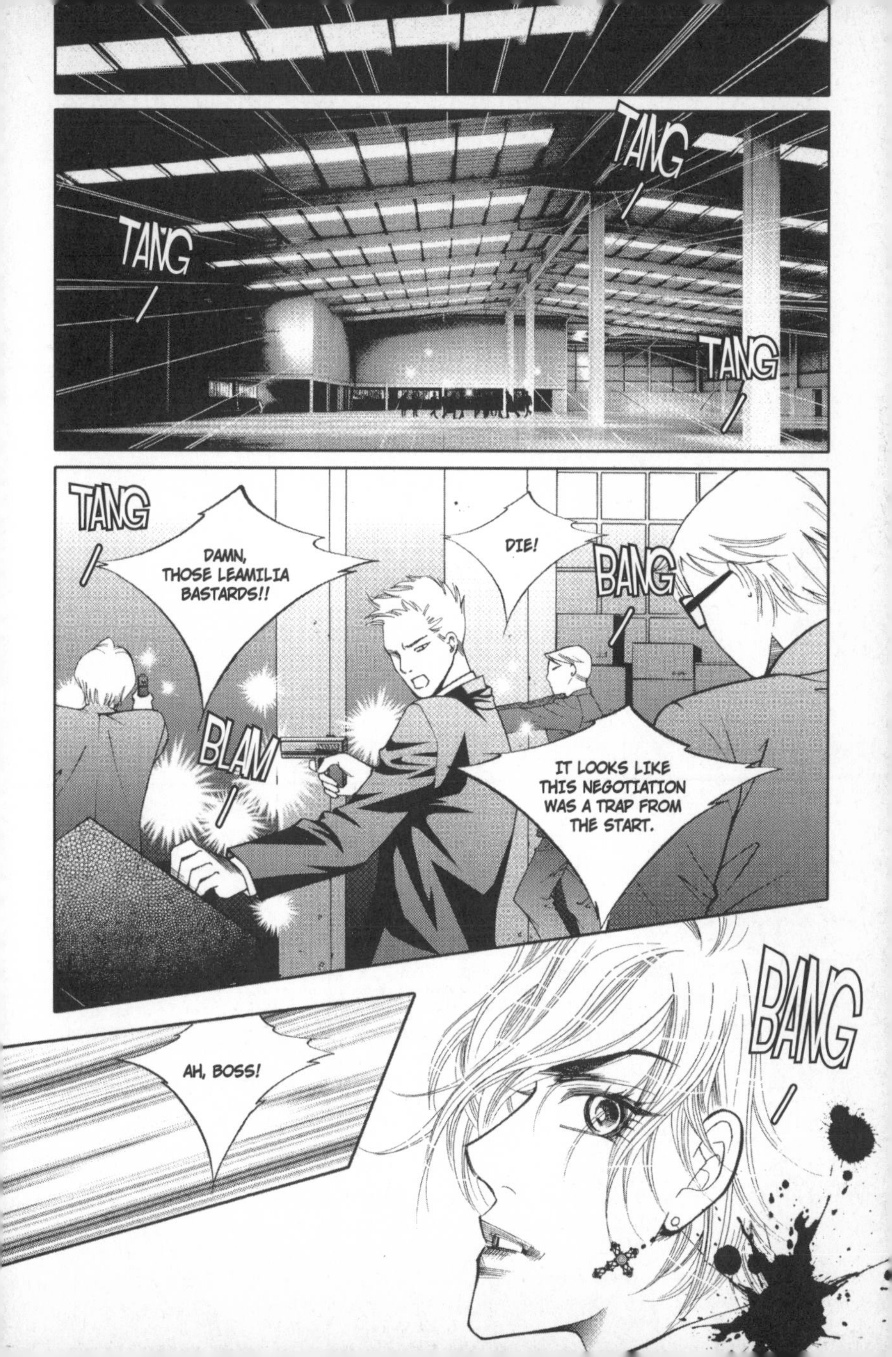
TANG
TANG
TANG
TANG
DAMN, THOSE LEAMILIA BASTARDS!!
DIE!
BANG
BLAM
IT LOOKS LIKE THIS NEGOTIATION WAS A TRAP FROM THE START.
AH, BOSS!
BANG

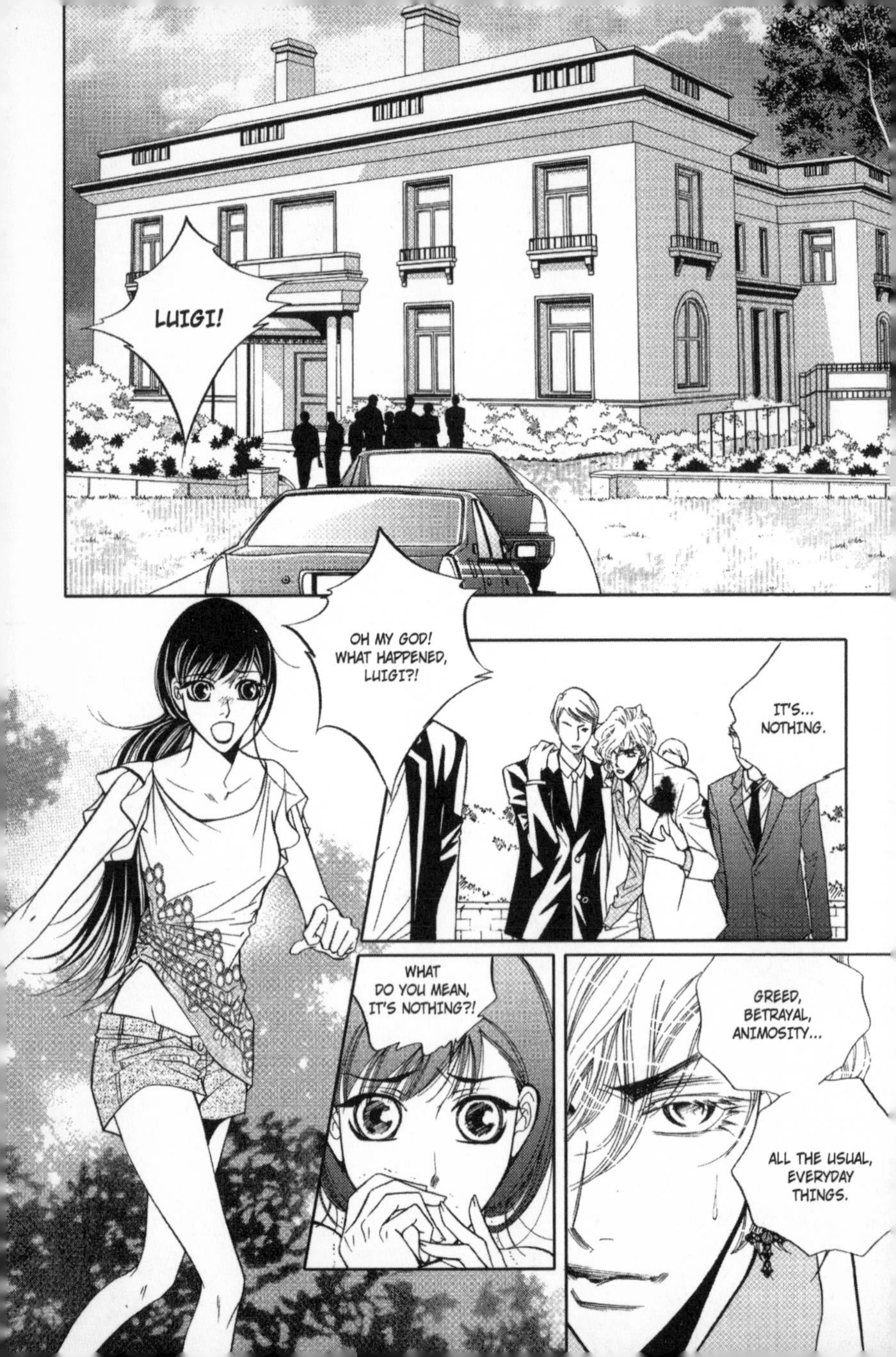
LUIGI!
OH MY GOD! WHAT HAPPENED, LUIGI?!
IT'S... NOTHING.
WHAT DO YOU MEAN, IT'S NOTHING?!
GREED, BETRAYAL, ANIMOSITY...
ALL THE USUAL, EVERYDAY THINGS.

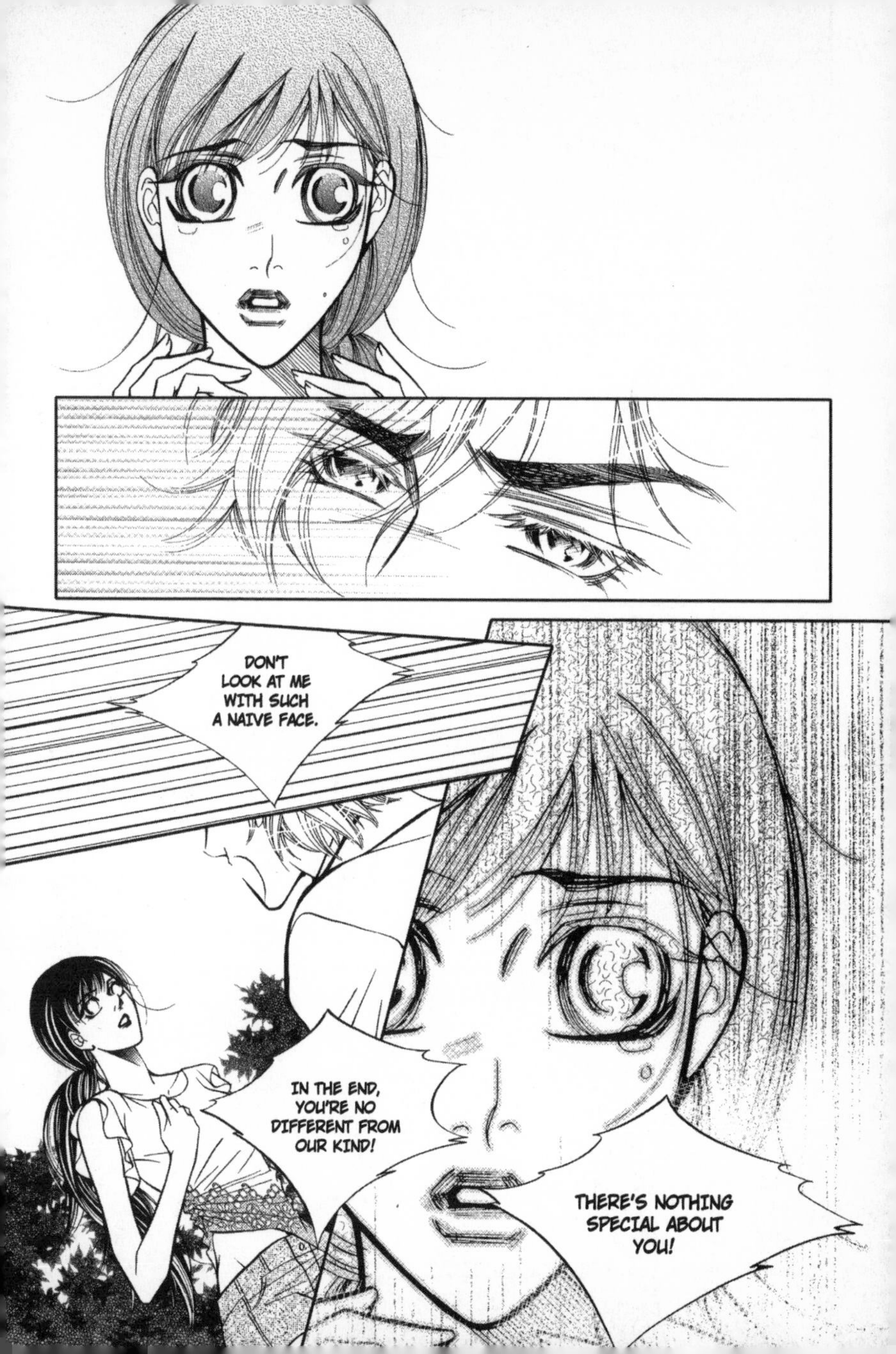
DON'T LOOK AT ME WITH SUCH A NAIVE FACE.
IN THE END, YOU'RE NO DIFFERENT FROM OUR KIND!
THERE'S NOTHING SPECIAL ABOUT YOU!

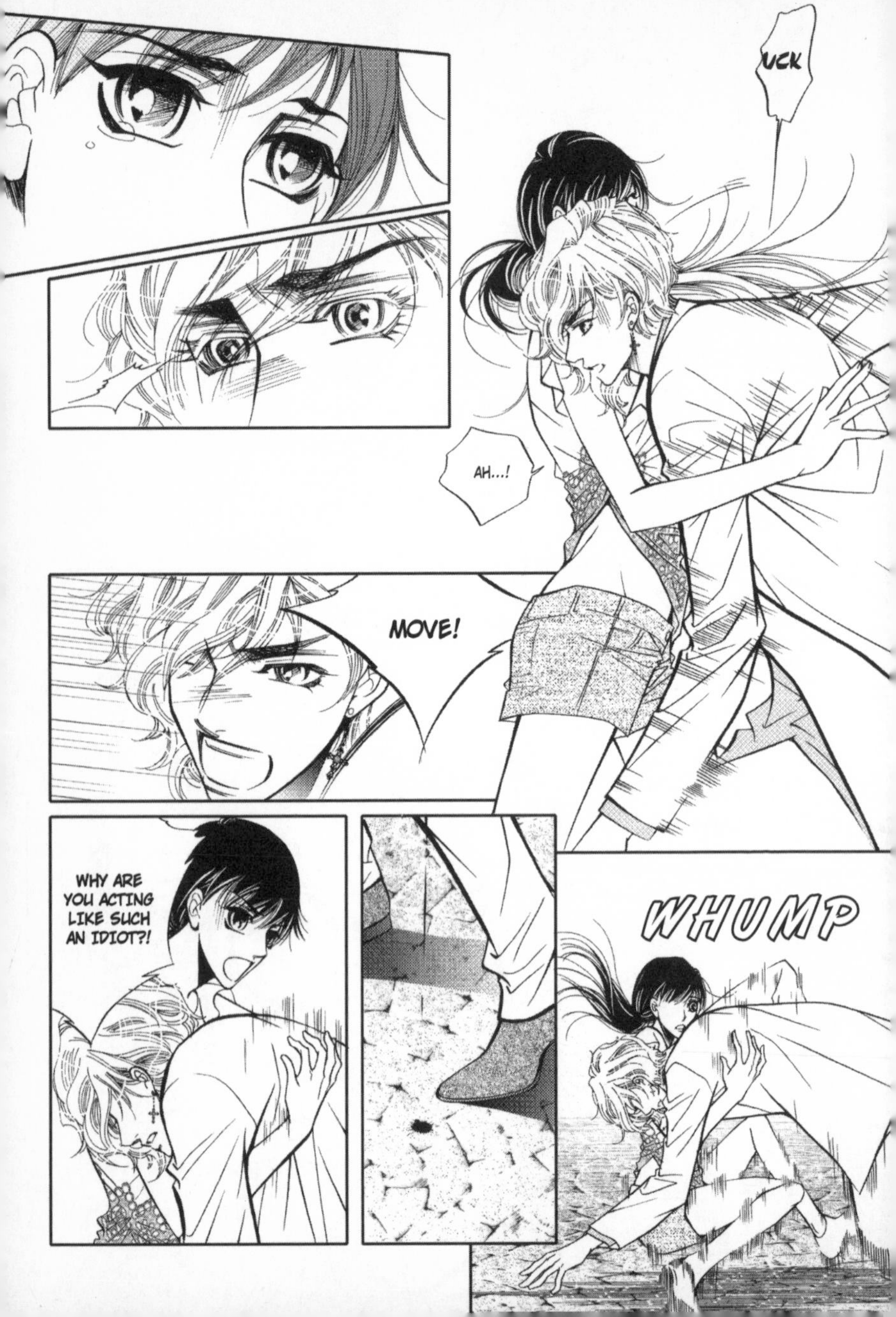
MOVE!
UCK
AH...!
WHY ARE YOU ACTING LIKE SUCH AN IDIOT?!
WHUMP

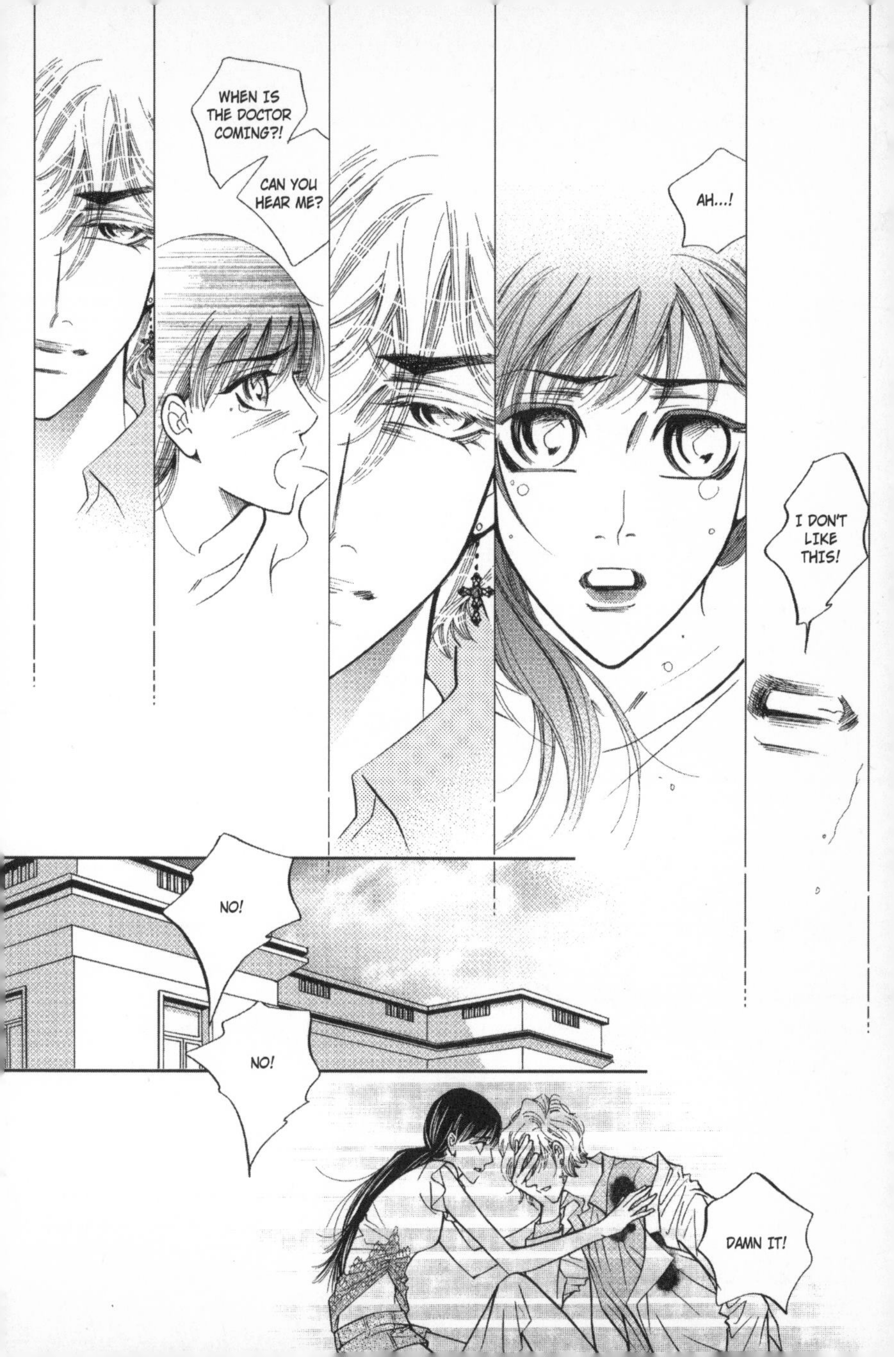
WHEN IS THE DOCTOR COMING?!
CAN YOU HEAR ME?
AH...!
I DON'T LIKE THIS!
NO!
NO!
DAMN IT!

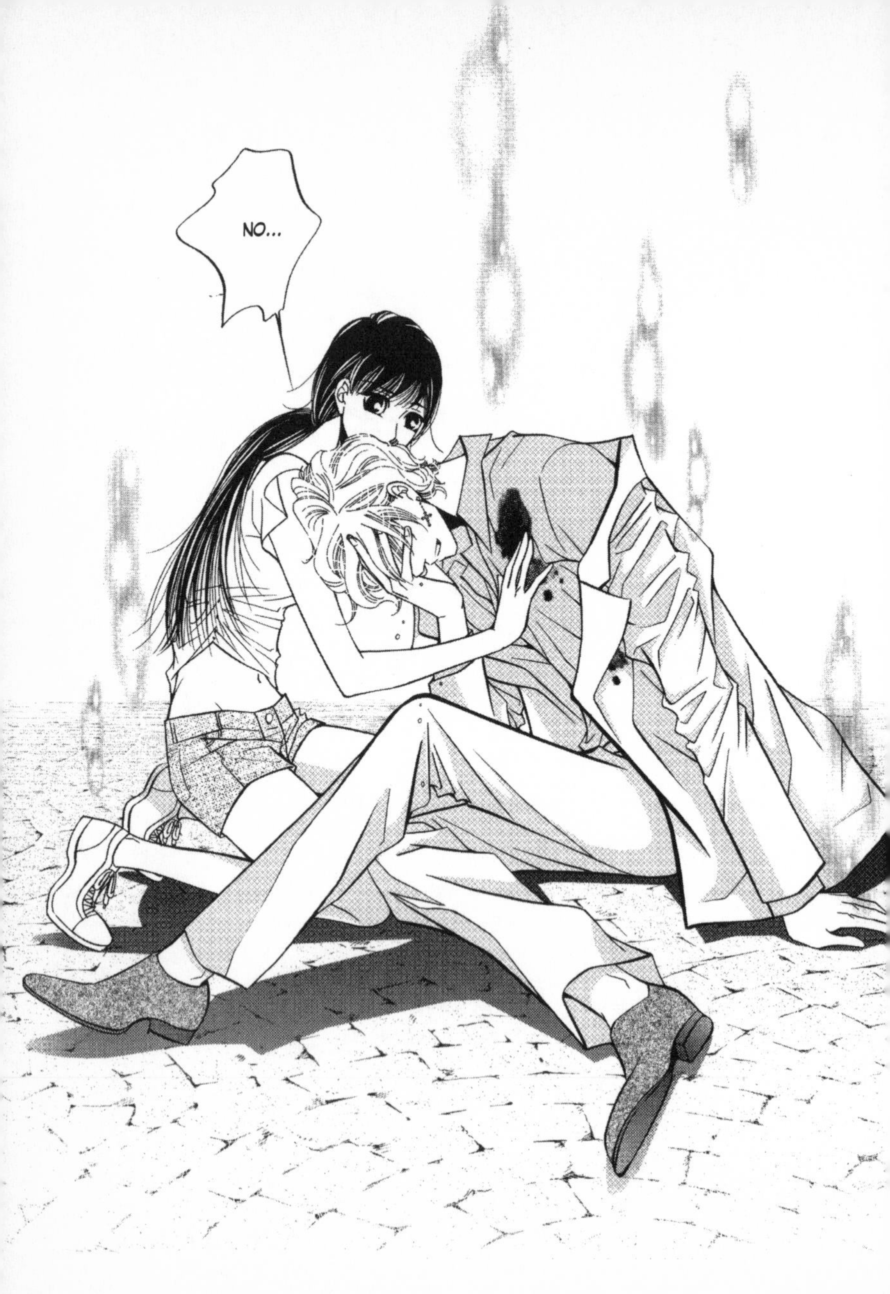
NO...

*I HATE THAT I'M FALLING
IN LOVE......*

HE SHOULD GET SOME REST FOR AWHILE...

THANK YOU. WE'LL WIRE THE MONEY TO THE USUAL ACCOUNT...

TU-CHUK

...HAVE YOU COMPLETELY FALLEN...

FOR THAT WOMAN?

PIETRO...

WELL--, IT IS REFRESHING, THIS RARE OPPORTUNITY TO SEE YOUR HUMAN SIDE.

DON'T GET TOO EXCITED.

A NAIVE WOMAN WHO SAVED YOUR LIFE, THAT'S REALLY ROMANTIC. YOU GUYS GO WELL TOGETHER.

CALL IT EVERY GANGSTER'S FANTASY.

HOW COULD YOU NOT BE MOVED?

BUT, THERE IS SOMETHING YOU DON'T KNOW, BOSS.

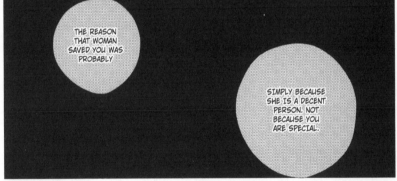

THE REASON THAT WOMAN SAVED YOU WAS PROBABLY

SIMPLY BECAUSE SHE IS A DECENT PERSON. NOT BECAUSE YOU ARE SPECIAL.

SHE WOULD HAVE TRIED TO SAVE ANYONE IN THAT SITUATION.

ANYONE!

WHAT DO YOU EXPECT FROM A DO-GOODER?

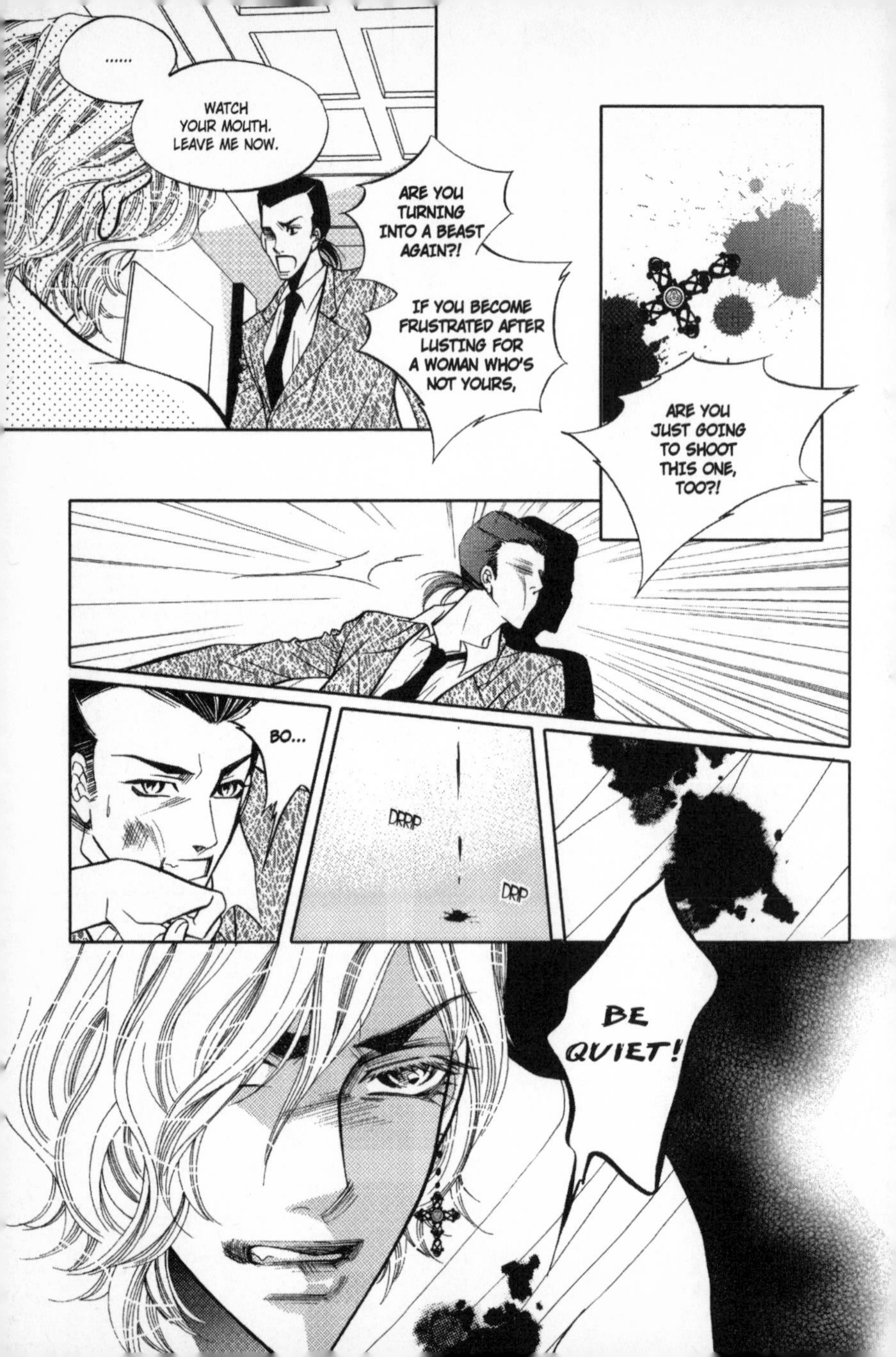
......
WATCH YOUR MOUTH. LEAVE ME NOW.
ARE YOU TURNING INTO A BEAST AGAIN?!
IF YOU BECOME FRUSTRATED AFTER LUSTING FOR A WOMAN WHO'S NOT YOURS,
ARE YOU JUST GOING TO SHOOT THIS ONE, TOO?!
BO...
DRRIP
DRIP
BE QUIET!

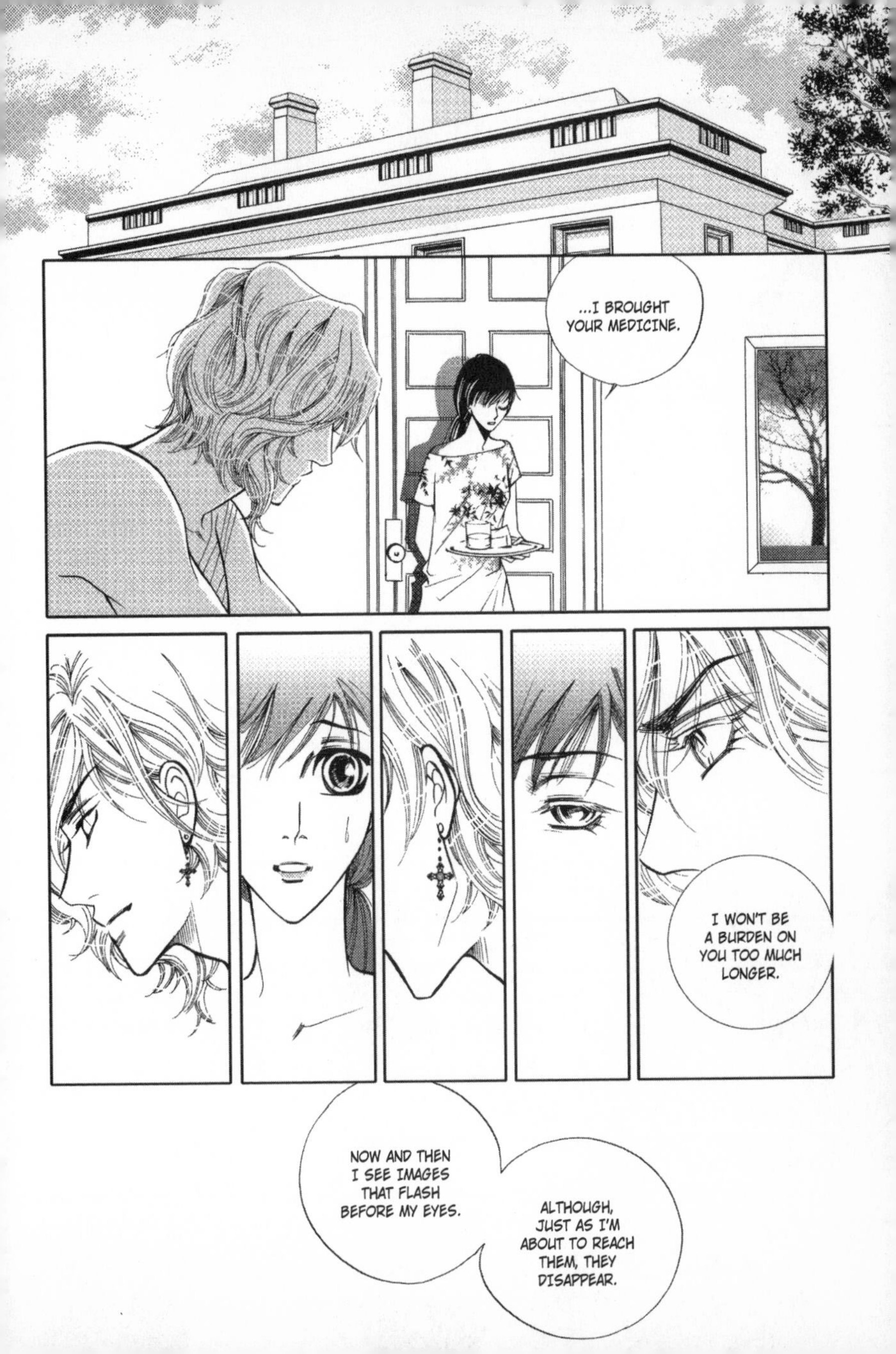
...I BROUGHT YOUR MEDICINE.
I WON'T BE A BURDEN ON YOU TOO MUCH LONGER.
NOW AND THEN I SEE IMAGES THAT FLASH BEFORE MY EYES.
ALTHOUGH, JUST AS I'M ABOUT TO REACH THEM, THEY DISAPPEAR.

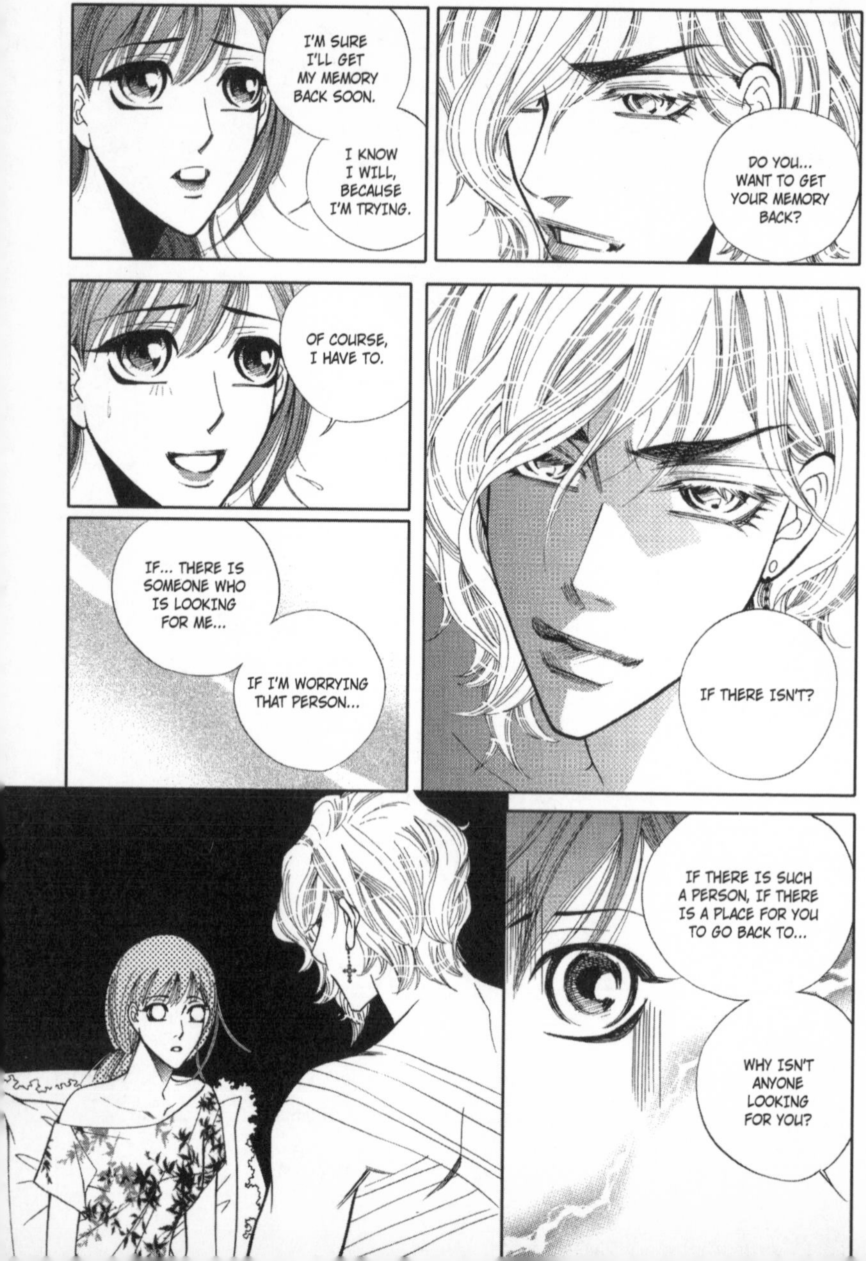
I'M SURE I'LL GET MY MEMORY BACK SOON.
I KNOW I WILL, BECAUSE I'M TRYING.
DO YOU... WANT TO GET YOUR MEMORY BACK?
OF COURSE, I HAVE TO.
IF... THERE IS SOMEONE WHO IS LOOKING FOR ME...
IF I'M WORRYING THAT PERSON...
IF THERE ISN'T?
IF THERE IS SUCH A PERSON, IF THERE IS A PLACE FOR YOU TO GO BACK TO...
WHY ISN'T ANYONE LOOKING FOR YOU?

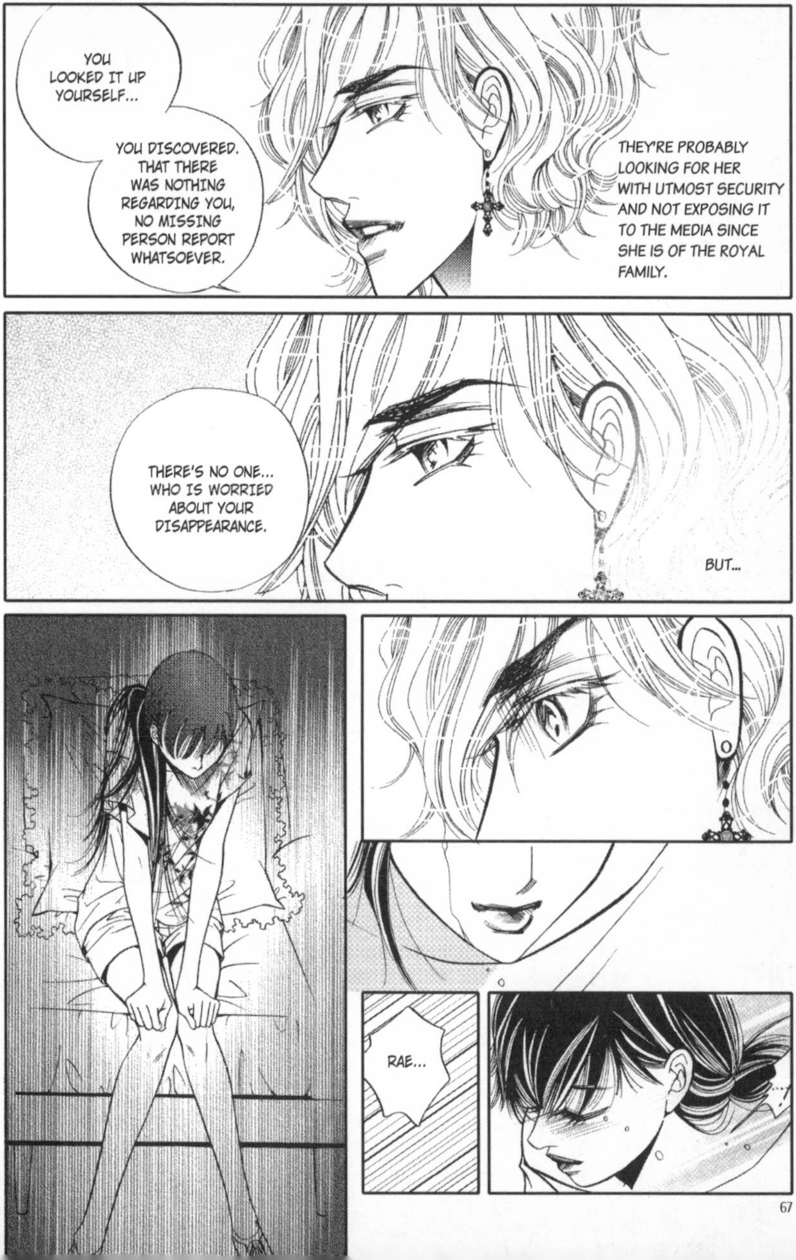
YOU LOOKED IT UP YOURSELF...
YOU DISCOVERED. THAT THERE WAS NOTHING REGARDING YOU, NO MISSING PERSON REPORT WHATSOEVER.
THEY'RE PROBABLY LOOKING FOR HER WITH UTMOST SECURITY AND NOT EXPOSING IT TO THE MEDIA SINCE SHE IS OF THE ROYAL FAMILY.
THERE'S NO ONE... WHO IS WORRIED ABOUT YOUR DISAPPEARANCE.
BUT...
RAE...

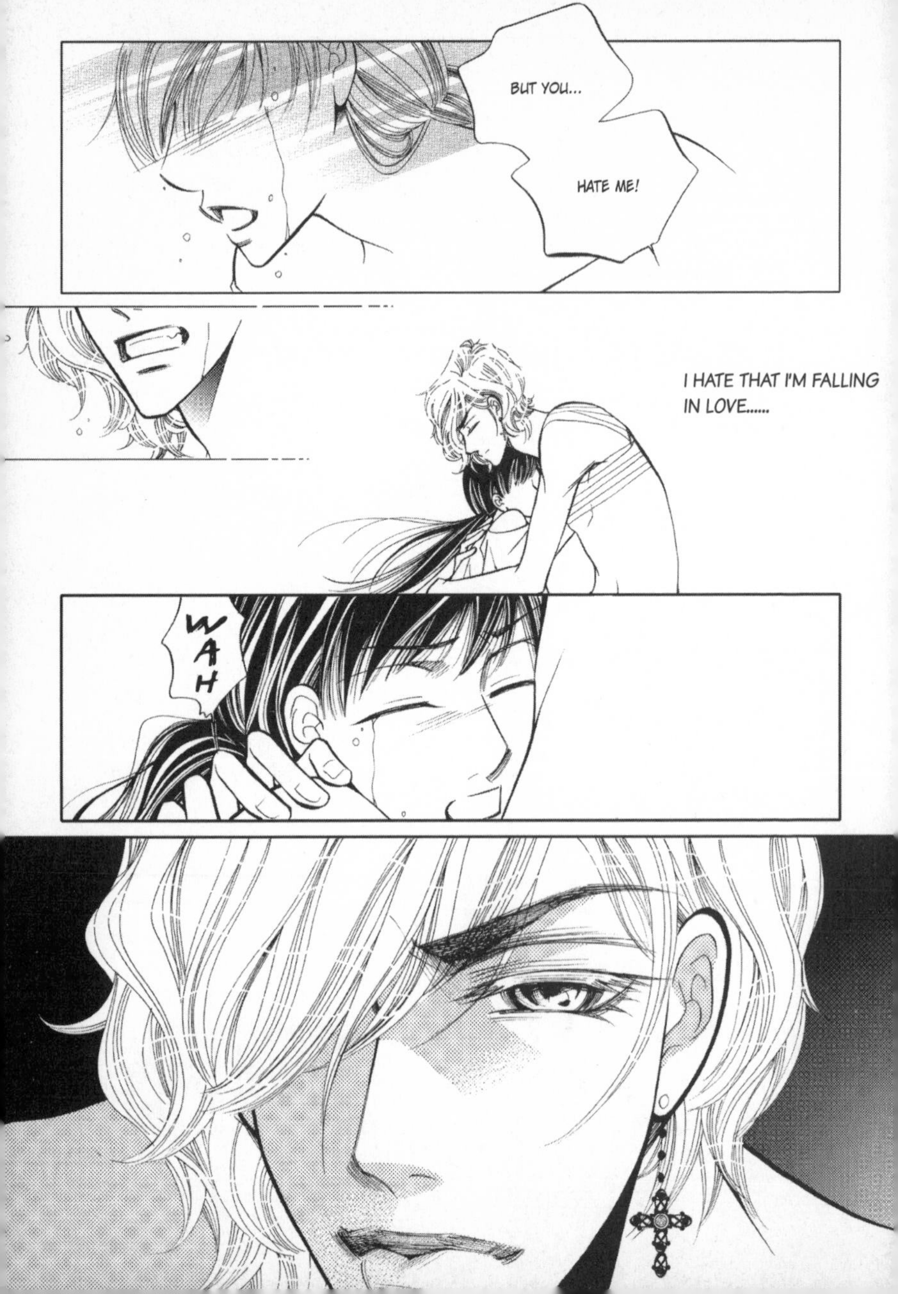
BUT YOU...
HATE ME!
I HATE THAT I'M FALLING IN LOVE......
WAH

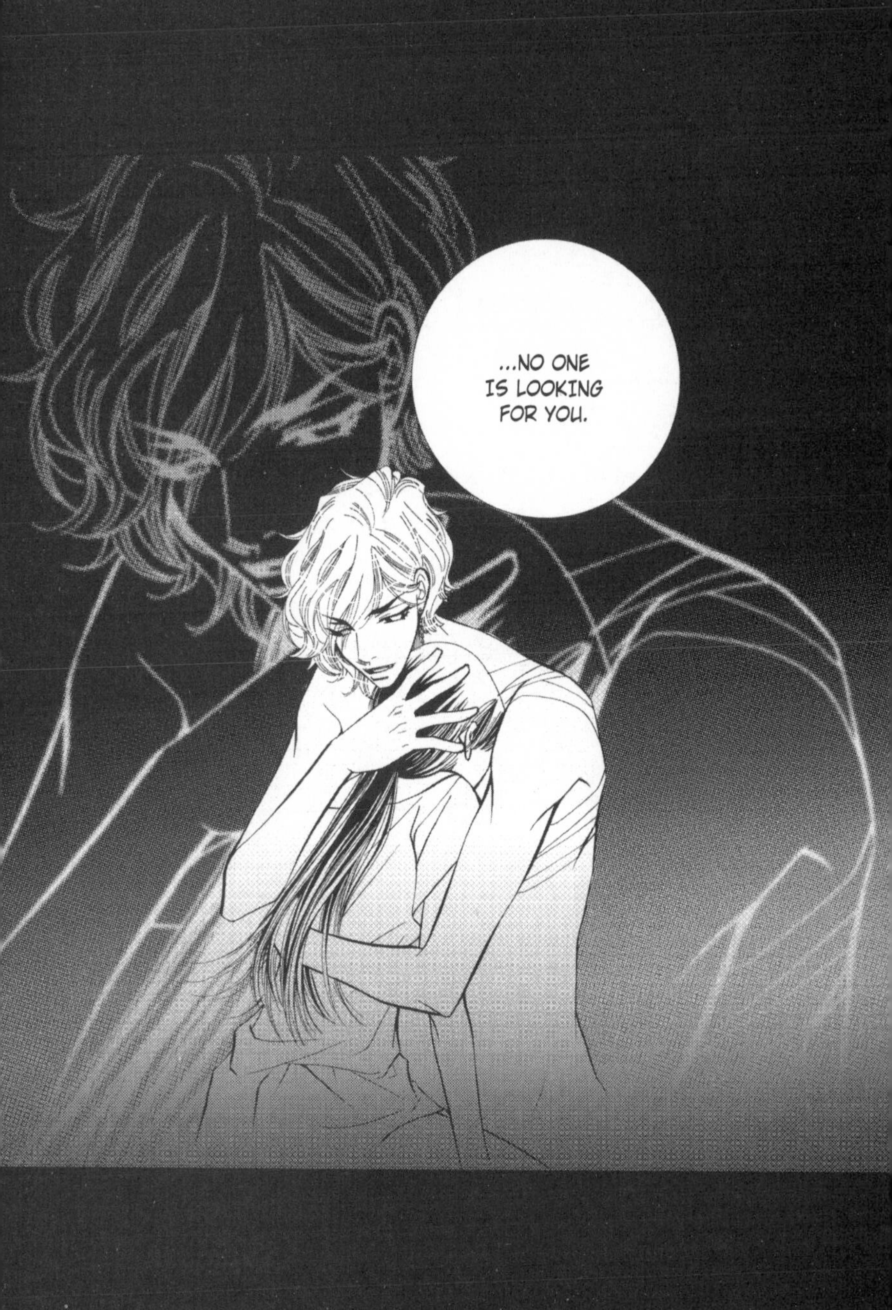
...NO ONE IS LOOKING FOR YOU.

I DON'T LIKE IT...

I DON'T LIKE
THAT I'M FALLING
IN LOVE.

I REALLY...

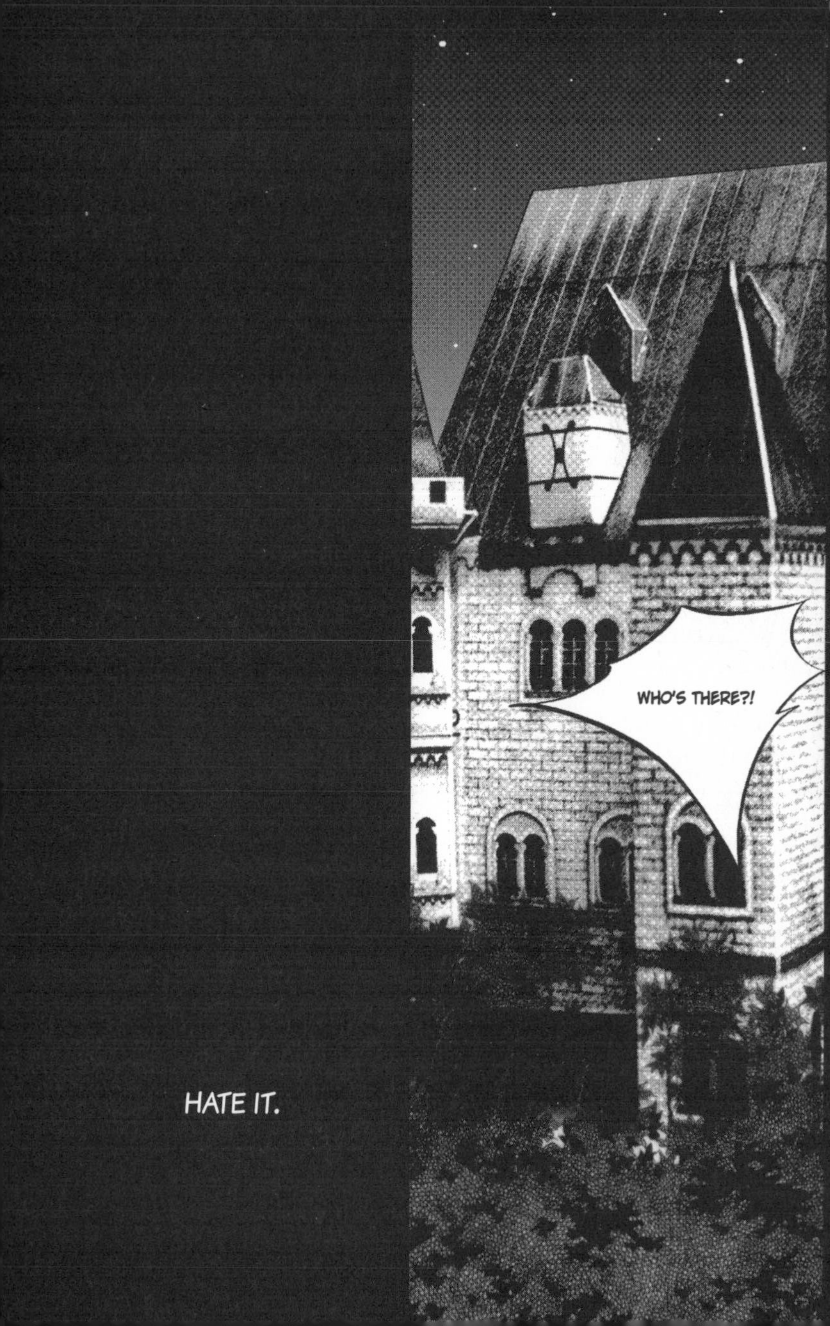
HATE IT.
WHO'S THERE?!

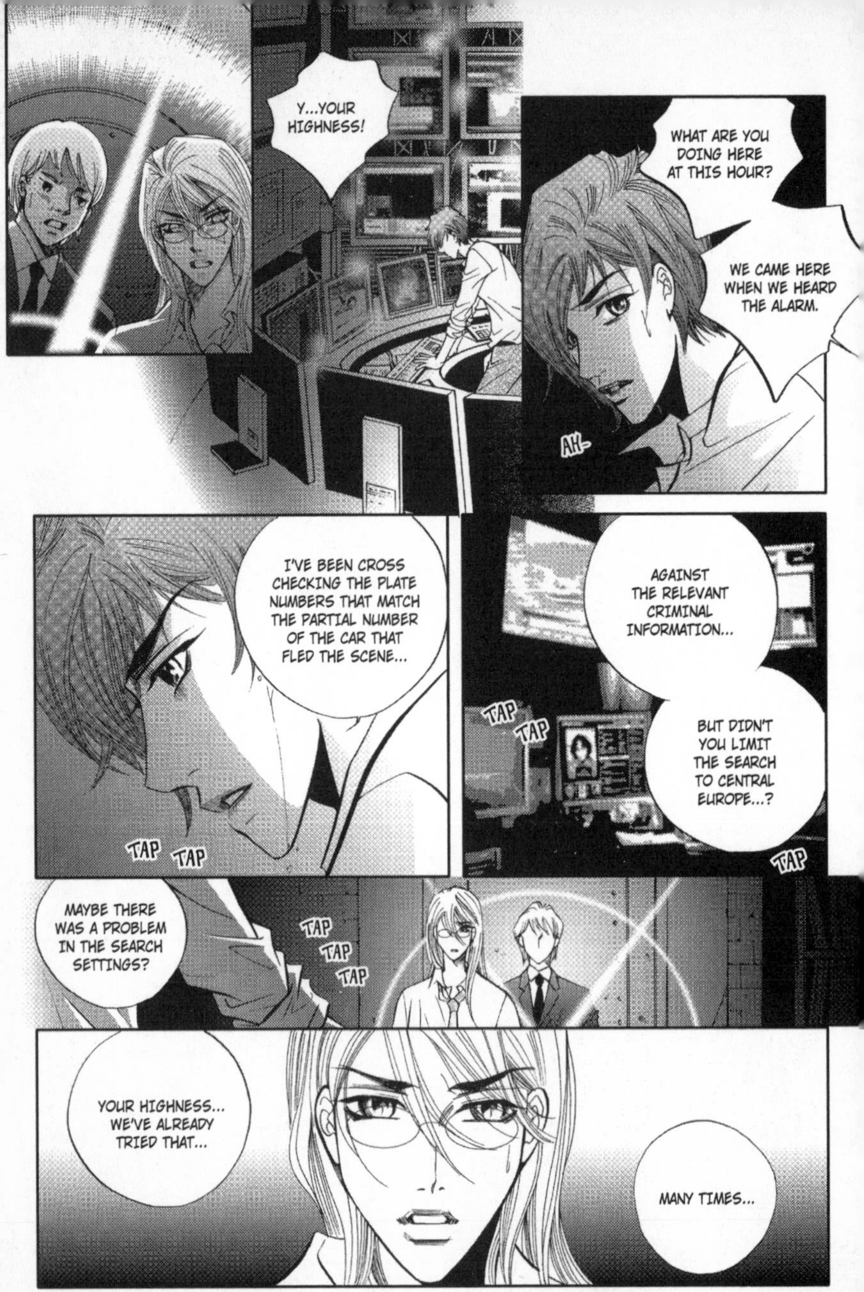
Y...YOUR HIGHNESS!
WHAT ARE YOU DOING HERE AT THIS HOUR?
WE CAME HERE WHEN WE HEARD THE ALARM.
AH-
I'VE BEEN CROSS CHECKING THE PLATE NUMBERS THAT MATCH THE PARTIAL NUMBER OF THE CAR THAT FLED THE SCENE...
TAP TAP
AGAINST THE RELEVANT CRIMINAL INFORMATION...
TAP TAP
BUT DIDN'T YOU LIMIT THE SEARCH TO CENTRAL EUROPE...?
TAP
MAYBE THERE WAS A PROBLEM IN THE SEARCH SETTINGS?
TAP TAP TAP
YOUR HIGHNESS... WE'VE ALREADY TRIED THAT...
MANY TIMES...

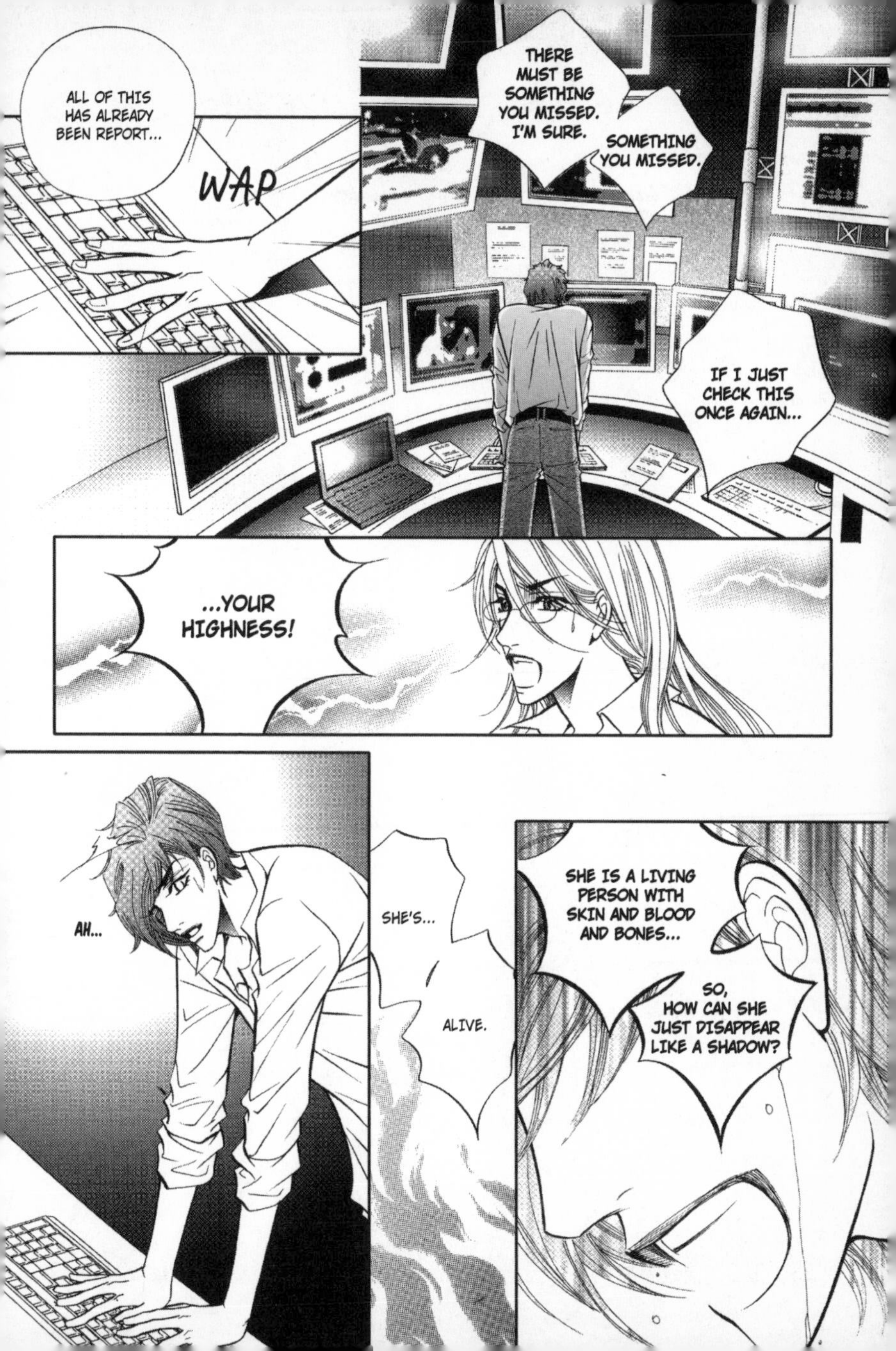
ALL OF THIS HAS ALREADY BEEN REPORT...
WAP
THERE MUST BE SOMETHING YOU MISSED. I'M SURE.
SOMETHING YOU MISSED.
IF I JUST CHECK THIS ONCE AGAIN...
...YOUR HIGHNESS!
AH...
SHE'S...
ALIVE.
SHE IS A LIVING PERSON WITH SKIN AND BLOOD AND BONES...
SO, HOW CAN SHE JUST DISAPPEAR LIKE A SHADOW?

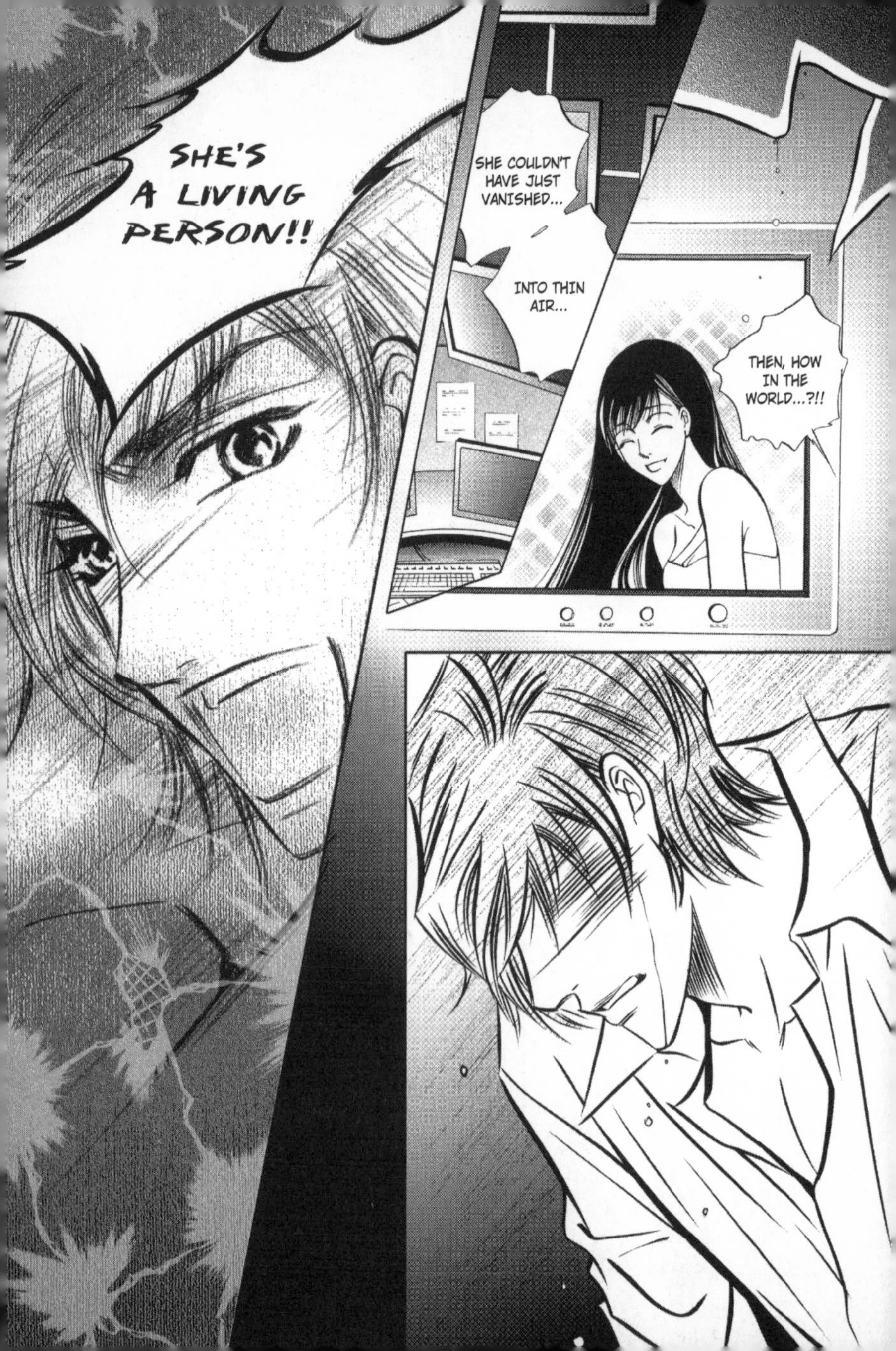
SHE'S A LIVING PERSON!!
SHE COULDN'T HAVE JUST VANISHED...
INTO THIN AIR...
THEN, HOW IN THE WORLD...?!!

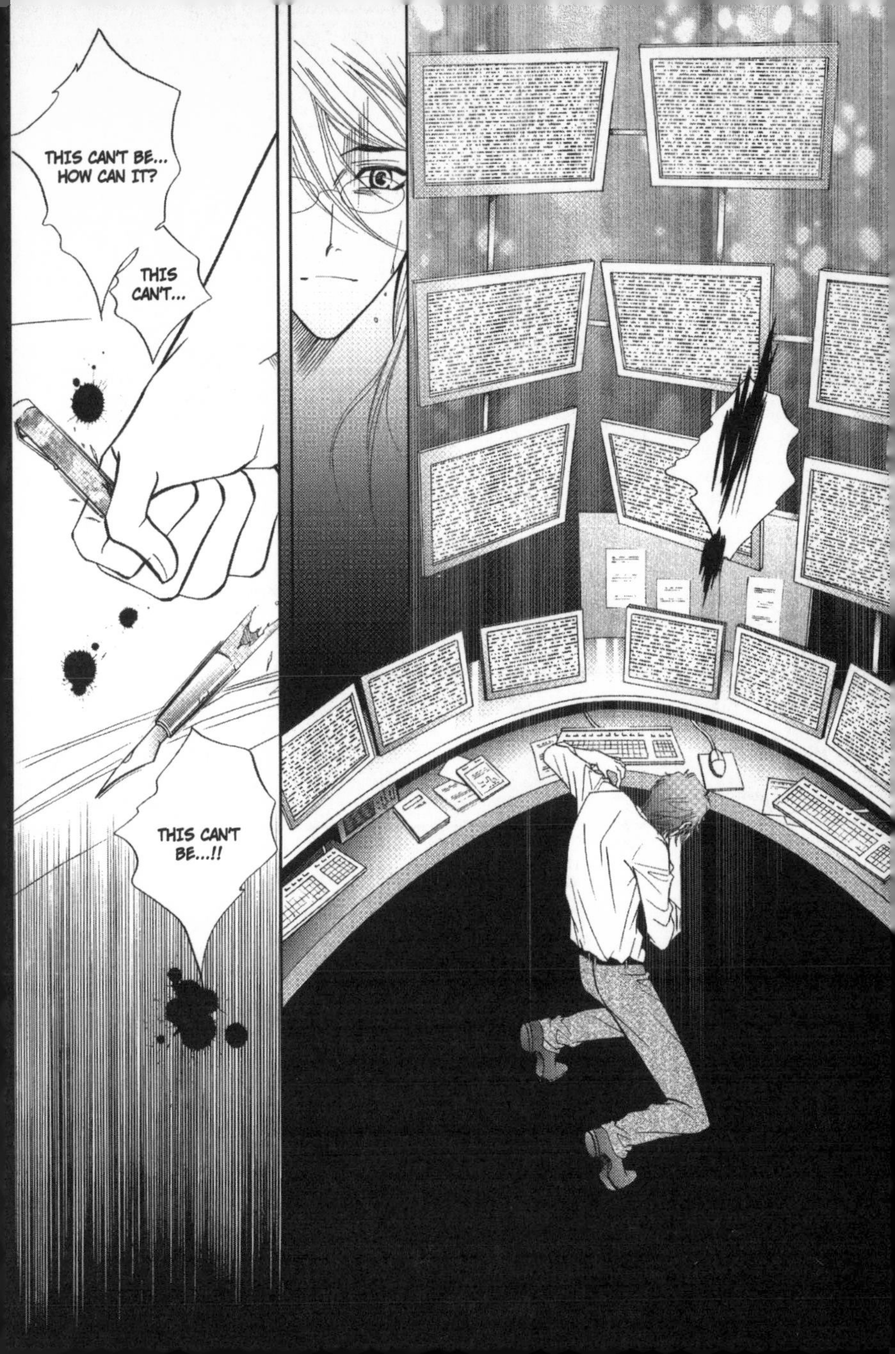
THIS CAN'T BE... HOW CAN IT?
THIS CAN'T...
THIS CAN'T BE...!!

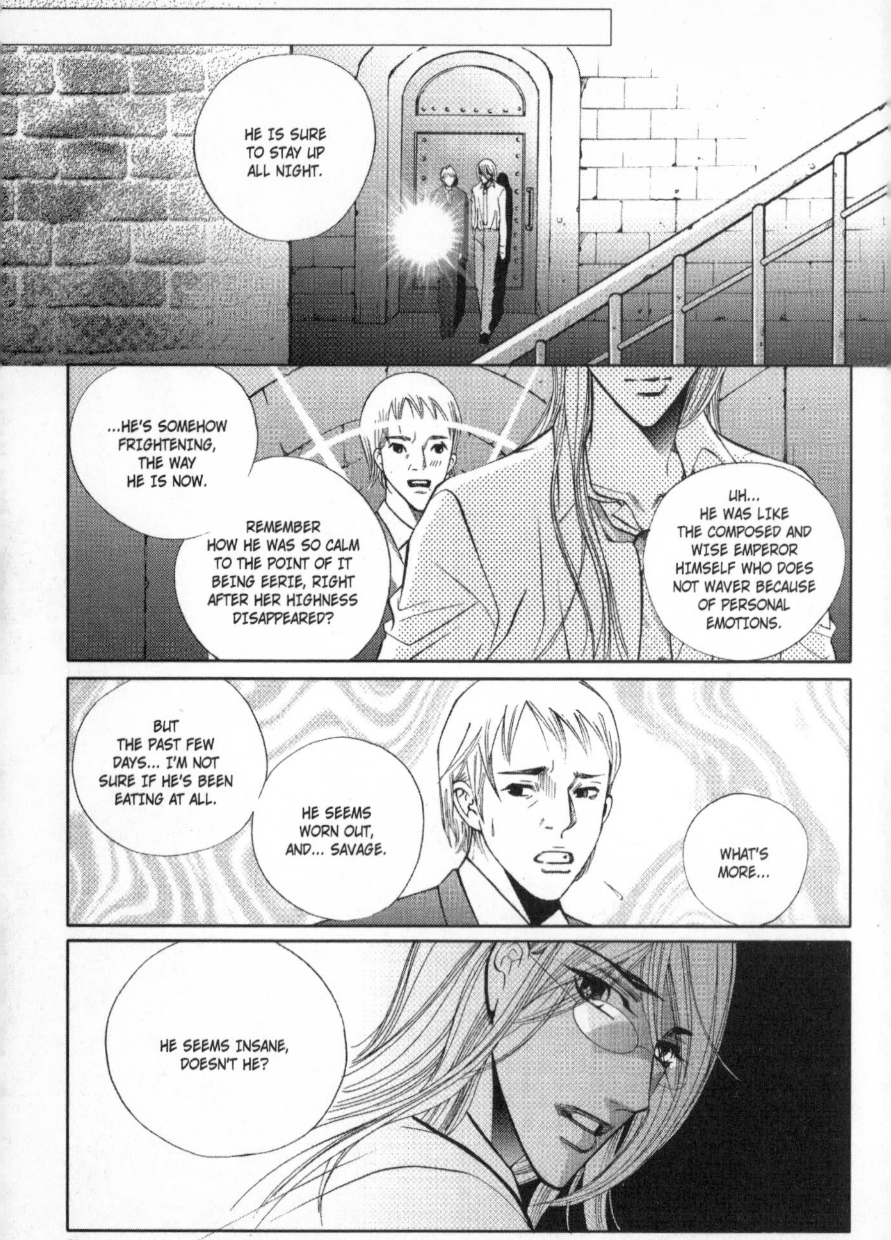
HE IS SURE TO STAY UP ALL NIGHT.
...HE'S SOMEHOW FRIGHTENING, THE WAY HE IS NOW.
REMEMBER HOW HE WAS SO CALM TO THE POINT OF IT BEING EERIE, RIGHT AFTER HER HIGHNESS DISAPPEARED?
UH... HE WAS LIKE THE COMPOSED AND WISE EMPEROR HIMSELF WHO DOES NOT WAVER BECAUSE OF PERSONAL EMOTIONS.
BUT THE PAST FEW DAYS... I'M NOT SURE IF HE'S BEEN EATING AT ALL.
HE SEEMS WORN OUT, AND... SAVAGE.
WHAT'S MORE...
HE SEEMS INSANE, DOESN'T HE?

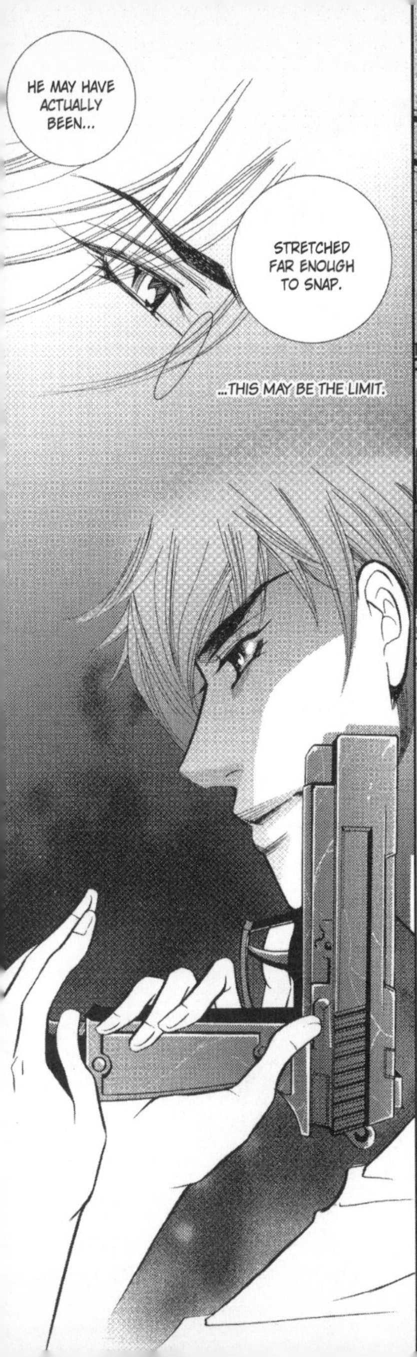
HE MAY HAVE ACTUALLY BEEN...
STRETCHED FAR ENOUGH TO SNAP.
...THIS MAY BE THE LIMIT.

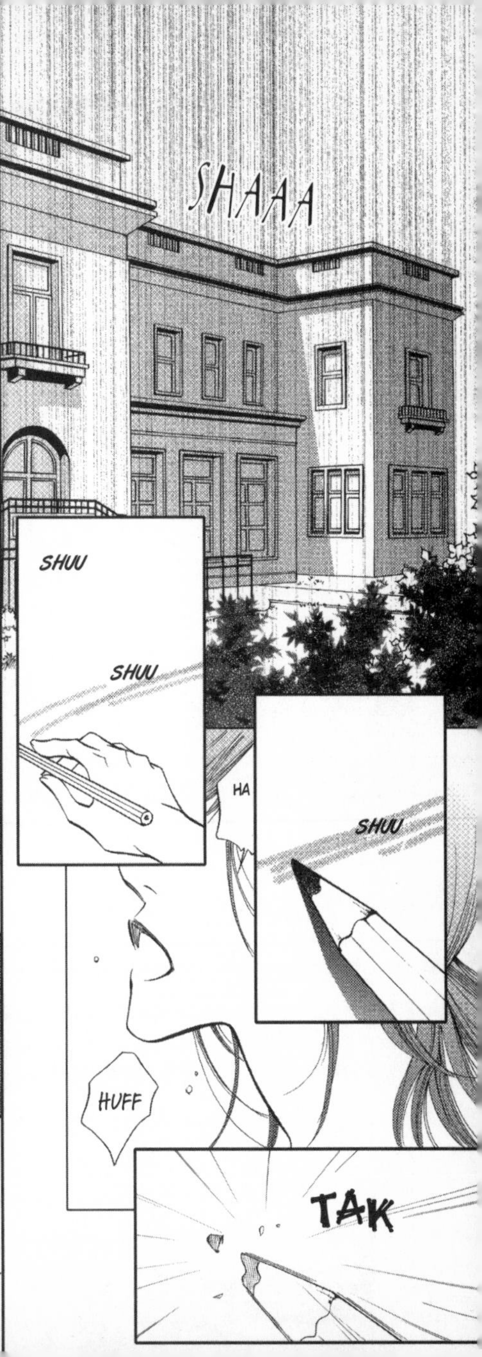
SHAAA
SHUU
SHUU
HA
SHUU
HUFF
TAK

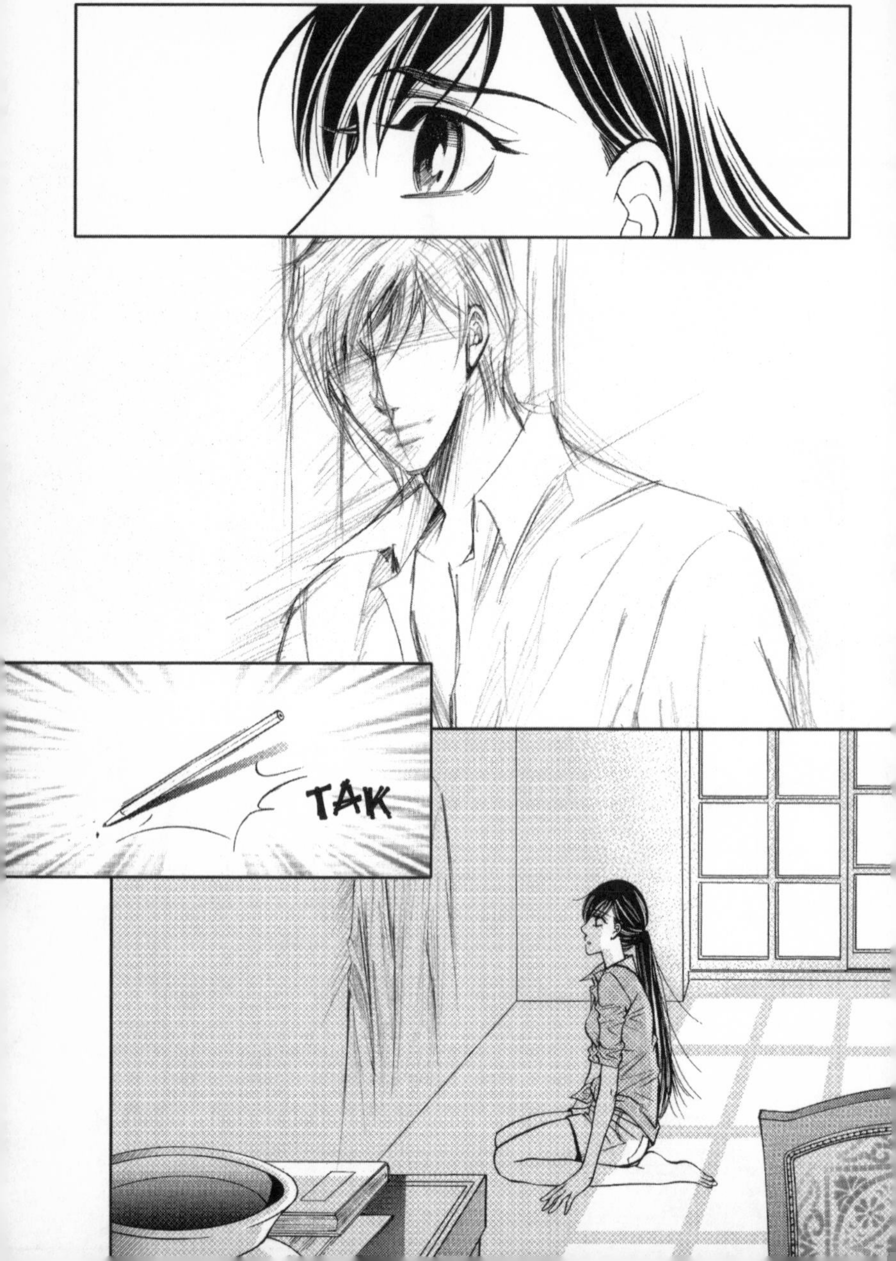
TAK

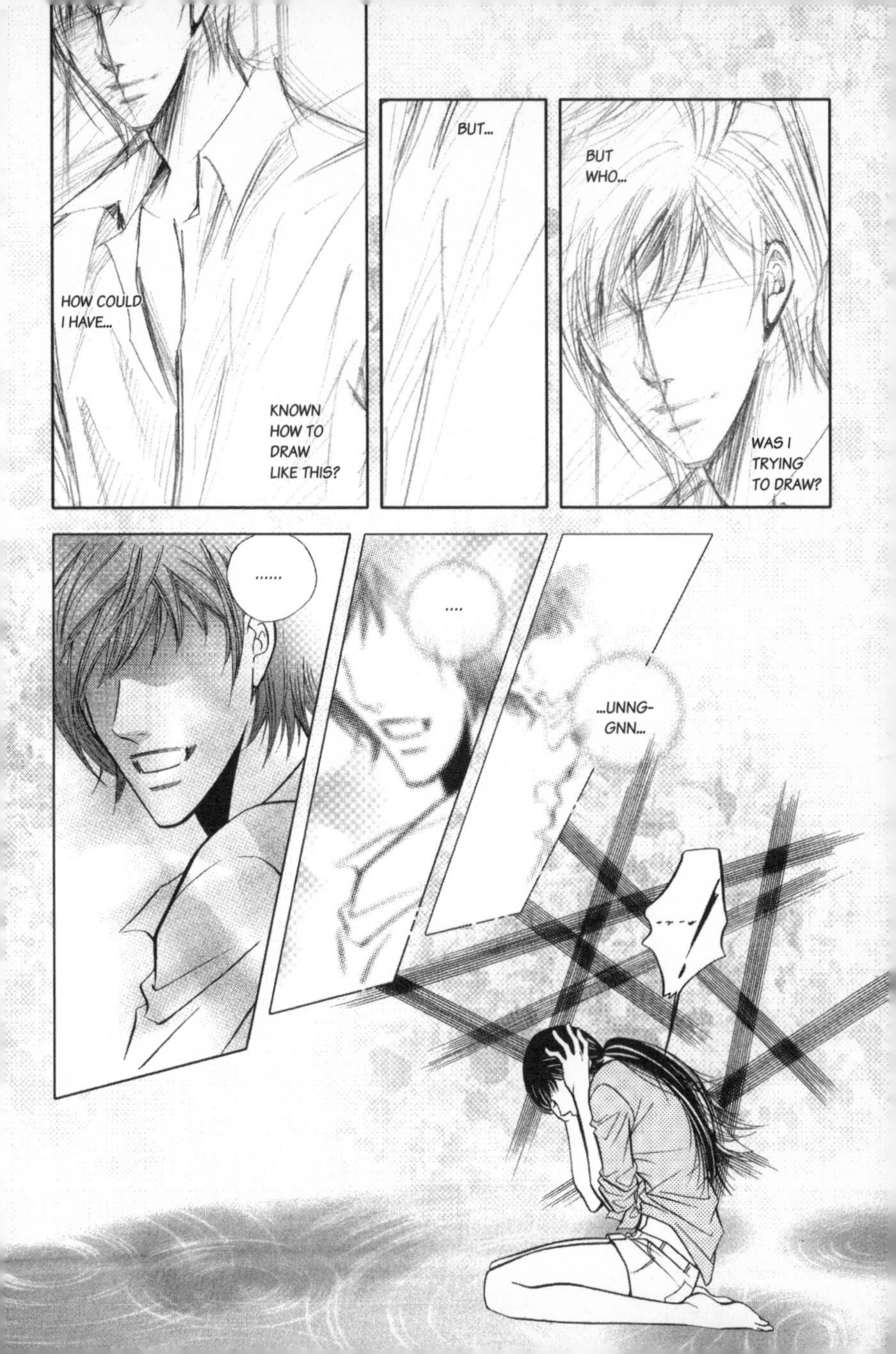
HOW COULD I HAVE...
KNOWN HOW TO DRAW LIKE THIS?
BUT...
BUT WHO...
WAS I TRYING TO DRAW?
......
....
...UNNG-GNN...

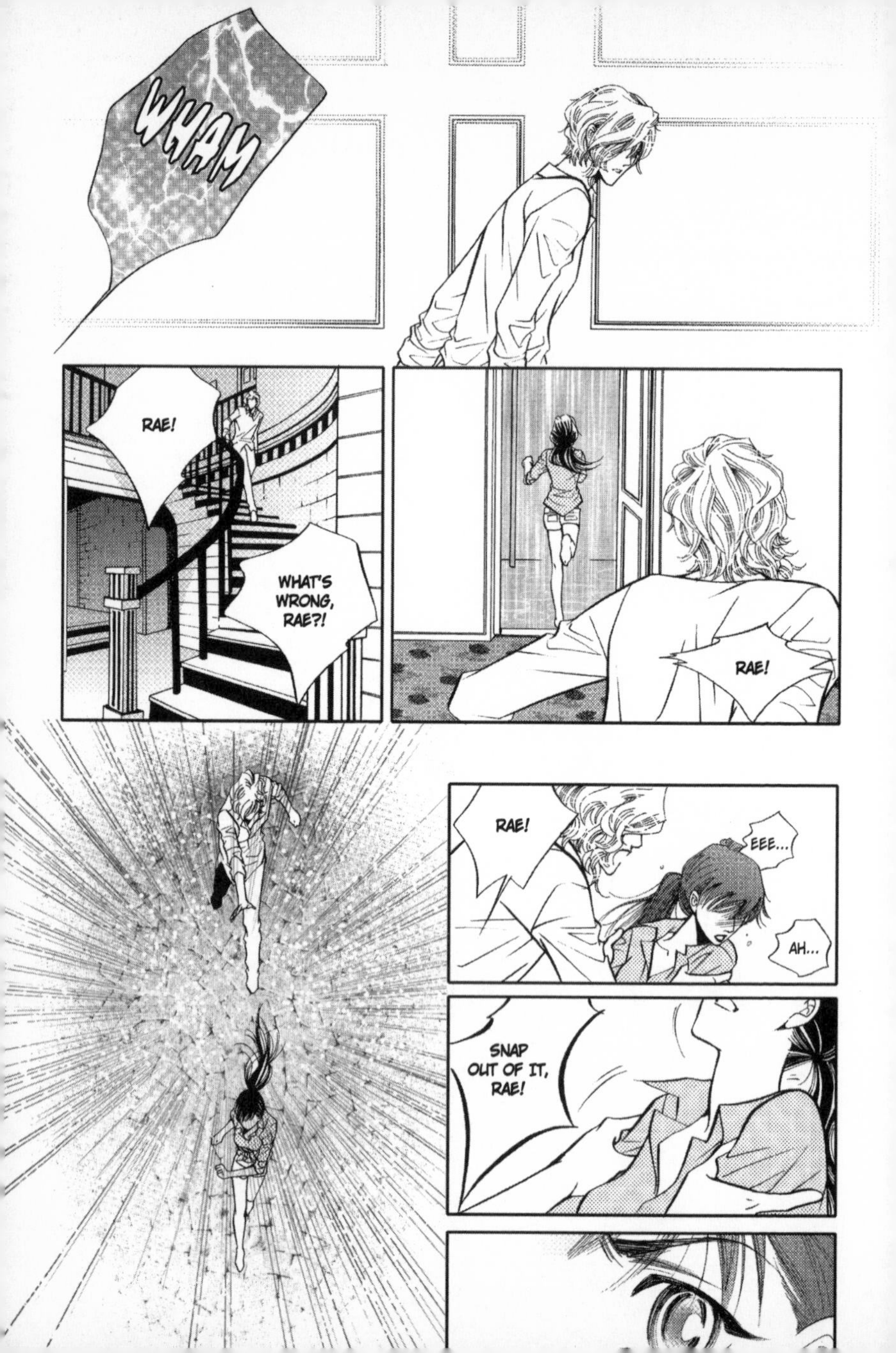
WHAM
RAE!
WHAT'S WRONG, RAE?!
RAE!
RAE!
EEE...
AH...
SNAP OUT OF IT, RAE!

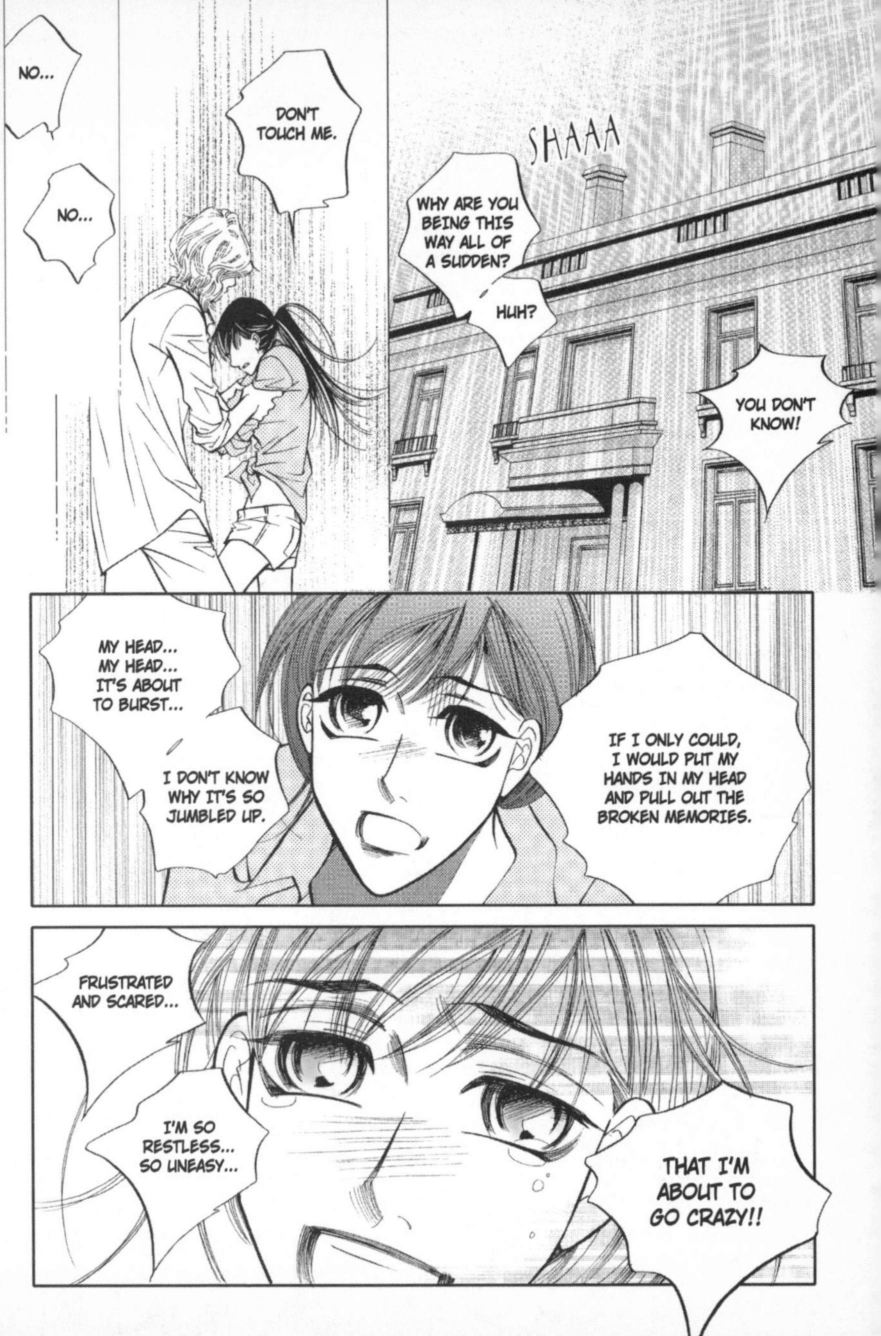
NO...
DON'T TOUCH ME.
NO...
SHAAA
WHY ARE YOU BEING THIS WAY ALL OF A SUDDEN?
HUH?
YOU DON'T KNOW!
MY HEAD... MY HEAD... IT'S ABOUT TO BURST...
I DON'T KNOW WHY IT'S SO JUMBLED UP.
IF I ONLY COULD, I WOULD PUT MY HANDS IN MY HEAD AND PULL OUT THE BROKEN MEMORIES.
FRUSTRATED AND SCARED...
I'M SO RESTLESS... SO UNEASY...
THAT I'M ABOUT TO GO CRAZY!!

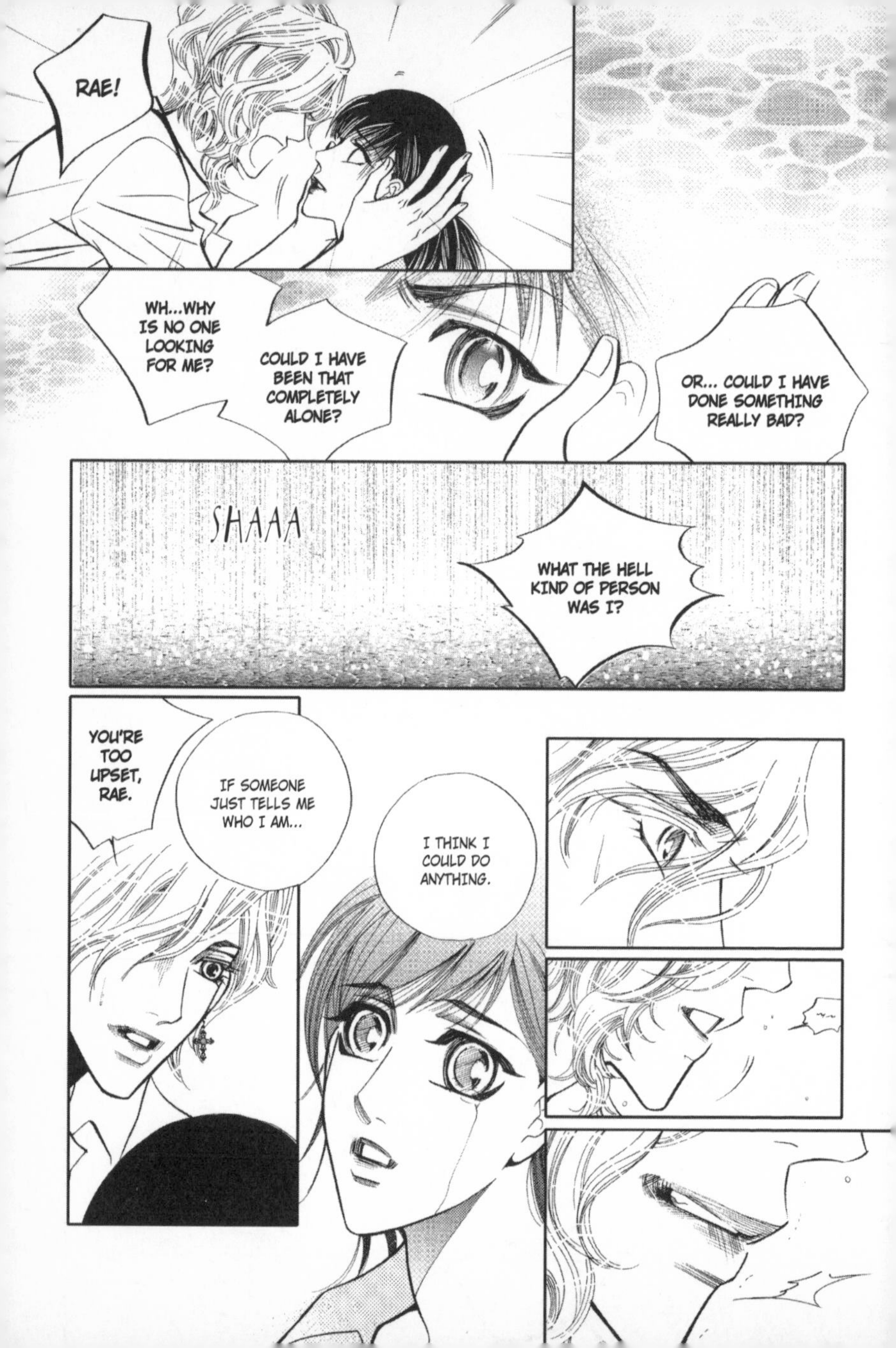
RAE!
WH...WHY IS NO ONE LOOKING FOR ME?
COULD I HAVE BEEN THAT COMPLETELY ALONE?
OR... COULD I HAVE DONE SOMETHING REALLY BAD?
SHAAA
WHAT THE HELL KIND OF PERSON WAS I?
YOU'RE TOO UPSET, RAE.
IF SOMEONE JUST TELLS ME WHO I AM...
I THINK I COULD DO ANYTHING.

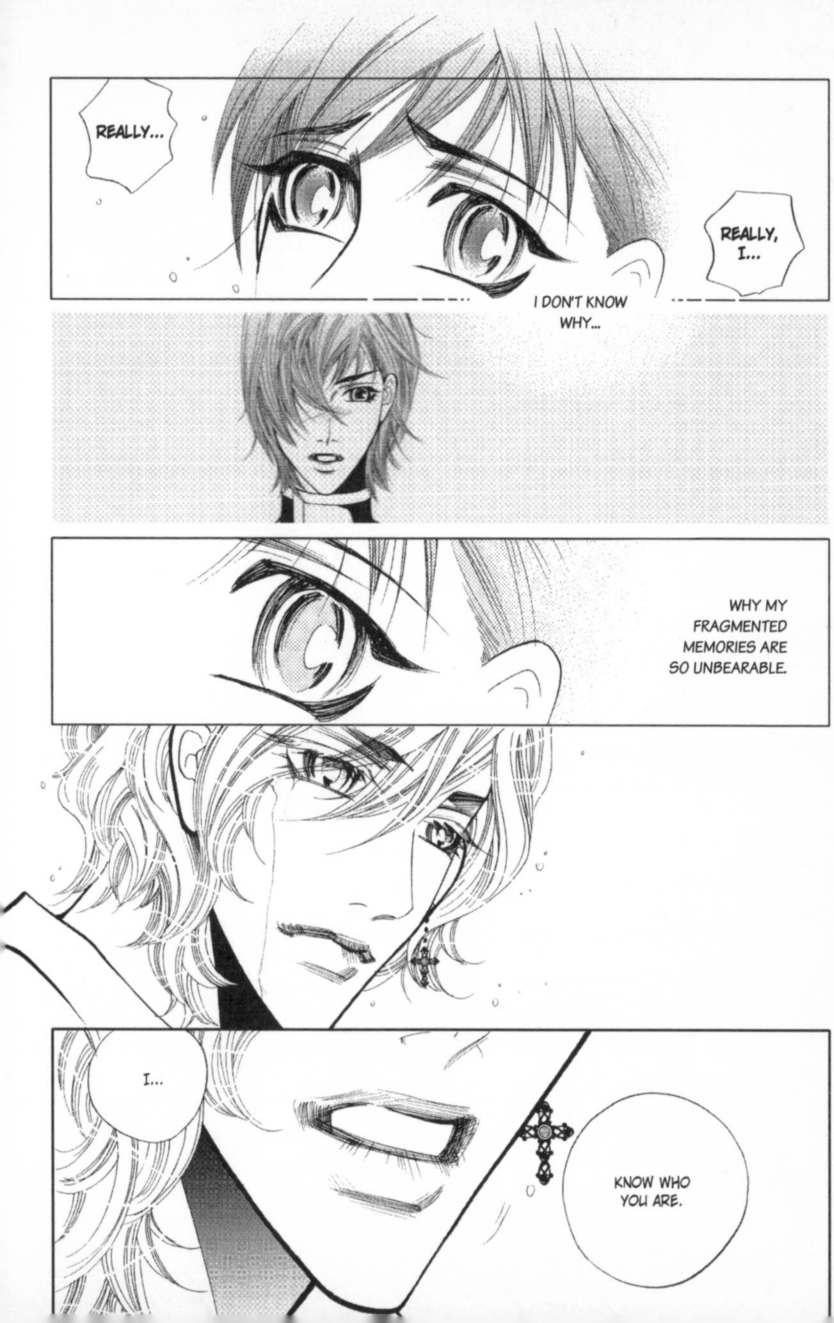
REALLY...
REALLY, I...
I DON'T KNOW WHY...
WHY MY FRAGMENTED MEMORIES ARE SO UNBEARABLE.
I...
KNOW WHO YOU ARE.

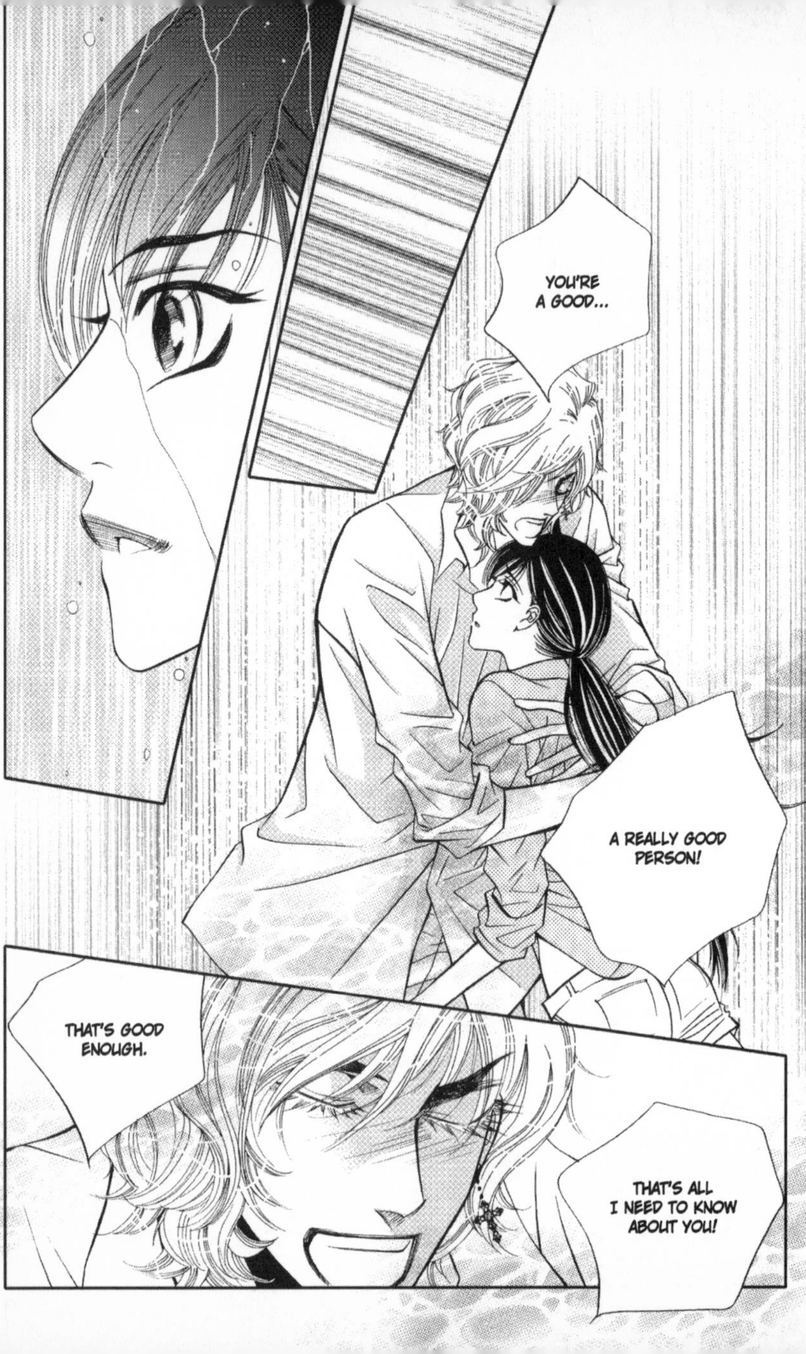

YOU'RE A GOOD...
A REALLY GOOD PERSON!
THAT'S GOOD ENOUGH.
THAT'S ALL I NEED TO KNOW ABOUT YOU!

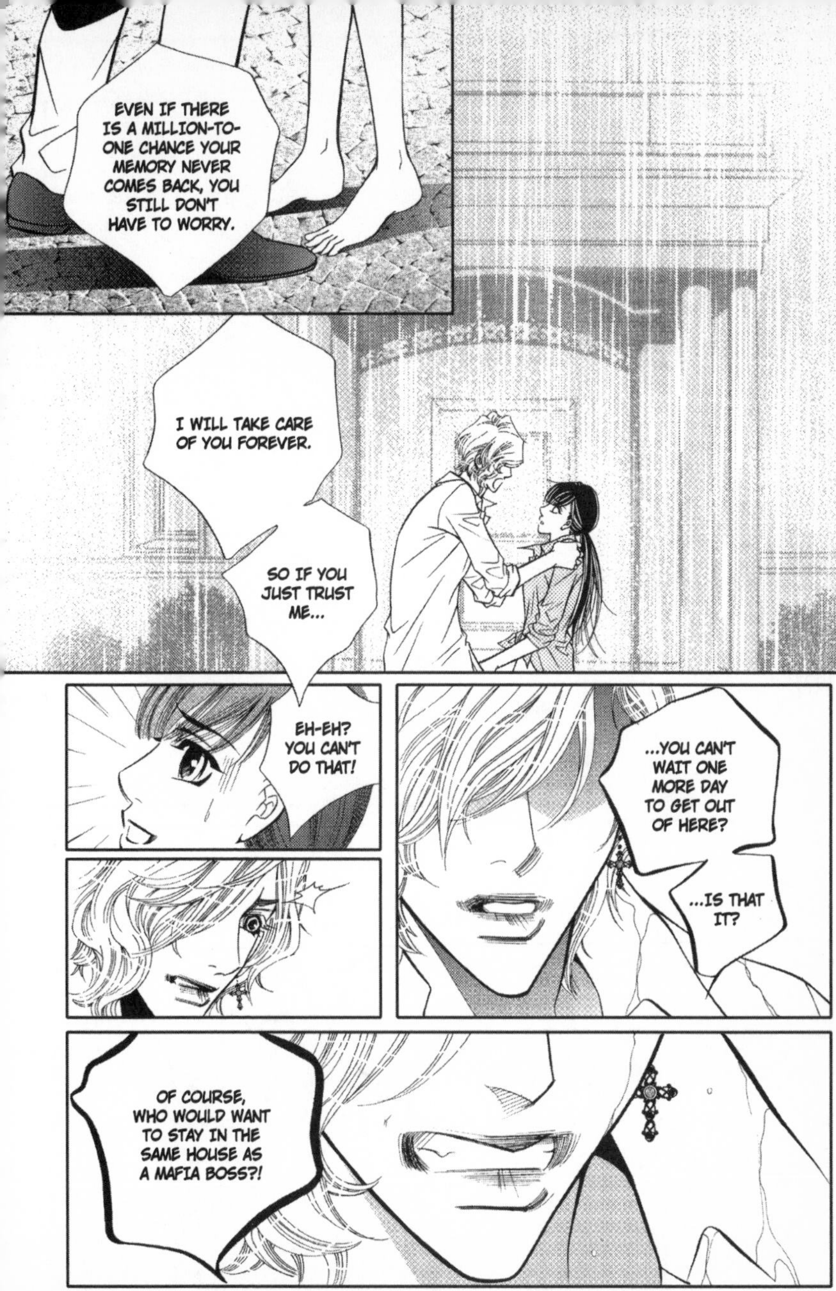
EVEN IF THERE IS A MILLION-TO-ONE CHANCE YOUR MEMORY NEVER COMES BACK, YOU STILL DON'T HAVE TO WORRY.
I WILL TAKE CARE OF YOU FOREVER.
SO IF YOU JUST TRUST ME...
EH-EH? YOU CAN'T DO THAT!
...YOU CAN'T WAIT ONE MORE DAY TO GET OUT OF HERE?
...IS THAT IT?
OF COURSE, WHO WOULD WANT TO STAY IN THE SAME HOUSE AS A MAFIA BOSS?!

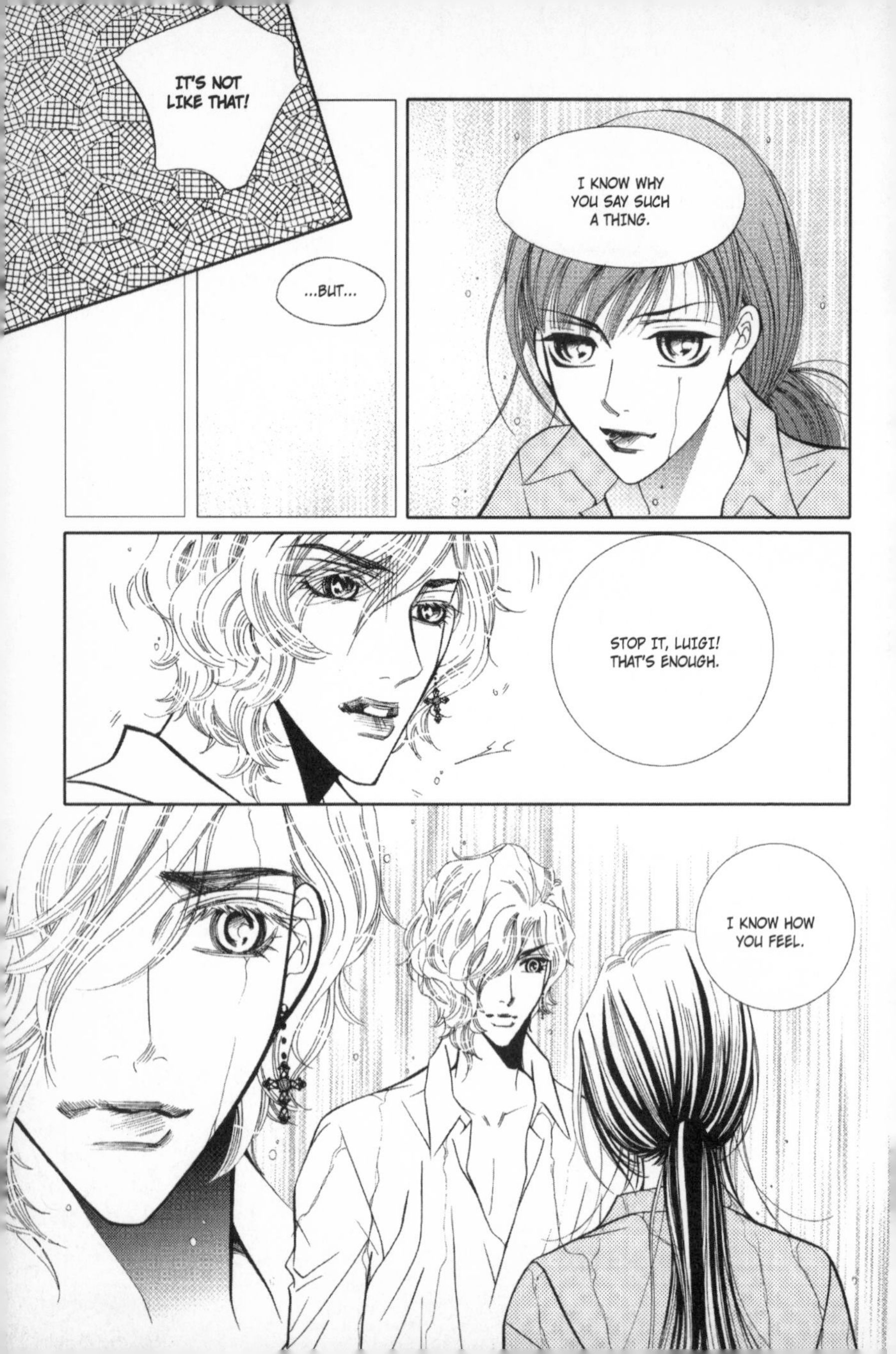
IT'S NOT LIKE THAT!
...BUT...
I KNOW WHY YOU SAY SUCH A THING.
STOP IT, LUIGI! THAT'S ENOUGH.
I KNOW HOW YOU FEEL.

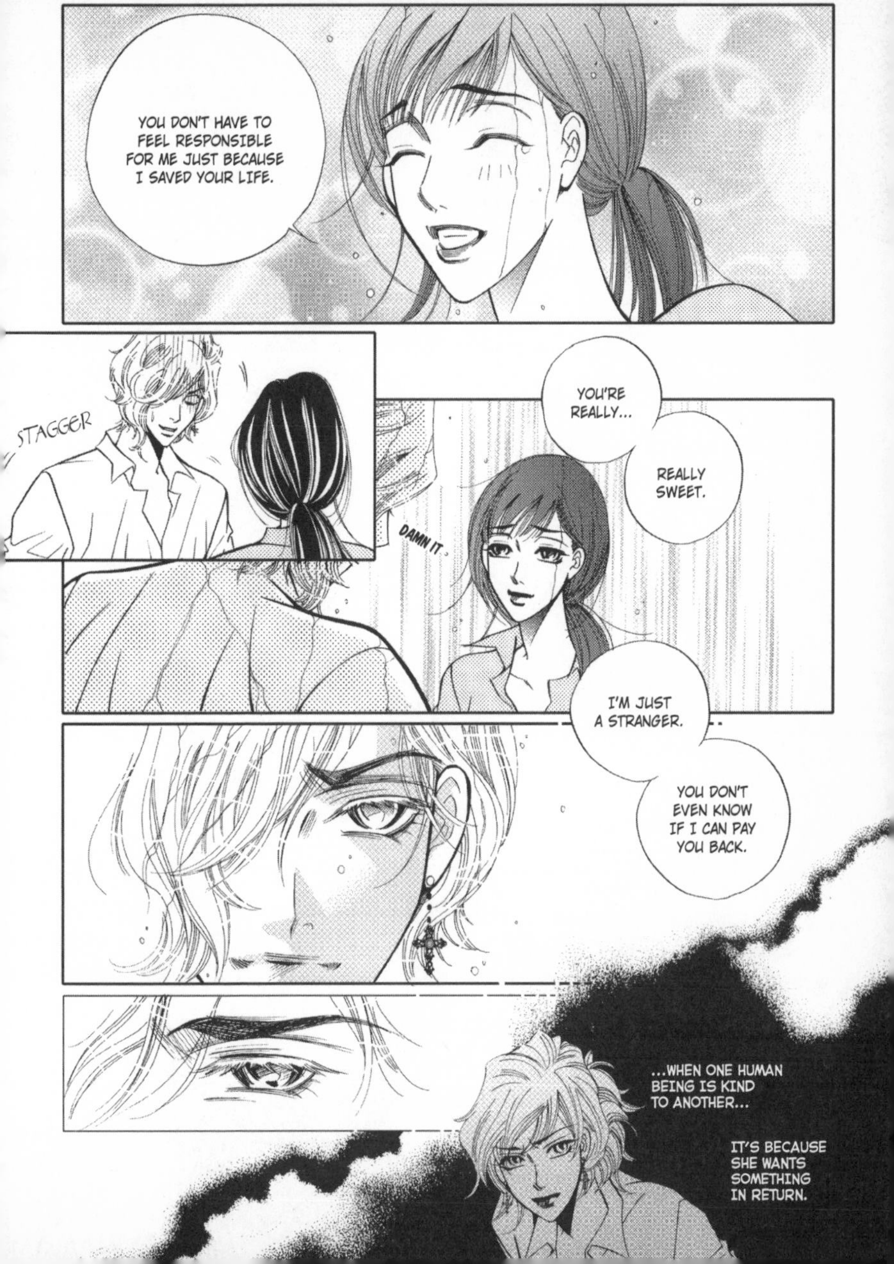
YOU DON'T HAVE TO FEEL RESPONSIBLE FOR ME JUST BECAUSE I SAVED YOUR LIFE.
STAGGER
YOU'RE REALLY...
REALLY SWEET.
DAMN IT
I'M JUST A STRANGER.
YOU DON'T EVEN KNOW IF I CAN PAY YOU BACK.
...WHEN ONE HUMAN BEING IS KIND TO ANOTHER...
IT'S BECAUSE SHE WANTS SOMETHING IN RETURN.

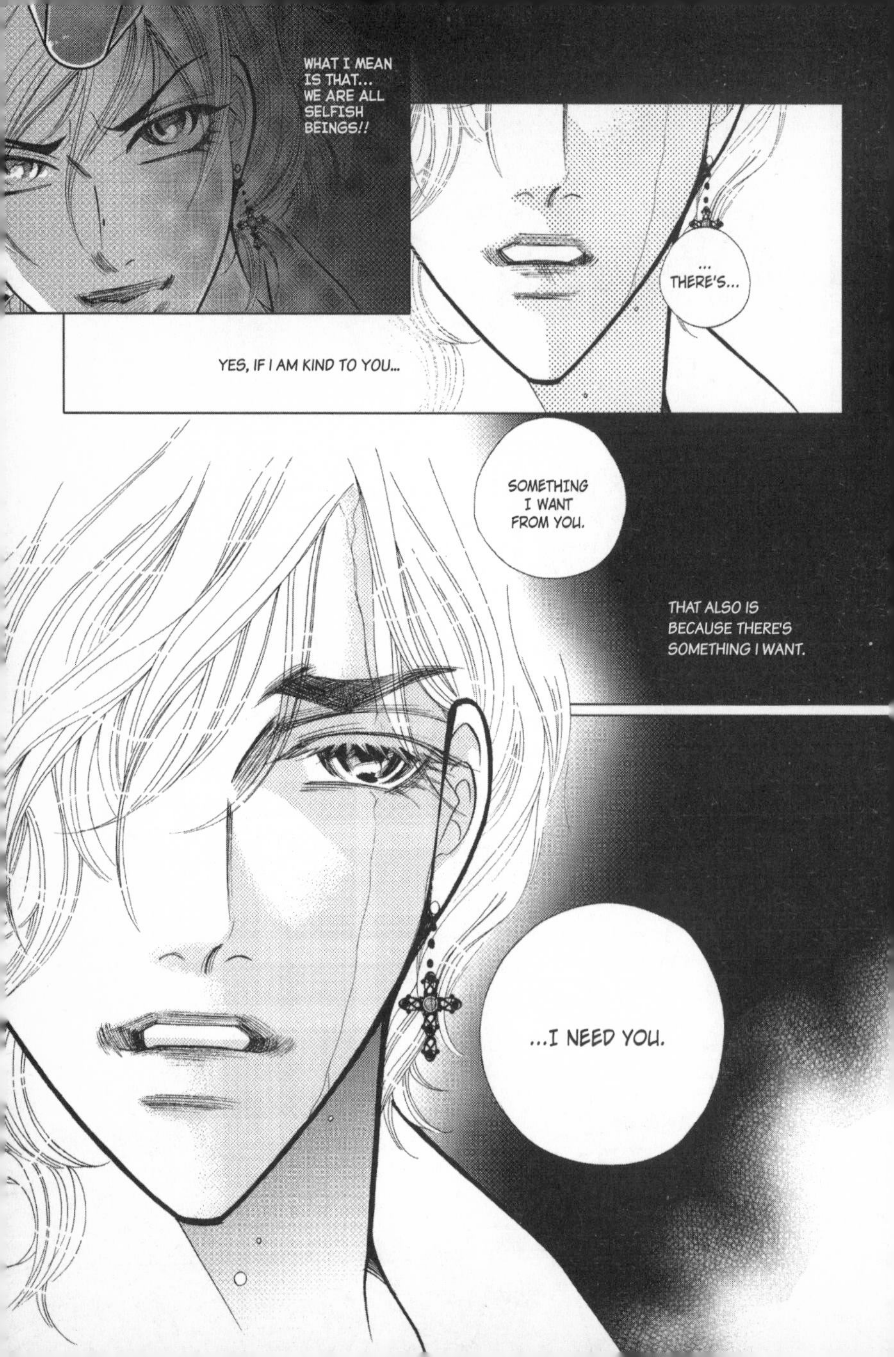
WHAT I MEAN IS THAT... WE ARE ALL SELFISH BEINGS!!
... THERE'S...
YES, IF I AM KIND TO YOU...
SOMETHING I WANT FROM YOU.
THAT ALSO IS BECAUSE THERE'S SOMETHING I WANT.
...I NEED YOU.

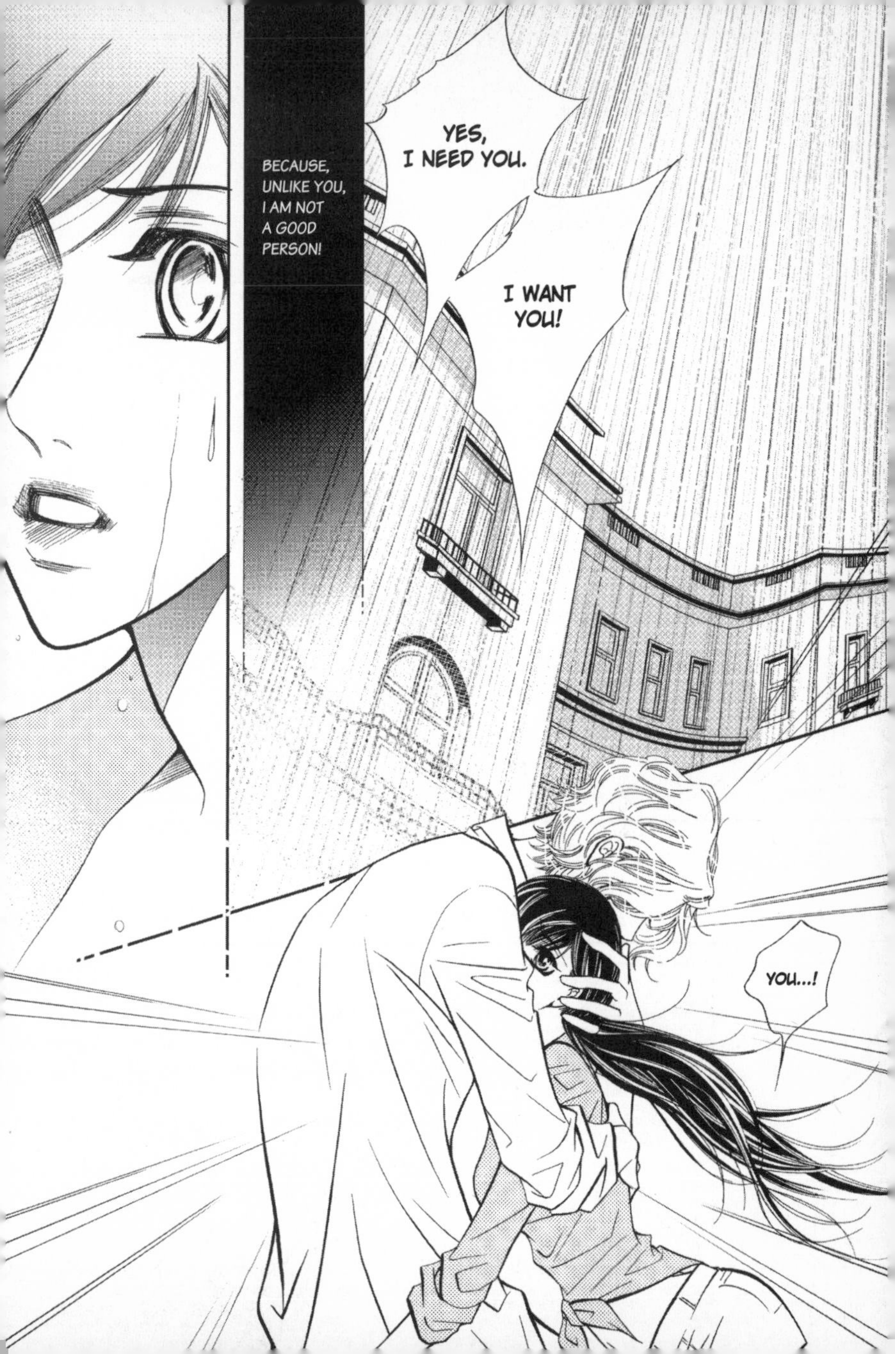
BECAUSE, UNLIKE YOU, I AM NOT A GOOD PERSON!
YES, I NEED YOU.
I WANT YOU!
YOU...!

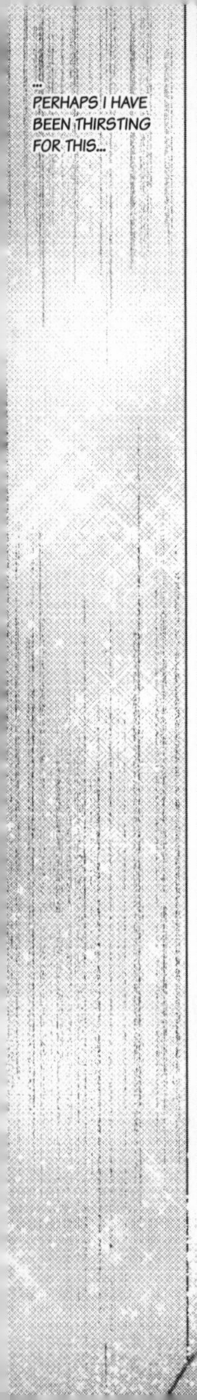
...
PERHAPS I HAVE BEEN THIRSTING FOR THIS...

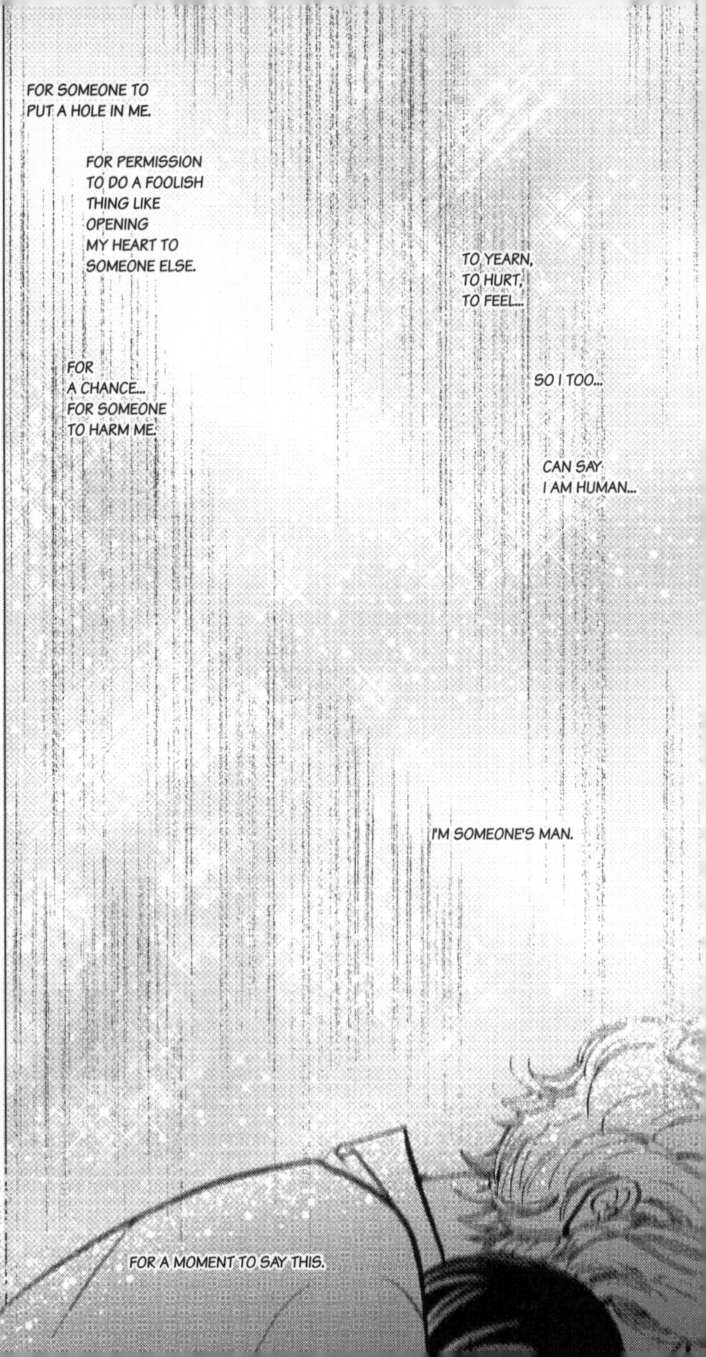
FOR SOMEONE TO PUT A HOLE IN ME.
FOR PERMISSION TO DO A FOOLISH THING LIKE OPENING MY HEART TO SOMEONE ELSE.
FOR A CHANCE... FOR SOMEONE TO HARM ME.
TO YEARN, TO HURT, TO FEEL...
SO I TOO...
CAN SAY I AM HUMAN...
I'M SOMEONE'S MAN.
FOR A MOMENT TO SAY THIS.

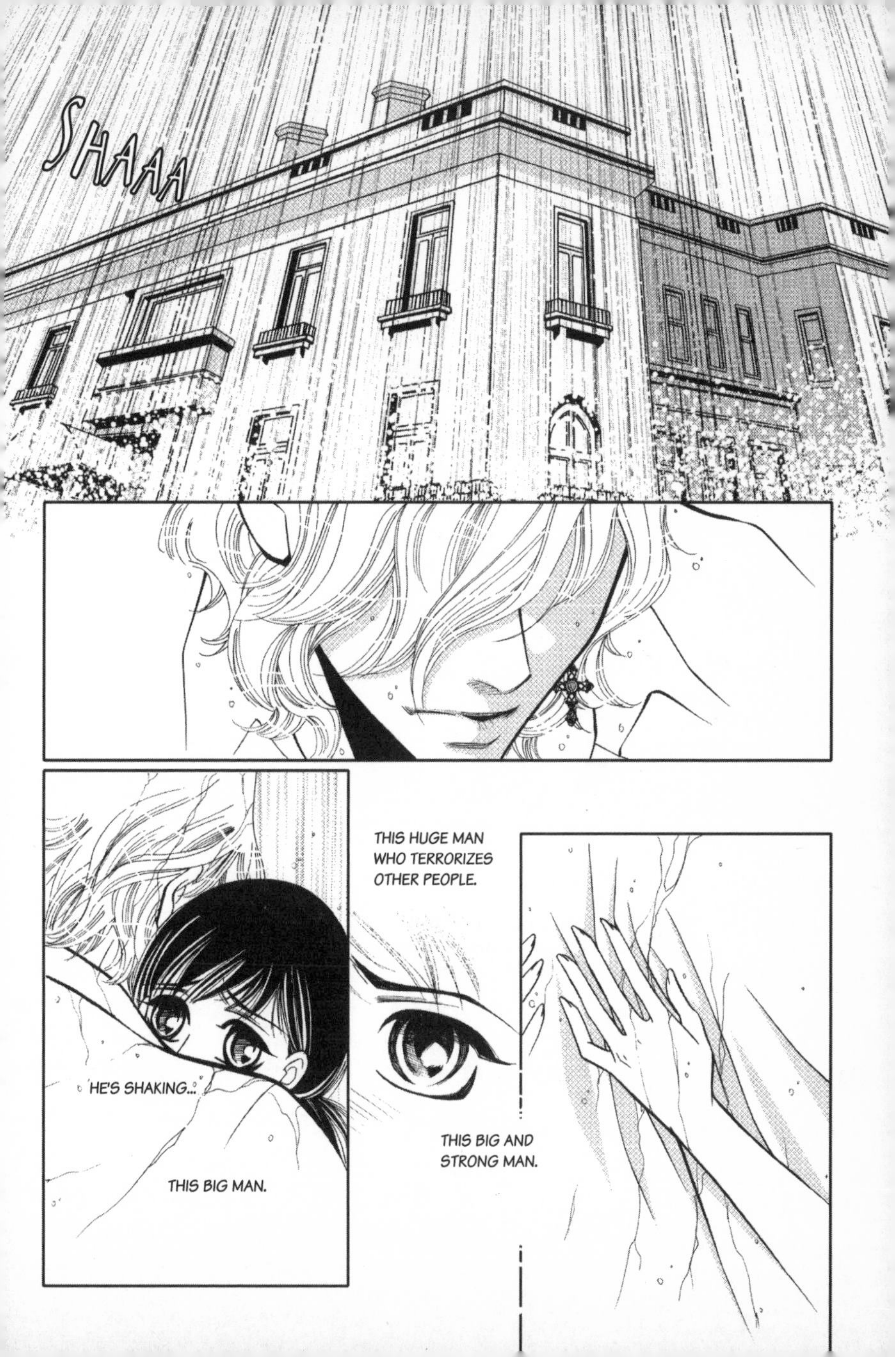
SHAAA
HE'S SHAKING...
THIS BIG MAN.
THIS HUGE MAN WHO TERRORIZES OTHER PEOPLE.
THIS BIG AND STRONG MAN.

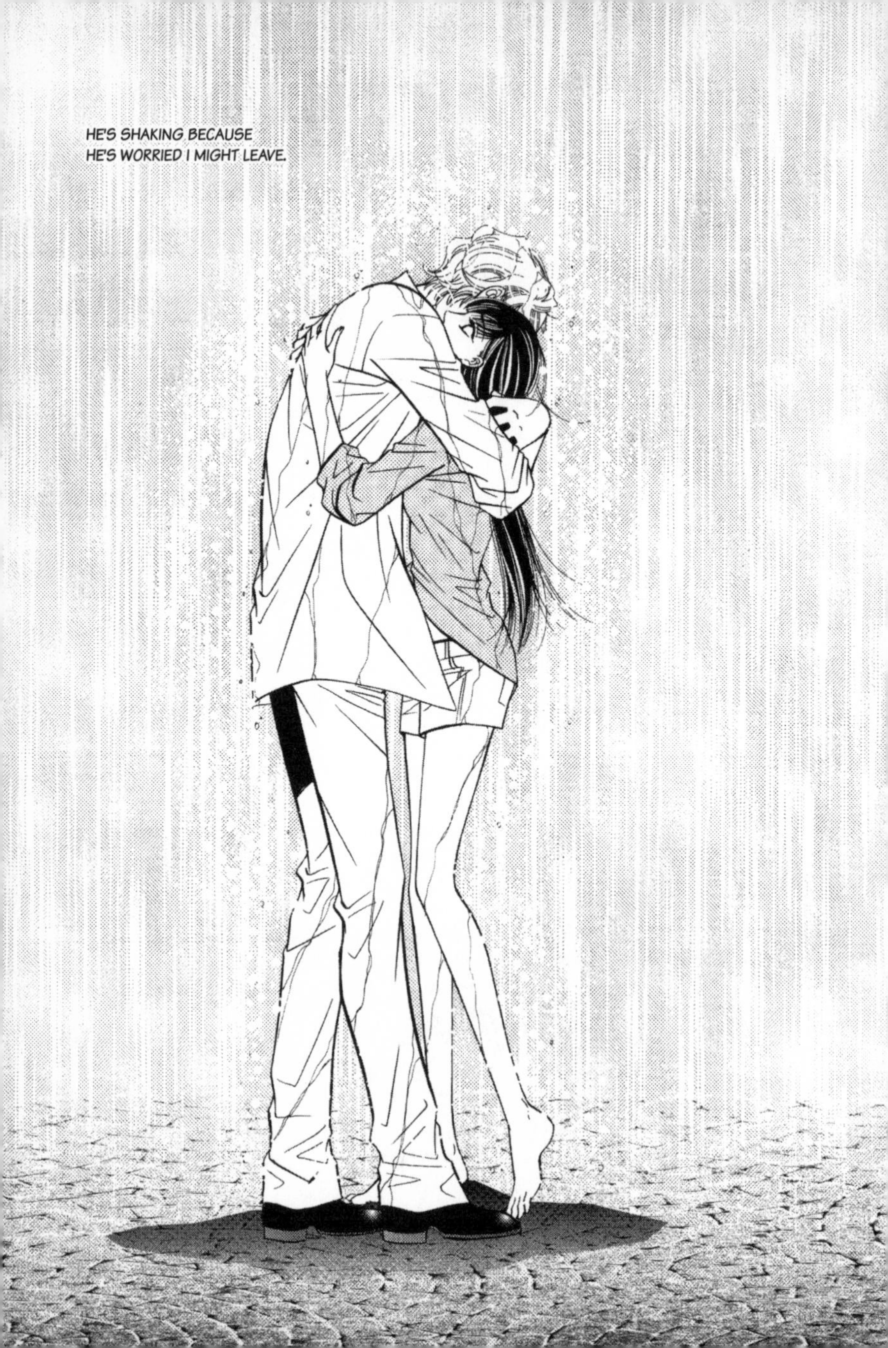
HE'S SHAKING BECAUSE
HE'S WORRIED I MIGHT LEAVE.

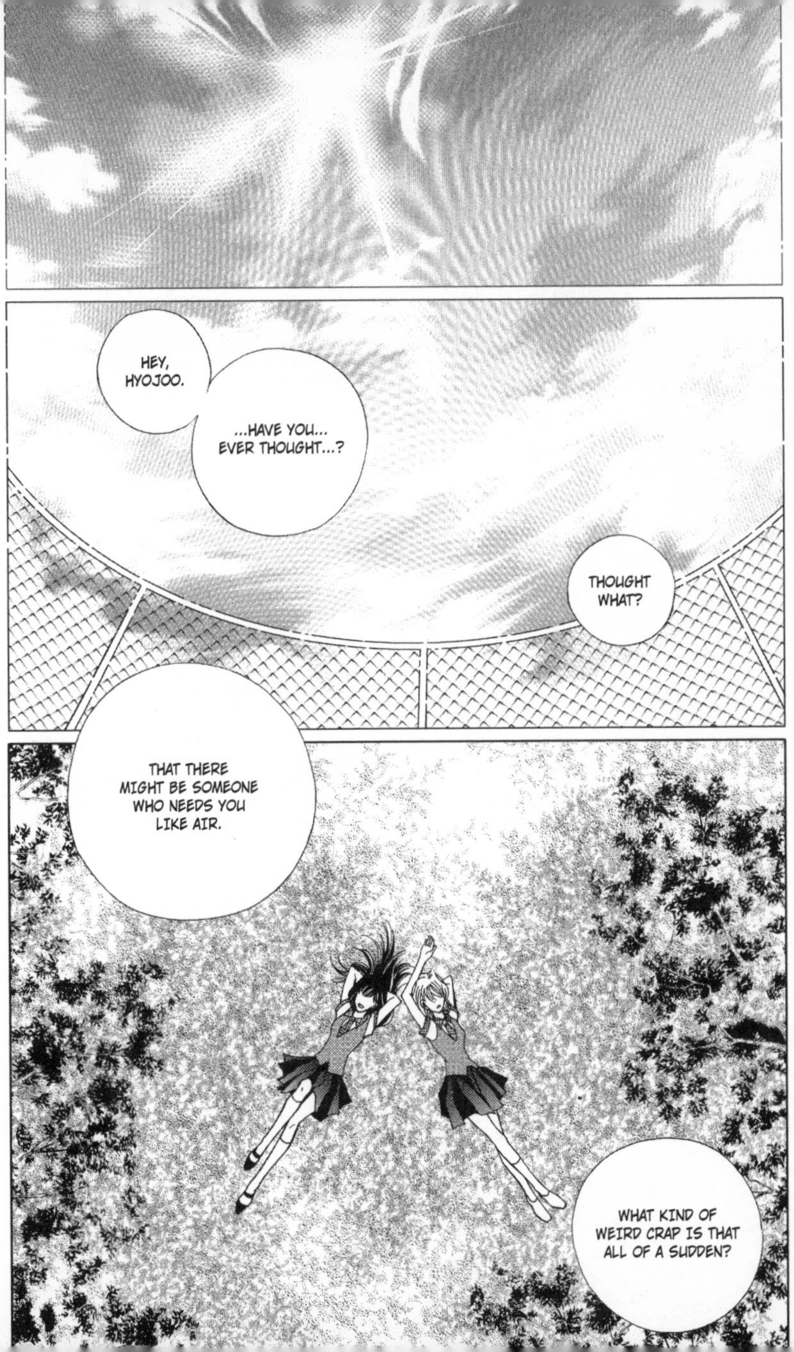
HEY, HYOJOO.
...HAVE YOU... EVER THOUGHT...?
THOUGHT WHAT?
THAT THERE MIGHT BE SOMEONE WHO NEEDS YOU LIKE AIR.
WHAT KIND OF WEIRD CRAP IS THAT ALL OF A SUDDEN?

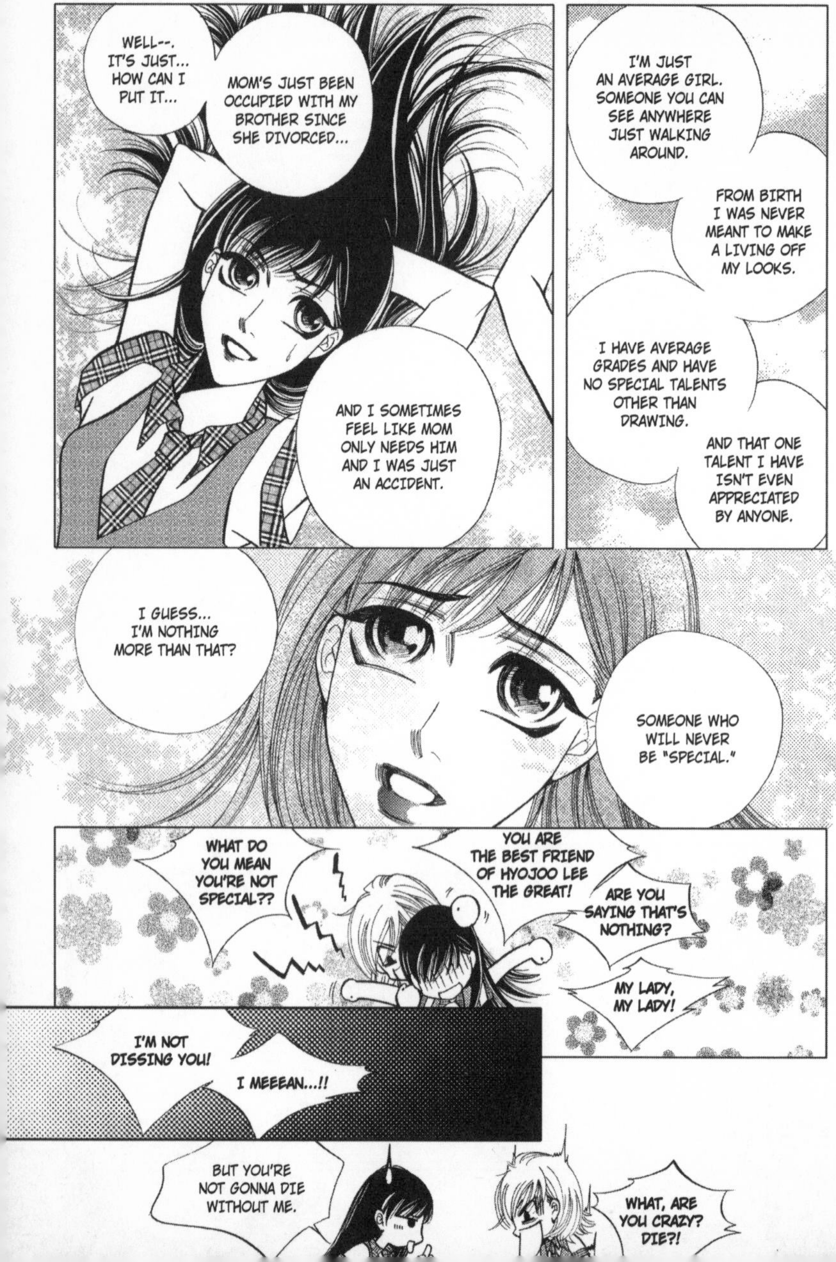
WELL--. IT'S JUST... HOW CAN I PUT IT...
MOM'S JUST BEEN OCCUPIED WITH MY BROTHER SINCE SHE DIVORCED...
AND I SOMETIMES FEEL LIKE MOM ONLY NEEDS HIM AND I WAS JUST AN ACCIDENT.
I'M JUST AN AVERAGE GIRL. SOMEONE YOU CAN SEE ANYWHERE JUST WALKING AROUND.
FROM BIRTH I WAS NEVER MEANT TO MAKE A LIVING OFF MY LOOKS.
I HAVE AVERAGE GRADES AND HAVE NO SPECIAL TALENTS OTHER THAN DRAWING.
AND THAT ONE TALENT I HAVE ISN'T EVEN APPRECIATED BY ANYONE.
I GUESS... I'M NOTHING MORE THAN THAT?
SOMEONE WHO WILL NEVER BE "SPECIAL."
WHAT DO YOU MEAN YOU'RE NOT SPECIAL??
YOU ARE THE BEST FRIEND OF HYOJOO LEE THE GREAT!
ARE YOU SAYING THAT'S NOTHING?
MY LADY, MY LADY!
I'M NOT DISSING YOU!
I MEEEAN...!!
BUT YOU'RE NOT GONNA DIE WITHOUT ME.
WHAT, ARE YOU CRAZY? DIE?!

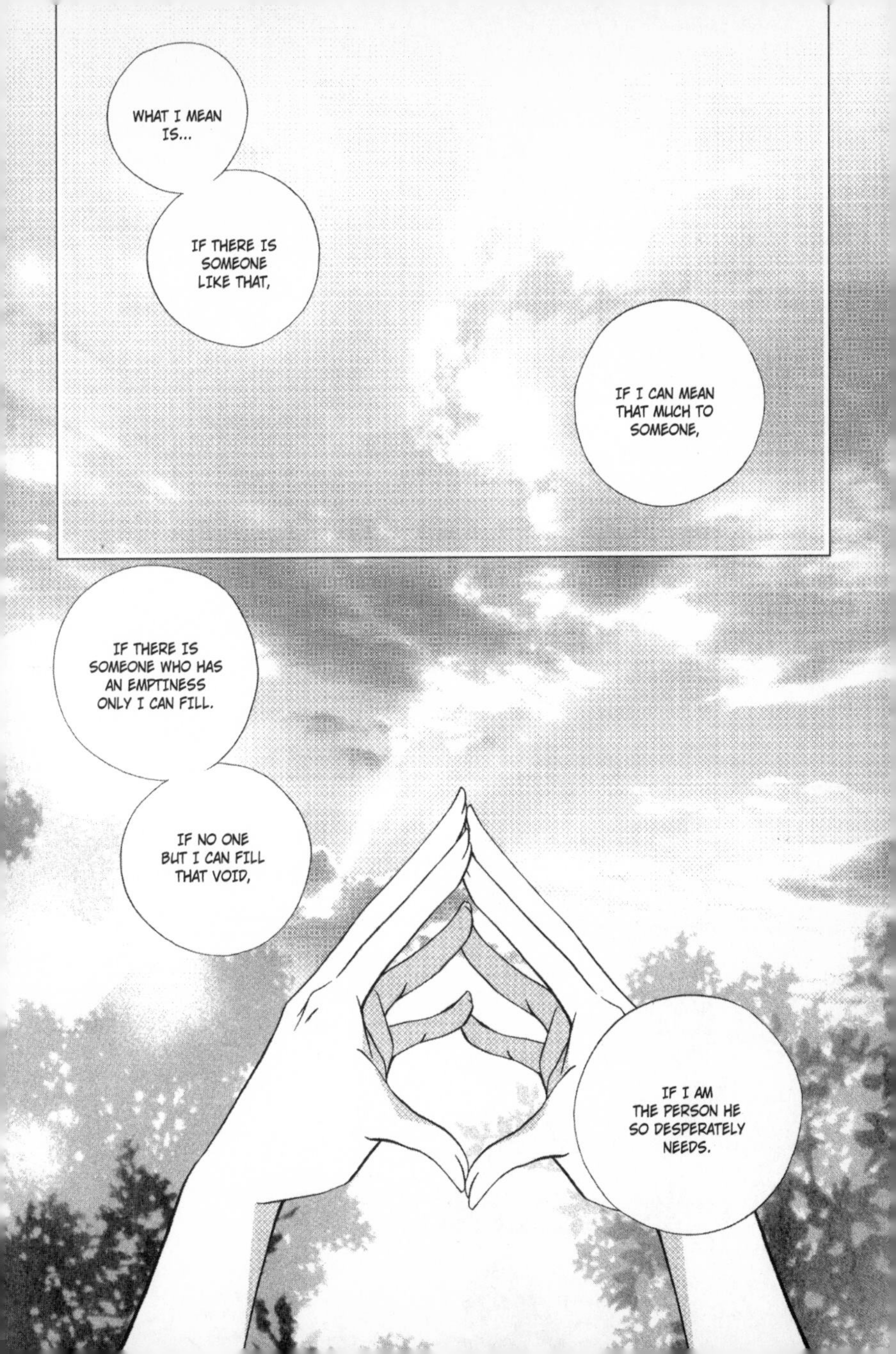
WHAT I MEAN IS...
IF THERE IS SOMEONE LIKE THAT,
IF I CAN MEAN THAT MUCH TO SOMEONE,
IF THERE IS SOMEONE WHO HAS AN EMPTINESS ONLY I CAN FILL.
IF NO ONE BUT I CAN FILL THAT VOID,
IF I AM THE PERSON HE SO DESPERATELY NEEDS.

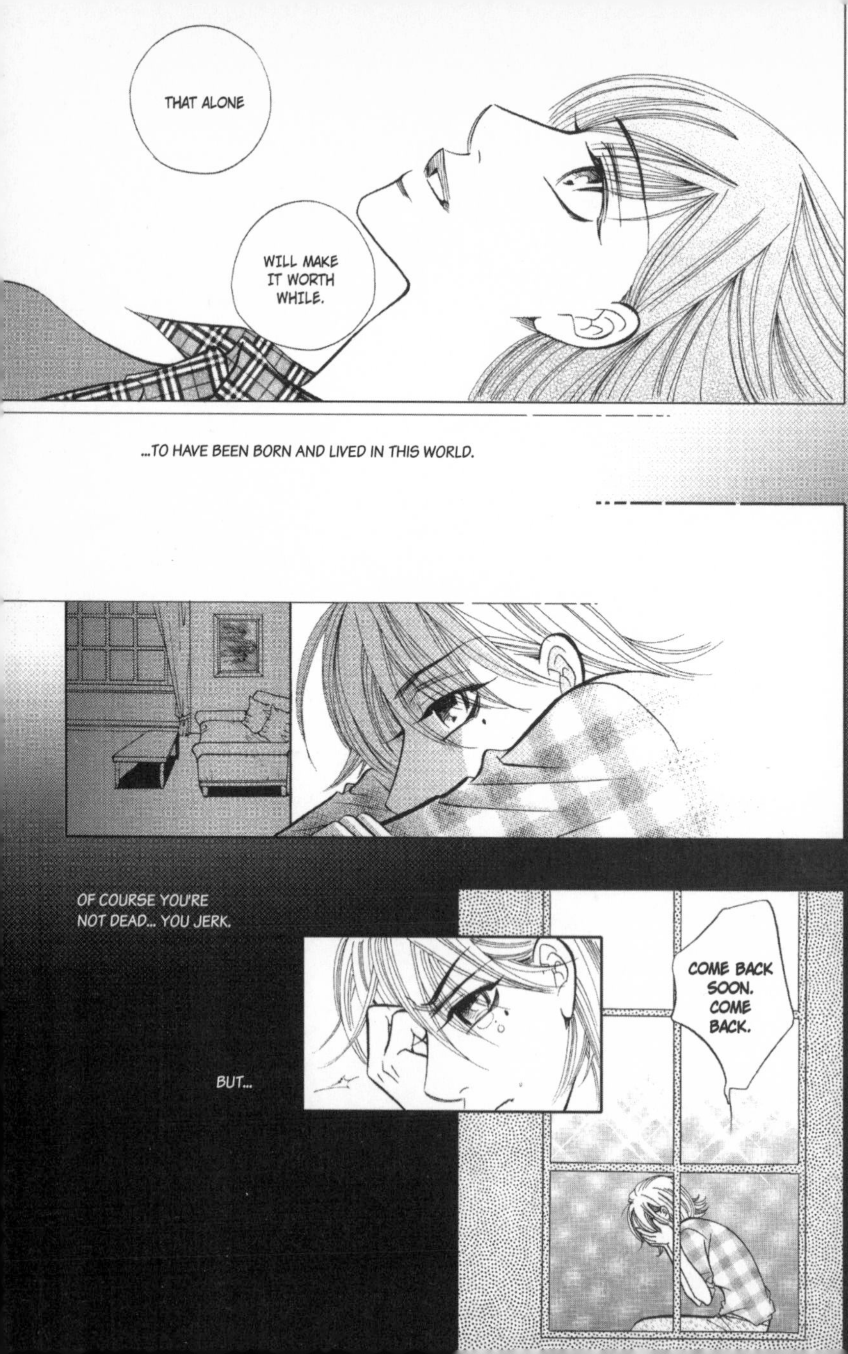
THAT ALONE
WILL MAKE IT WORTH WHILE.
...TO HAVE BEEN BORN AND LIVED IN THIS WORLD.
OF COURSE YOU'RE NOT DEAD... YOU JERK.
BUT...
COME BACK SOON. COME BACK.

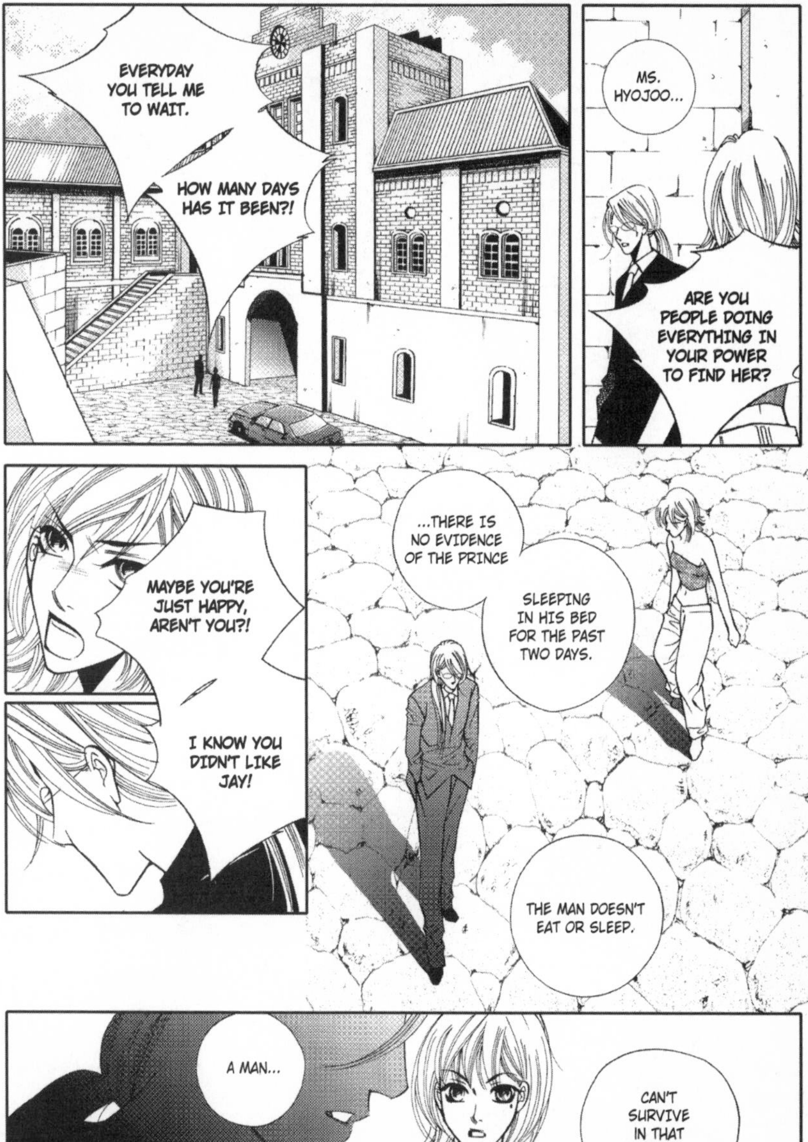
EVERYDAY YOU TELL ME TO WAIT.
HOW MANY DAYS HAS IT BEEN?!
MS. HYOJOO...
ARE YOU PEOPLE DOING EVERYTHING IN YOUR POWER TO FIND HER?
MAYBE YOU'RE JUST HAPPY, AREN'T YOU?!
I KNOW YOU DIDN'T LIKE JAY!
...THERE IS NO EVIDENCE OF THE PRINCE
SLEEPING IN HIS BED FOR THE PAST TWO DAYS.
THE MAN DOESN'T EAT OR SLEEP.
A MAN...
CAN'T SURVIVE IN THAT CONDITION.

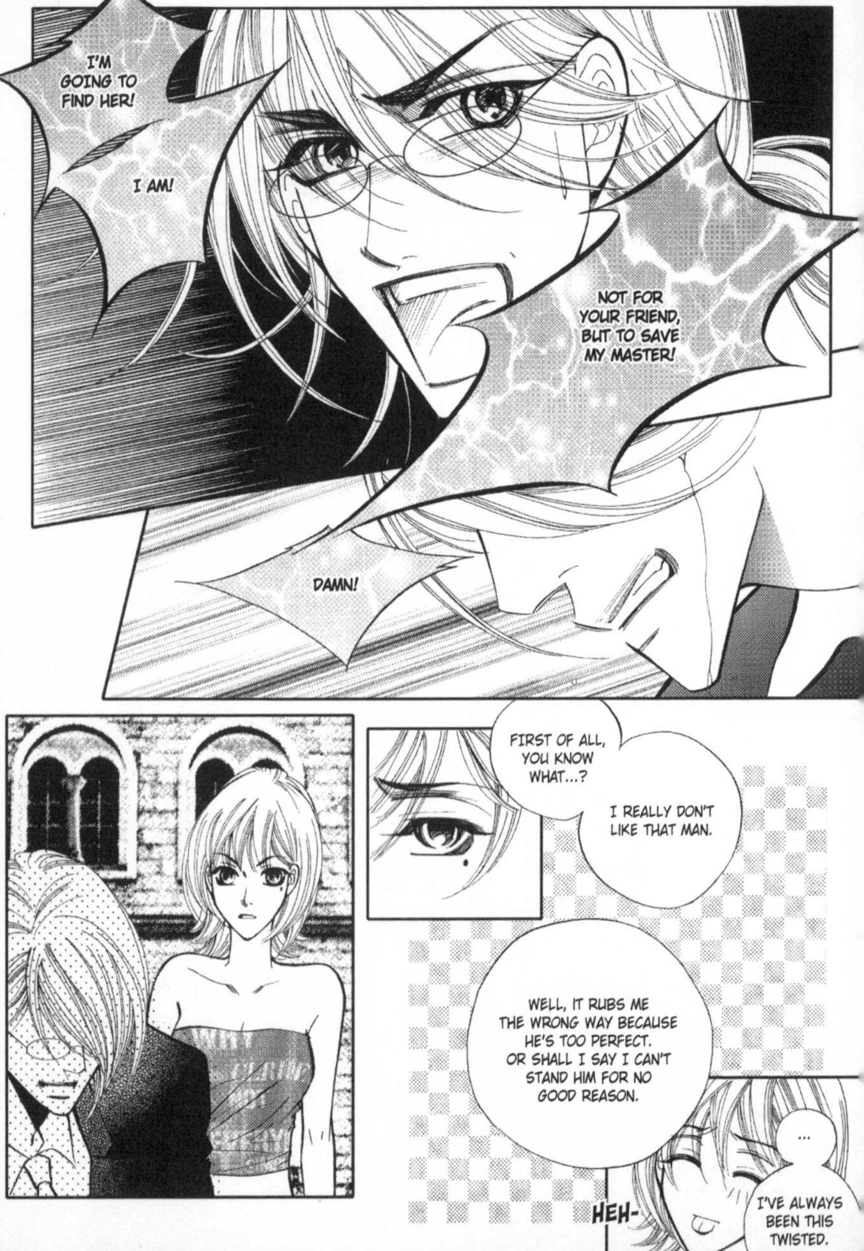
I'M GOING TO FIND HER!
I AM!
NOT FOR YOUR FRIEND, BUT TO SAVE MY MASTER!
DAMN!
FIRST OF ALL, YOU KNOW WHAT...?
I REALLY DON'T LIKE THAT MAN.
WELL, IT RUBS ME THE WRONG WAY BECAUSE HE'S TOO PERFECT. OR SHALL I SAY I CAN'T STAND HIM FOR NO GOOD REASON.
HEH-
...
I'VE ALWAYS BEEN THIS TWISTED.

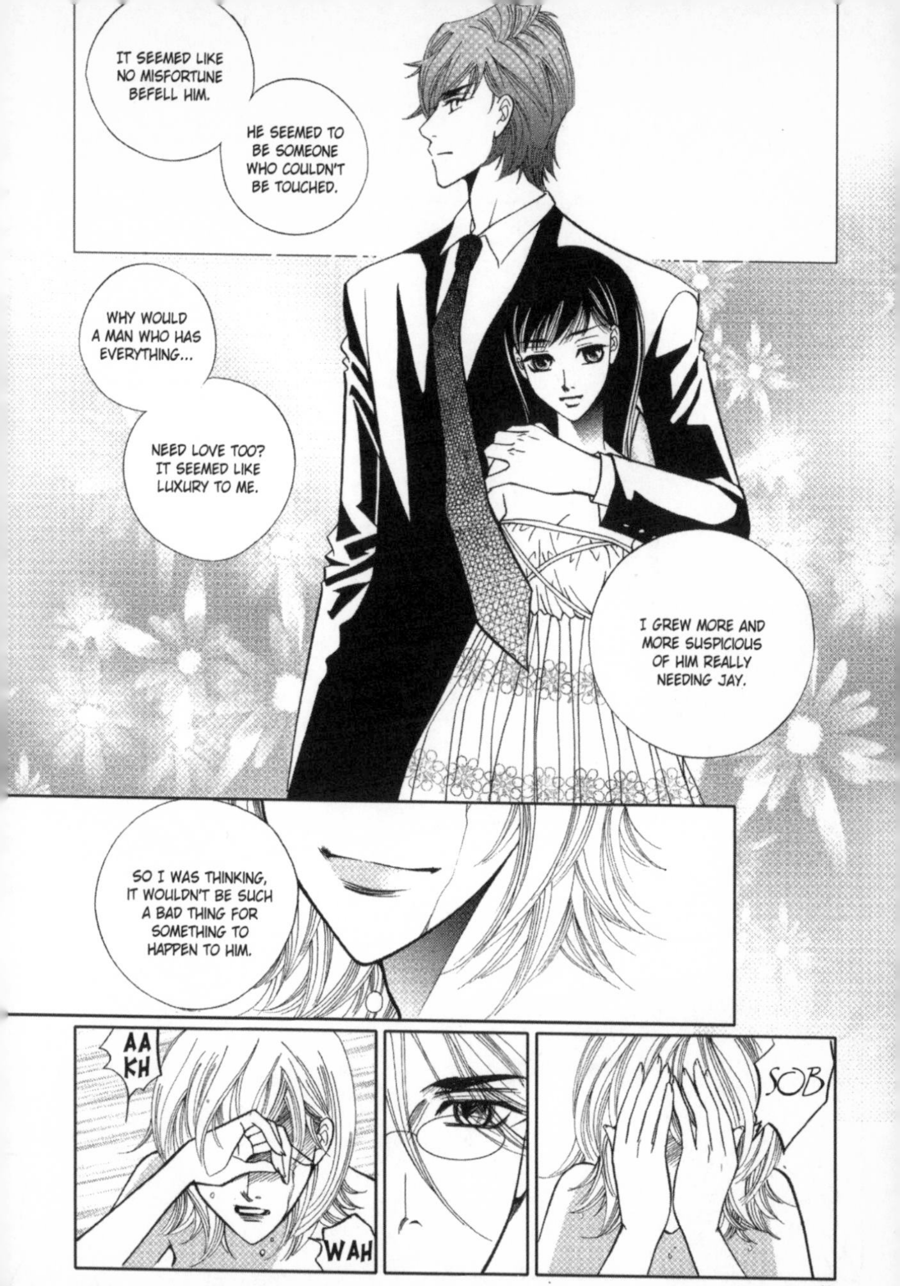
IT SEEMED LIKE NO MISFORTUNE BEFELL HIM.
HE SEEMED TO BE SOMEONE WHO COULDN'T BE TOUCHED.
WHY WOULD A MAN WHO HAS EVERYTHING...
NEED LOVE TOO? IT SEEMED LIKE LUXURY TO ME.
I GREW MORE AND MORE SUSPICIOUS OF HIM REALLY NEEDING JAY.
SO I WAS THINKING, IT WOULDN'T BE SUCH A BAD THING FOR SOMETHING TO HAPPEN TO HIM.
AAKH
WAH
SOB

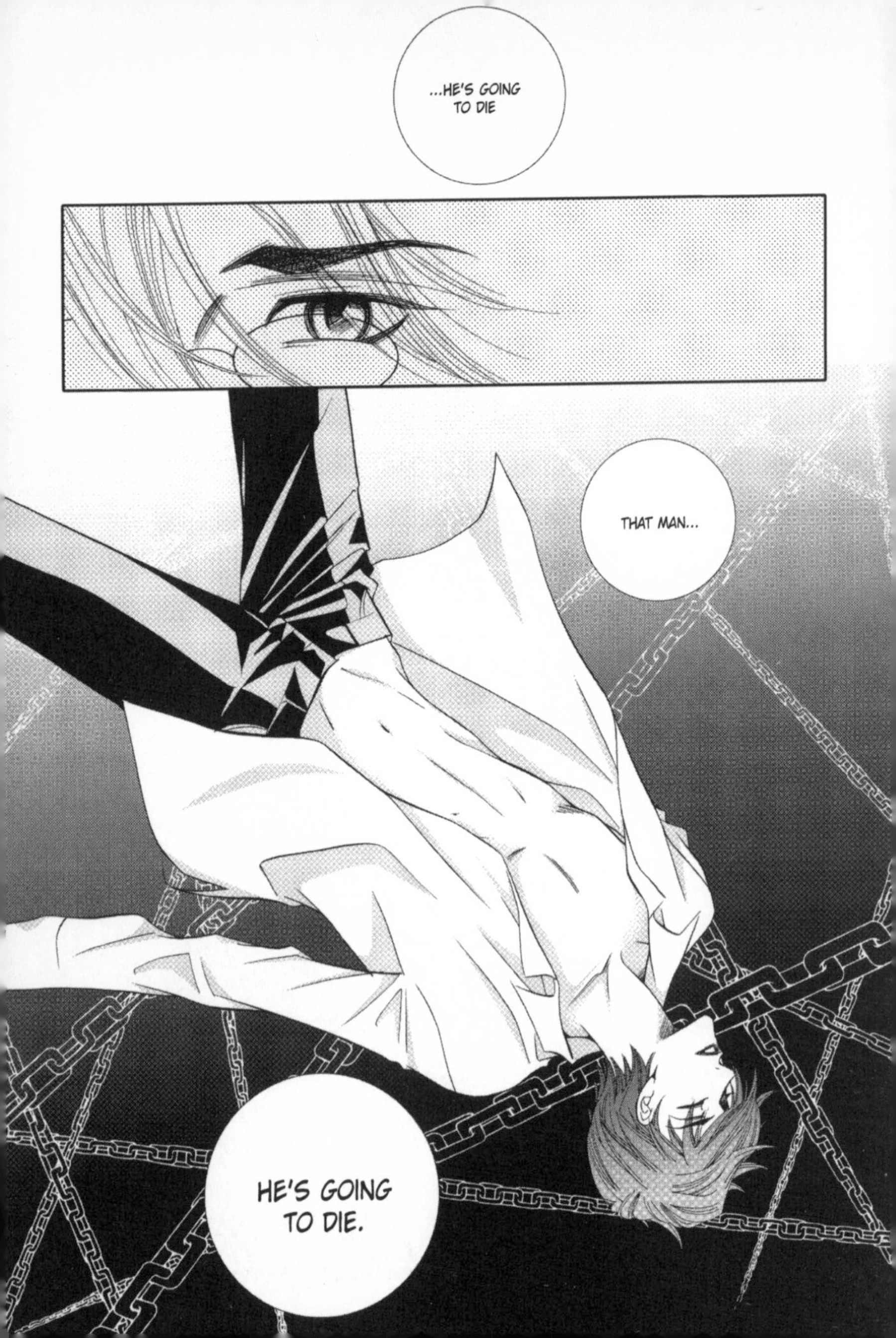
...HE'S GOING TO DIE
THAT MAN...
HE'S GOING TO DIE.

6. RECOVERY

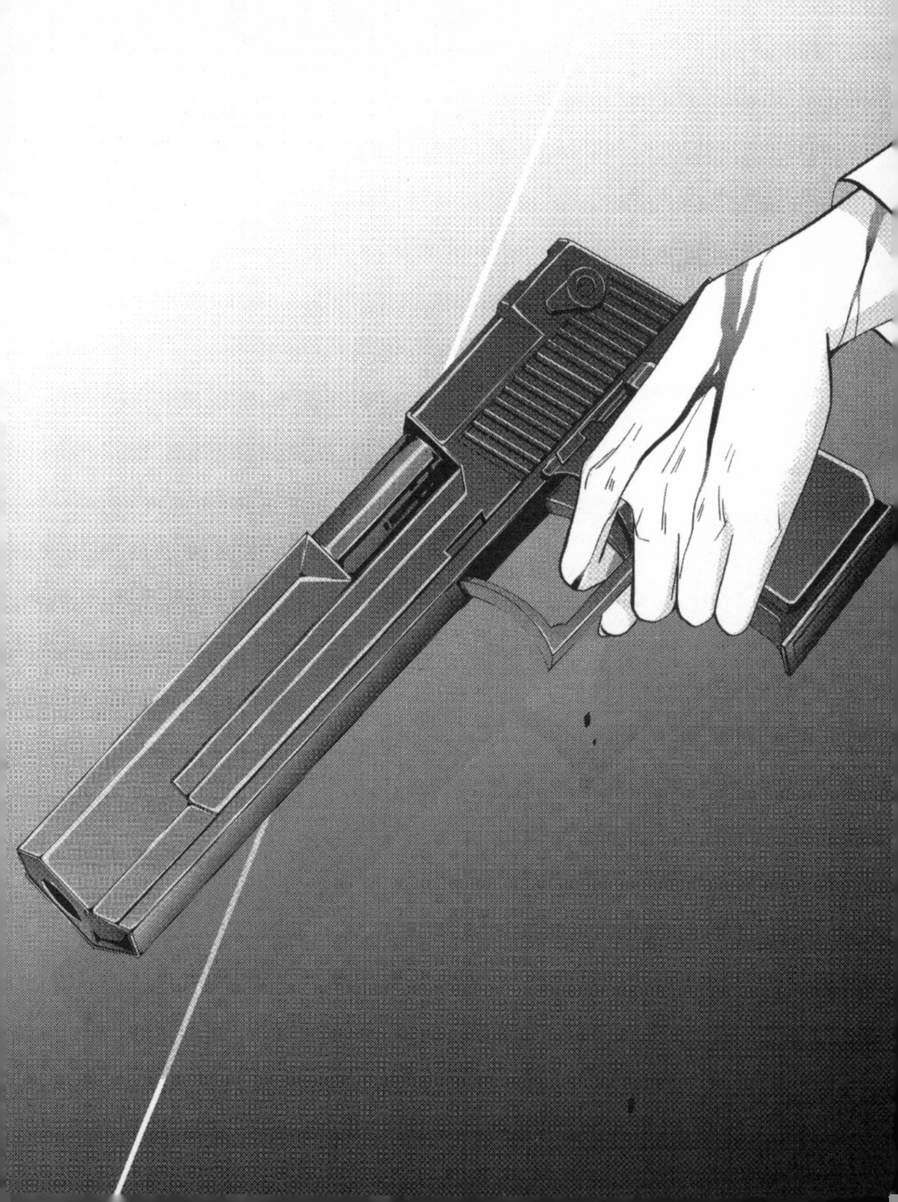

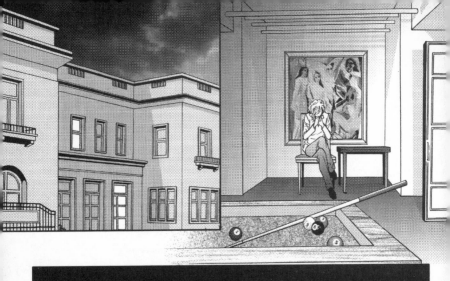

THE REASON
THAT WOMAN SAVED
YOU WAS PROBABLY

SIMPLY BECAUSE
SHE IS A *DECENT* PERSON.

NOT BECAUSE
YOU ARE SPECIAL.

TAK

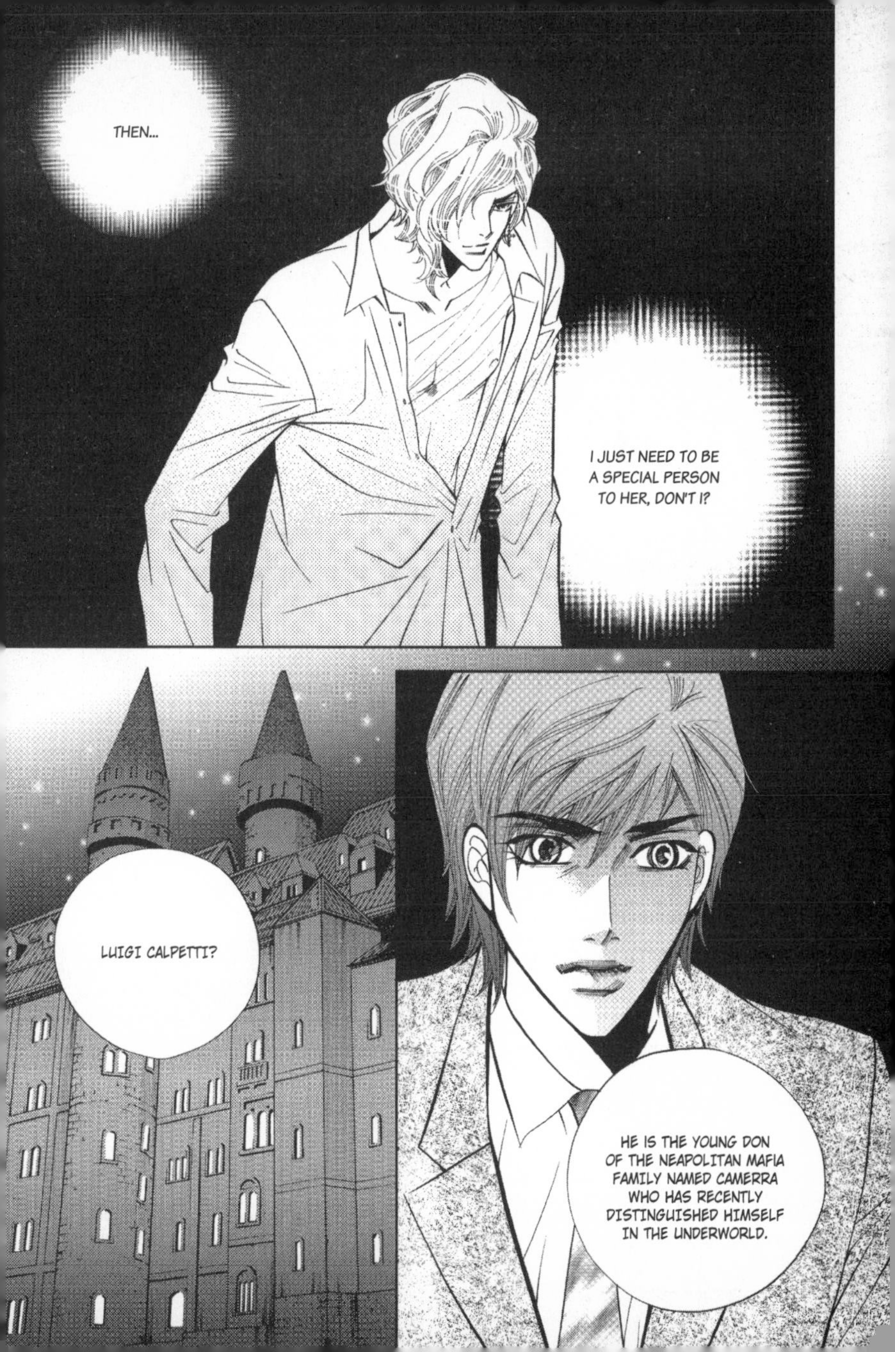
THEN...
I JUST NEED TO BE A SPECIAL PERSON TO HER, DON'T I?
LUIGI CALPETTI?
HE IS THE YOUNG DON OF THE NEAPOLITAN MAFIA FAMILY NAMED CAMERRA WHO HAS RECENTLY DISTINGUISHED HIMSELF IN THE UNDERWORLD.

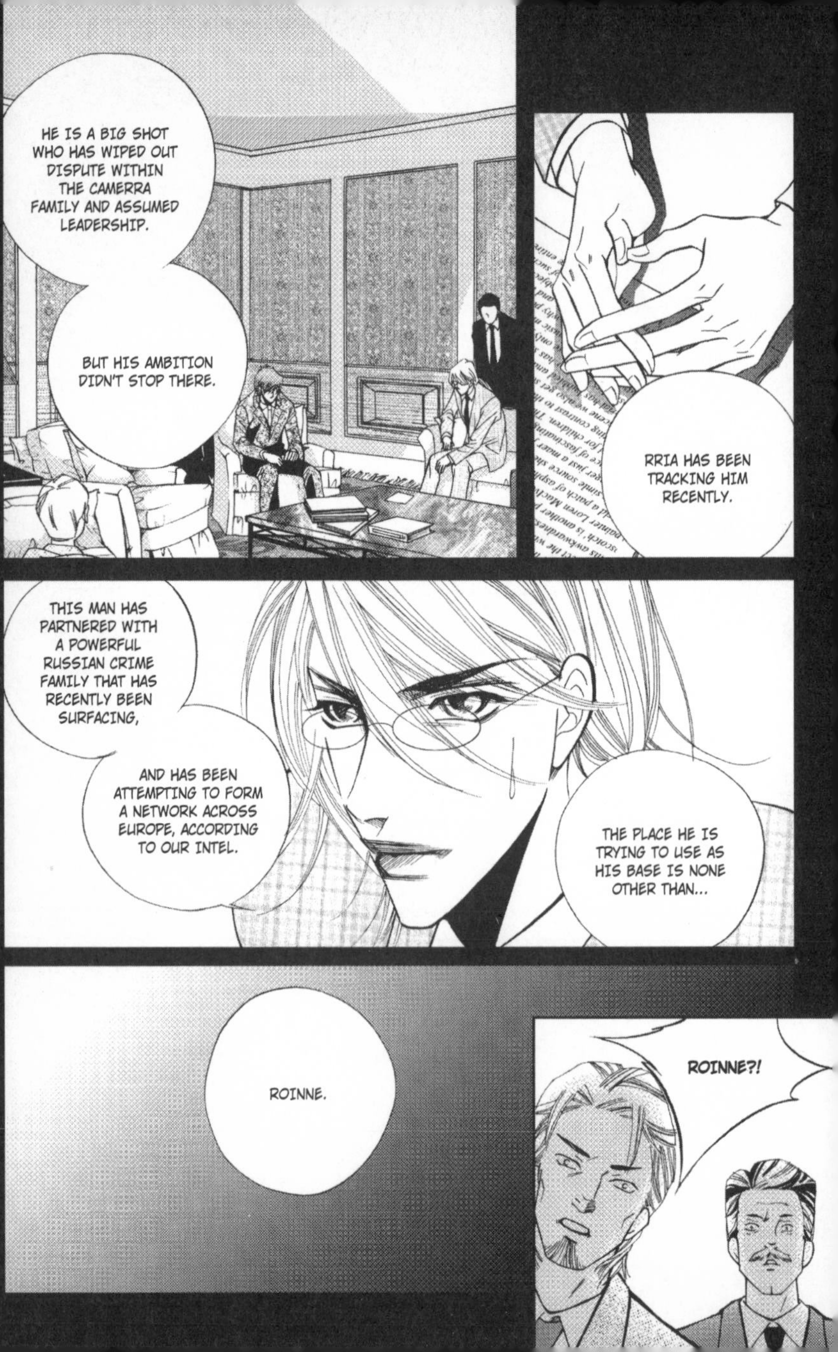
HE IS A BIG SHOT WHO HAS WIPED OUT DISPUTE WITHIN THE CAMERRA FAMILY AND ASSUMED LEADERSHIP.
BUT HIS AMBITION DIDN'T STOP THERE.
RRIA HAS BEEN TRACKING HIM RECENTLY.
THIS MAN HAS PARTNERED WITH A POWERFUL RUSSIAN CRIME FAMILY THAT HAS RECENTLY BEEN SURFACING,
AND HAS BEEN ATTEMPTING TO FORM A NETWORK ACROSS EUROPE, ACCORDING TO OUR INTEL.
THE PLACE HE IS TRYING TO USE AS HIS BASE IS NONE OTHER THAN...
ROINNE.
ROINNE?!

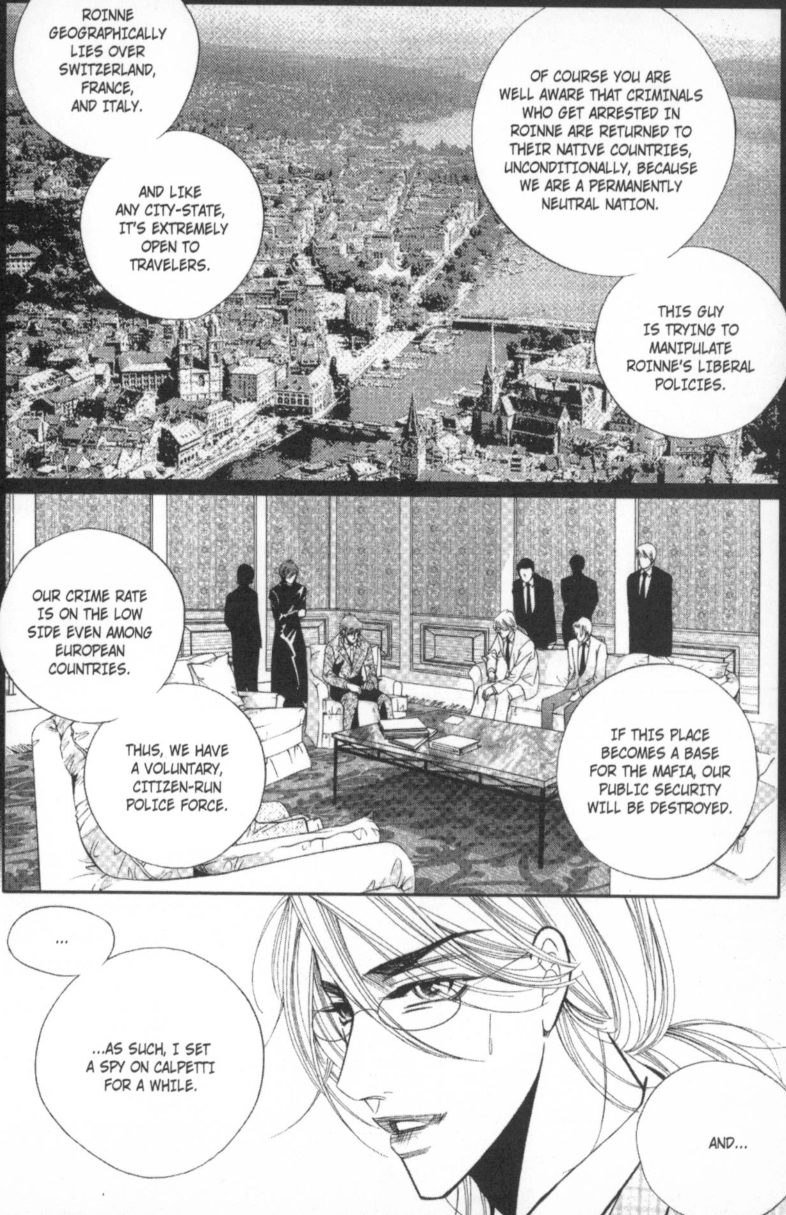
ROINNE GEOGRAPHICALLY LIES OVER SWITZERLAND, FRANCE, AND ITALY.
AND LIKE ANY CITY-STATE, IT'S EXTREMELY OPEN TO TRAVELERS.
OF COURSE YOU ARE WELL AWARE THAT CRIMINALS WHO GET ARRESTED IN ROINNE ARE RETURNED TO THEIR NATIVE COUNTRIES, UNCONDITIONALLY, BECAUSE WE ARE A PERMANENTLY NEUTRAL NATION.
THIS GUY IS TRYING TO MANIPULATE ROINNE'S LIBERAL POLICIES.
OUR CRIME RATE IS ON THE LOW SIDE EVEN AMONG EUROPEAN COUNTRIES.
THUS, WE HAVE A VOLUNTARY, CITIZEN-RUN POLICE FORCE.
IF THIS PLACE BECOMES A BASE FOR THE MAFIA, OUR PUBLIC SECURITY WILL BE DESTROYED.
...
...AS SUCH, I SET A SPY ON CALPETTI FOR A WHILE.
AND...

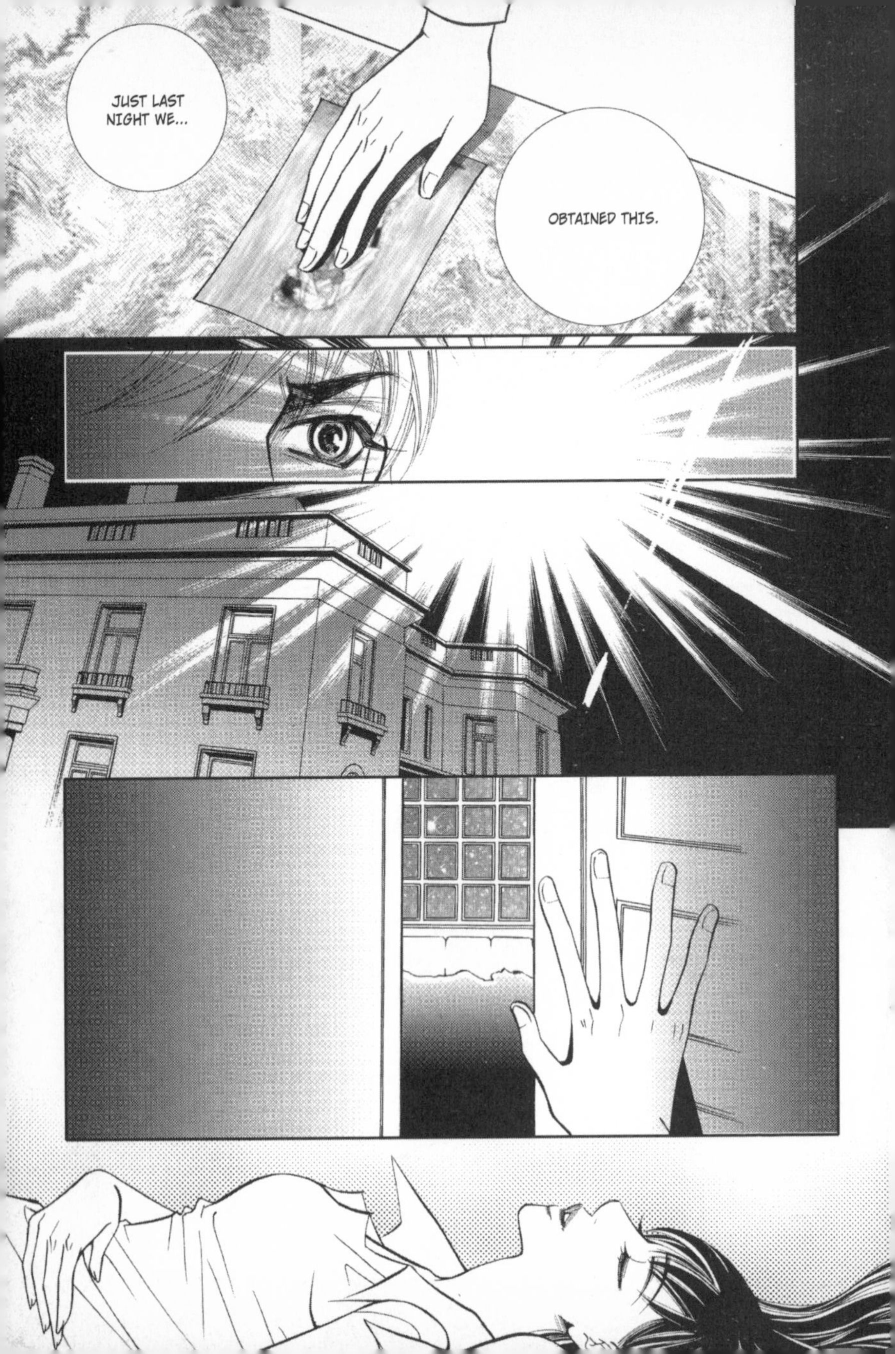
JUST LAST NIGHT WE...
OBTAINED THIS.

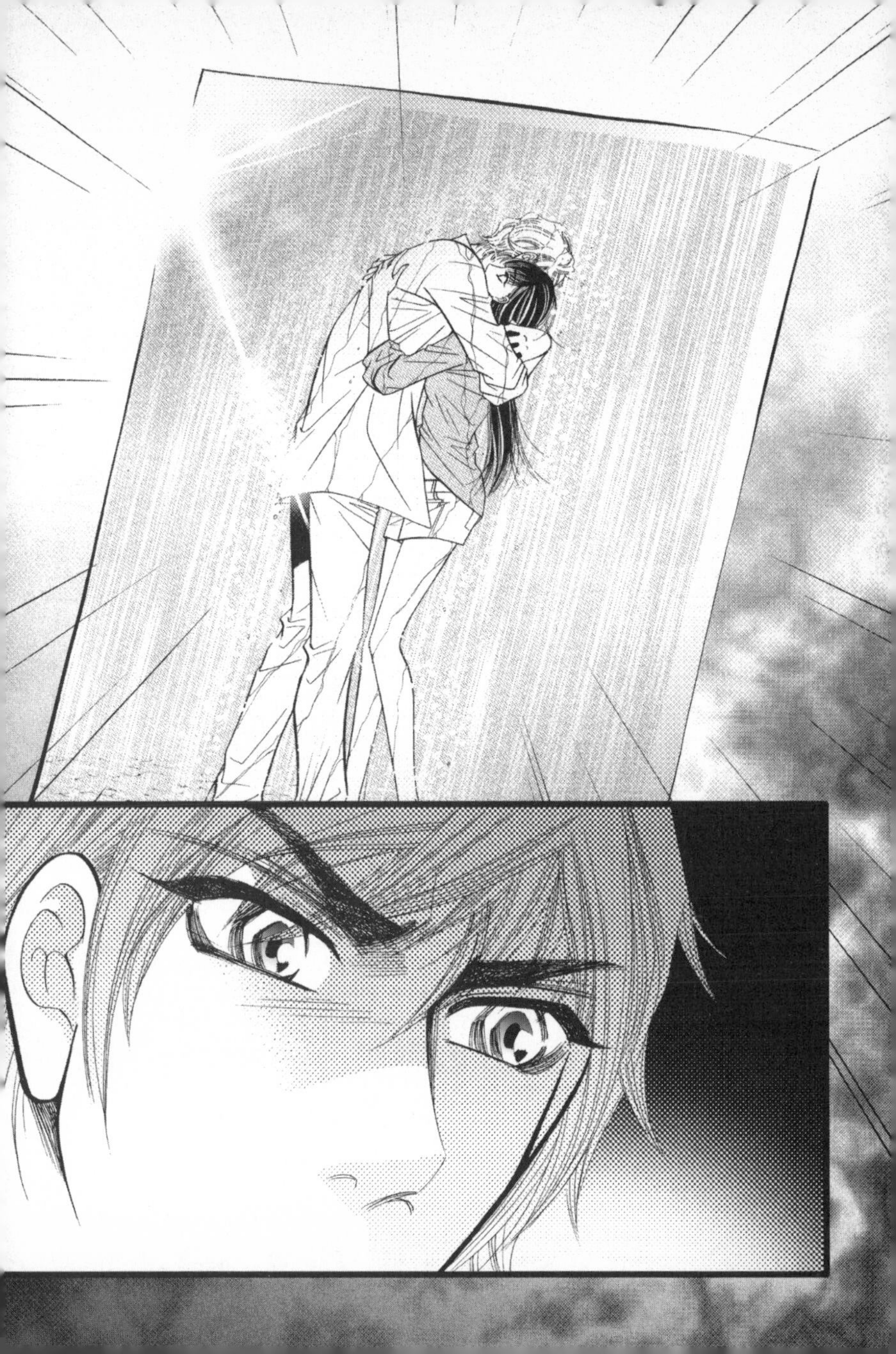

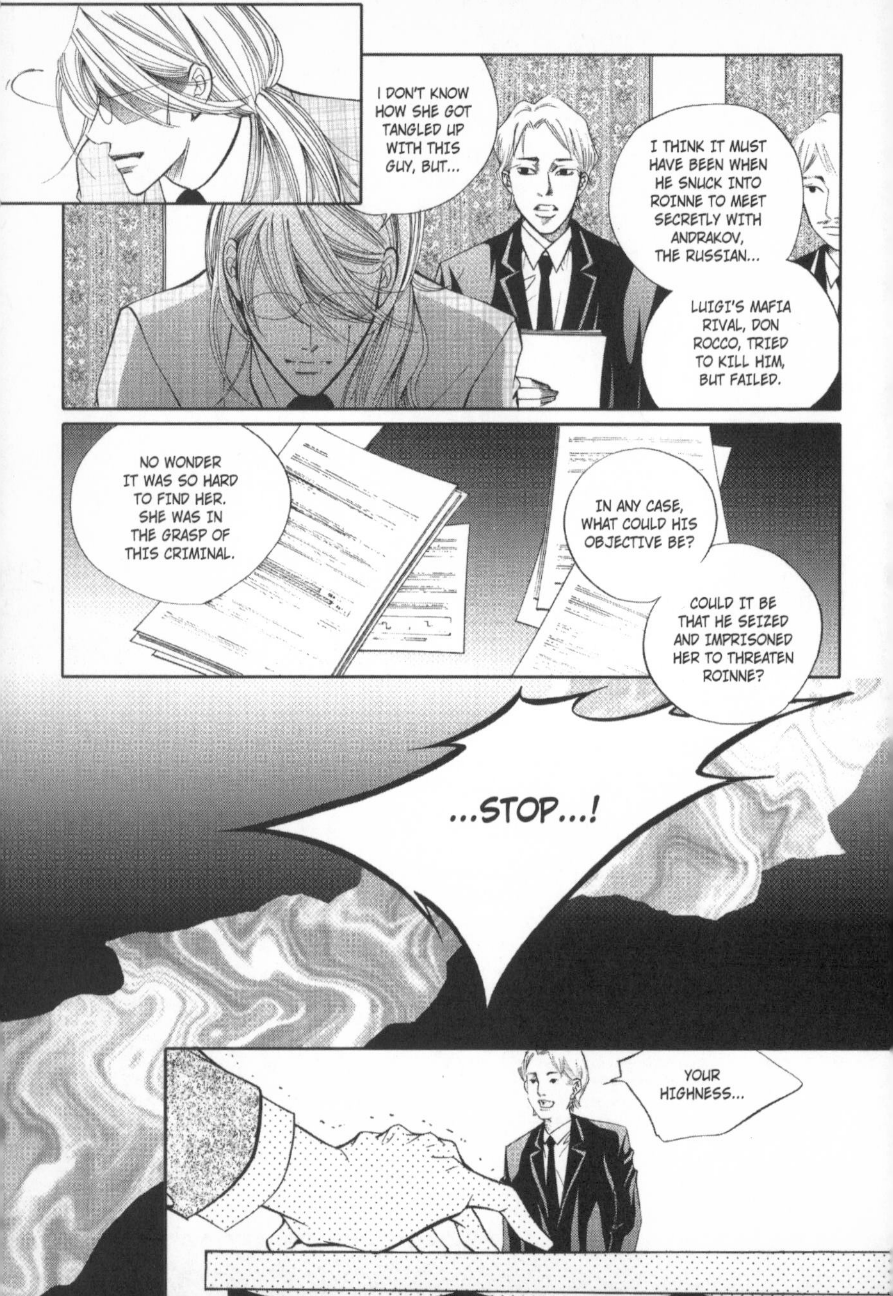
I DON'T KNOW HOW SHE GOT TANGLED UP WITH THIS GUY, BUT...
I THINK IT MUST HAVE BEEN WHEN HE SNUCK INTO ROINNE TO MEET SECRETLY WITH ANDRAKOV, THE RUSSIAN...
LUIGI'S MAFIA RIVAL, DON ROCCO, TRIED TO KILL HIM, BUT FAILED.
NO WONDER IT WAS SO HARD TO FIND HER. SHE WAS IN THE GRASP OF THIS CRIMINAL.
IN ANY CASE, WHAT COULD HIS OBJECTIVE BE?
COULD IT BE THAT HE SEIZED AND IMPRISONED HER TO THREATEN ROINNE?
...STOP...!
YOUR HIGHNESS...

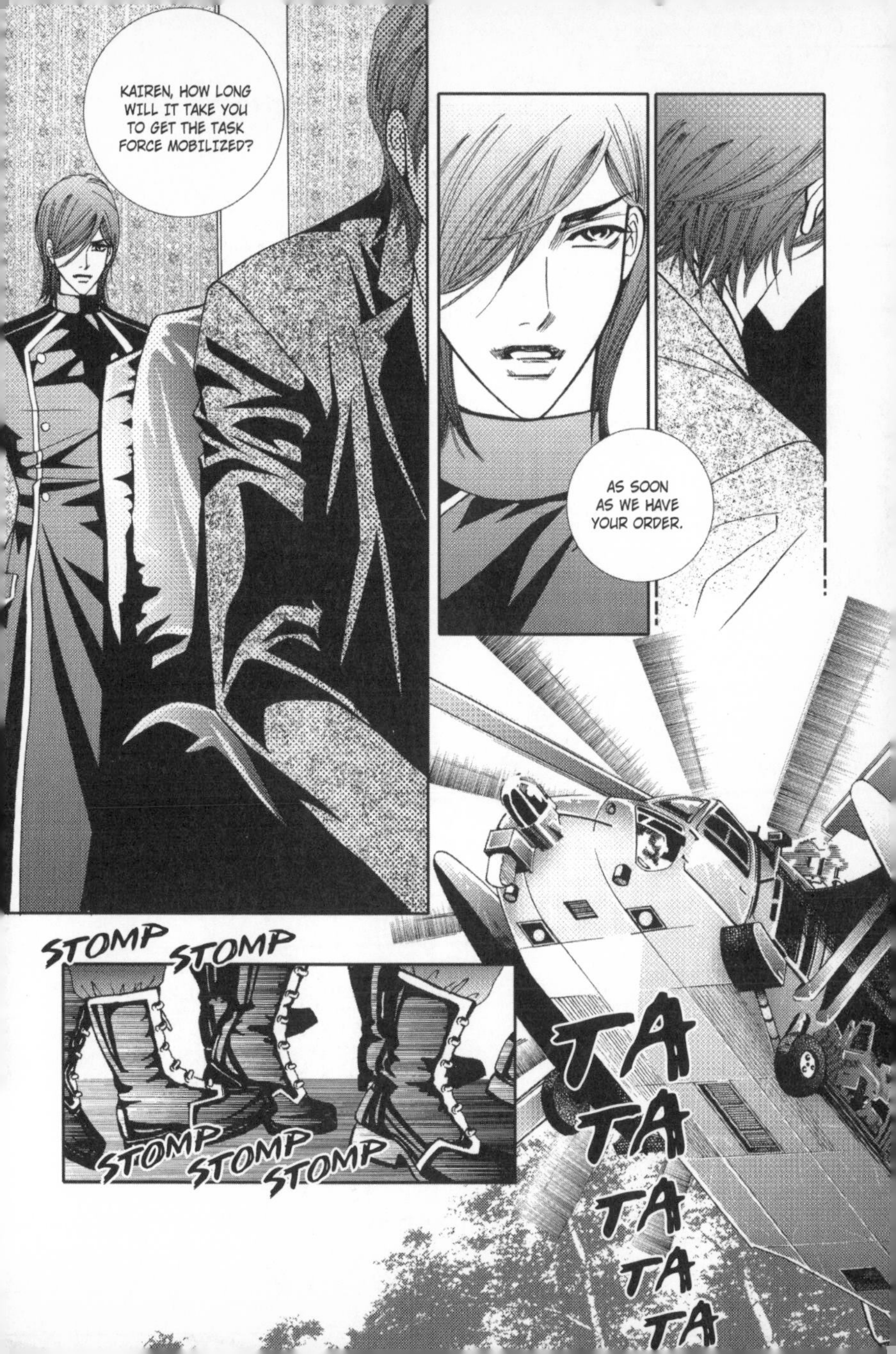
KAIREN, HOW LONG WILL IT TAKE YOU TO GET THE TASK FORCE MOBILIZED?
AS SOON AS WE HAVE YOUR ORDER.
STOMP STOMP
STOMP STOMP STOMP
TA TA TA TA TA TA

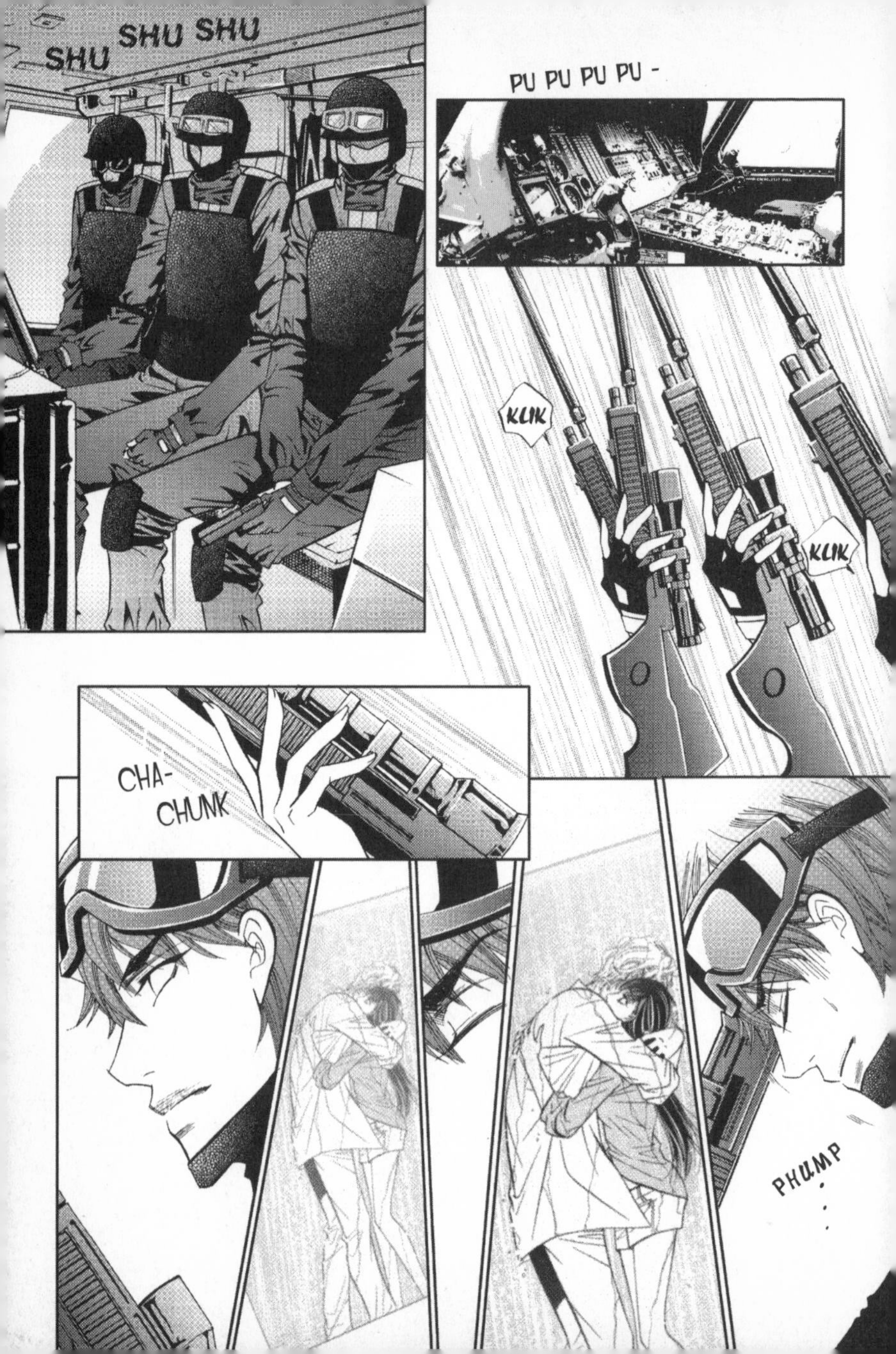
SHU SHU SHU
PU PU PU PU -
KLIK
KLIK
CHA-
CHUNK
PHUMP
. . .

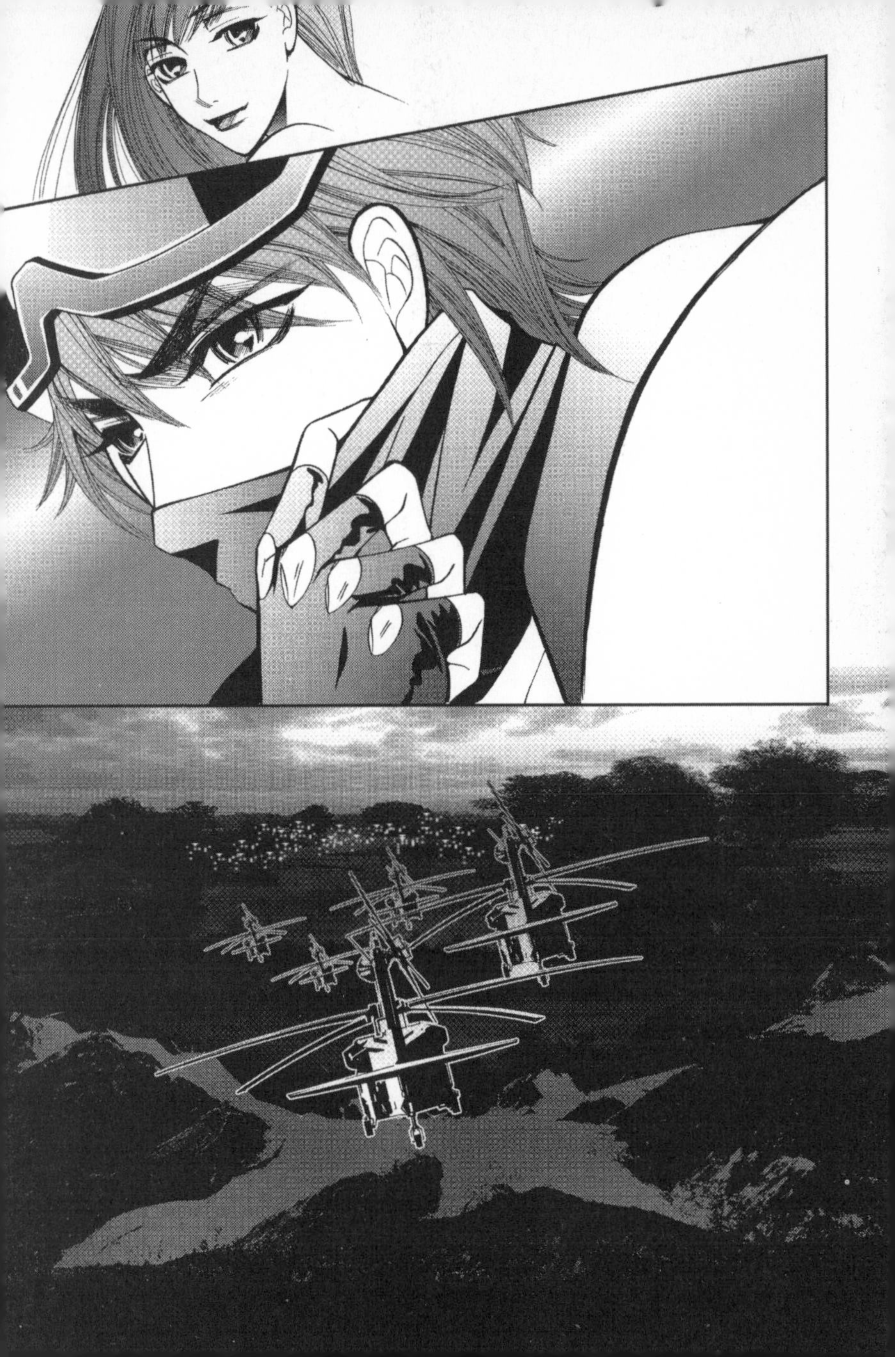

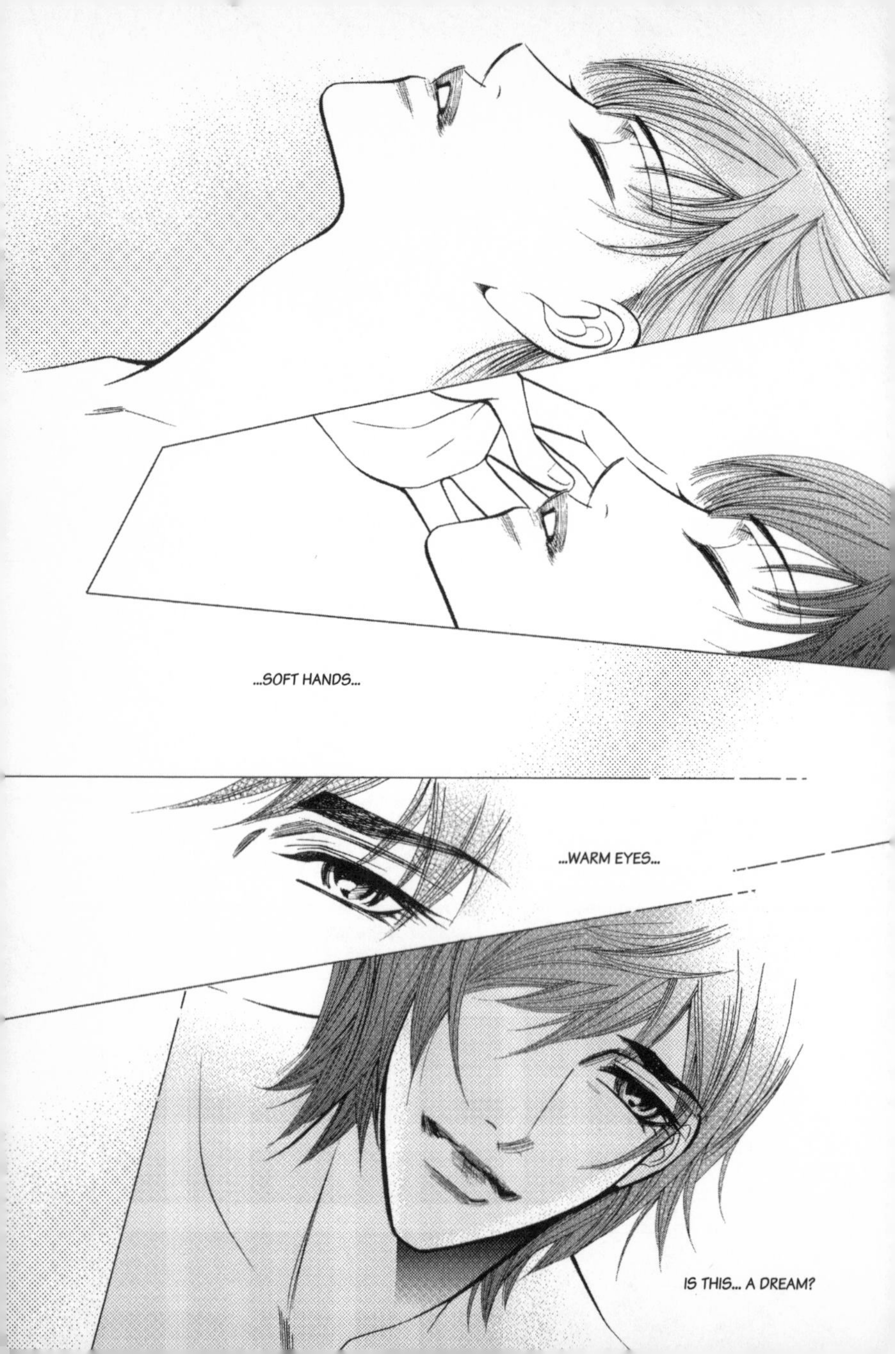
...SOFT HANDS...
...WARM EYES...
IS THIS... A DREAM?

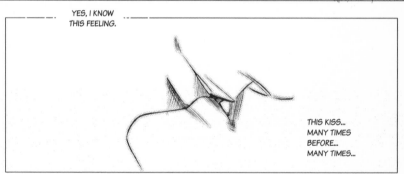

YES, I KNOW
THIS FEELING.

THIS KISS...
MANY TIMES
BEFORE...
MANY TIMES...

YOU...

IS THAT YOU?

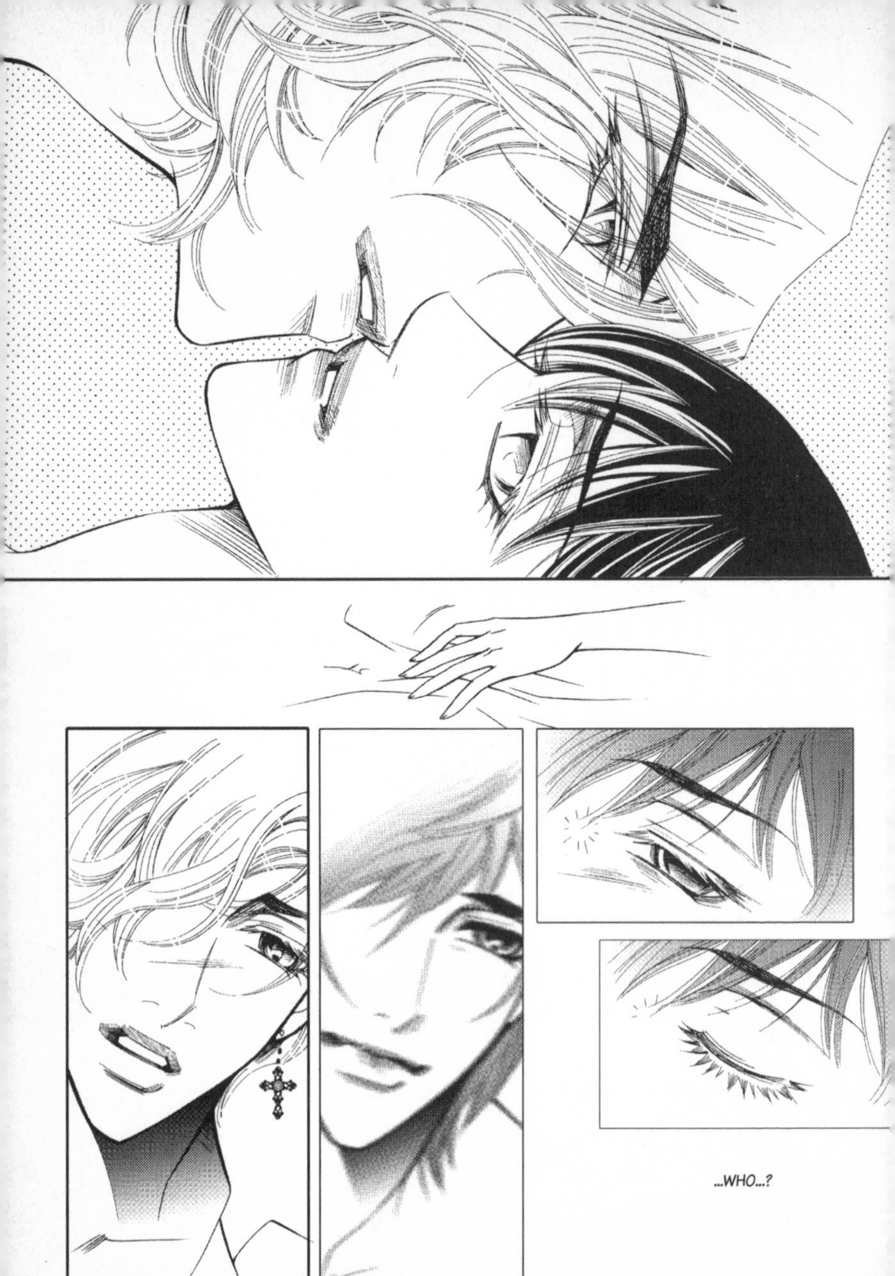
...WHO...?

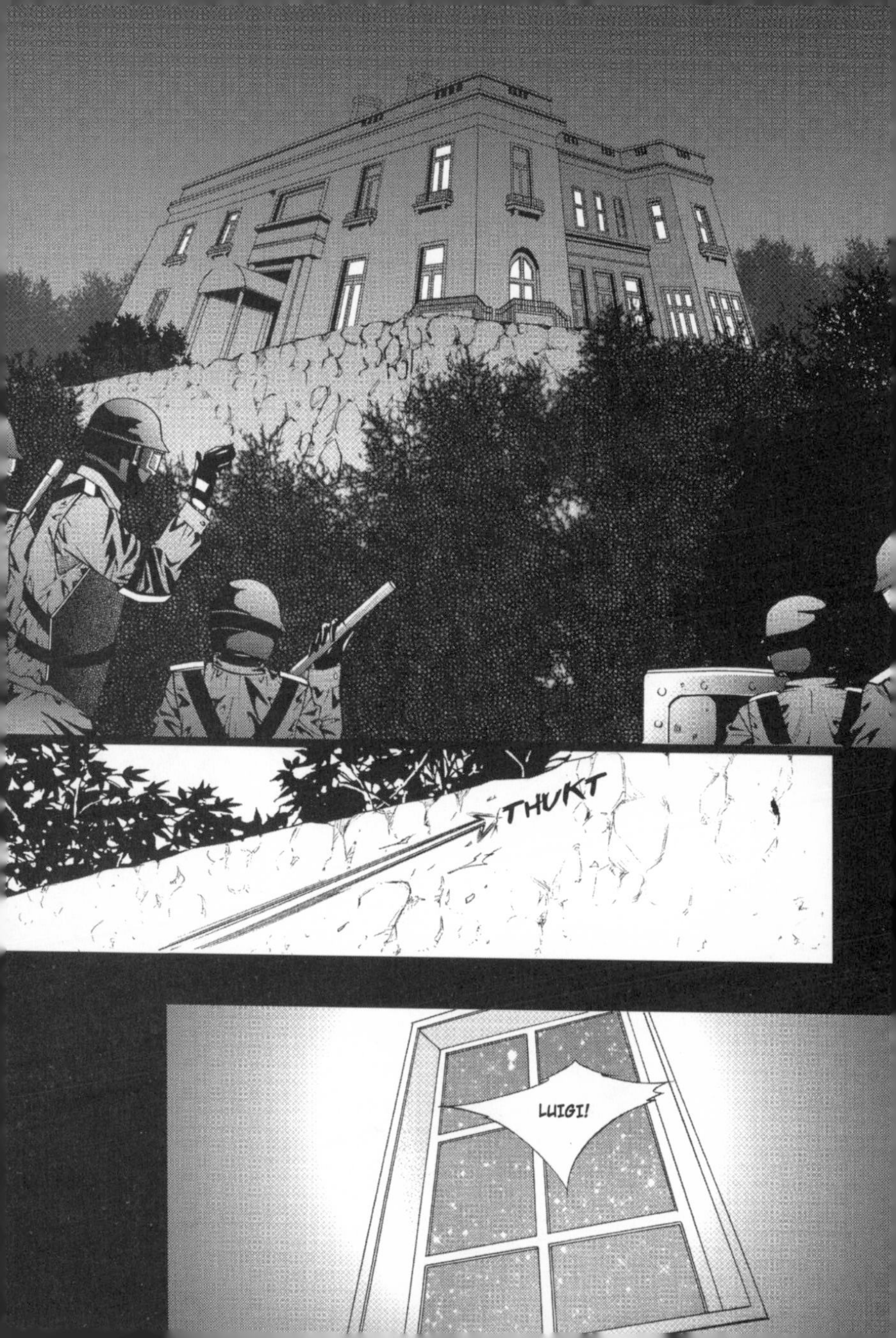
THUKT
LUIGI!

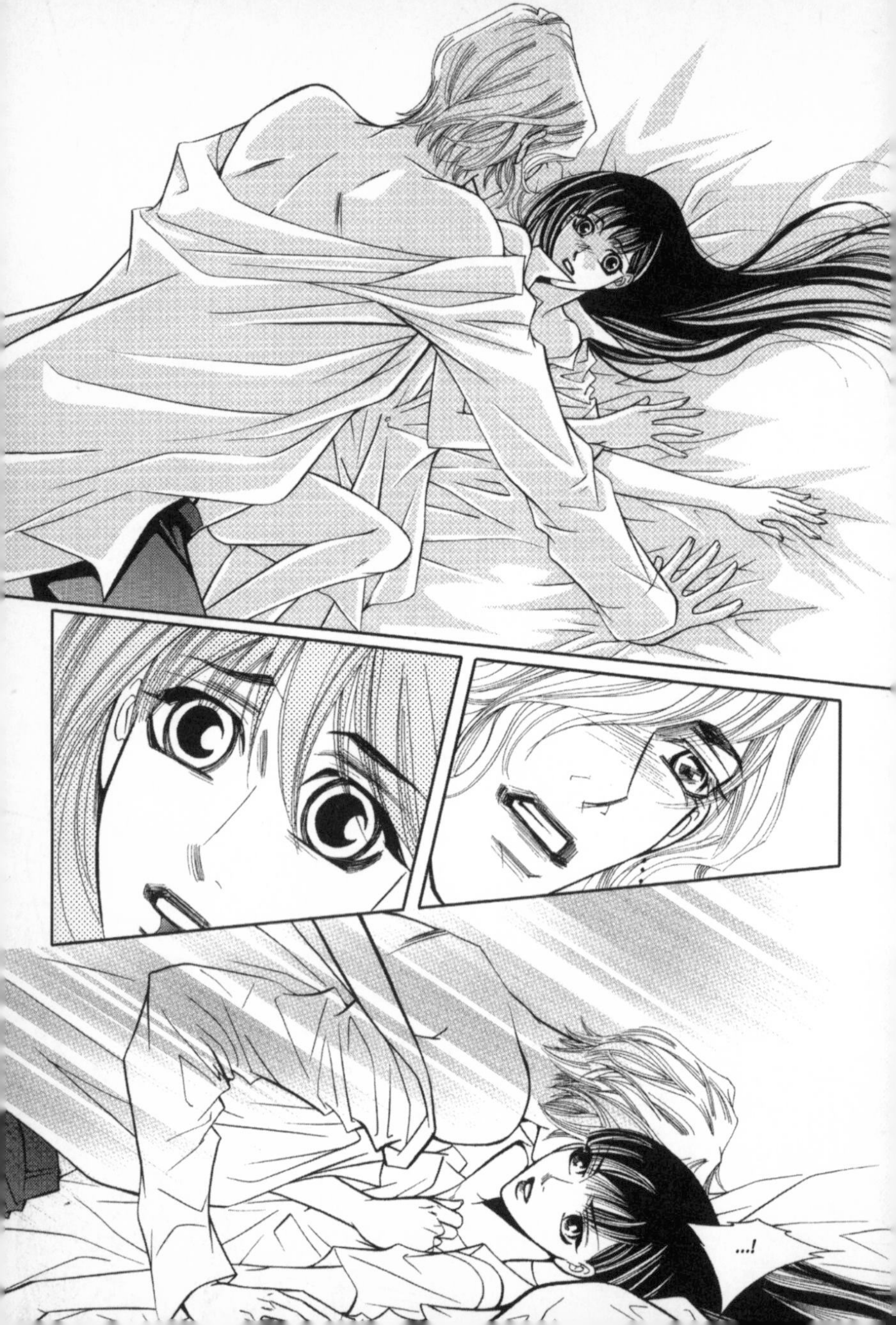
...!

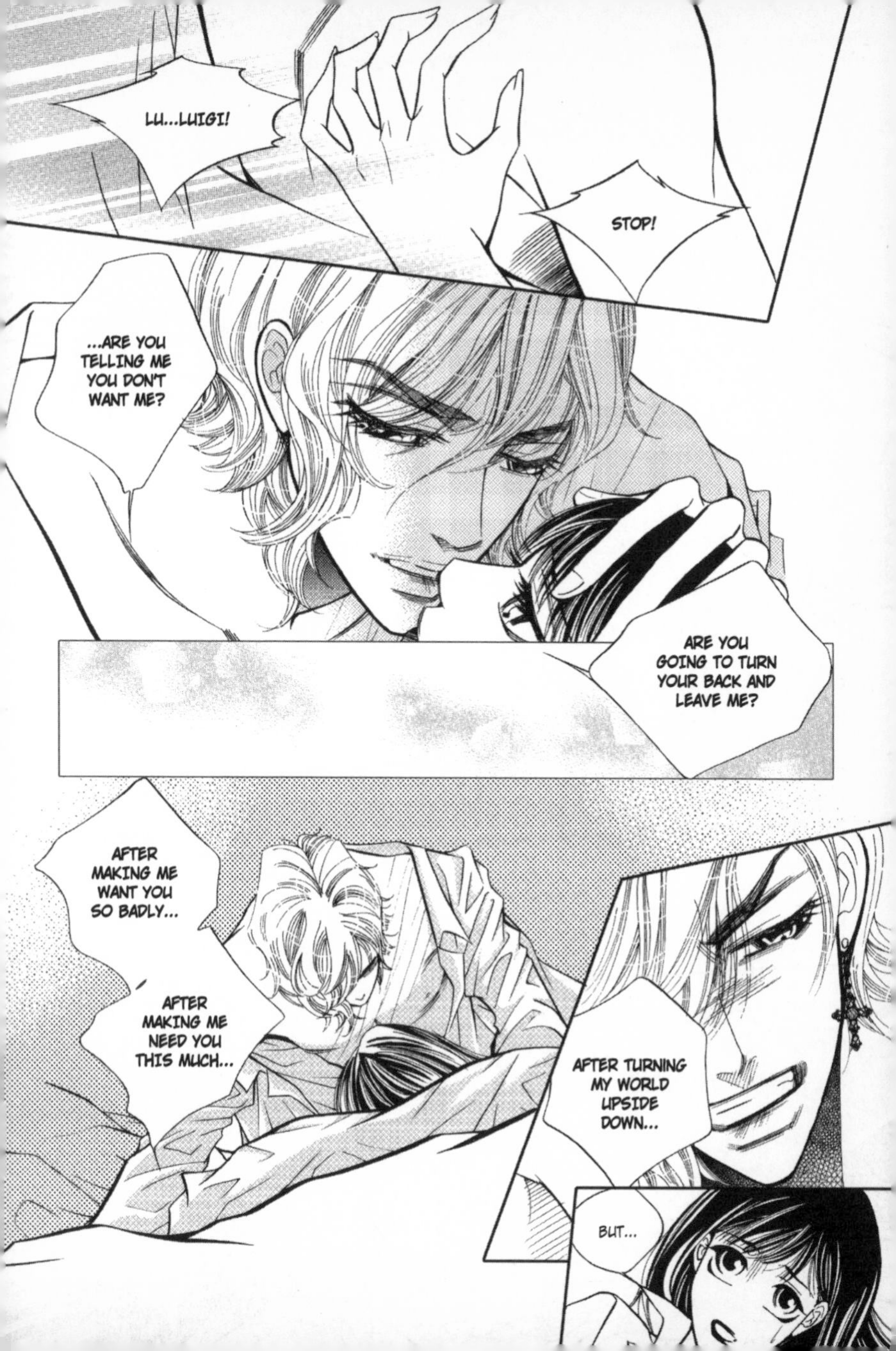
LU...LUIGI!
STOP!
...ARE YOU TELLING ME YOU DON'T WANT ME?
ARE YOU GOING TO TURN YOUR BACK AND LEAVE ME?
AFTER MAKING ME WANT YOU SO BADLY...
AFTER MAKING ME NEED YOU THIS MUCH...
AFTER TURNING MY WORLD UPSIDE DOWN...
BUT...

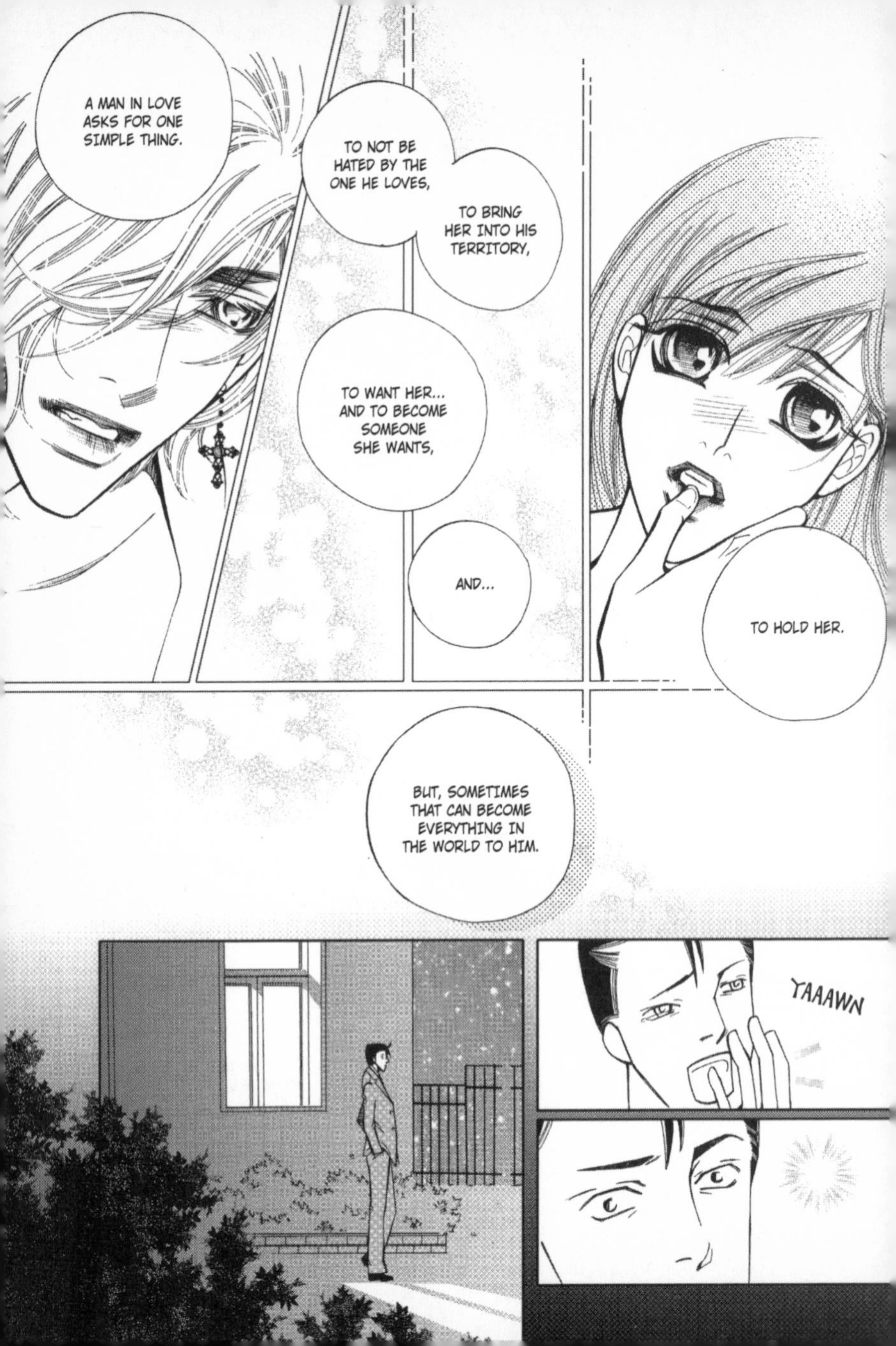
A MAN IN LOVE ASKS FOR ONE SIMPLE THING.
TO NOT BE HATED BY THE ONE HE LOVES,
TO BRING HER INTO HIS TERRITORY,
TO WANT HER... AND TO BECOME SOMEONE SHE WANTS,
AND...
TO HOLD HER.
BUT, SOMETIMES THAT CAN BECOME EVERYTHING IN THE WORLD TO HIM.
YAAAWN

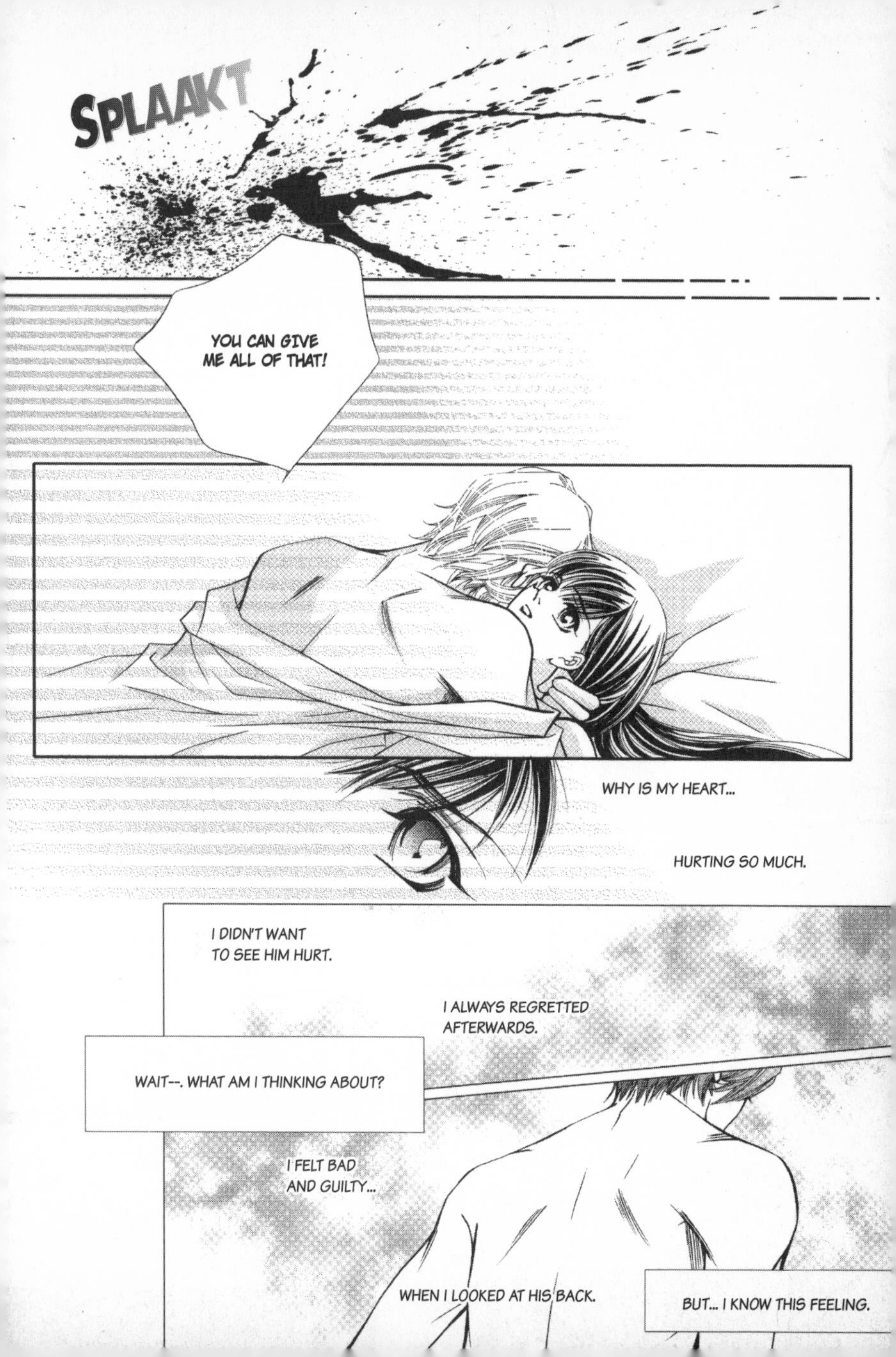
SPLAAKT
YOU CAN GIVE ME ALL OF THAT!
WHY IS MY HEART...
HURTING SO MUCH.
I DIDN'T WANT TO SEE HIM HURT.
I ALWAYS REGRETTED AFTERWARDS.
WAIT--. WHAT AM I THINKING ABOUT?
I FELT BAD AND GUILTY...
WHEN I LOOKED AT HIS BACK.
BUT... I KNOW THIS FEELING.

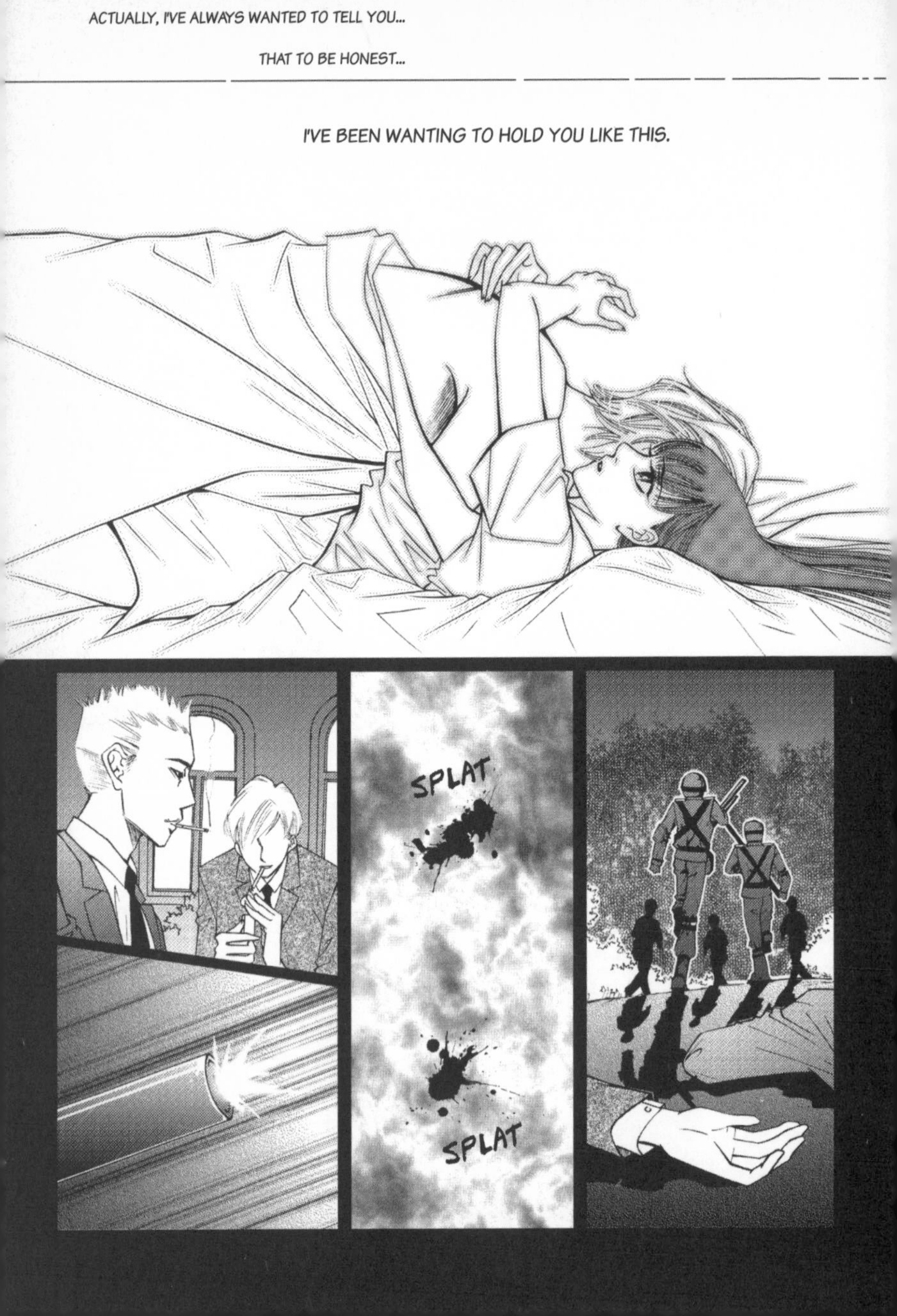
ACTUALLY, I'VE ALWAYS WANTED TO TELL YOU...
THAT TO BE HONEST...
I'VE BEEN WANTING TO HOLD YOU LIKE THIS.
SPLAT
SPLAT

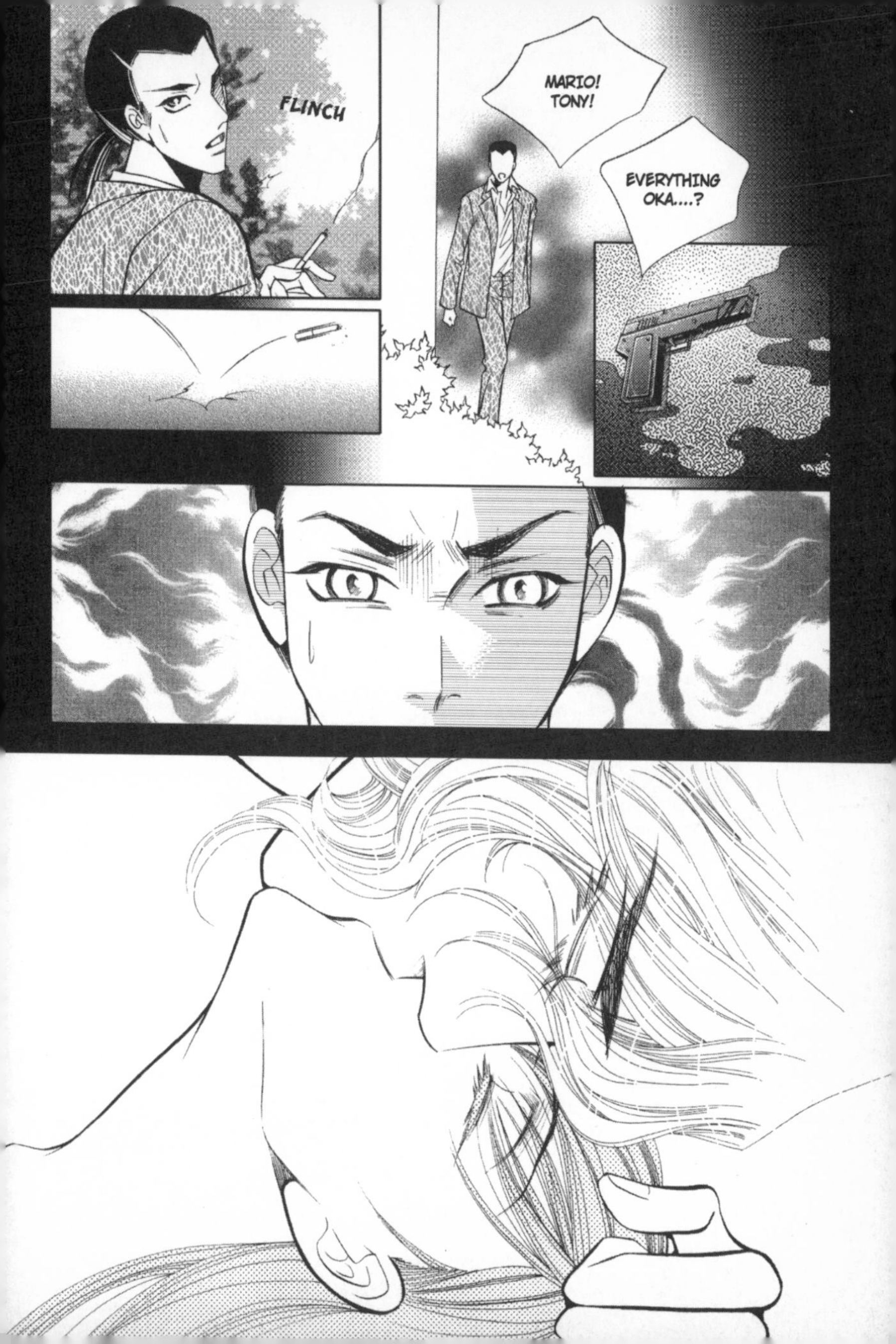
FLINCH
MARIO! TONY!
EVERYTHING OKA....?

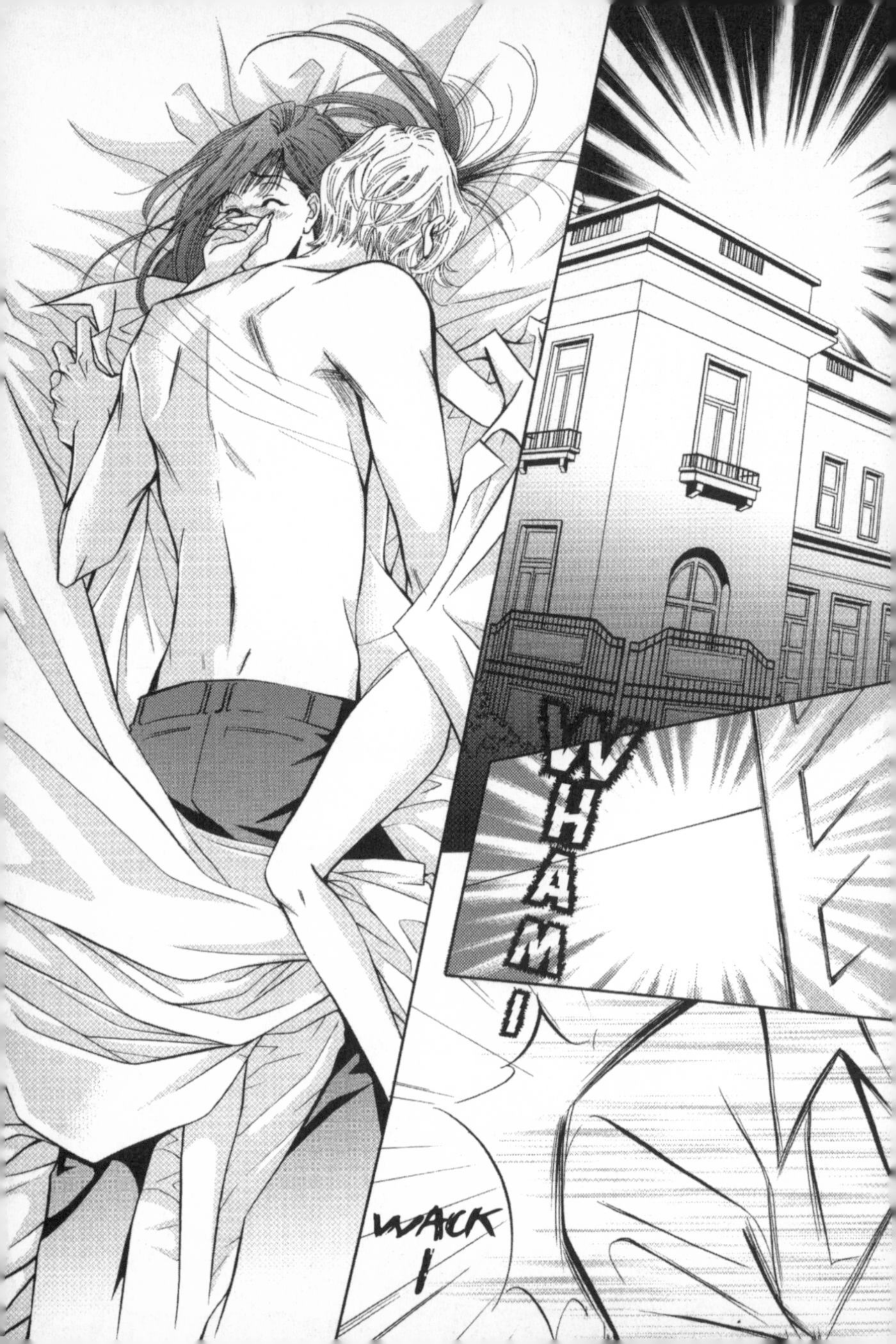
WHAM!
WACK!

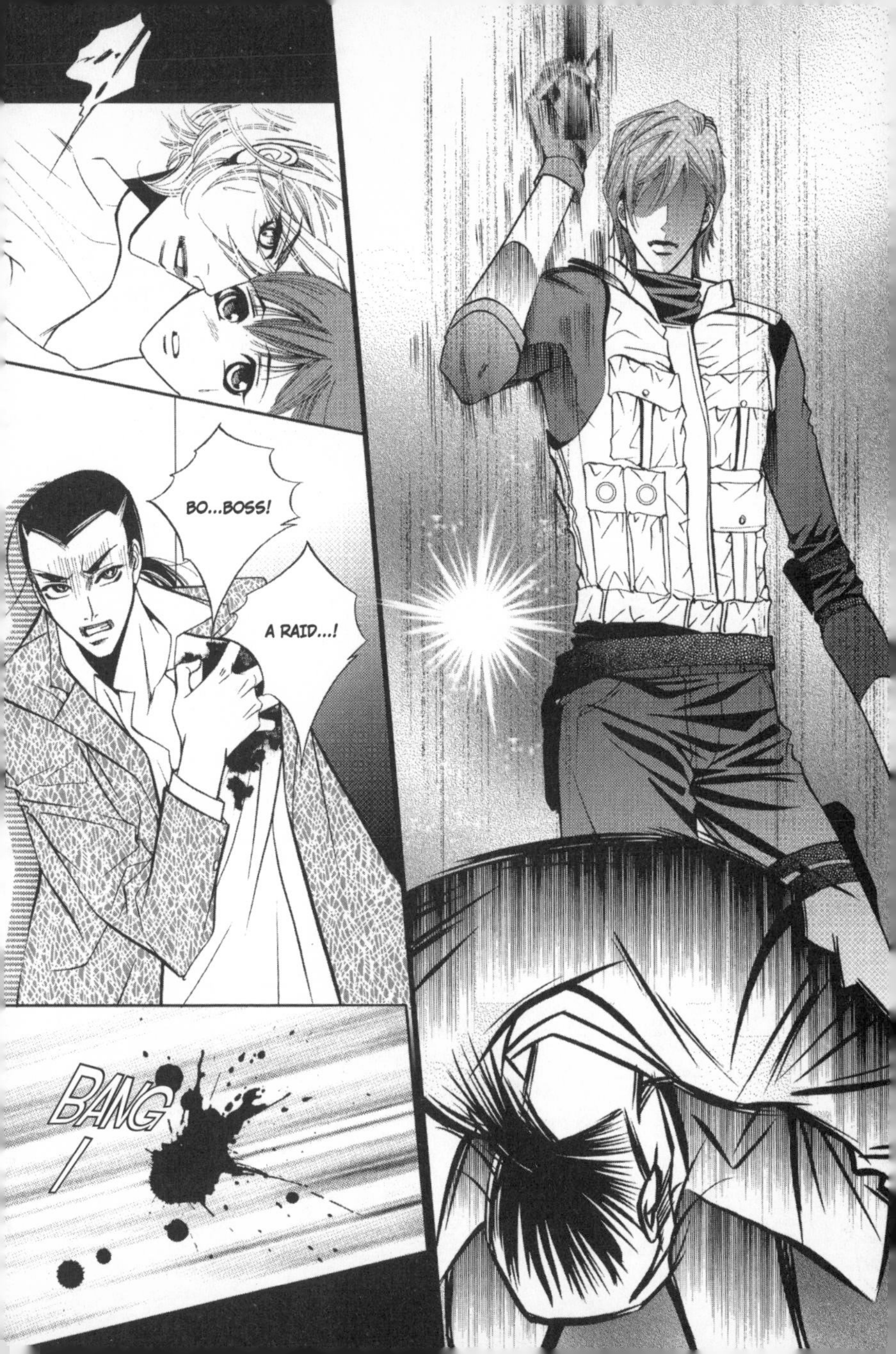
BO...BOSS!
A RAID...!
BANG!

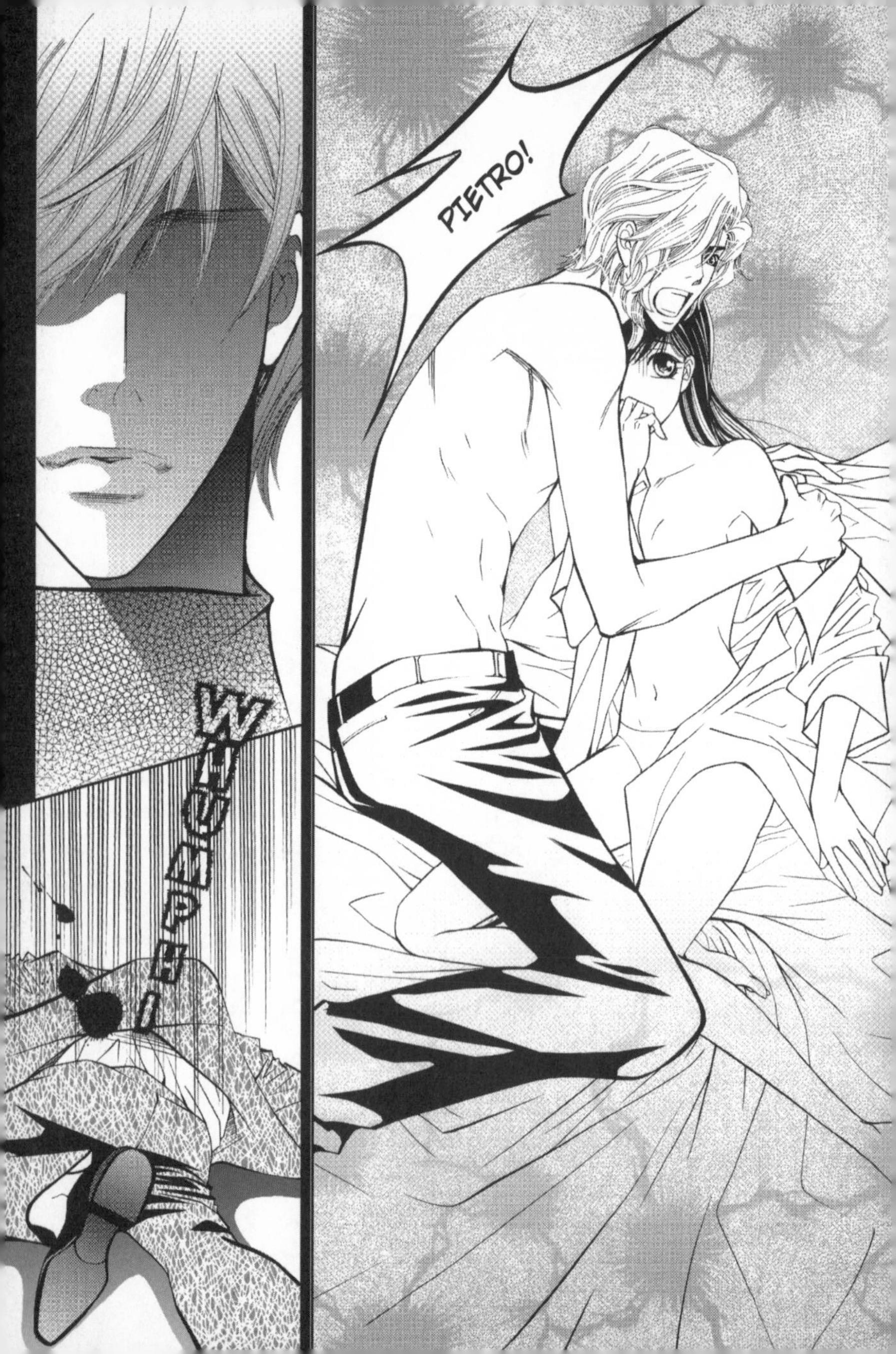
WHUMPF!
PIETRO!

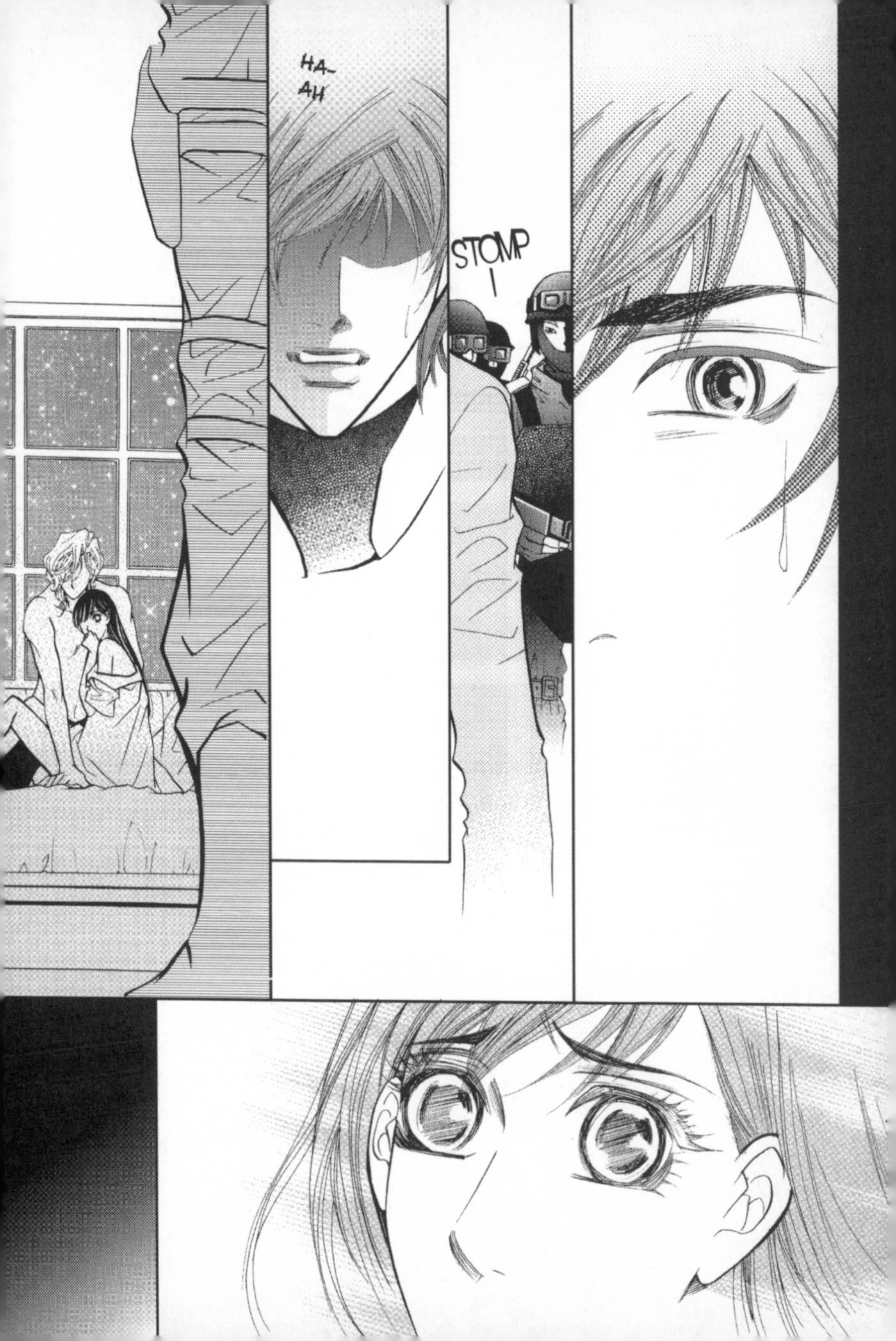
HA-AH
STOMP

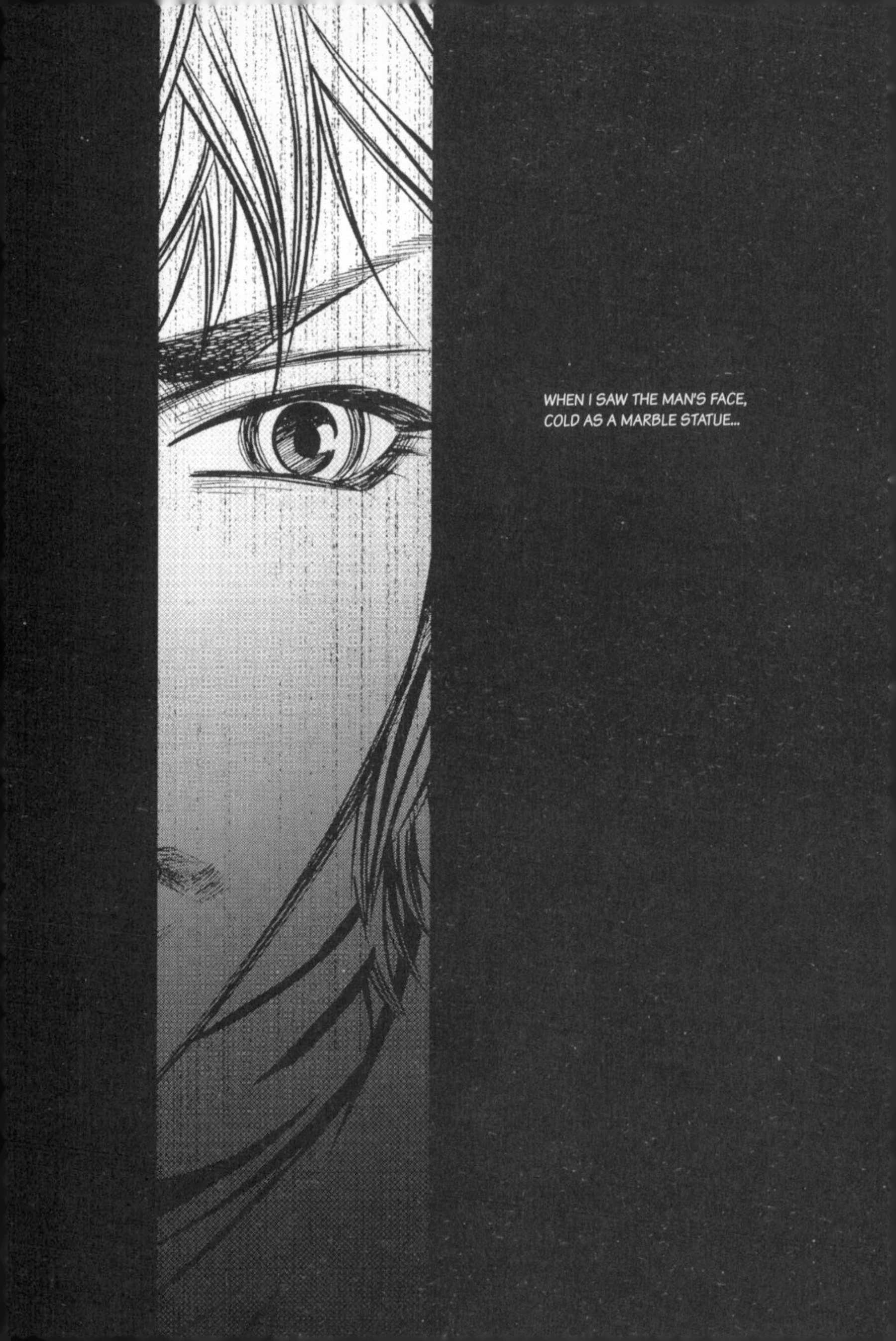
WHEN I SAW THE MAN'S FACE, COLD AS A MARBLE STATUE...

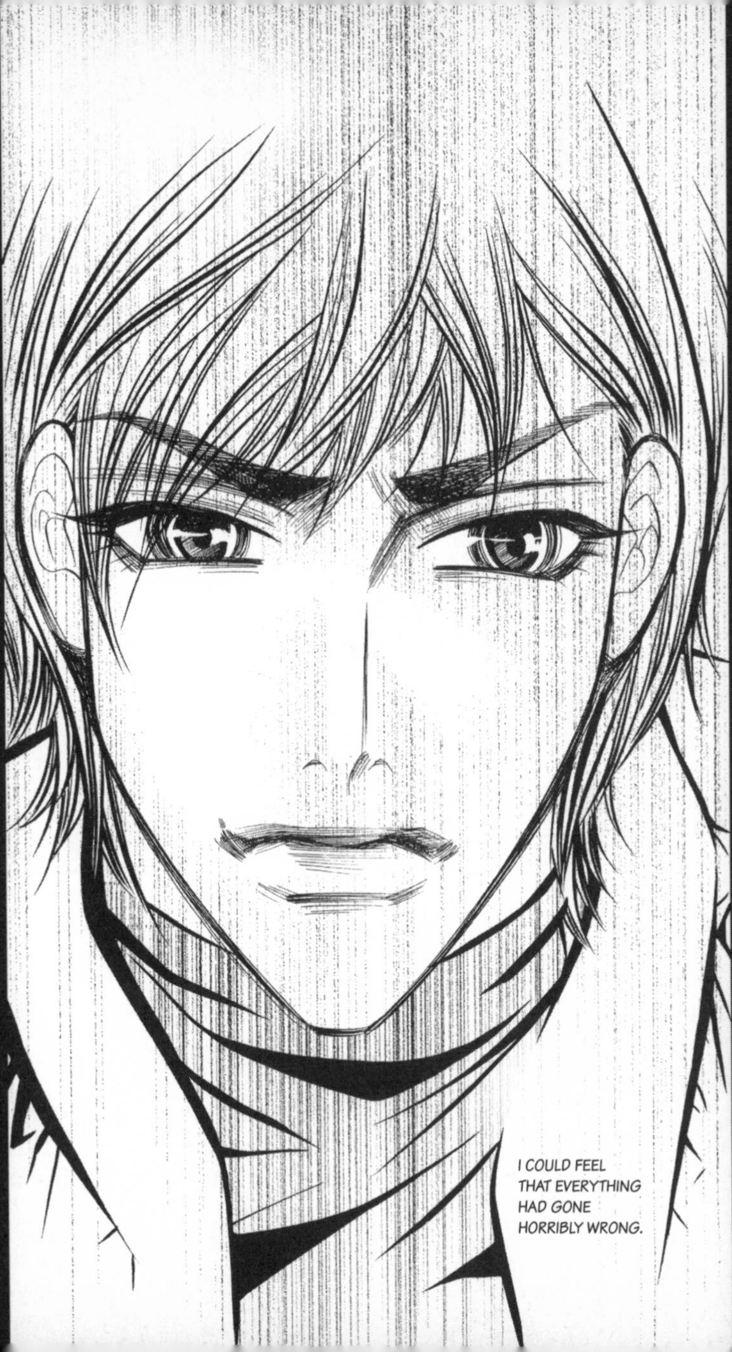
I COULD FEEL THAT EVERYTHING HAD GONE HORRIBLY WRONG.

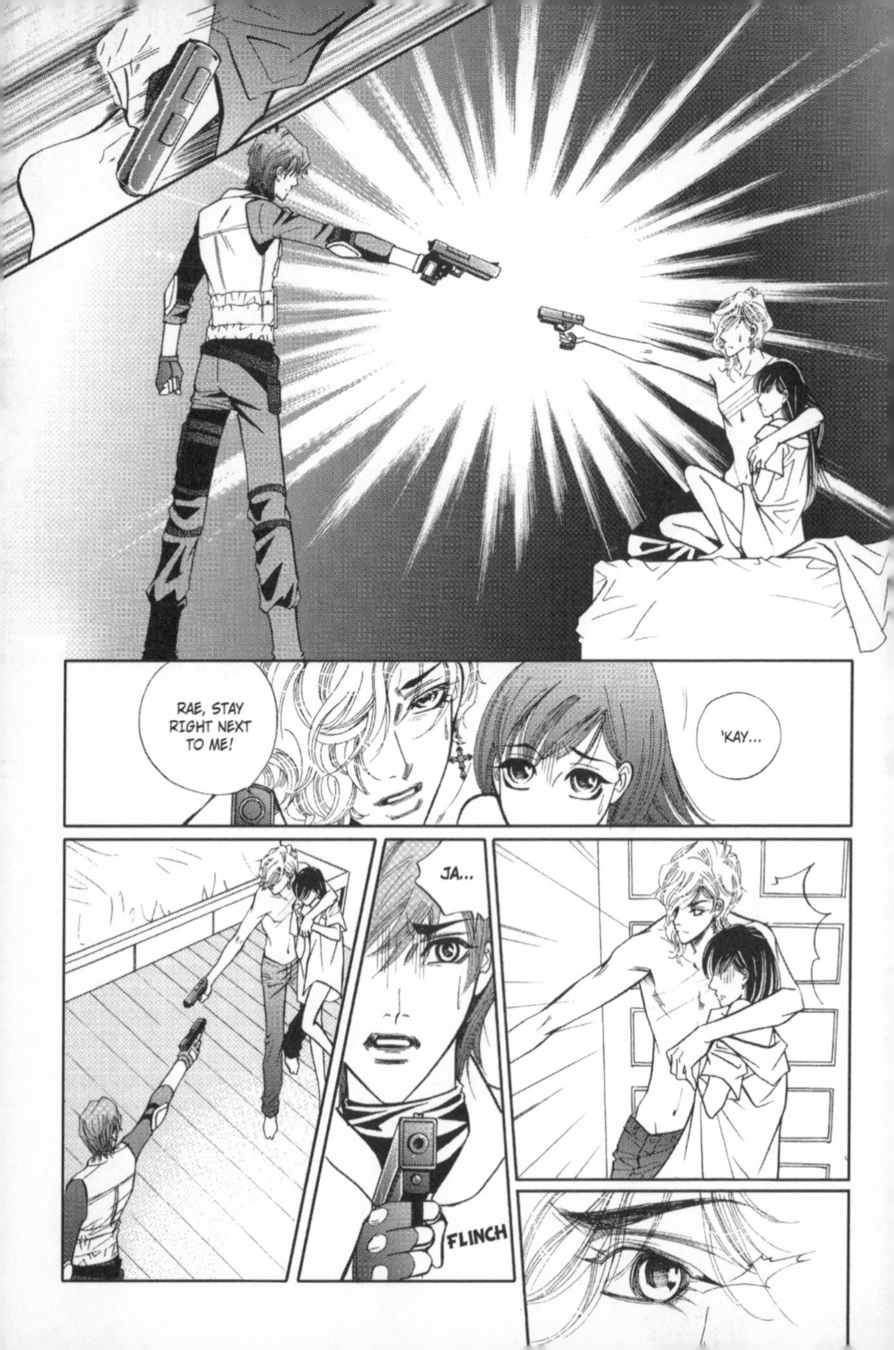
RAE, STAY RIGHT NEXT TO ME!
'KAY...
JA...
FLINCH

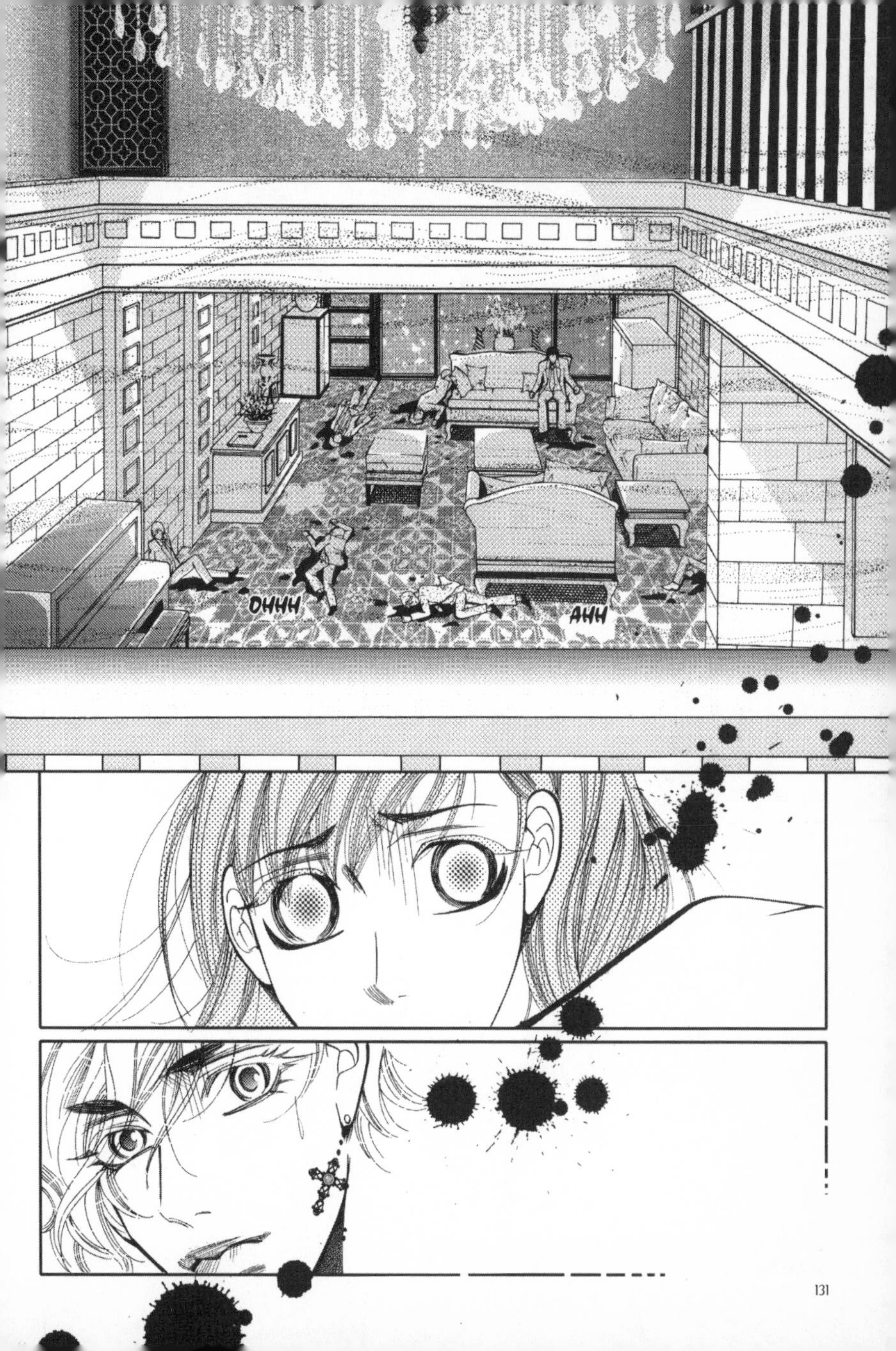
OHHH
AHH

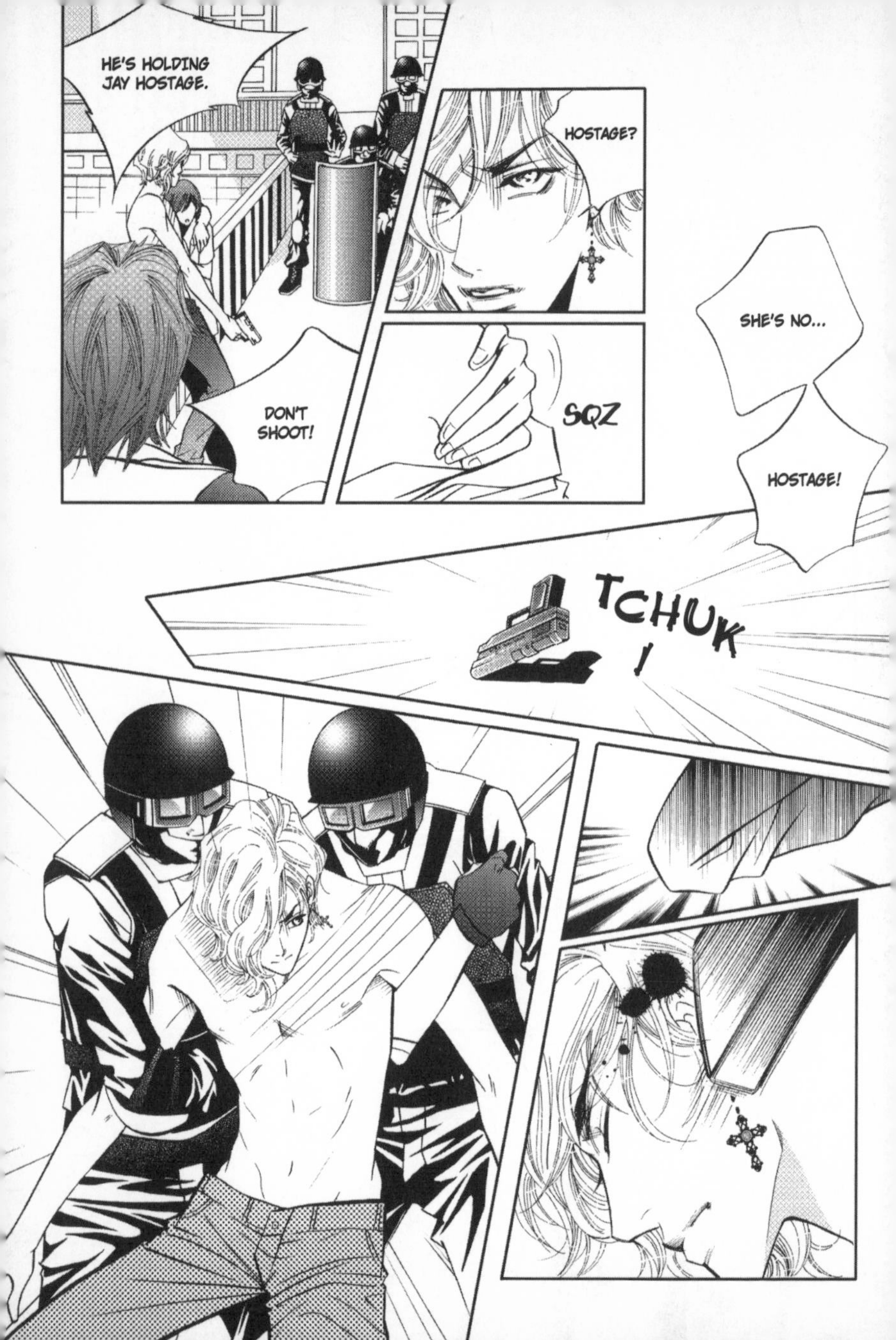
HE'S HOLDING JAY HOSTAGE.
DON'T SHOOT!
HOSTAGE?
SQZ
SHE'S NO...
HOSTAGE!
TCHUK!

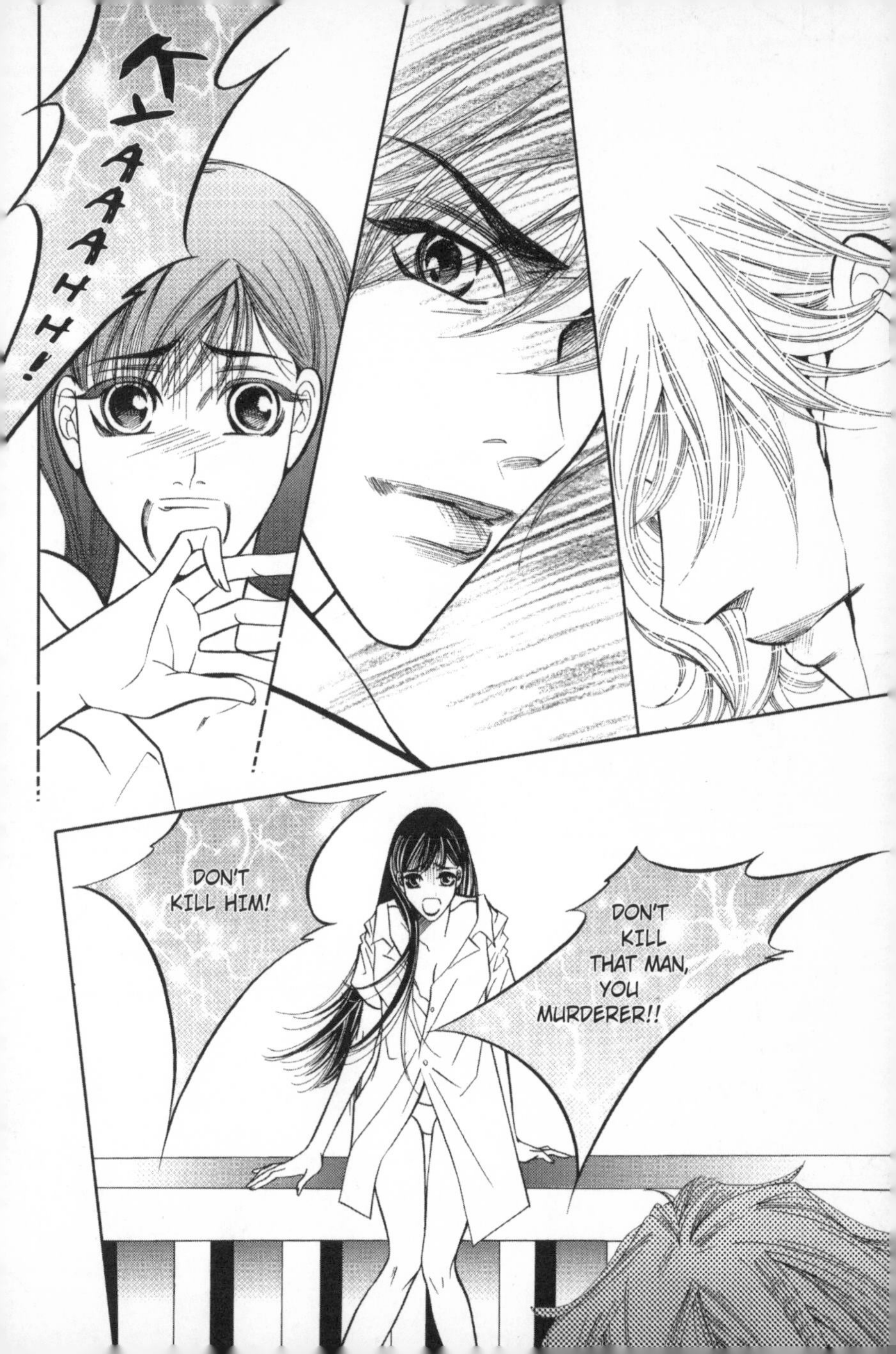
KYAAAAHH!!
DON'T KILL HIM!
DON'T KILL THAT MAN, YOU MURDERER!!

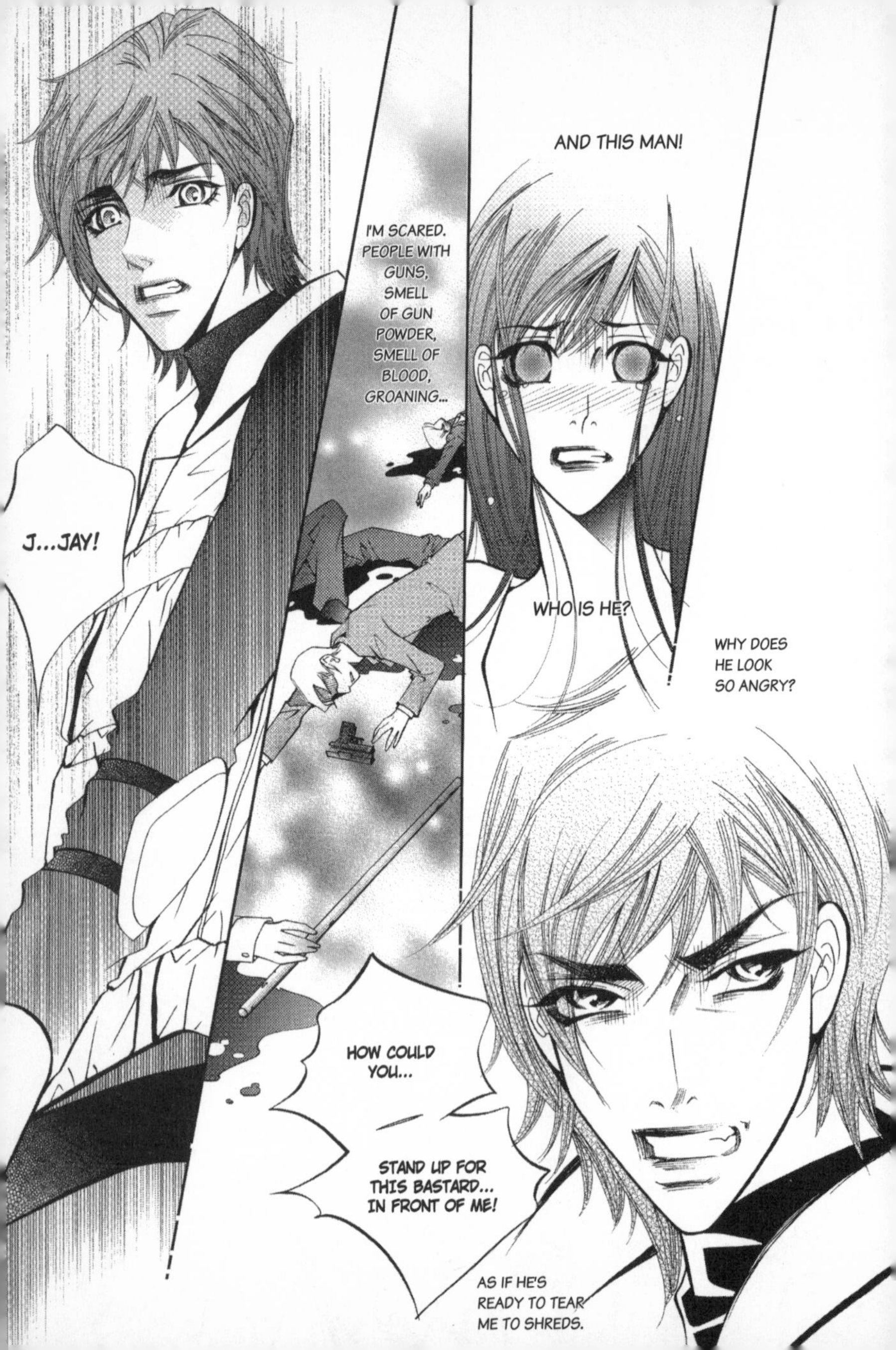
AND THIS MAN!
I'M SCARED. PEOPLE WITH GUNS, SMELL OF GUN POWDER, SMELL OF BLOOD, GROANING...
J...JAY!
WHO IS HE?
WHY DOES HE LOOK SO ANGRY?
HOW COULD YOU...
STAND UP FOR THIS BASTARD... IN FRONT OF ME!
AS IF HE'S READY TO TEAR ME TO SHREDS.

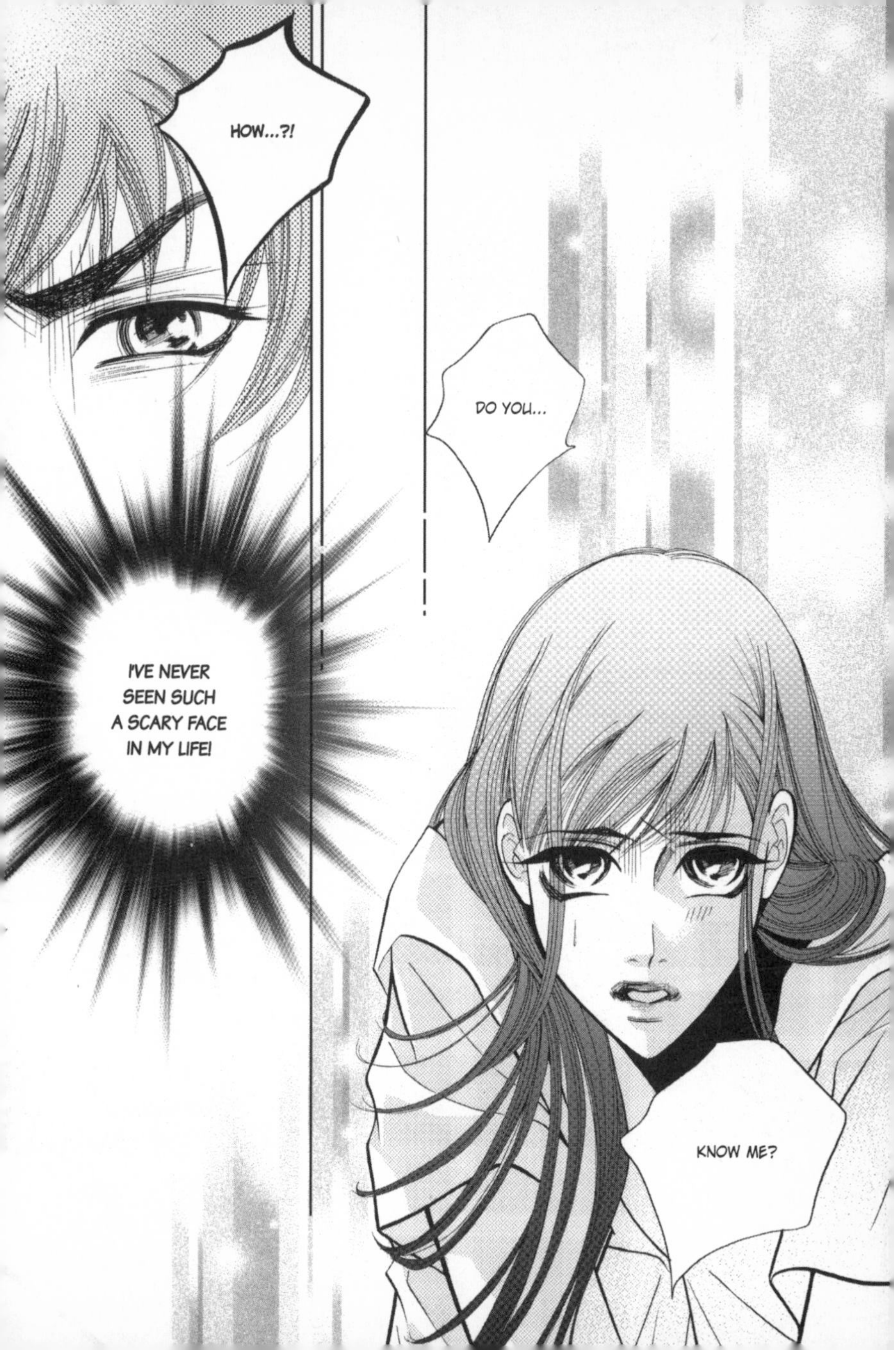
HOW...?!
I'VE NEVER SEEN SUCH A SCARY FACE IN MY LIFE!
DO YOU...
KNOW ME?

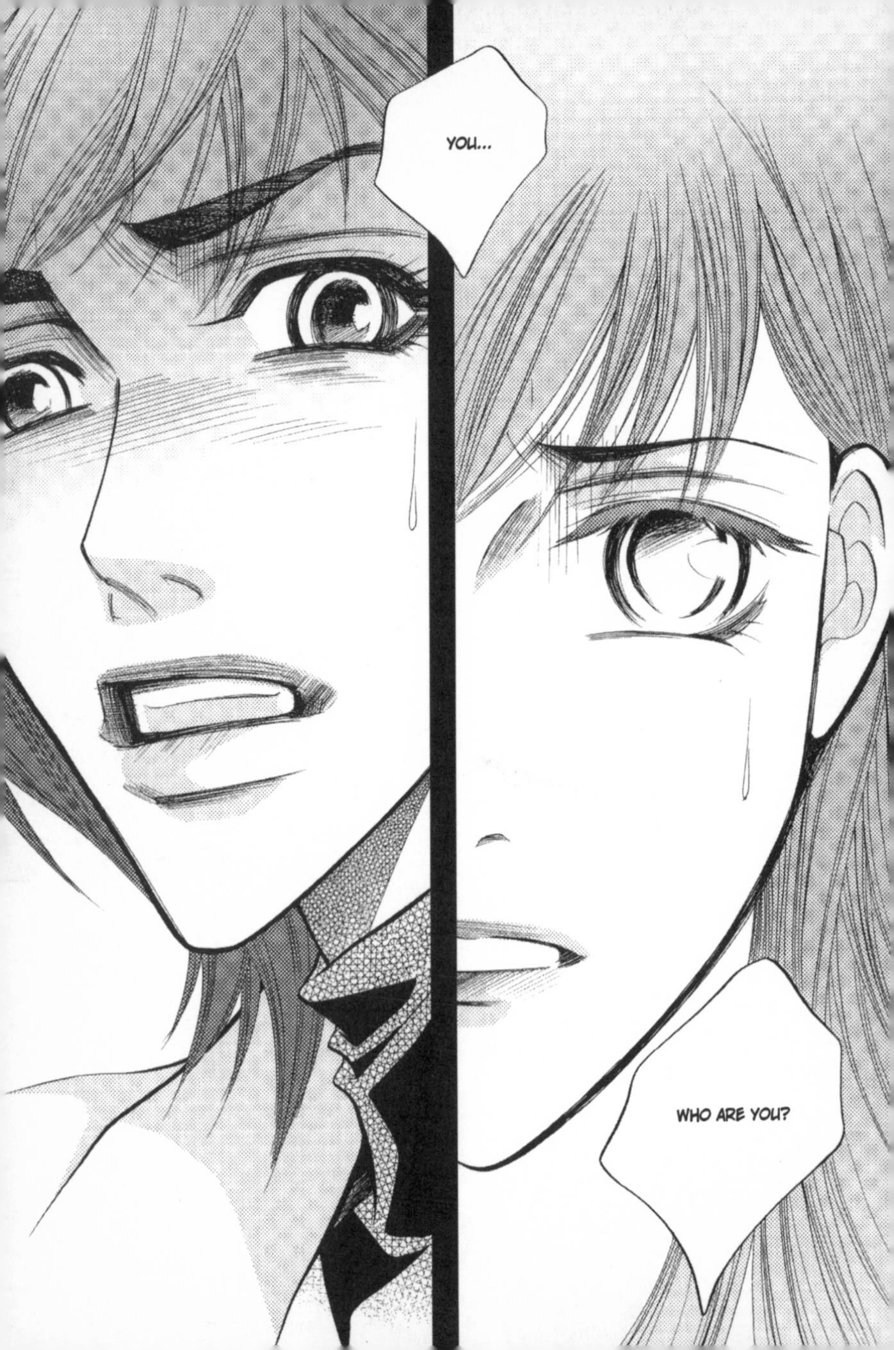
YOU...
WHO ARE YOU?

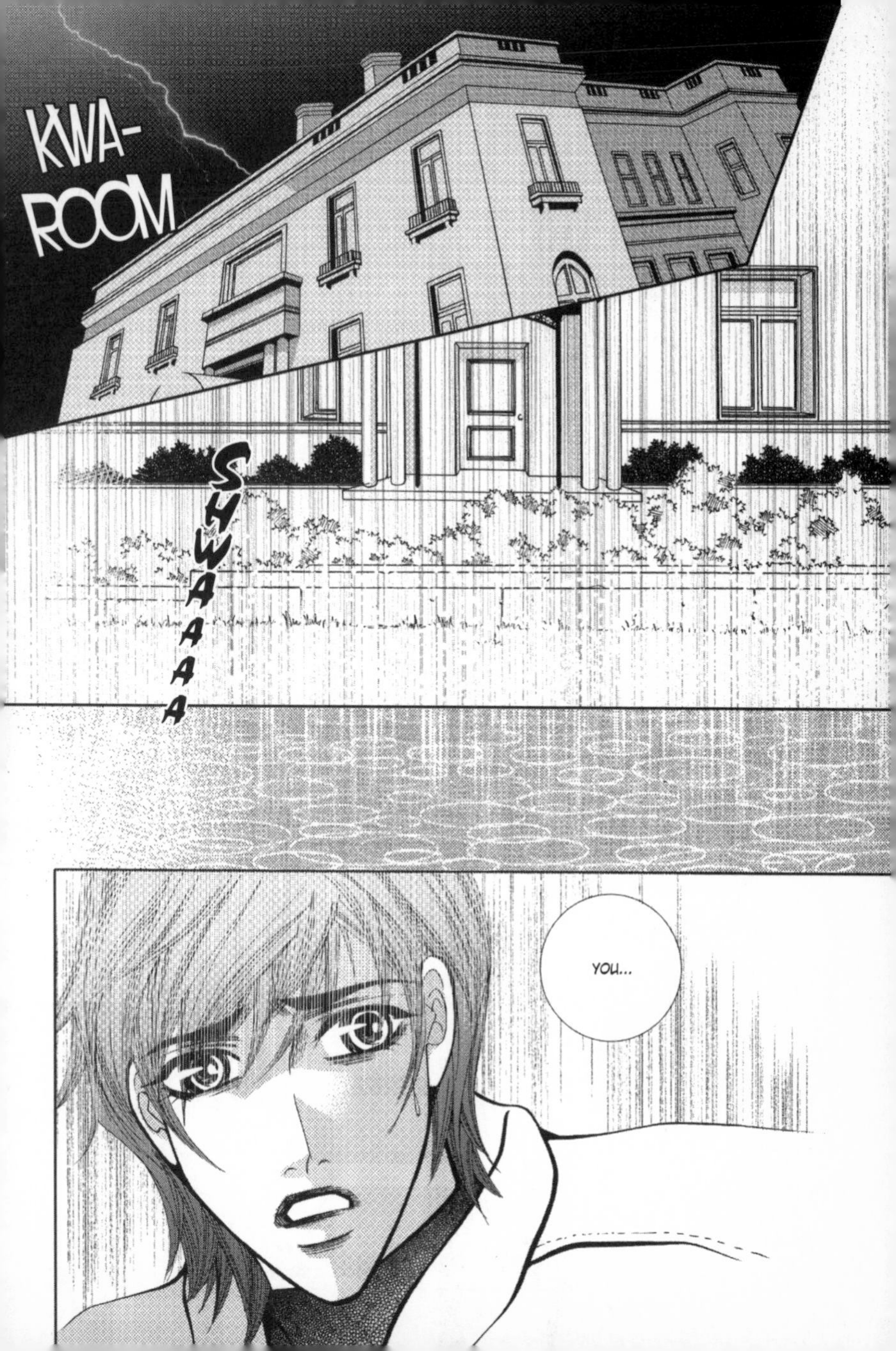
KWA-
ROOM
SHWAAAAAA
YOU...

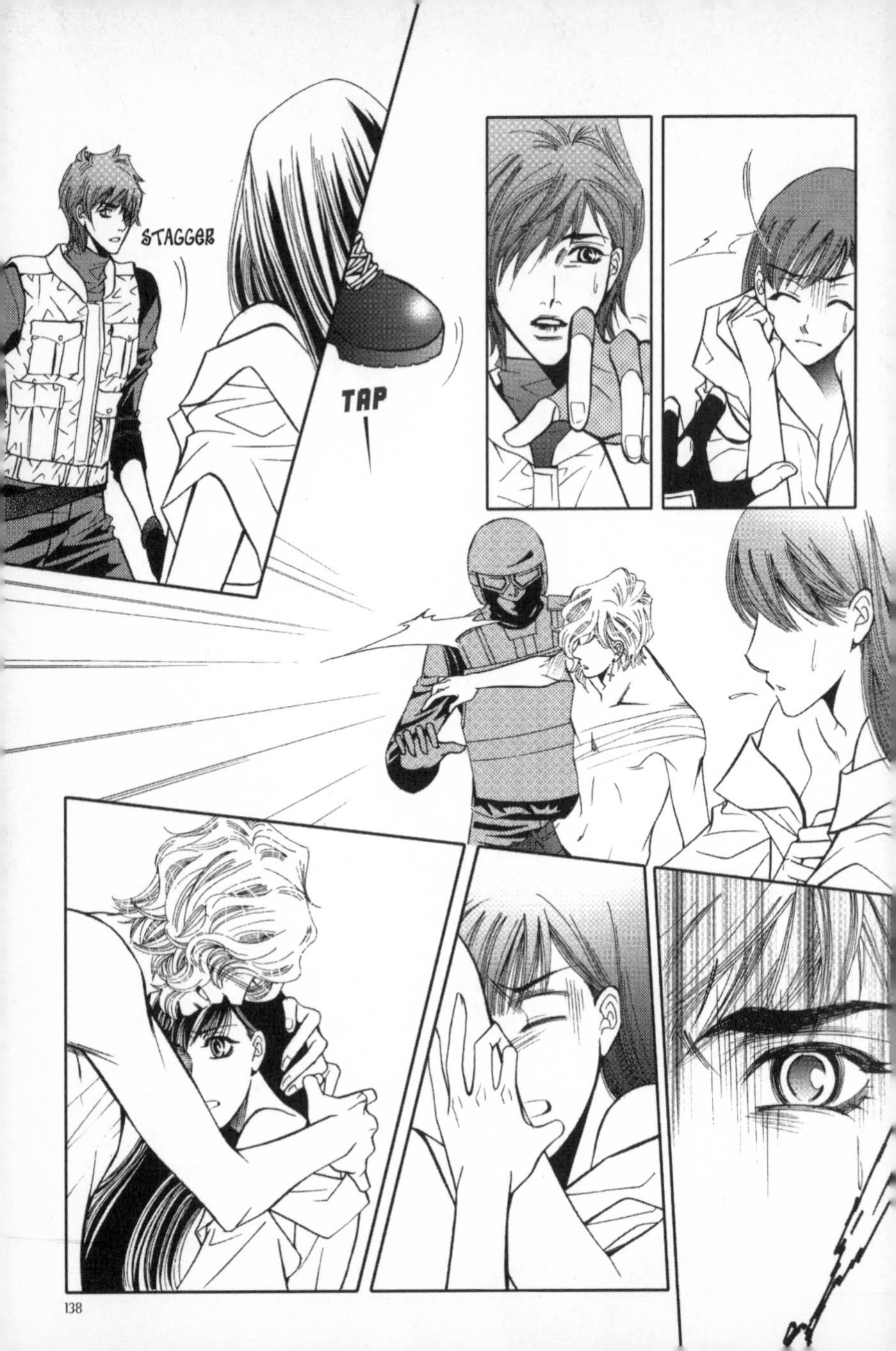
STAGGER
TAP

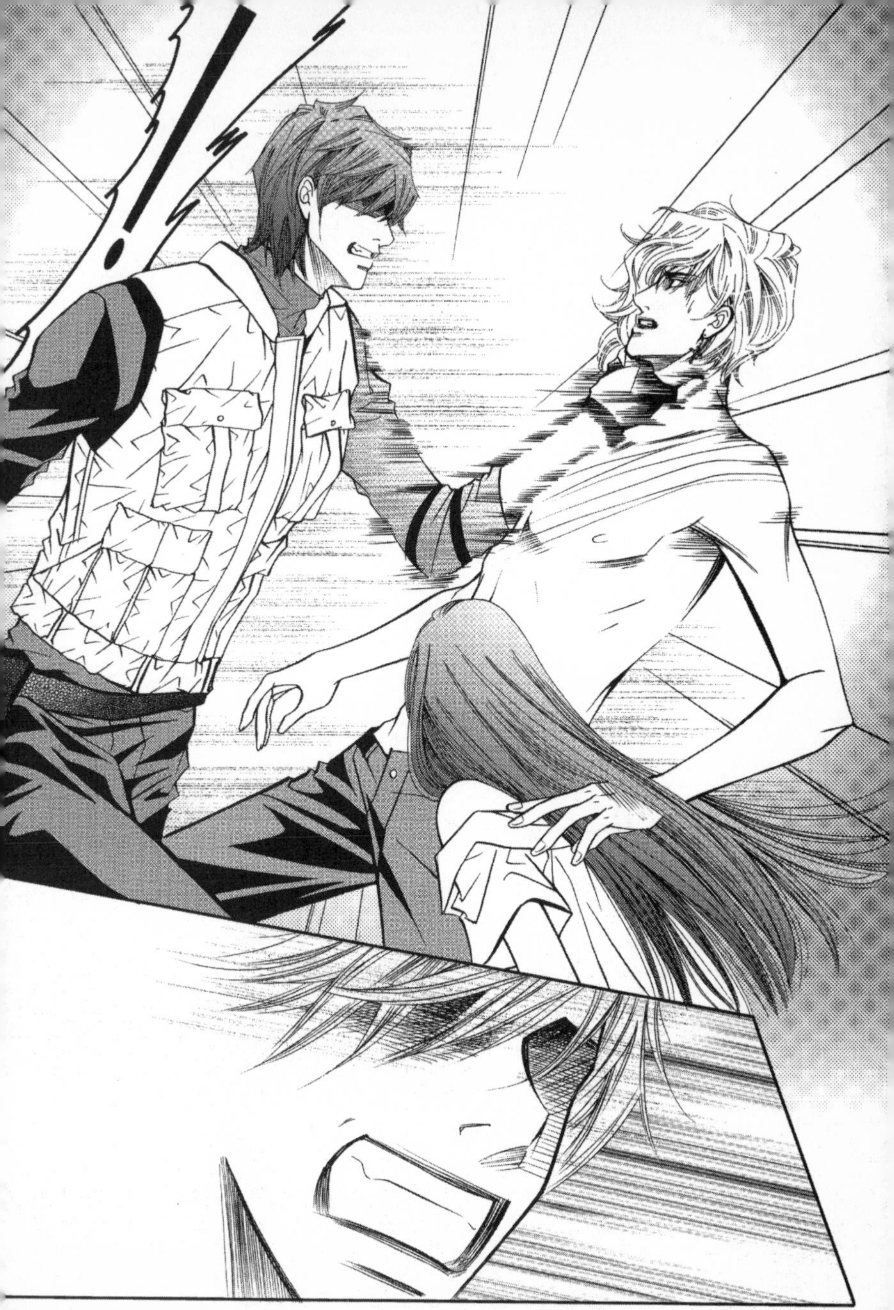

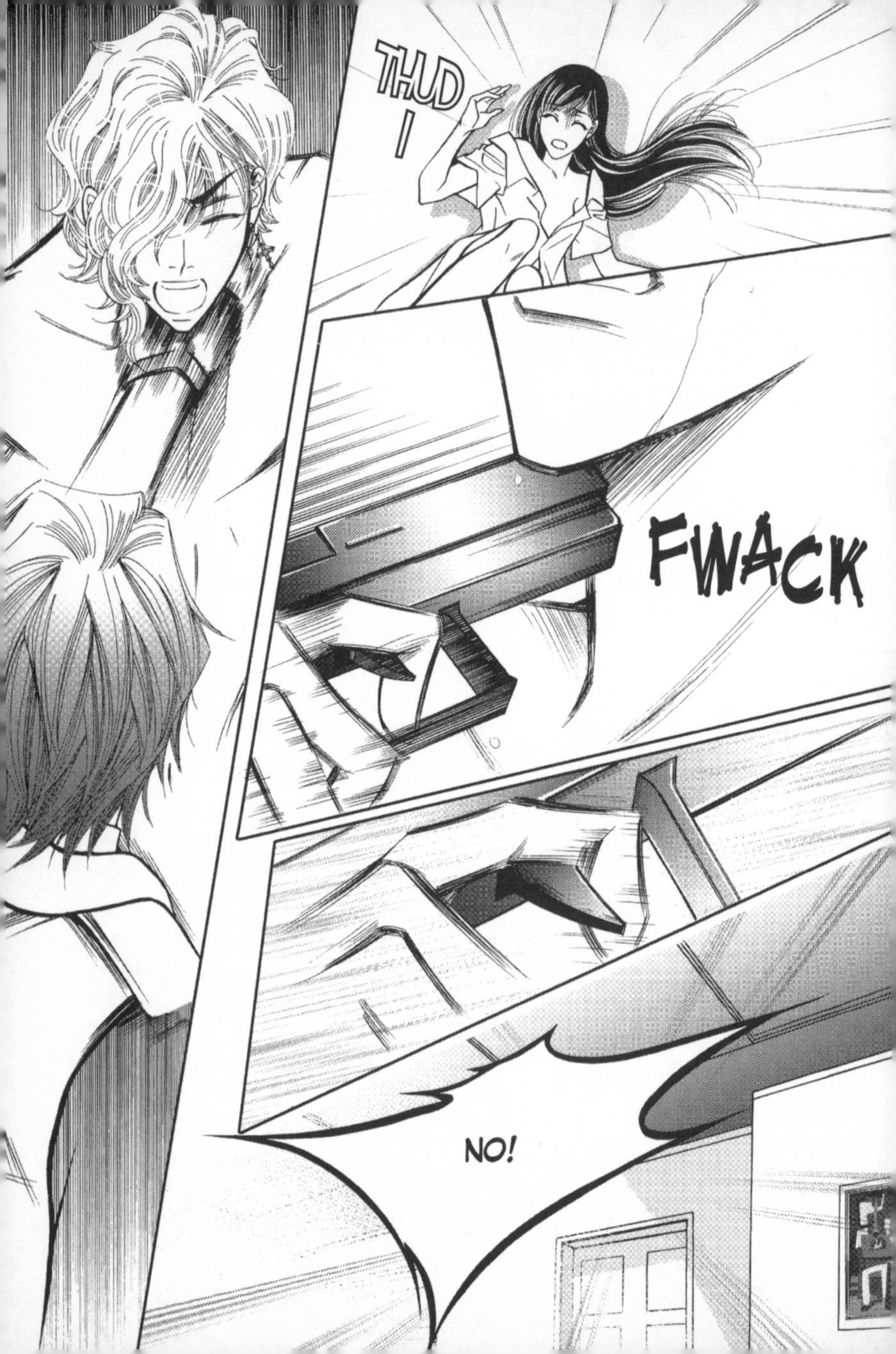
THUD
FWACK
NO!

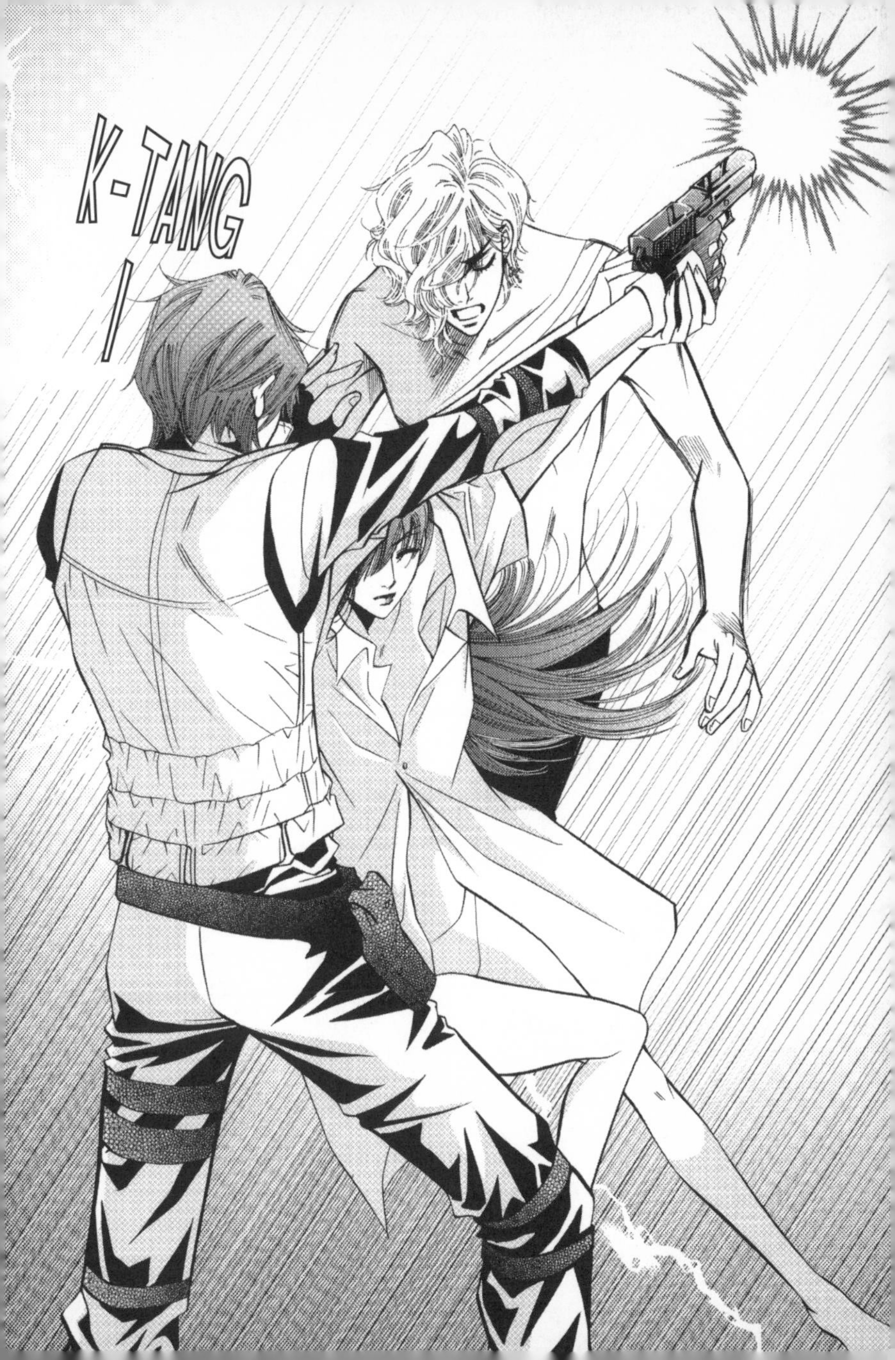
K-TANG!

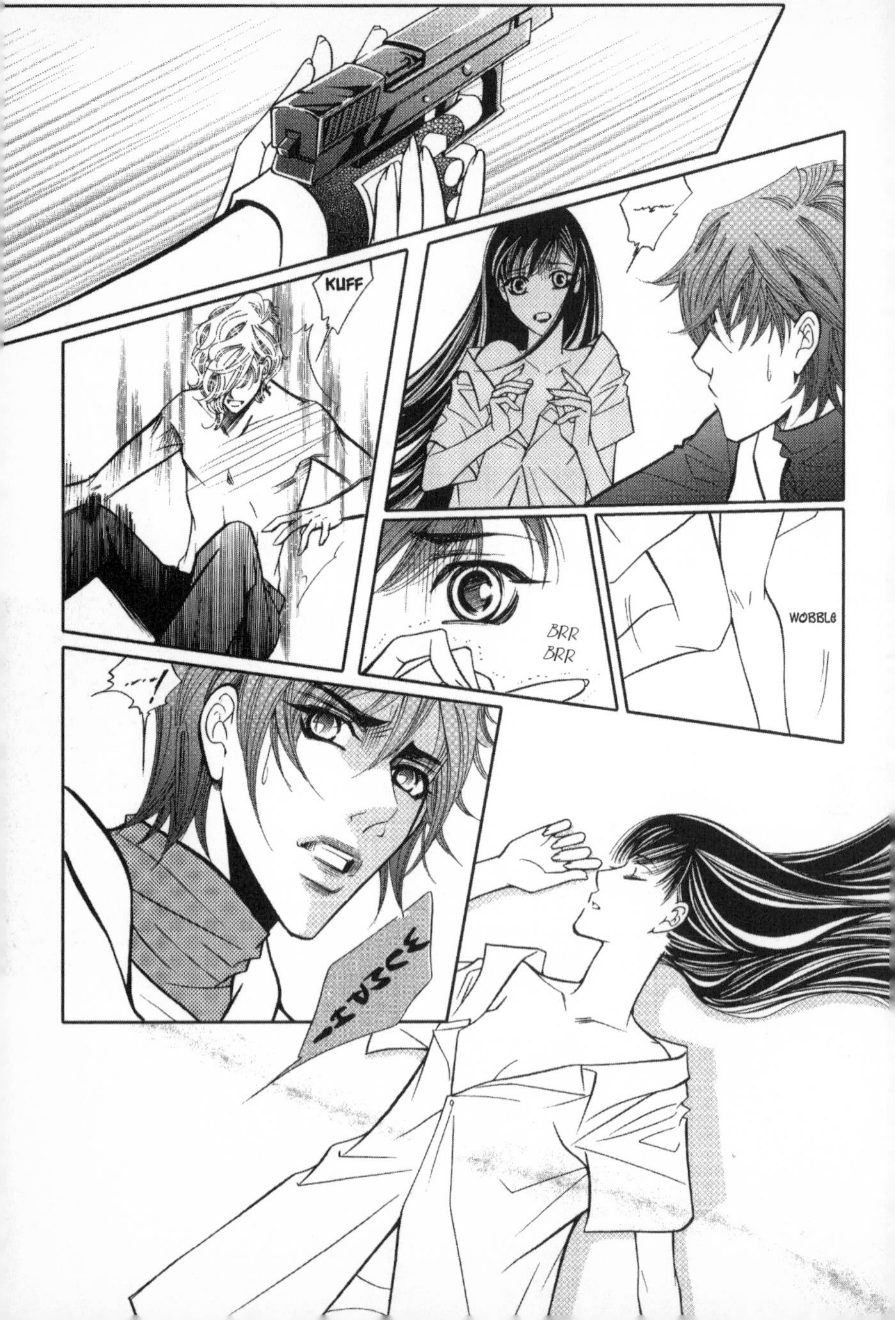
KUFF
...
BRR
BRR
WOBBLE
...!

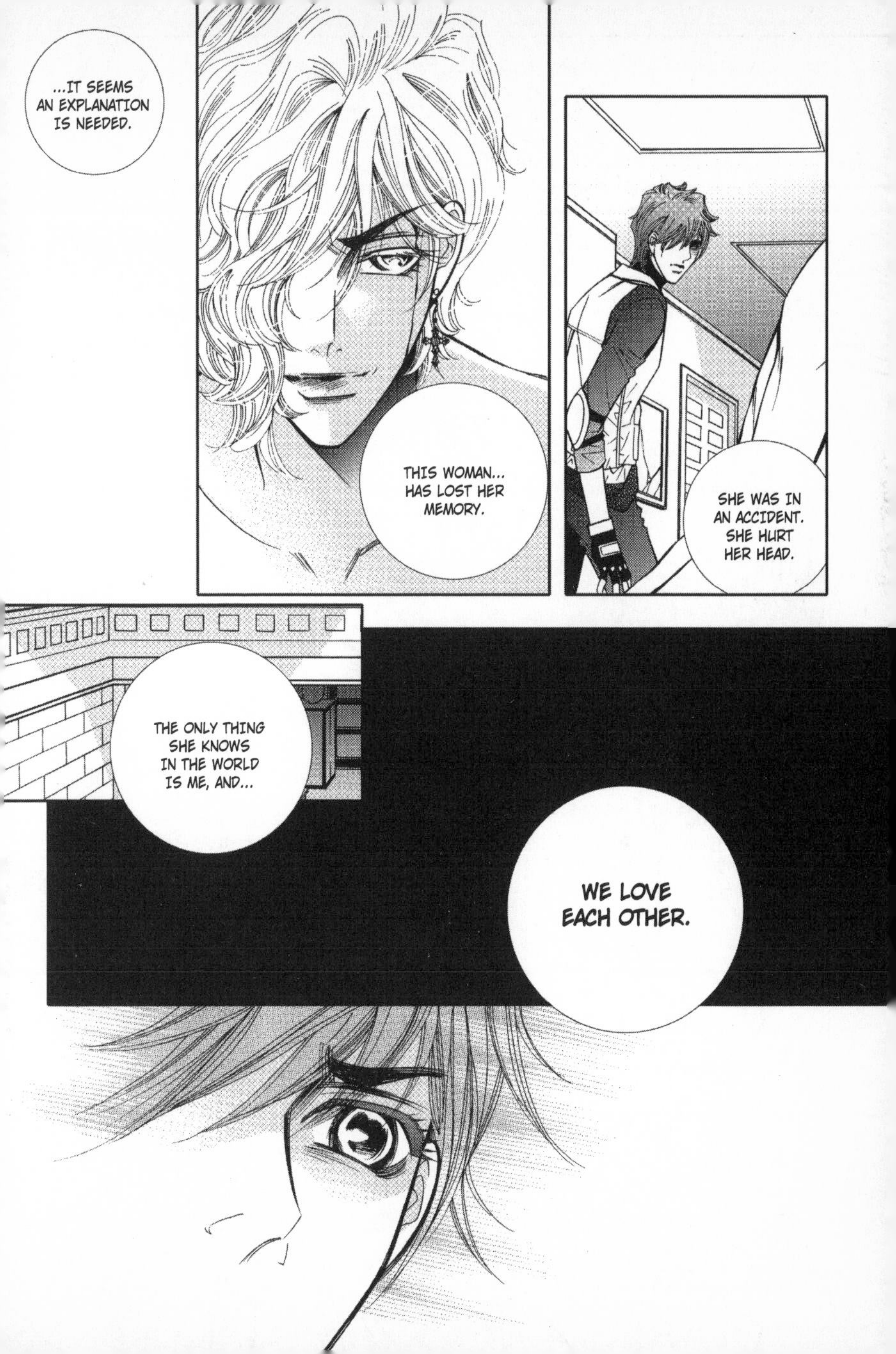
...IT SEEMS AN EXPLANATION IS NEEDED.
THIS WOMAN... HAS LOST HER MEMORY.
SHE WAS IN AN ACCIDENT. SHE HURT HER HEAD.
THE ONLY THING SHE KNOWS IN THE WORLD IS ME, AND...
WE LOVE EACH OTHER.

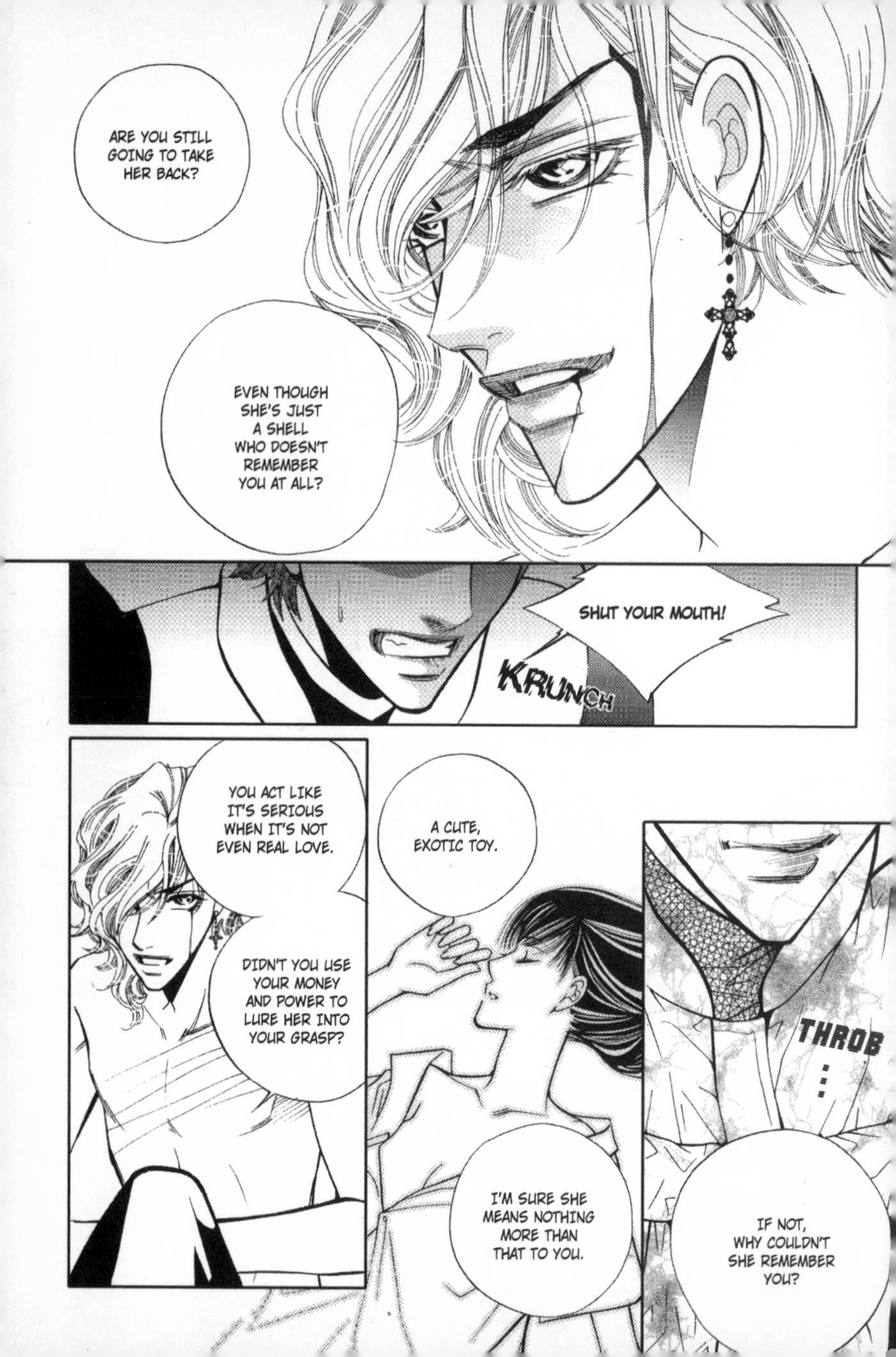
ARE YOU STILL GOING TO TAKE HER BACK?
EVEN THOUGH SHE'S JUST A SHELL WHO DOESN'T REMEMBER YOU AT ALL?
SHUT YOUR MOUTH!
KRUNCH
YOU ACT LIKE IT'S SERIOUS WHEN IT'S NOT EVEN REAL LOVE.
DIDN'T YOU USE YOUR MONEY AND POWER TO LURE HER INTO YOUR GRASP?
A CUTE, EXOTIC TOY.
I'M SURE SHE MEANS NOTHING MORE THAN THAT TO YOU.
THROB
IF NOT, WHY COULDN'T SHE REMEMBER YOU?

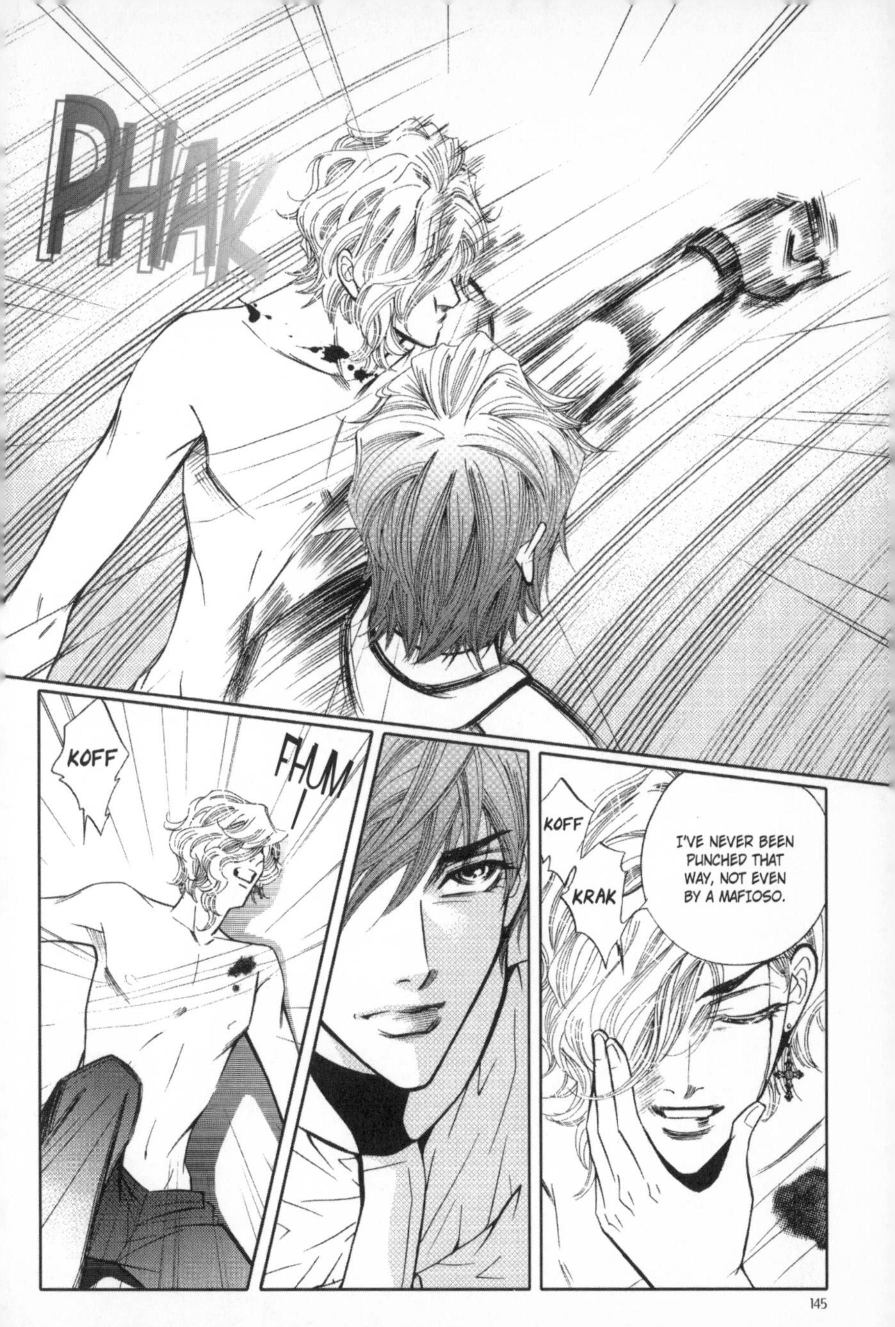
PHAK
KOFF
FHUM
KOFF
KRAK
I'VE NEVER BEEN PUNCHED THAT WAY, NOT EVEN BY A MAFIOSO.

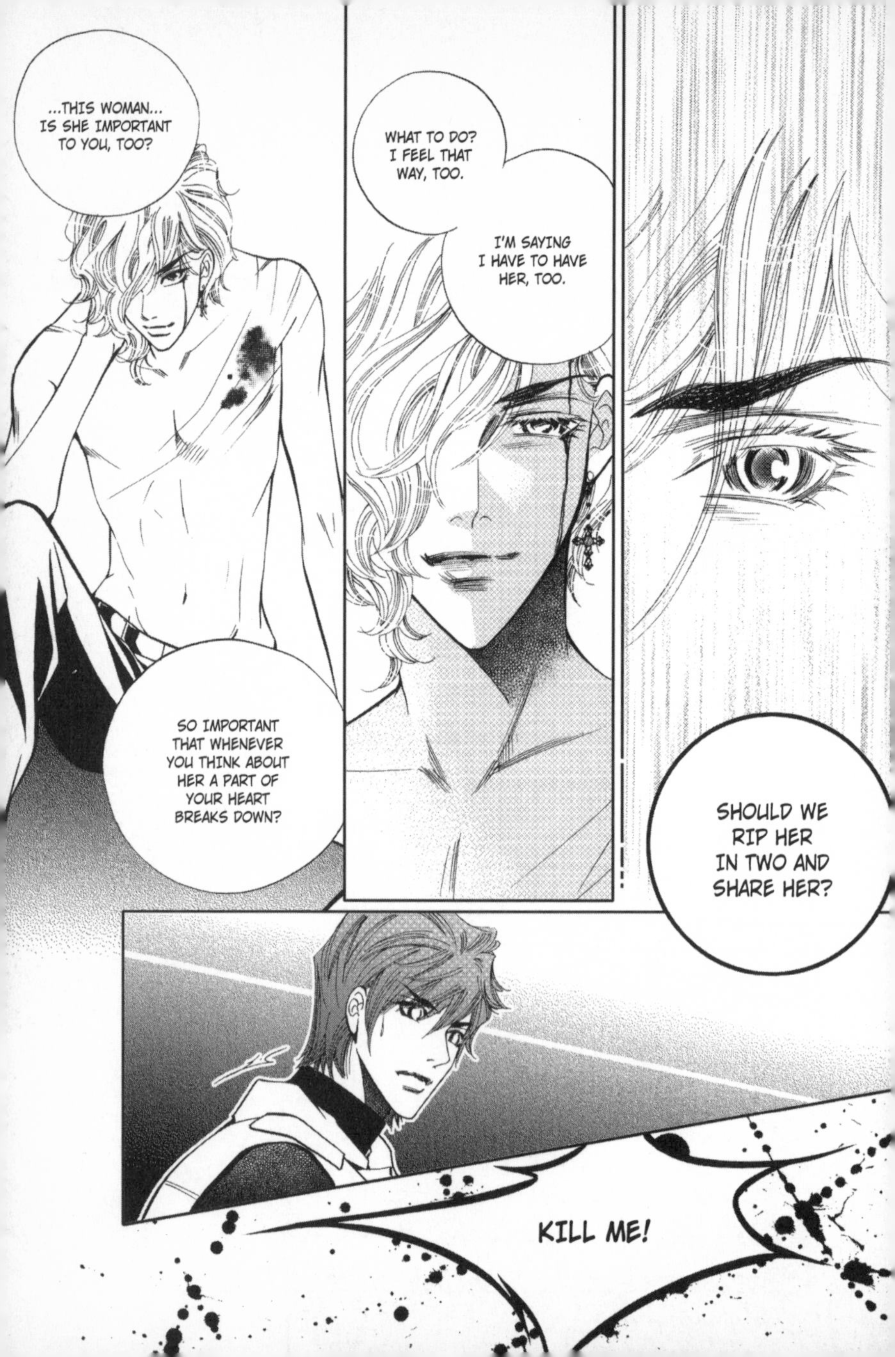
...THIS WOMAN... IS SHE IMPORTANT TO YOU, TOO?
SO IMPORTANT THAT WHENEVER YOU THINK ABOUT HER A PART OF YOUR HEART BREAKS DOWN?
WHAT TO DO? I FEEL THAT WAY, TOO.
I'M SAYING I HAVE TO HAVE HER, TOO.
SHOULD WE RIP HER IN TWO AND SHARE HER?
KILL ME!

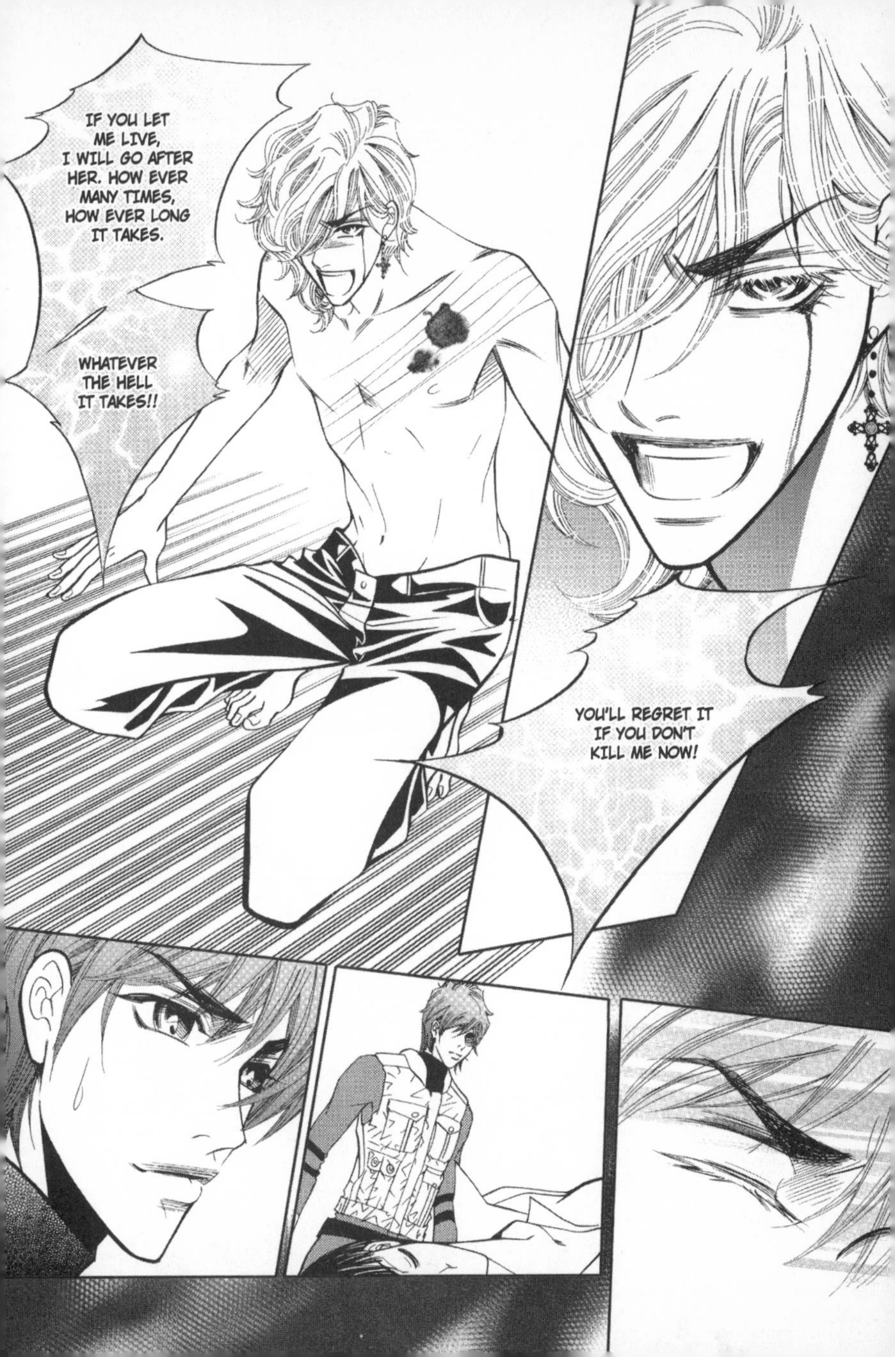
IF YOU LET ME LIVE, I WILL GO AFTER HER. HOW EVER MANY TIMES, HOW EVER LONG IT TAKES.
WHATEVER THE HELL IT TAKES!!
YOU'LL REGRET IT IF YOU DON'T KILL ME NOW!

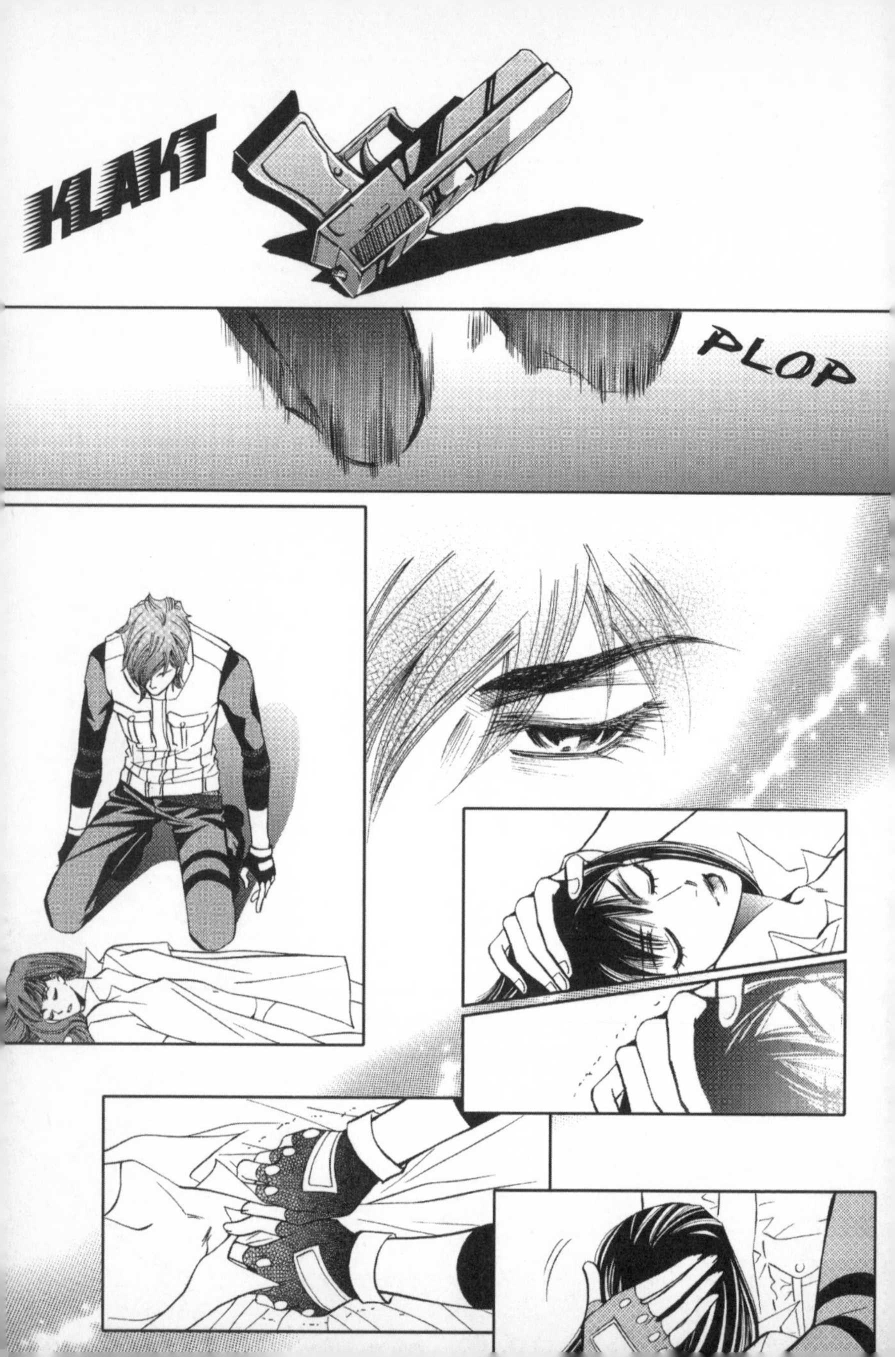
KLAKT
PLOP

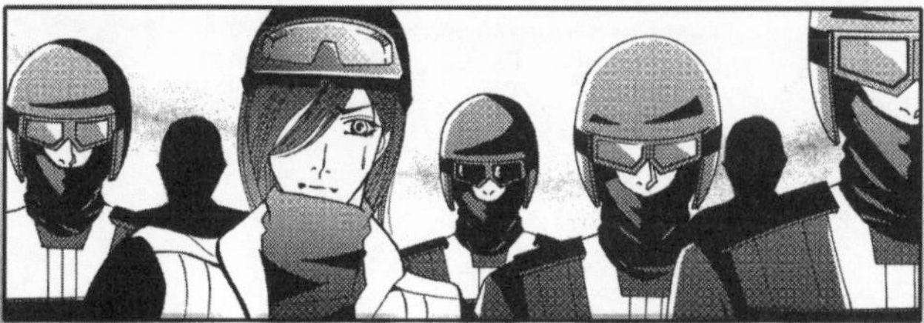
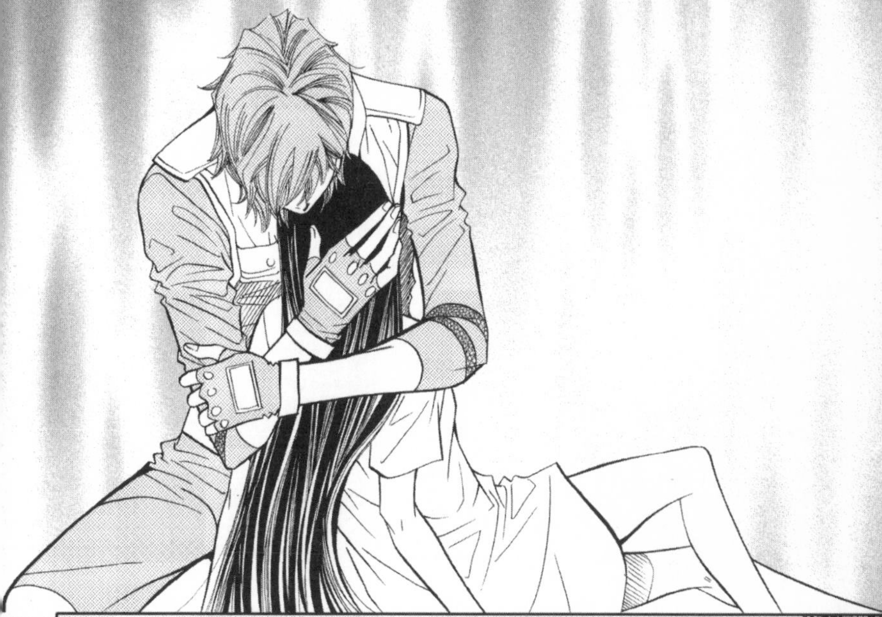
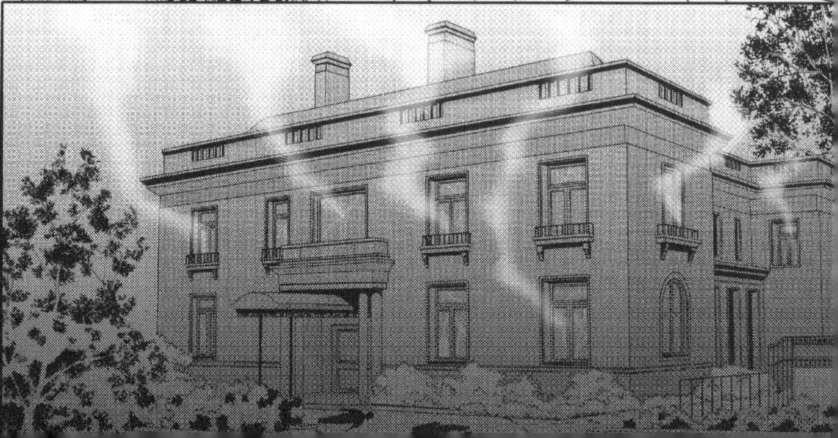

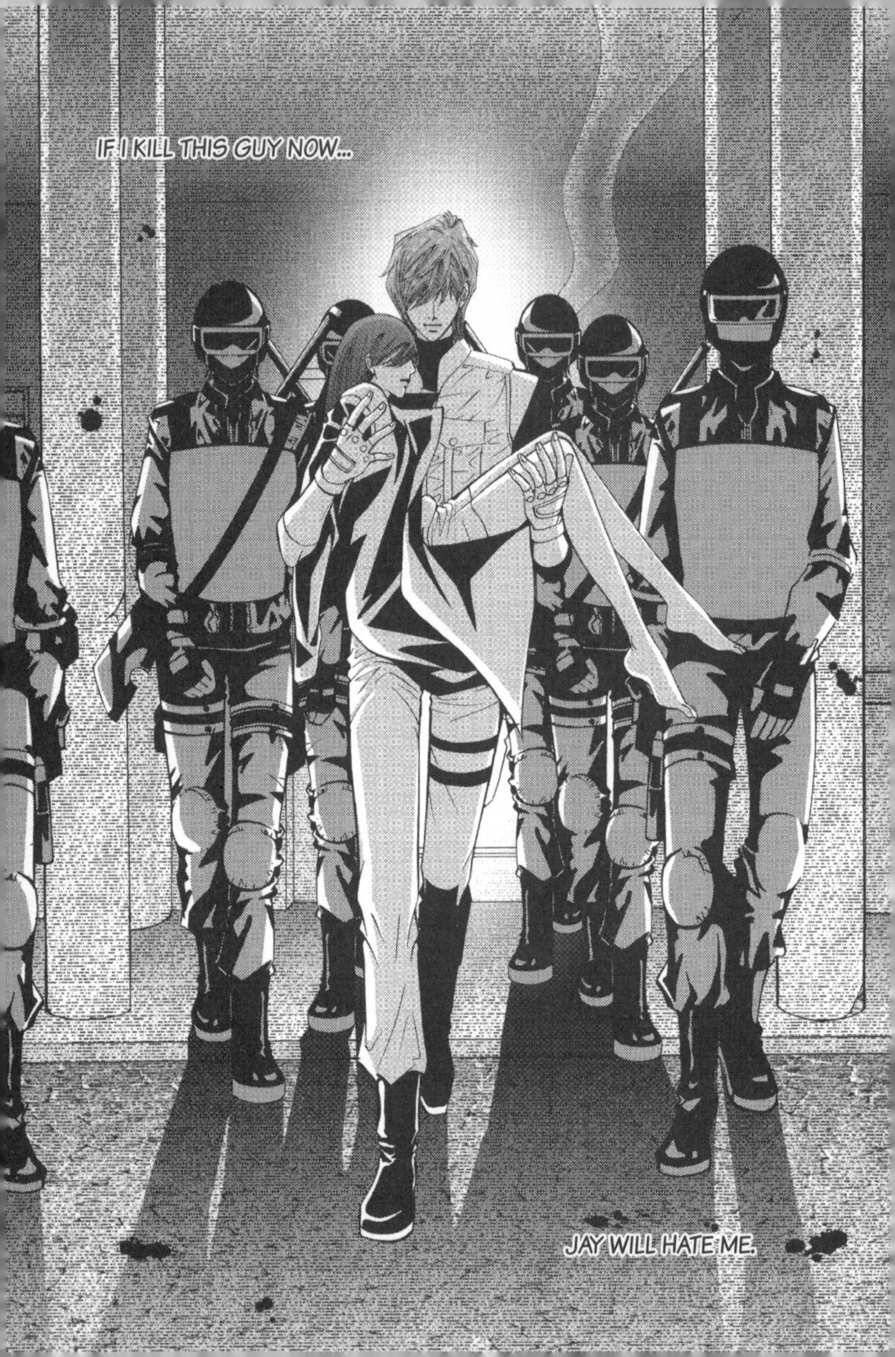
IF I KILL THIS GUY NOW...
JAY WILL HATE ME.

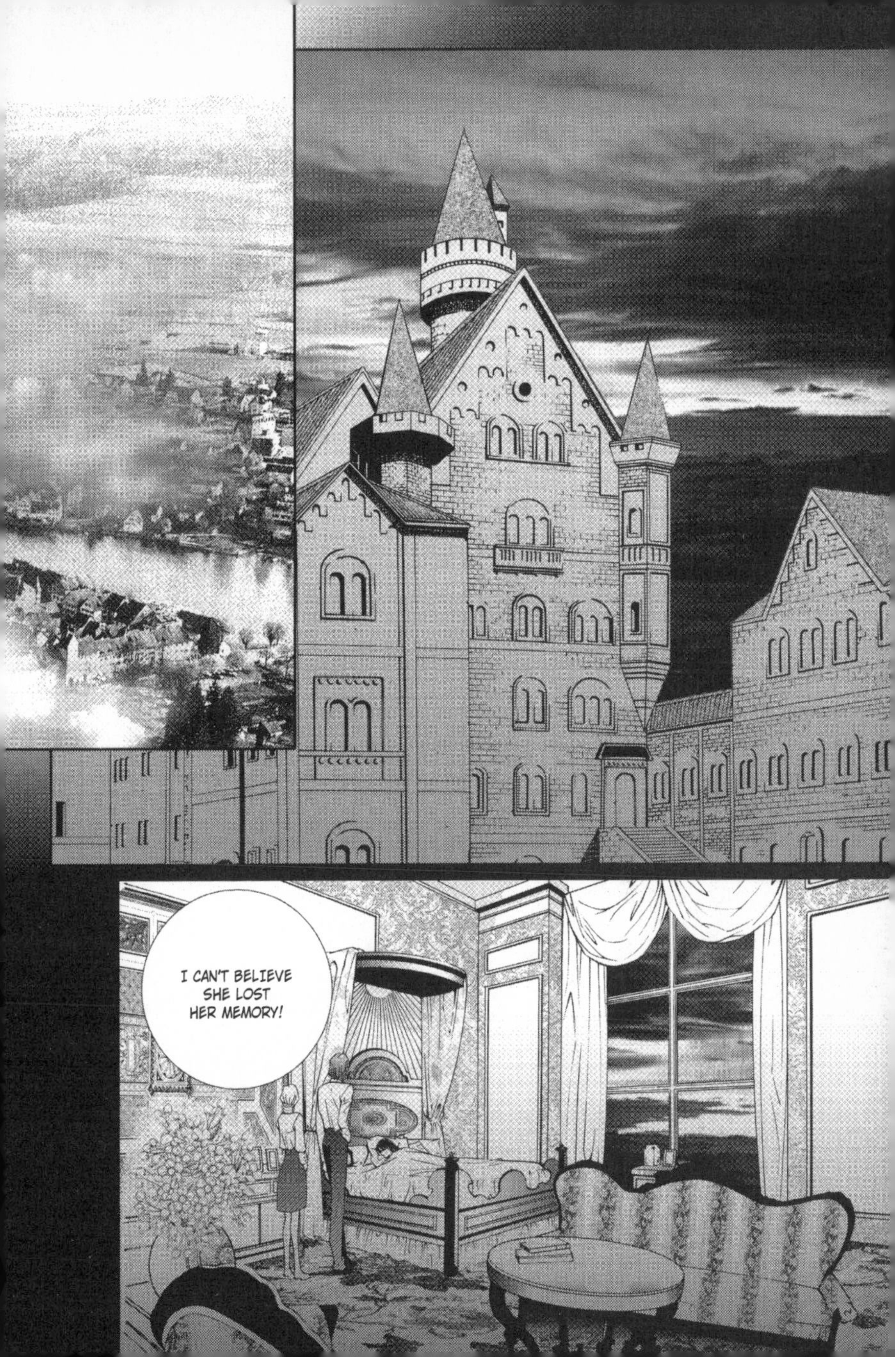
I CAN'T BELIEVE SHE LOST HER MEMORY!

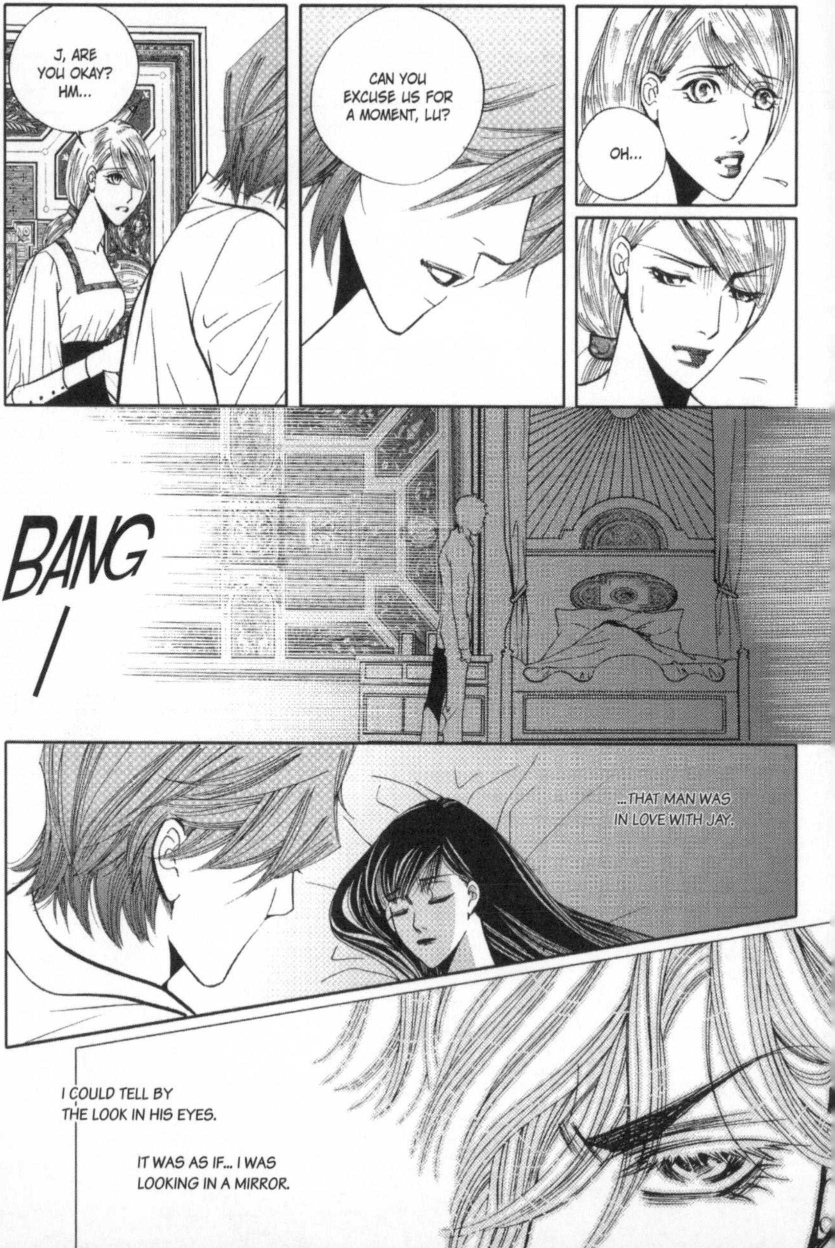
J, ARE YOU OKAY? HM...
CAN YOU EXCUSE US FOR A MOMENT, LU?
OH...
BANG
...THAT MAN WAS IN LOVE WITH JAY.
I COULD TELL BY THE LOOK IN HIS EYES.
IT WAS AS IF... I WAS LOOKING IN A MIRROR.

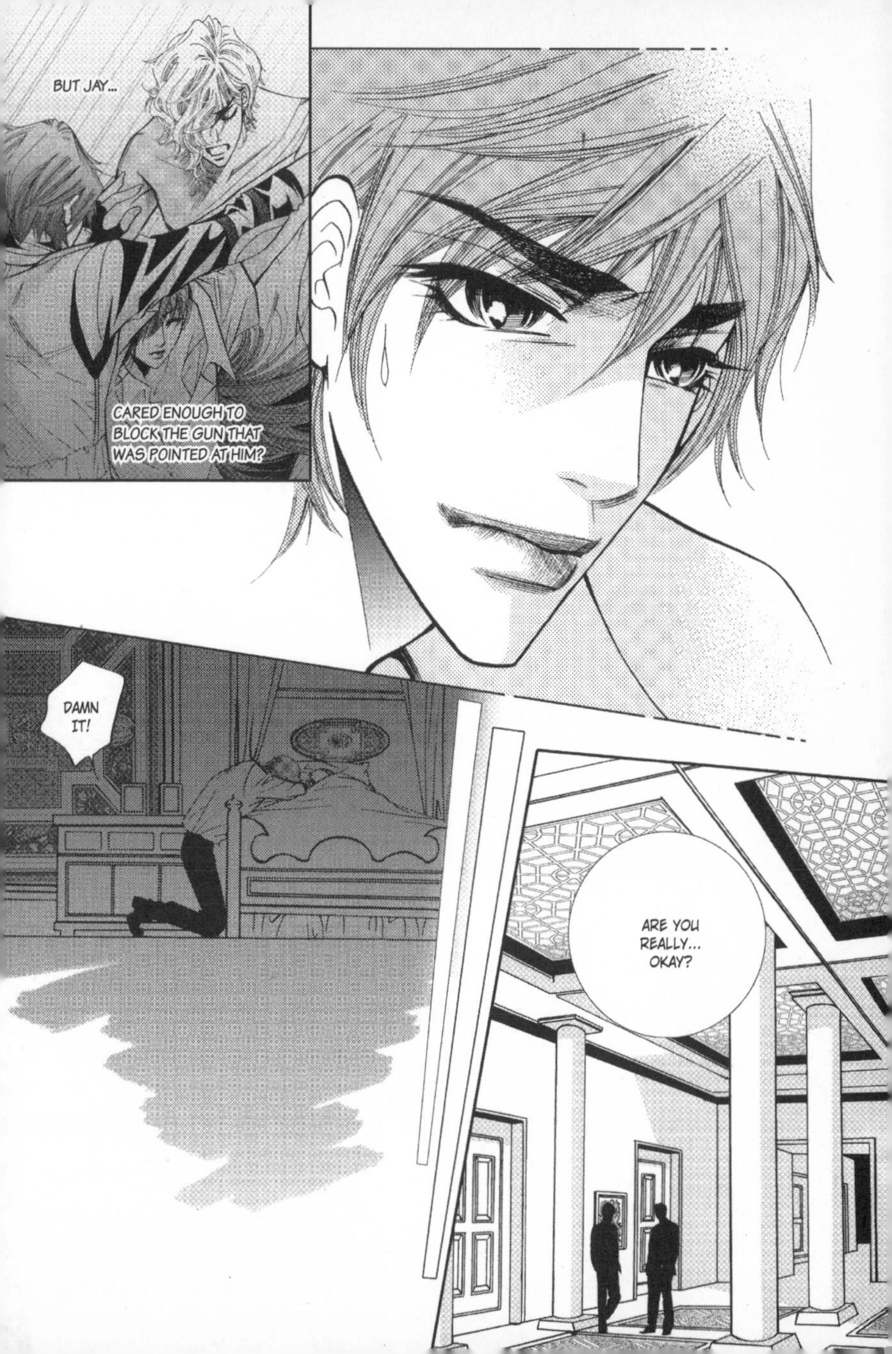
BUT JAY...
CARED ENOUGH TO BLOCK THE GUN THAT WAS POINTED AT HIM?
DAMN IT!
ARE YOU REALLY... OKAY?

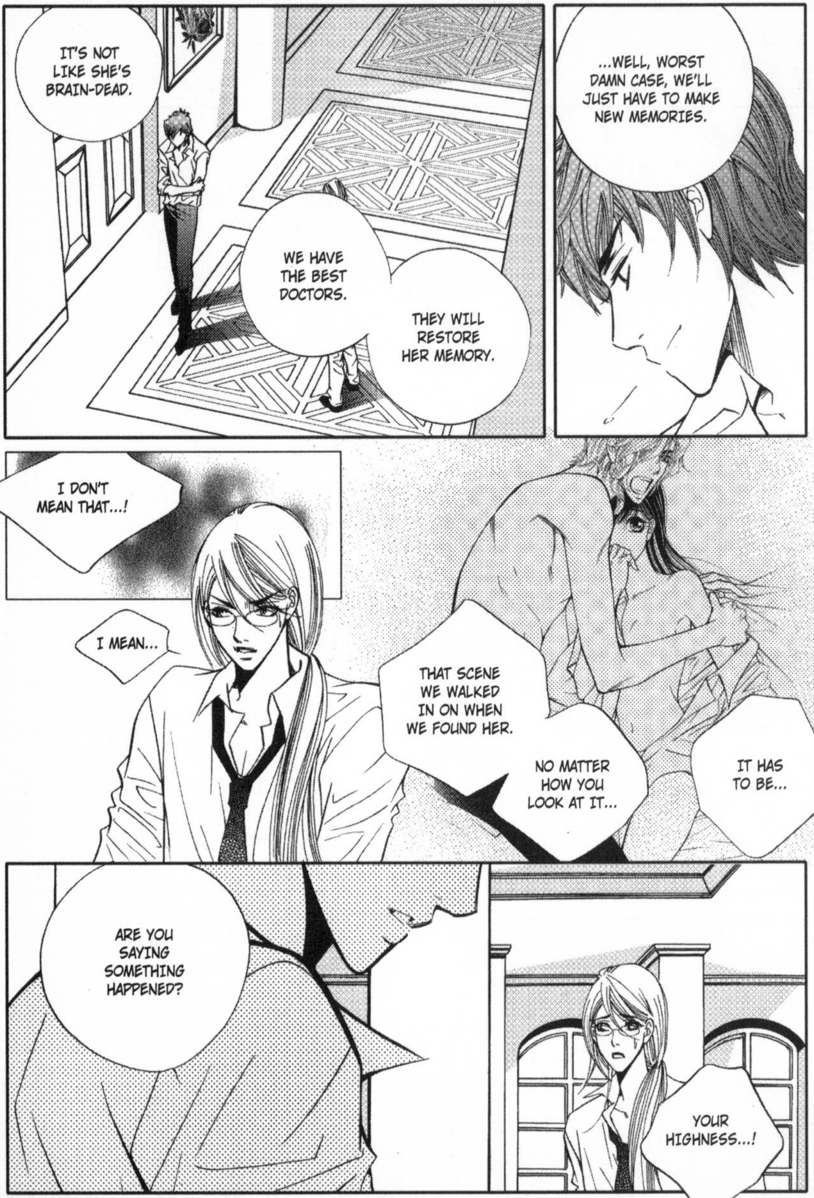
IT'S NOT LIKE SHE'S BRAIN-DEAD.
WE HAVE THE BEST DOCTORS.
THEY WILL RESTORE HER MEMORY.
...WELL, WORST DAMN CASE, WE'LL JUST HAVE TO MAKE NEW MEMORIES.
I DON'T MEAN THAT...!
I MEAN...
THAT SCENE WE WALKED IN ON WHEN WE FOUND HER.
NO MATTER HOW YOU LOOK AT IT...
IT HAS TO BE...
ARE YOU SAYING SOMETHING HAPPENED?
YOUR HIGHNESS...!

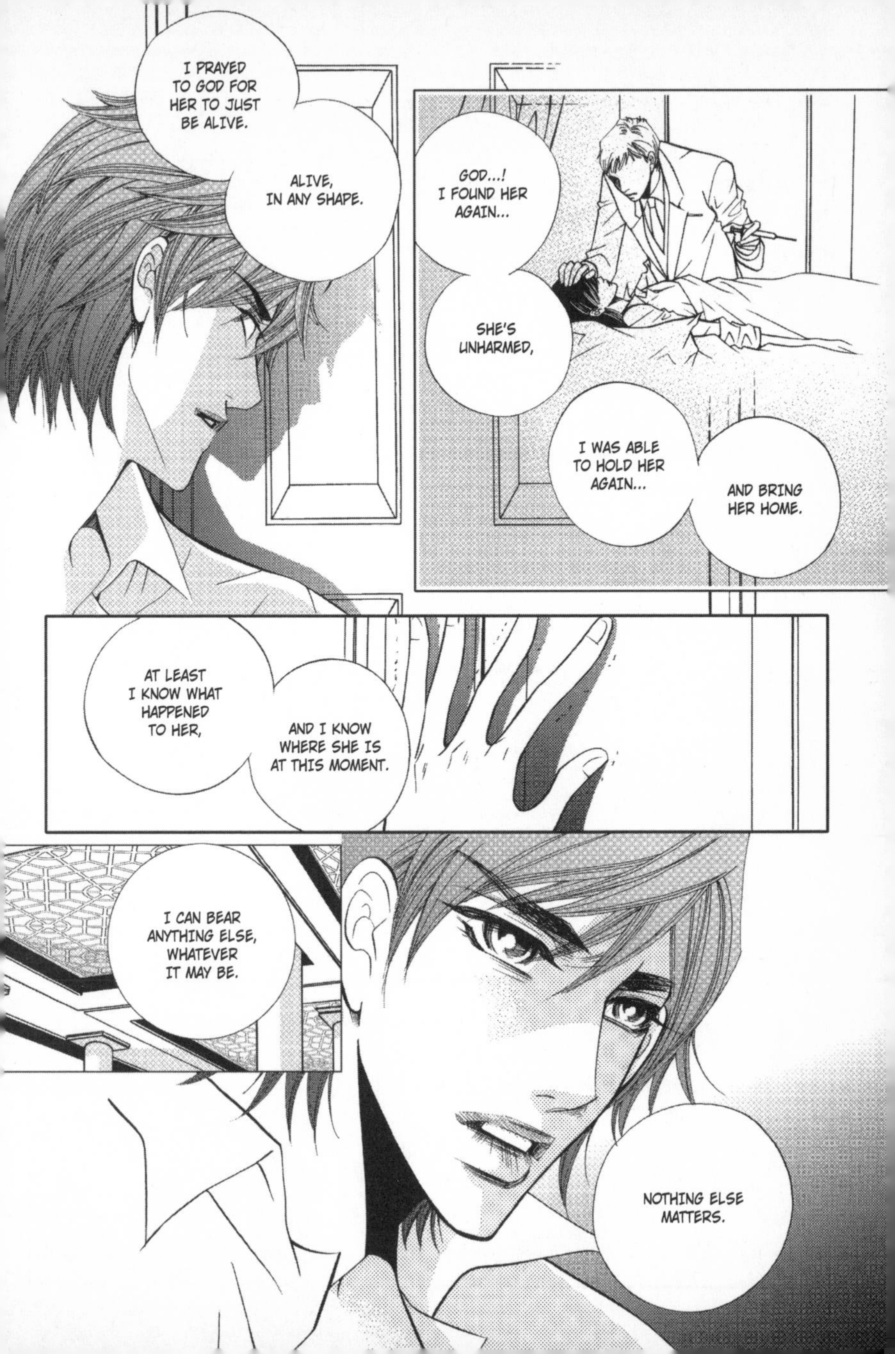
I PRAYED TO GOD FOR HER TO JUST BE ALIVE.
ALIVE, IN ANY SHAPE.
GOD...! I FOUND HER AGAIN...
SHE'S UNHARMED,
I WAS ABLE TO HOLD HER AGAIN...
AND BRING HER HOME.
AT LEAST I KNOW WHAT HAPPENED TO HER,
AND I KNOW WHERE SHE IS AT THIS MOMENT.
I CAN BEAR ANYTHING ELSE, WHATEVER IT MAY BE.
NOTHING ELSE MATTERS.

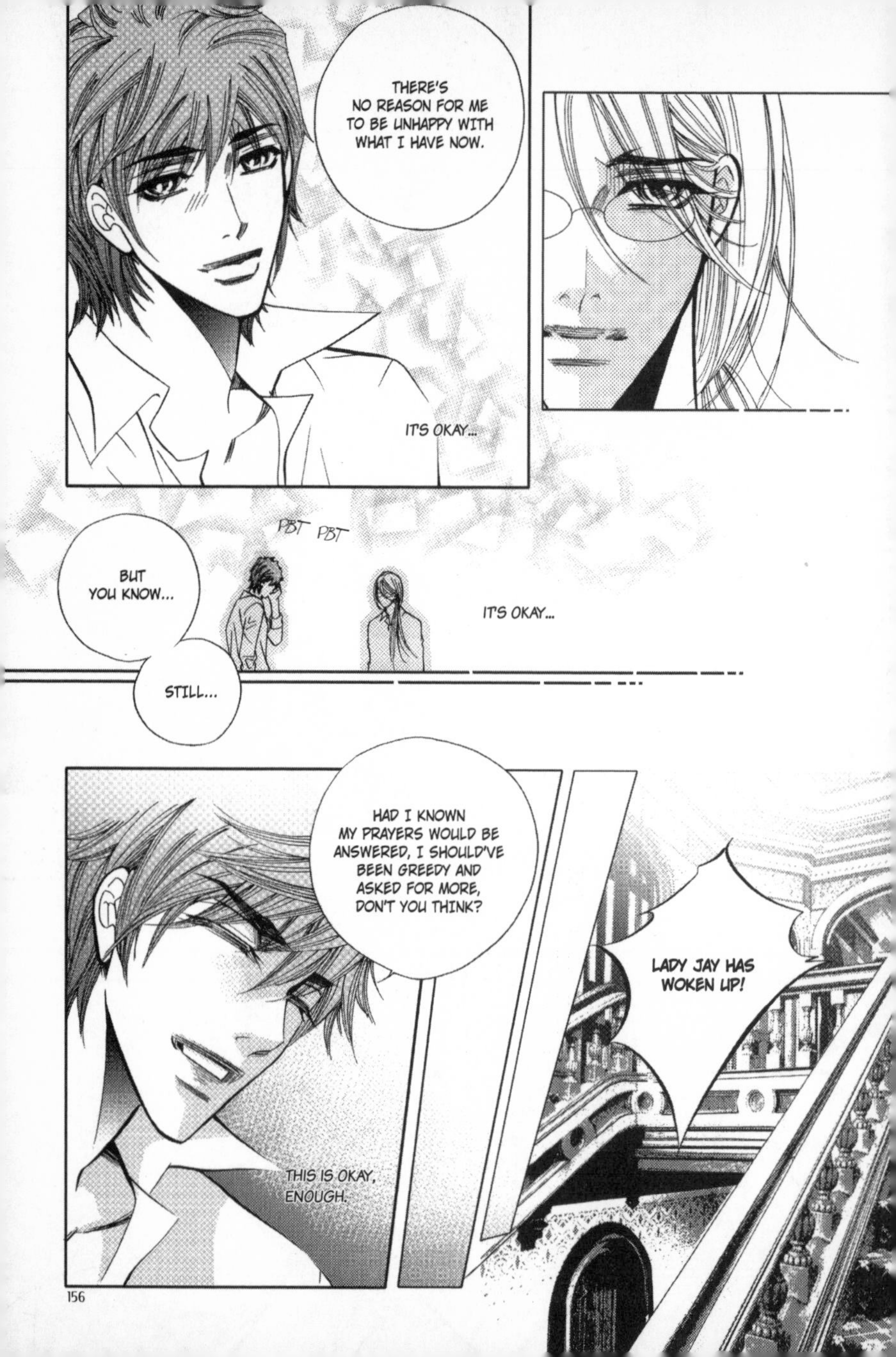
THERE'S NO REASON FOR ME TO BE UNHAPPY WITH WHAT I HAVE NOW.
IT'S OKAY...
PBT PBT
BUT YOU KNOW...
IT'S OKAY...
STILL...
HAD I KNOWN MY PRAYERS WOULD BE ANSWERED, I SHOULD'VE BEEN GREEDY AND ASKED FOR MORE, DON'T YOU THINK?
THIS IS OKAY, ENOUGH.
LADY JAY HAS WOKEN UP!

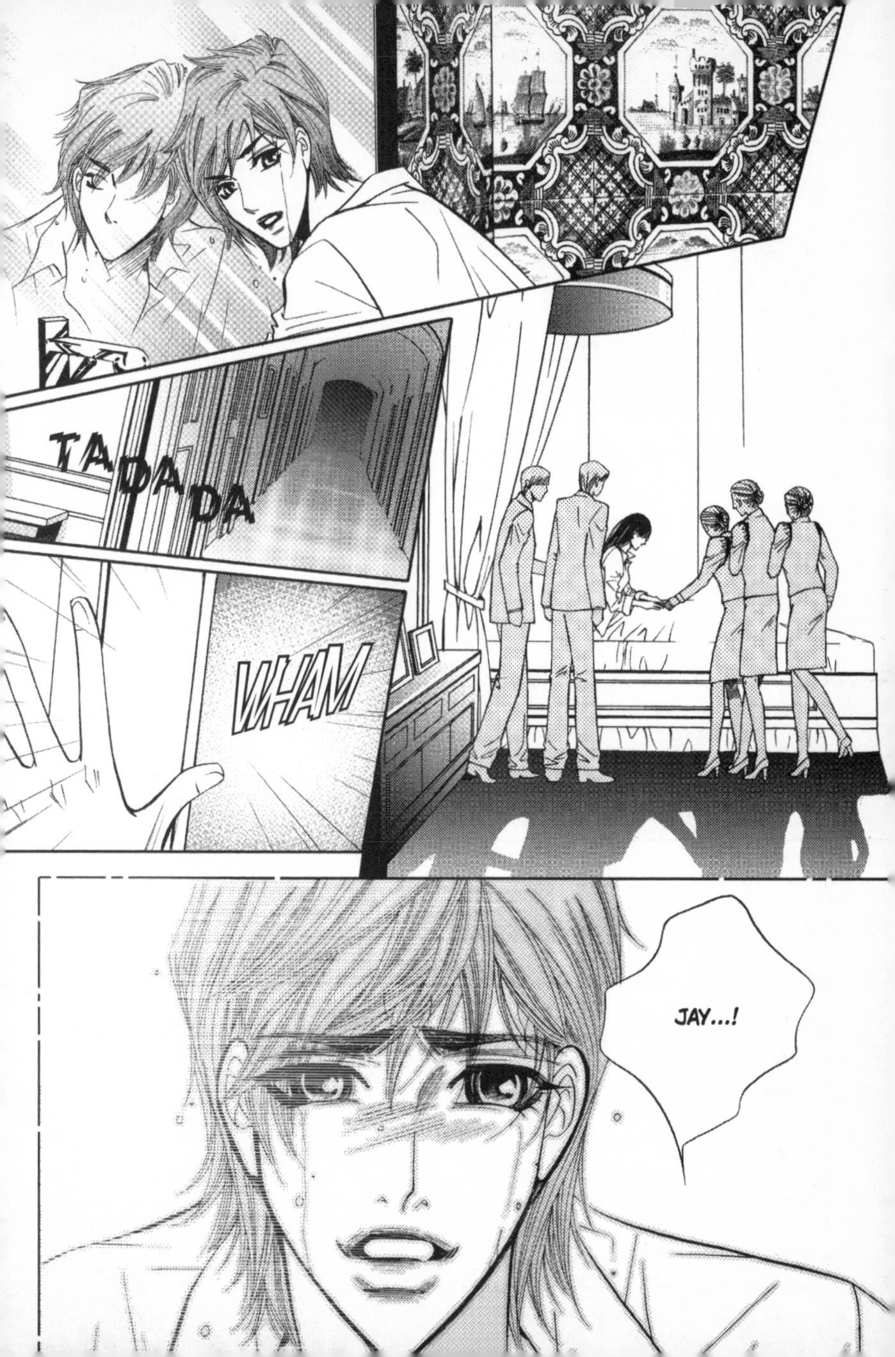
TA DA DA DA
WHAM
JAY...!

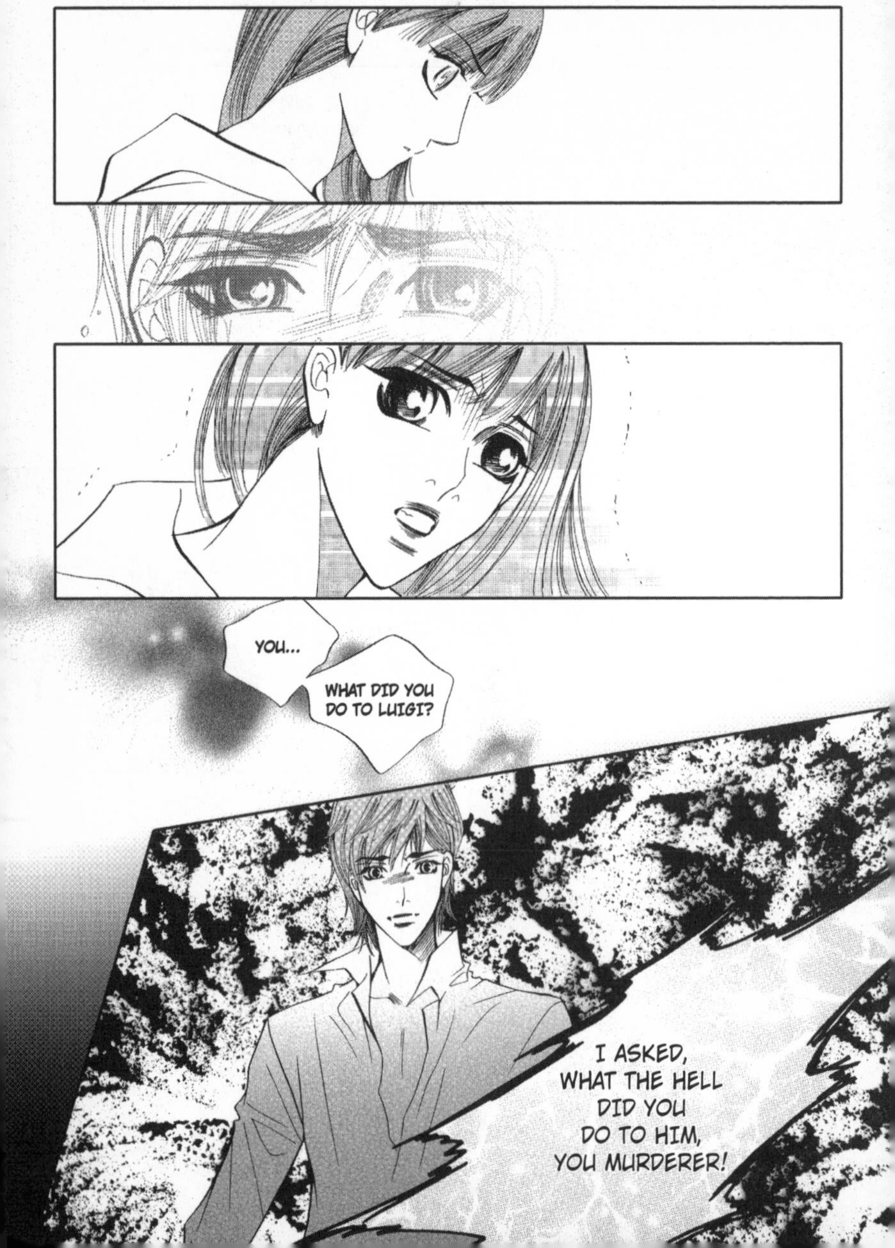
YOU...
WHAT DID YOU DO TO LUIGI?
I ASKED, WHAT THE HELL DID YOU DO TO HIM, YOU MURDERER!

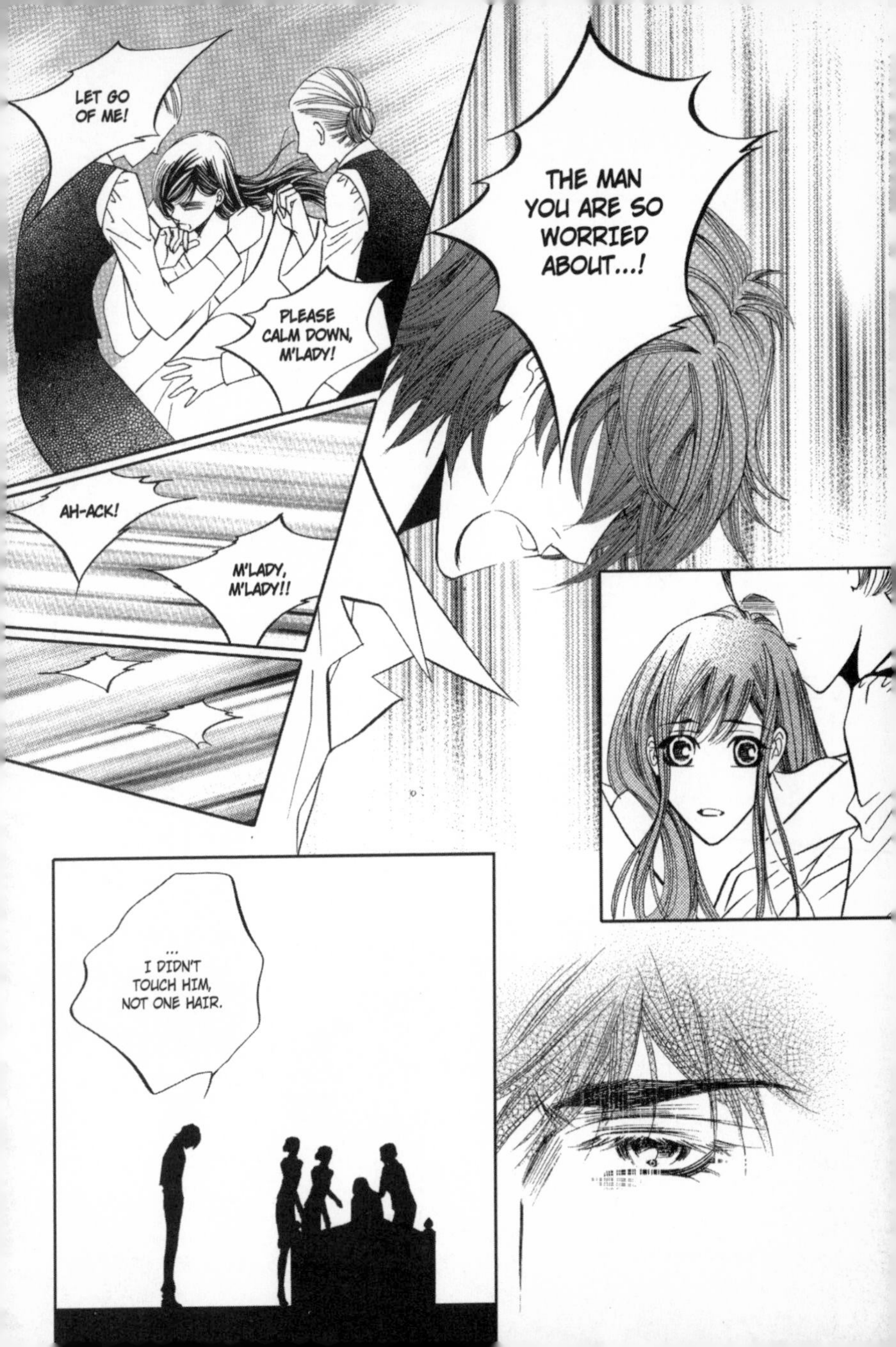
LET GO OF ME!
PLEASE CALM DOWN, M'LADY!
THE MAN YOU ARE SO WORRIED ABOUT...!
AH-ACK!
M'LADY, M'LADY!!
... I DIDN'T TOUCH HIM, NOT ONE HAIR.

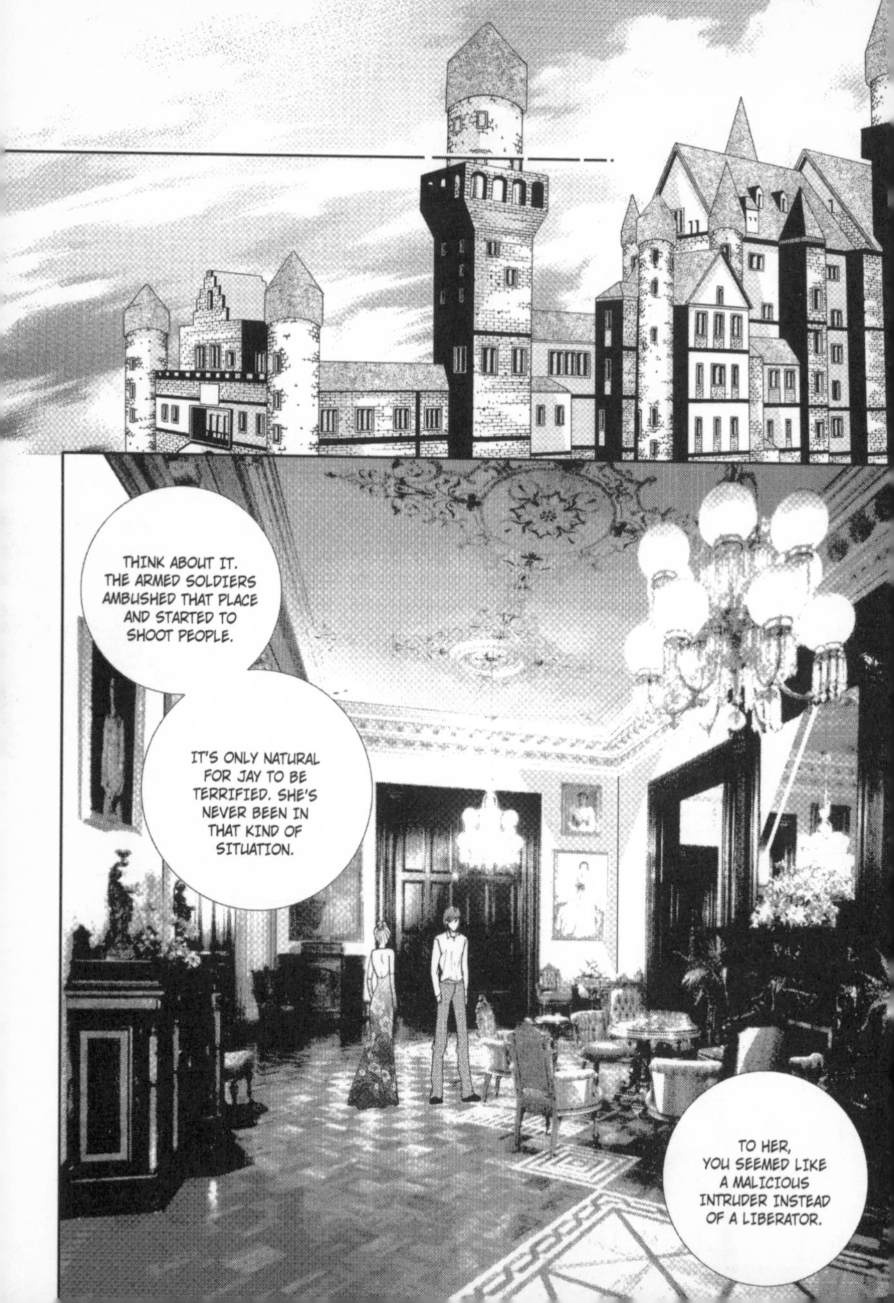
THINK ABOUT IT. THE ARMED SOLDIERS AMBUSHED THAT PLACE AND STARTED TO SHOOT PEOPLE.
IT'S ONLY NATURAL FOR JAY TO BE TERRIFIED. SHE'S NEVER BEEN IN THAT KIND OF SITUATION.
TO HER, YOU SEEMED LIKE A MALICIOUS INTRUDER INSTEAD OF A LIBERATOR.

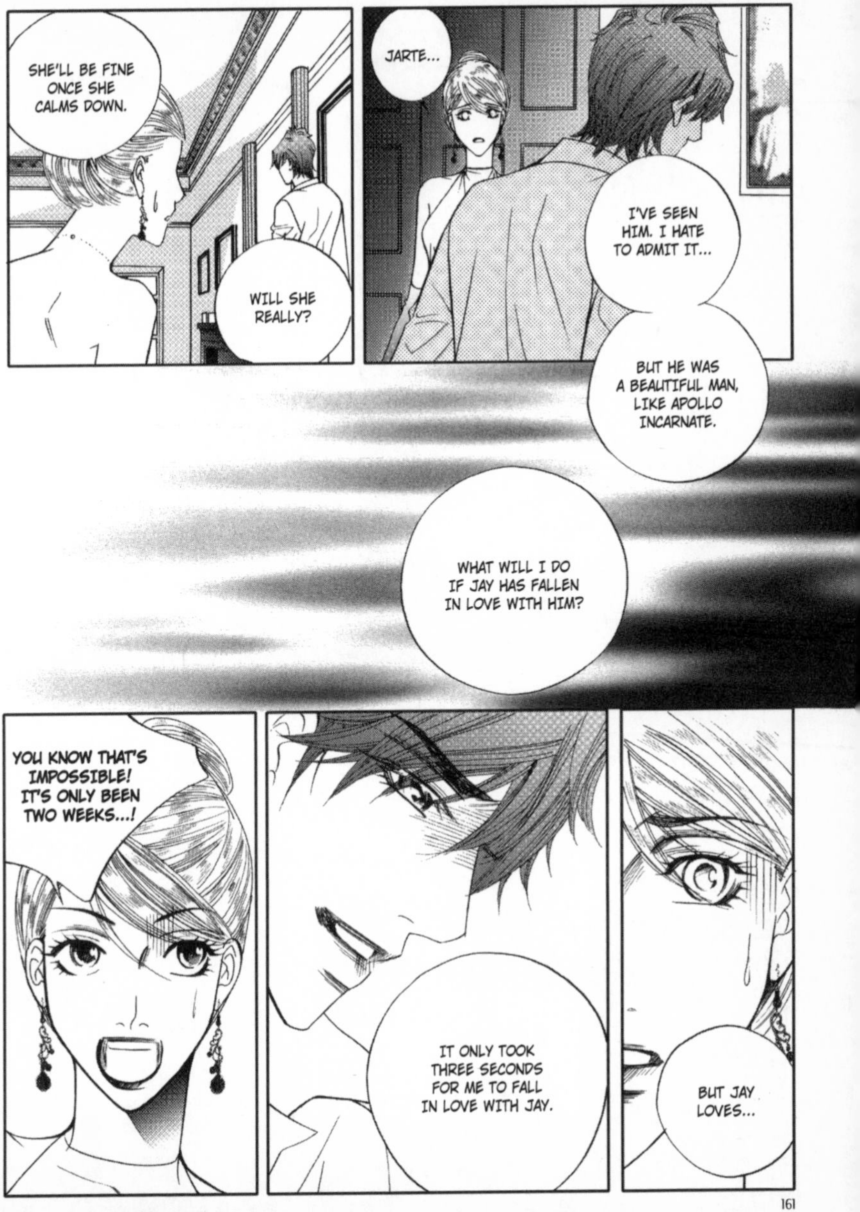
SHE'LL BE FINE ONCE SHE CALMS DOWN.
WILL SHE REALLY?
JARTE...
I'VE SEEN HIM. I HATE TO ADMIT IT...
BUT HE WAS A BEAUTIFUL MAN, LIKE APOLLO INCARNATE.
WHAT WILL I DO IF JAY HAS FALLEN IN LOVE WITH HIM?
YOU KNOW THAT'S IMPOSSIBLE! IT'S ONLY BEEN TWO WEEKS...!
IT ONLY TOOK THREE SECONDS FOR ME TO FALL IN LOVE WITH JAY.
BUT JAY LOVES...

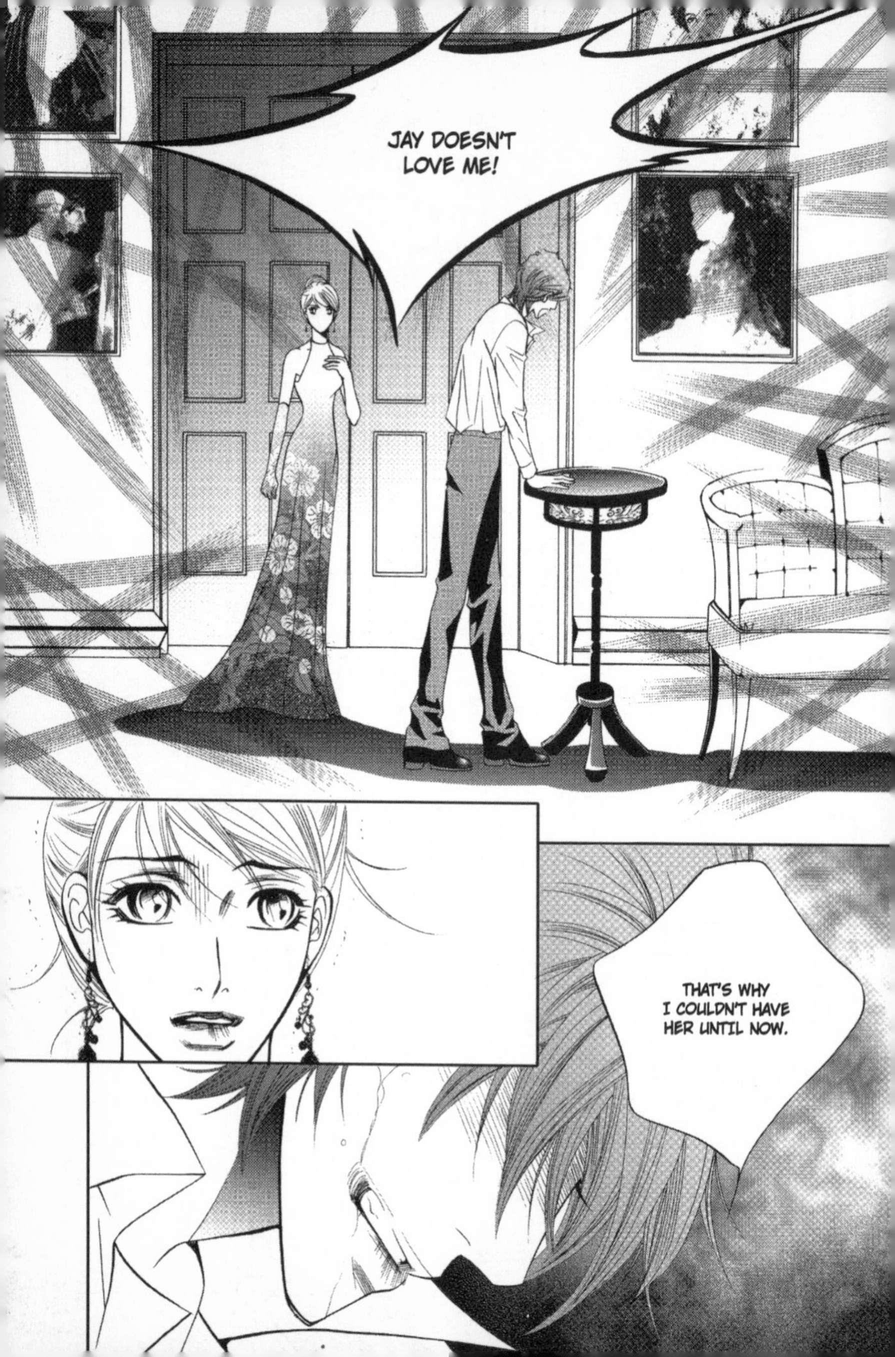
JAY DOESN'T LOVE ME!
THAT'S WHY I COULDN'T HAVE HER UNTIL NOW.

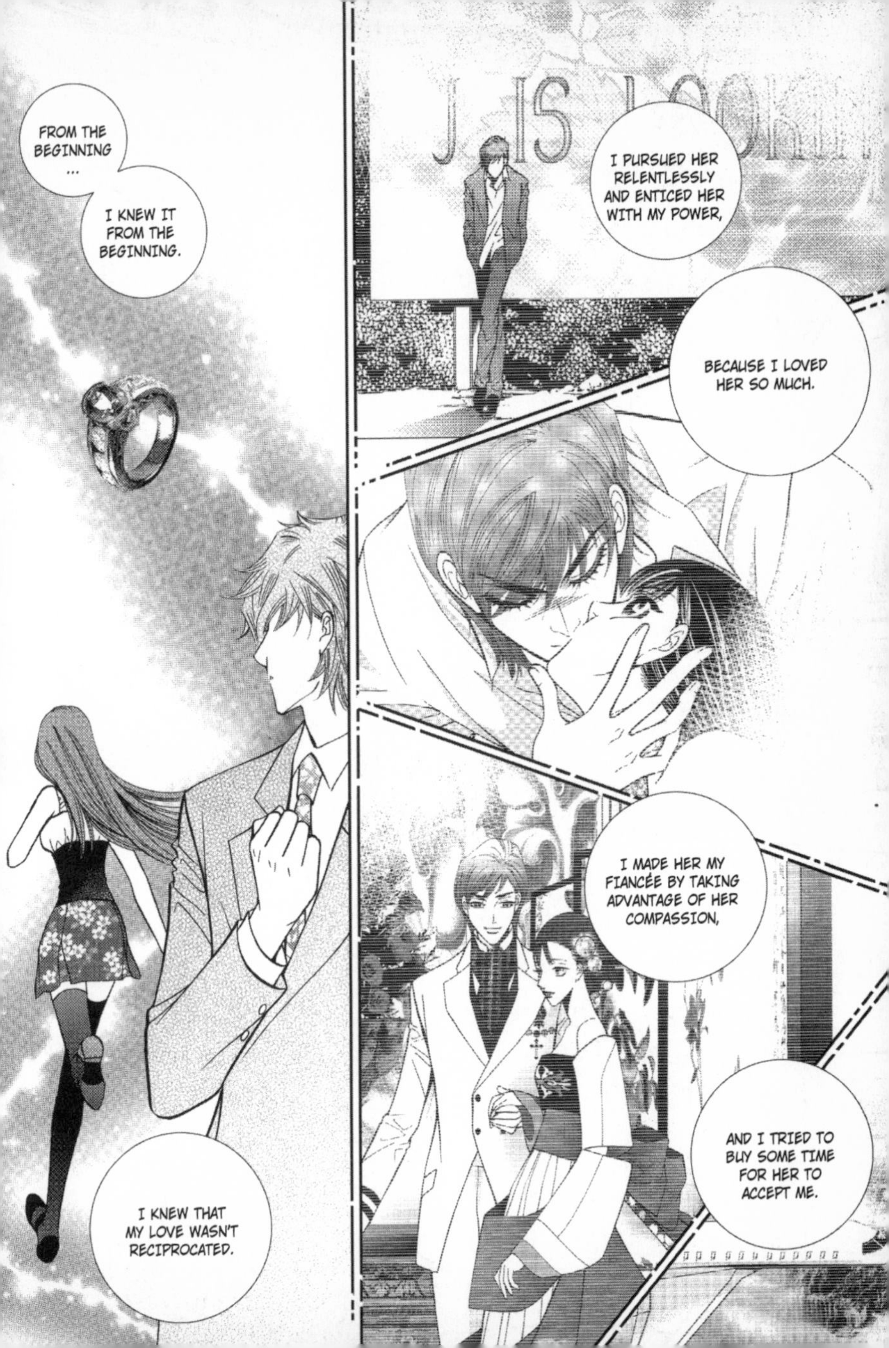
FROM THE BEGINNING ...
I KNEW IT FROM THE BEGINNING.
I KNEW THAT MY LOVE WASN'T RECIPROCATED.
I PURSUED HER RELENTLESSLY AND ENTICED HER WITH MY POWER,
BECAUSE I LOVED HER SO MUCH.
I MADE HER MY FIANCÉE BY TAKING ADVANTAGE OF HER COMPASSION,
AND I TRIED TO BUY SOME TIME FOR HER TO ACCEPT ME.

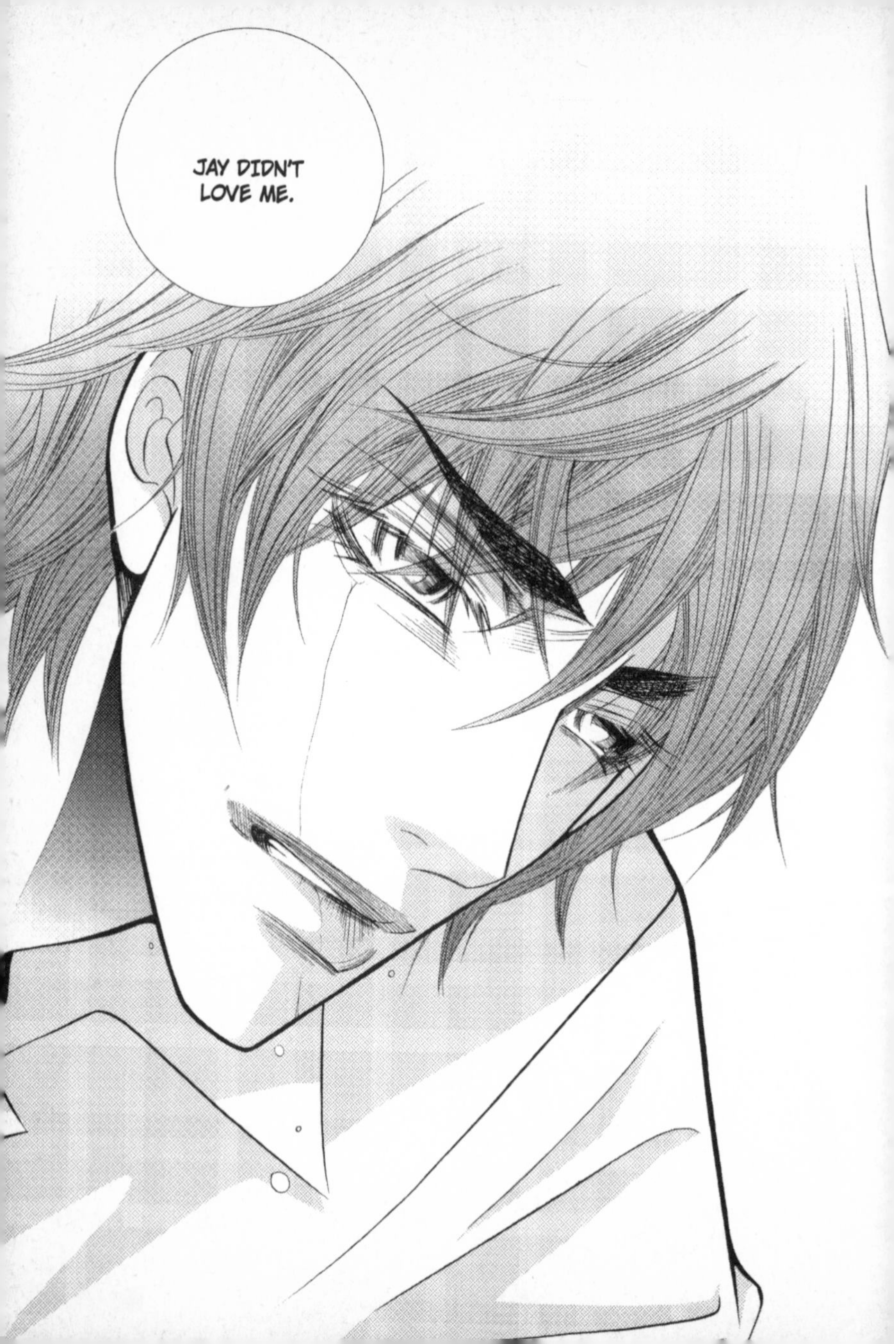
JAY DIDN'T LOVE ME.

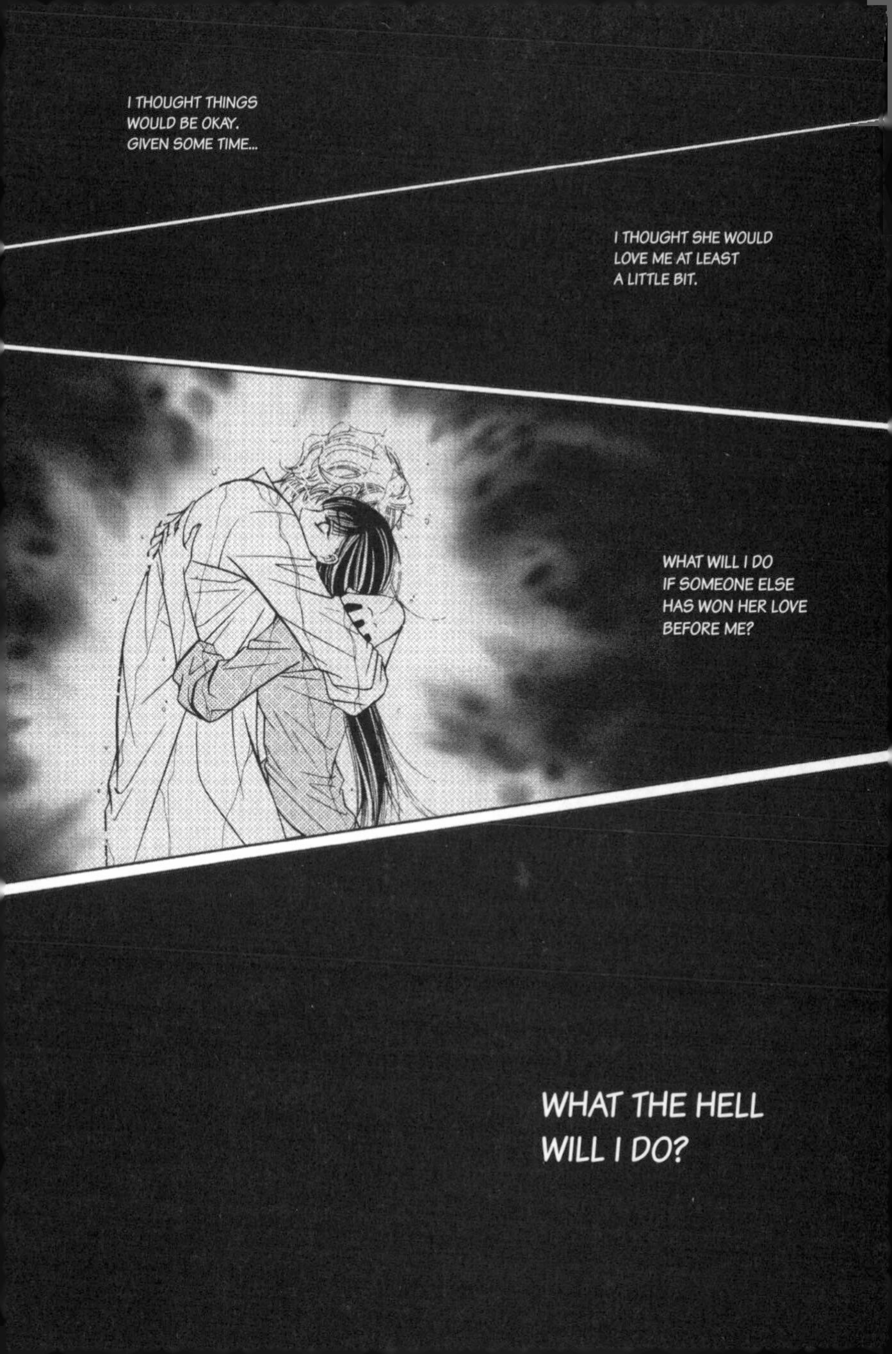
I THOUGHT THINGS WOULD BE OKAY. GIVEN SOME TIME...
I THOUGHT SHE WOULD LOVE ME AT LEAST A LITTLE BIT.
WHAT WILL I DO IF SOMEONE ELSE HAS WON HER LOVE BEFORE ME?
WHAT THE HELL WILL I DO?

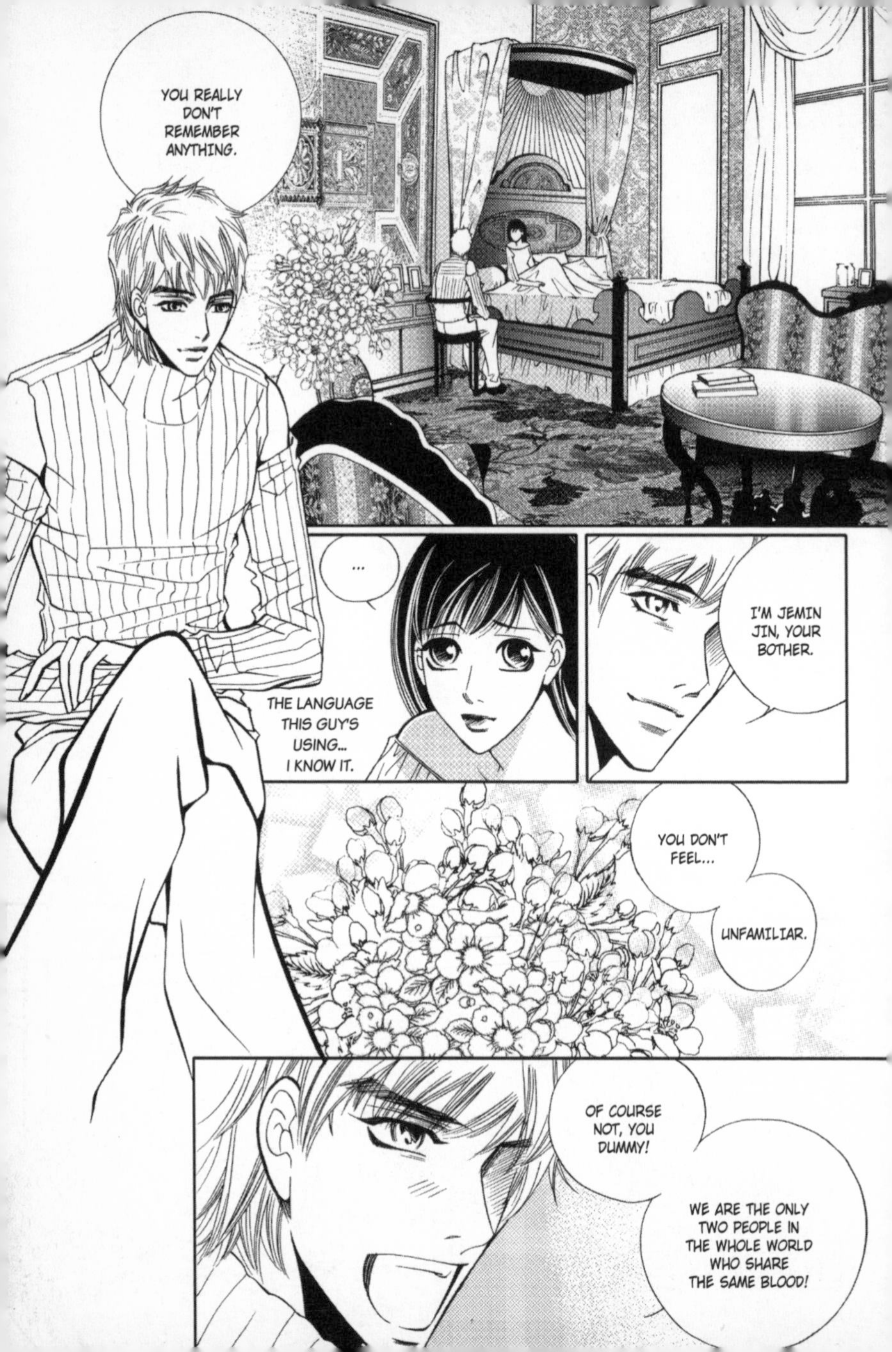
YOU REALLY DON'T REMEMBER ANYTHING.
...
THE LANGUAGE THIS GUY'S USING... I KNOW IT.
I'M JEMIN JIN, YOUR BOTHER.
YOU DON'T FEEL...
UNFAMILIAR.
OF COURSE NOT, YOU DUMMY!
WE ARE THE ONLY TWO PEOPLE IN THE WHOLE WORLD WHO SHARE THE SAME BLOOD!

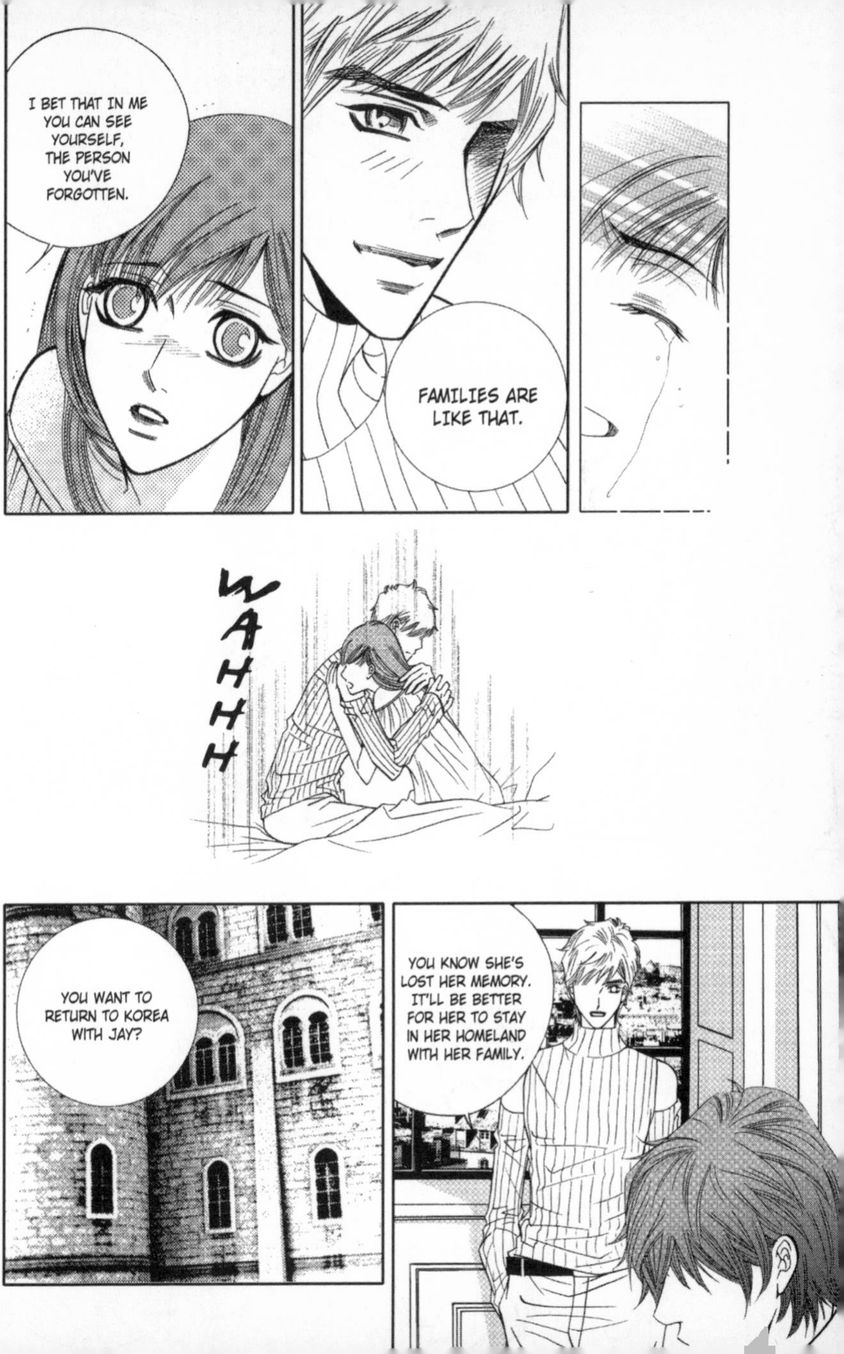
I BET THAT IN ME YOU CAN SEE YOURSELF, THE PERSON YOU'VE FORGOTTEN.
FAMILIES ARE LIKE THAT.
WAHHHH
YOU WANT TO RETURN TO KOREA WITH JAY?
YOU KNOW SHE'S LOST HER MEMORY. IT'LL BE BETTER FOR HER TO STAY IN HER HOMELAND WITH HER FAMILY.

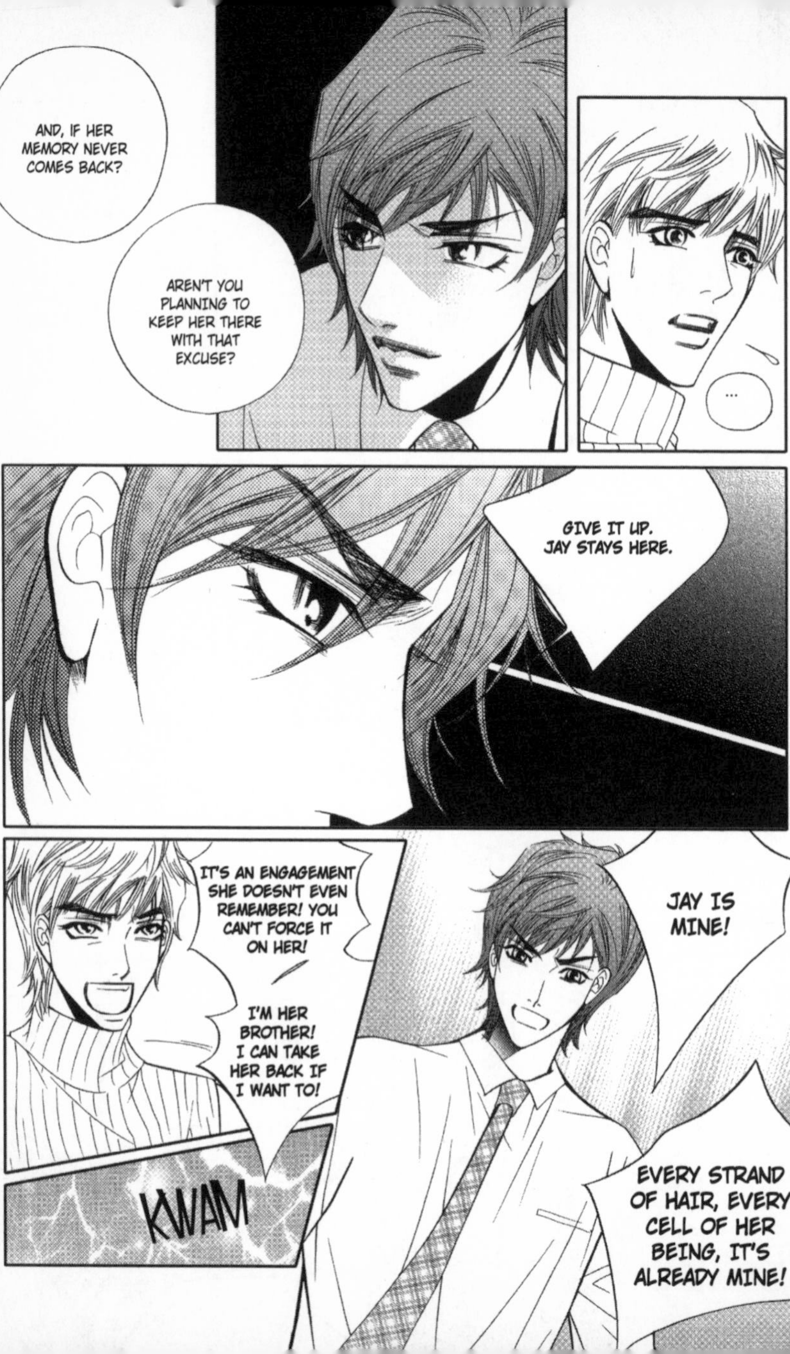

AND, IF HER MEMORY NEVER COMES BACK?
AREN'T YOU PLANNING TO KEEP HER THERE WITH THAT EXCUSE?
...
GIVE IT UP. JAY STAYS HERE.
IT'S AN ENGAGEMENT SHE DOESN'T EVEN REMEMBER! YOU CAN'T FORCE IT ON HER!
I'M HER BROTHER! I CAN TAKE HER BACK IF I WANT TO!
KWAM
JAY IS MINE!
EVERY STRAND OF HAIR, EVERY CELL OF HER BEING, IT'S ALREADY MINE!

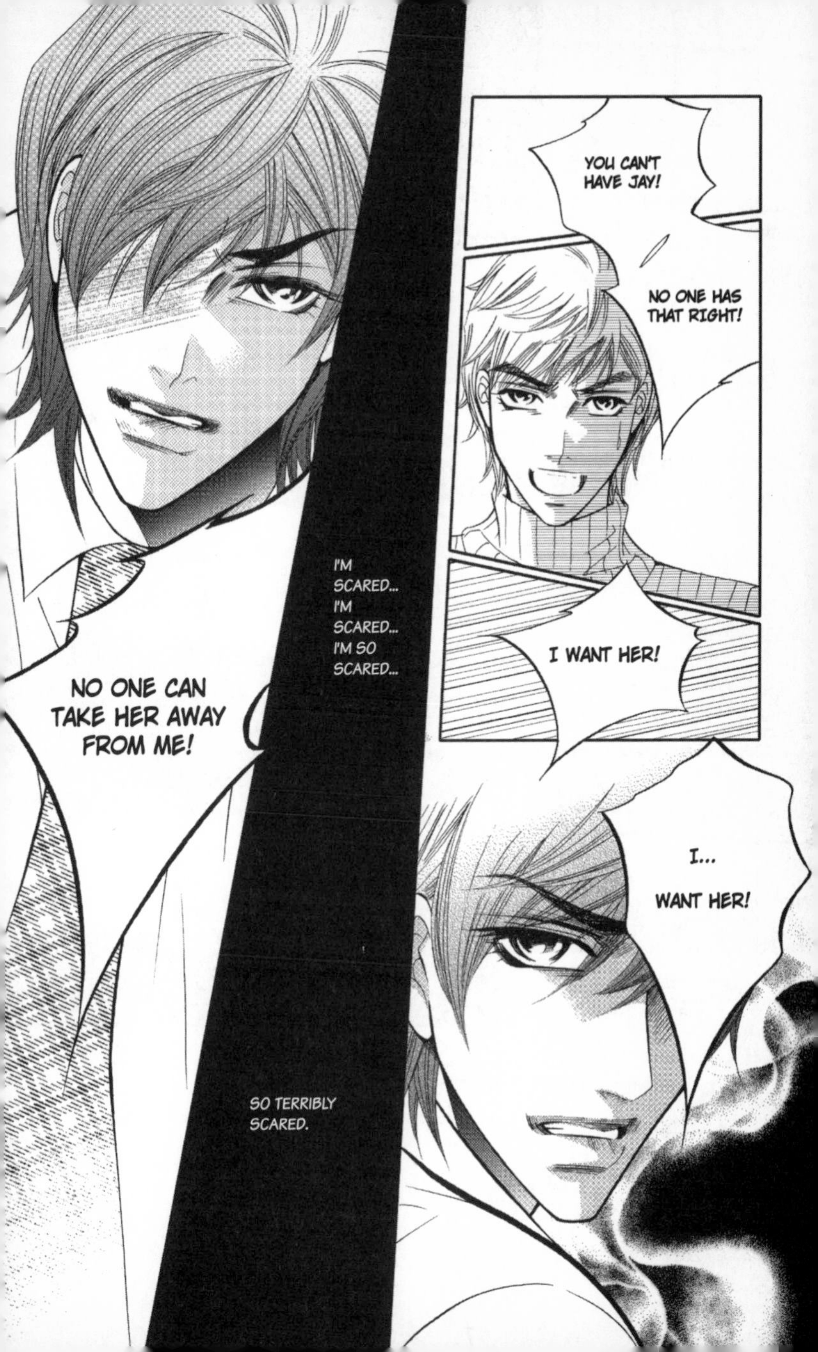
NO ONE CAN TAKE HER AWAY FROM ME!
I'M SCARED... I'M SCARED... I'M SO SCARED...
SO TERRIBLY SCARED.
YOU CAN'T HAVE JAY!
NO ONE HAS THAT RIGHT!
I WANT HER!
I... WANT HER!

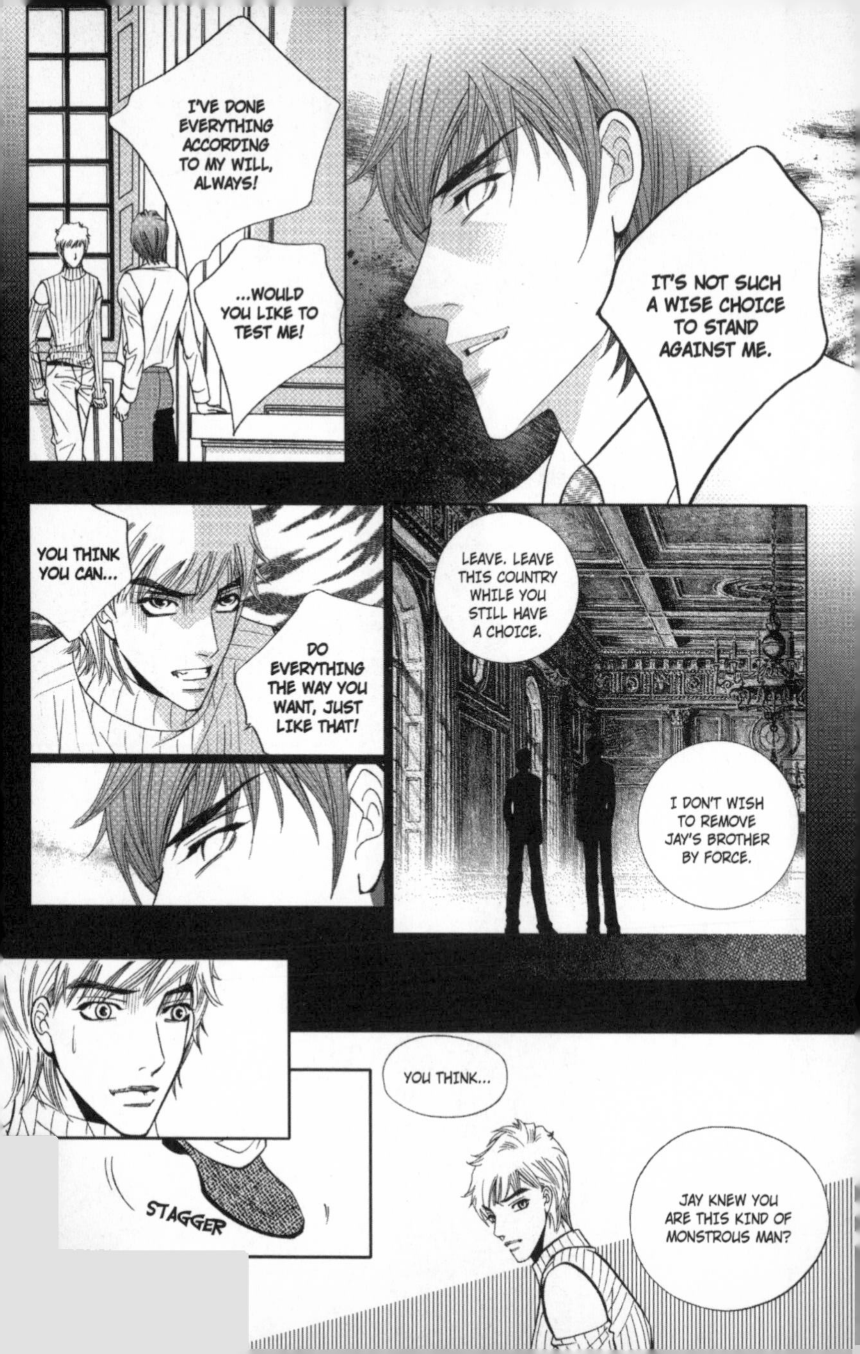

I'VE DONE EVERYTHING ACCORDING TO MY WILL, ALWAYS!
...WOULD YOU LIKE TO TEST ME!
IT'S NOT SUCH A WISE CHOICE TO STAND AGAINST ME.
YOU THINK YOU CAN...
DO EVERYTHING THE WAY YOU WANT, JUST LIKE THAT!
LEAVE. LEAVE THIS COUNTRY WHILE YOU STILL HAVE A CHOICE.
I DON'T WISH TO REMOVE JAY'S BROTHER BY FORCE.
STAGGER
YOU THINK...
JAY KNEW YOU ARE THIS KIND OF MONSTROUS MAN?

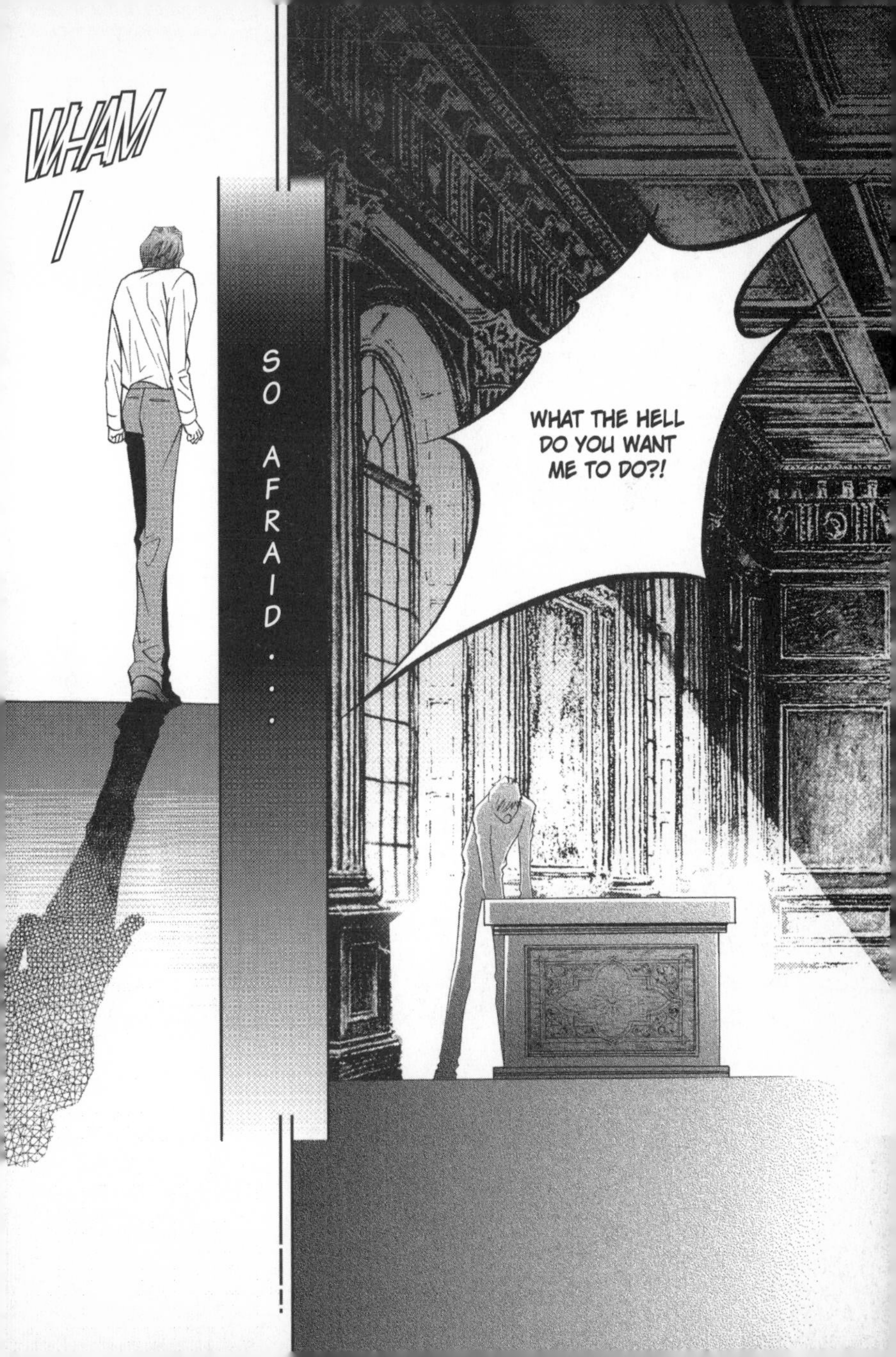
WHAM
SO AFRAID...
WHAT THE HELL DO YOU WANT ME TO DO?!

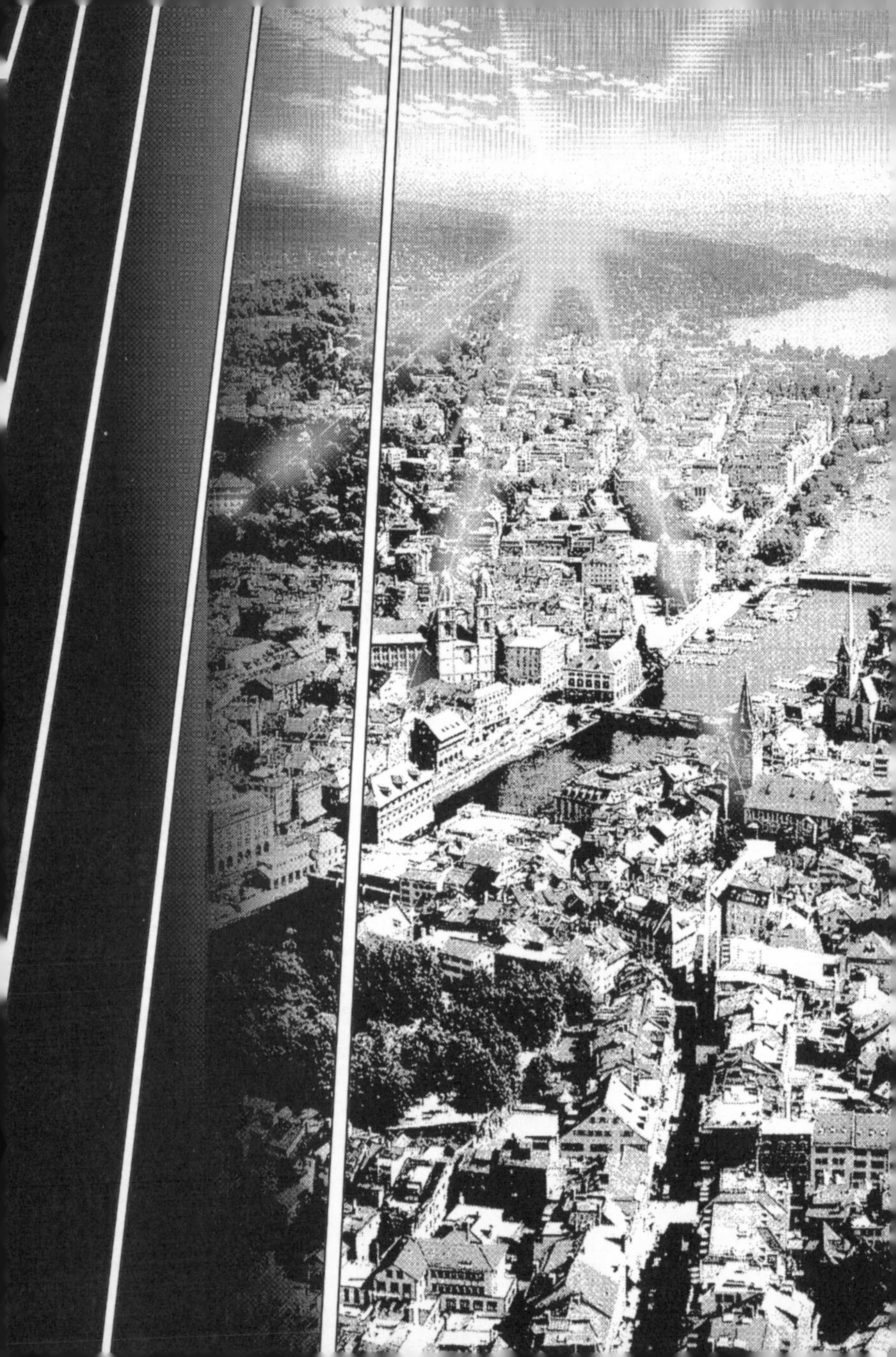

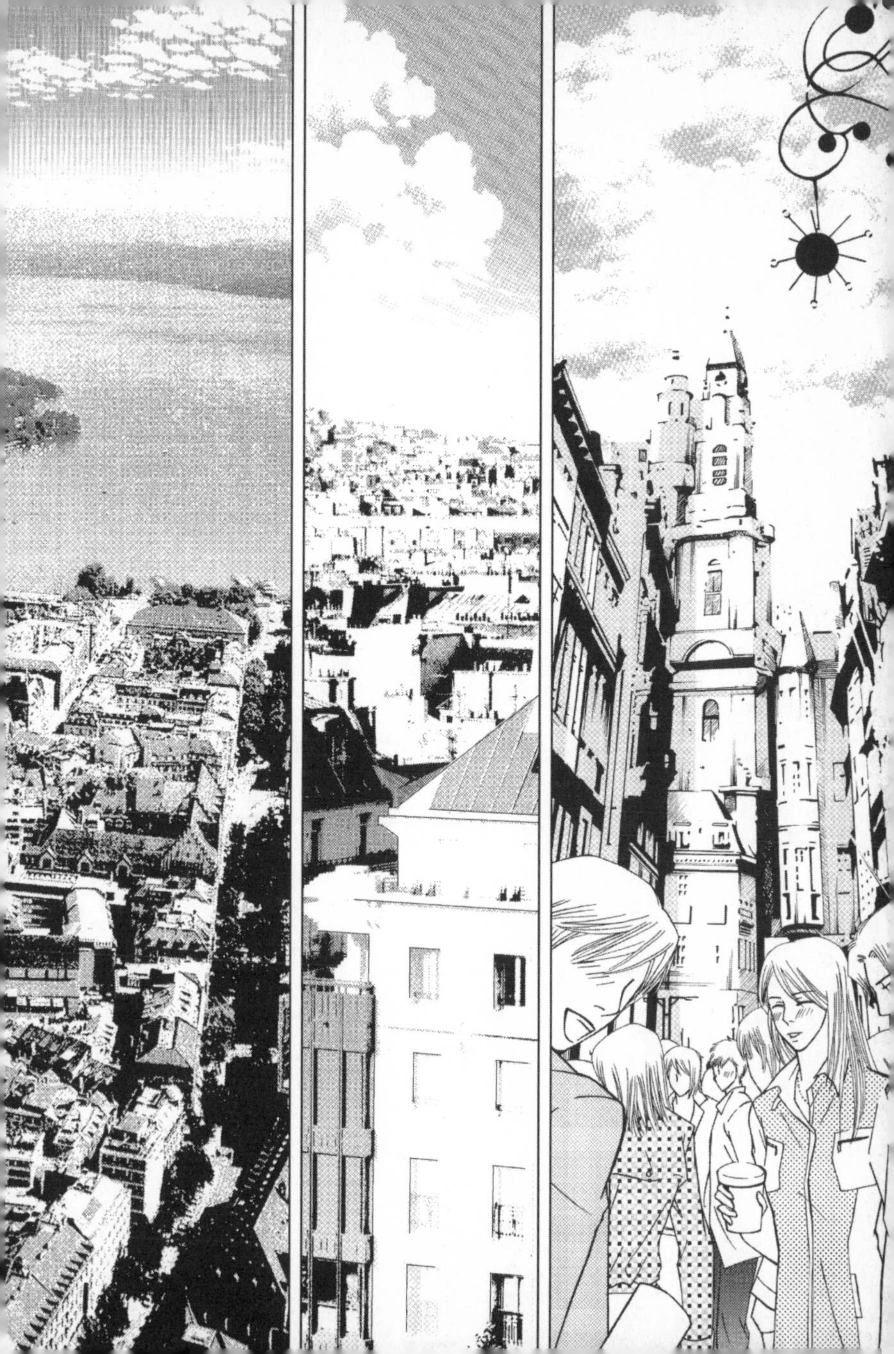

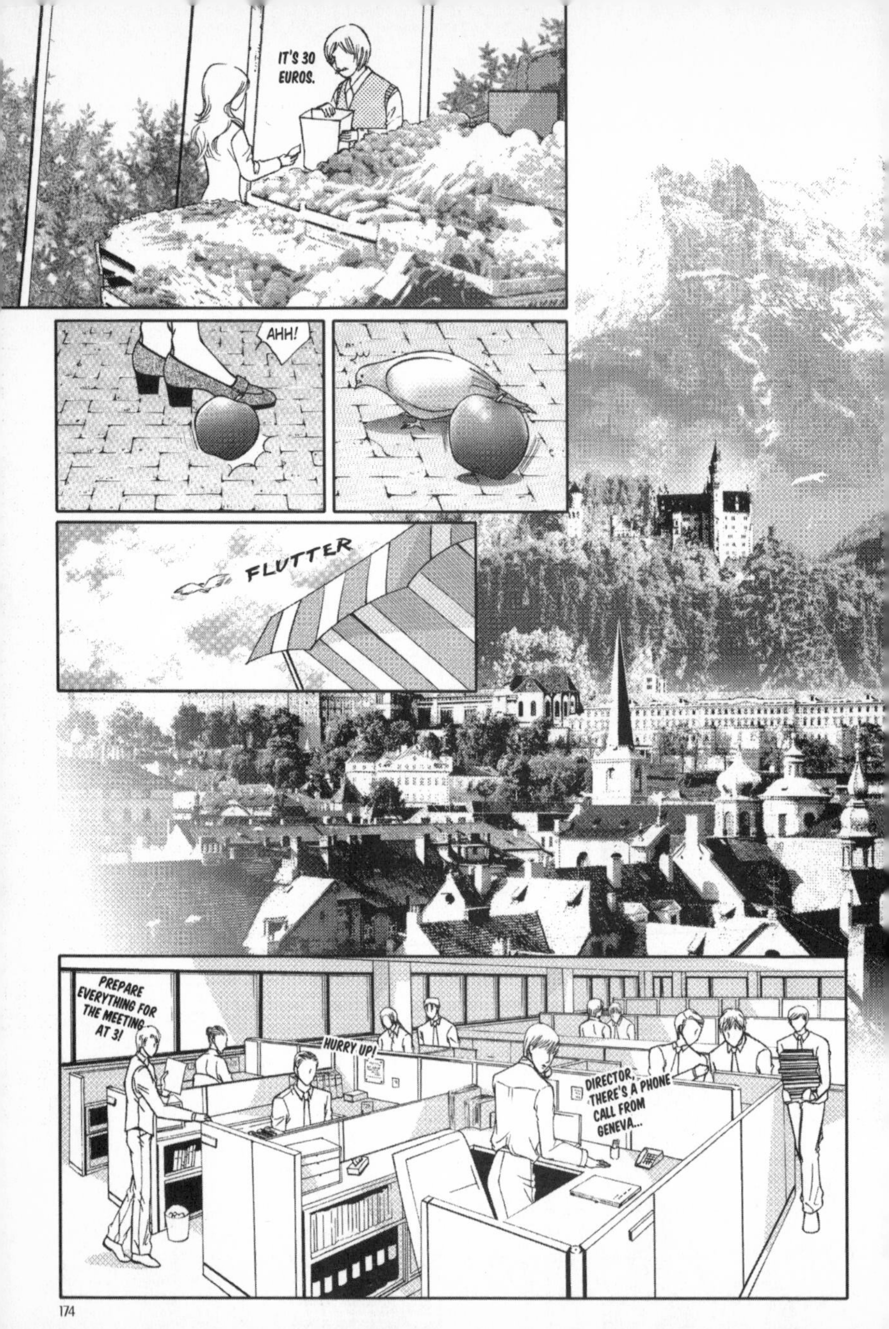
IT'S 30 EUROS.
AHH!
FLUTTER
PREPARE EVERYTHING FOR THE MEETING AT 3!
HURRY UP!
DIRECTOR, THERE'S A PHONE CALL FROM GENEVA...

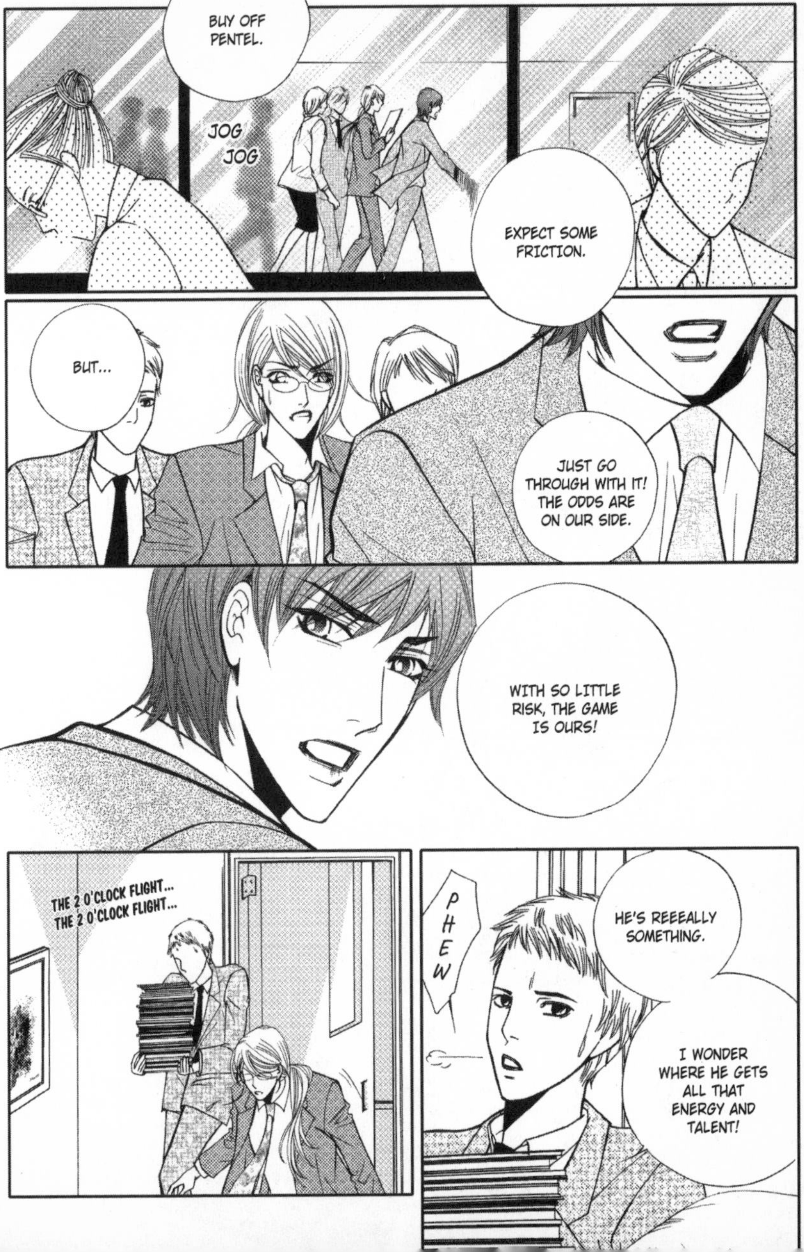
BUY OFF PENTEL.
JOG JOG
EXPECT SOME FRICTION.
BUT...
JUST GO THROUGH WITH IT! THE ODDS ARE ON OUR SIDE.
WITH SO LITTLE RISK, THE GAME IS OURS!
THE 2 O'CLOCK FLIGHT... THE 2 O'CLOCK FLIGHT...
PHEW
HE'S REEEALLY SOMETHING.
I WONDER WHERE HE GETS ALL THAT ENERGY AND TALENT!

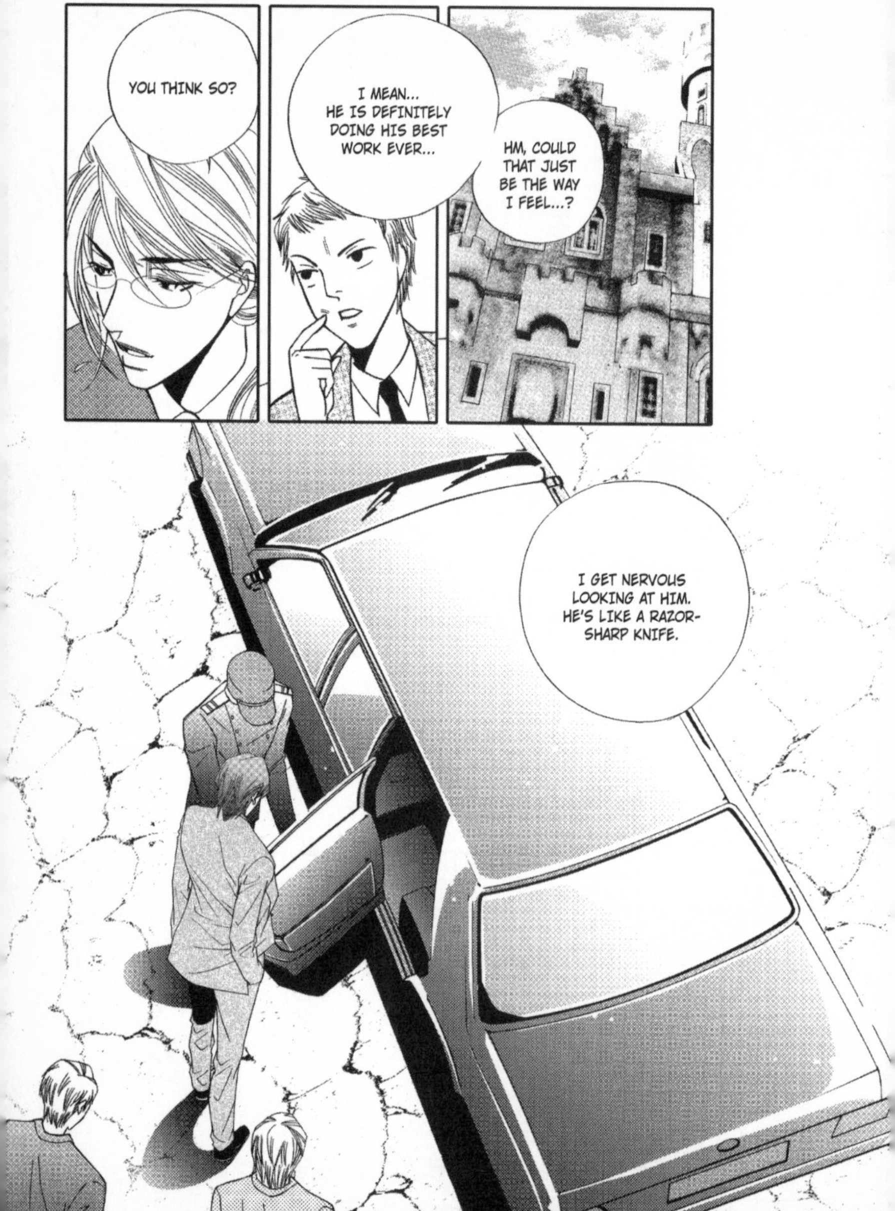
YOU THINK SO?
I MEAN... HE IS DEFINITELY DOING HIS BEST WORK EVER...
HM, COULD THAT JUST BE THE WAY I FEEL...?
I GET NERVOUS LOOKING AT HIM. HE'S LIKE A RAZOR-SHARP KNIFE.

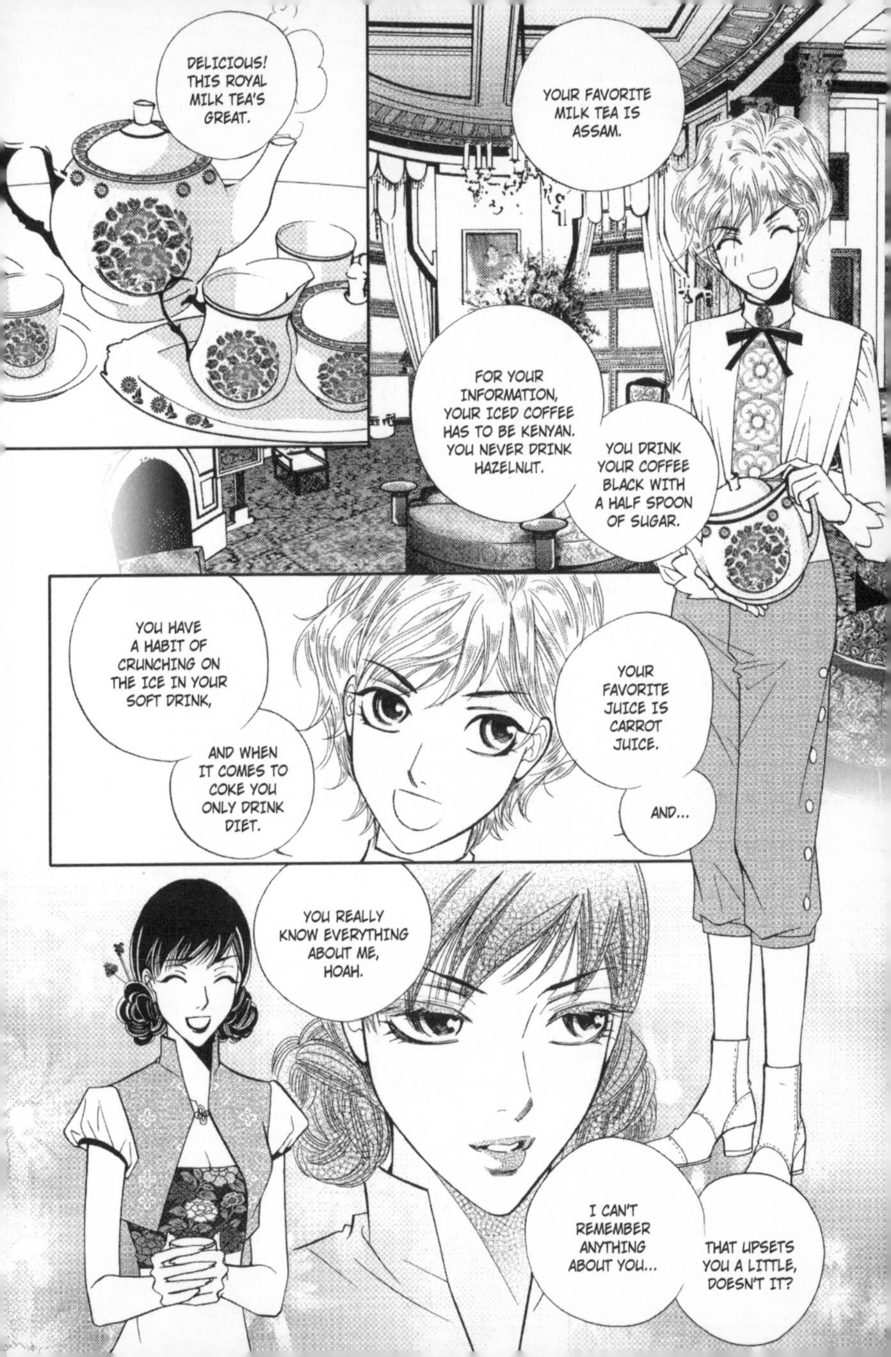
DELICIOUS! THIS ROYAL MILK TEA'S GREAT.
YOUR FAVORITE MILK TEA IS ASSAM.
FOR YOUR INFORMATION, YOUR ICED COFFEE HAS TO BE KENYAN. YOU NEVER DRINK HAZELNUT.
YOU DRINK YOUR COFFEE BLACK WITH A HALF SPOON OF SUGAR.
YOU HAVE A HABIT OF CRUNCHING ON THE ICE IN YOUR SOFT DRINK,
AND WHEN IT COMES TO COKE YOU ONLY DRINK DIET.
YOUR FAVORITE JUICE IS CARROT JUICE.
AND...
YOU REALLY KNOW EVERYTHING ABOUT ME, HOAH.
I CAN'T REMEMBER ANYTHING ABOUT YOU...
THAT UPSETS YOU A LITTLE, DOESN'T IT?

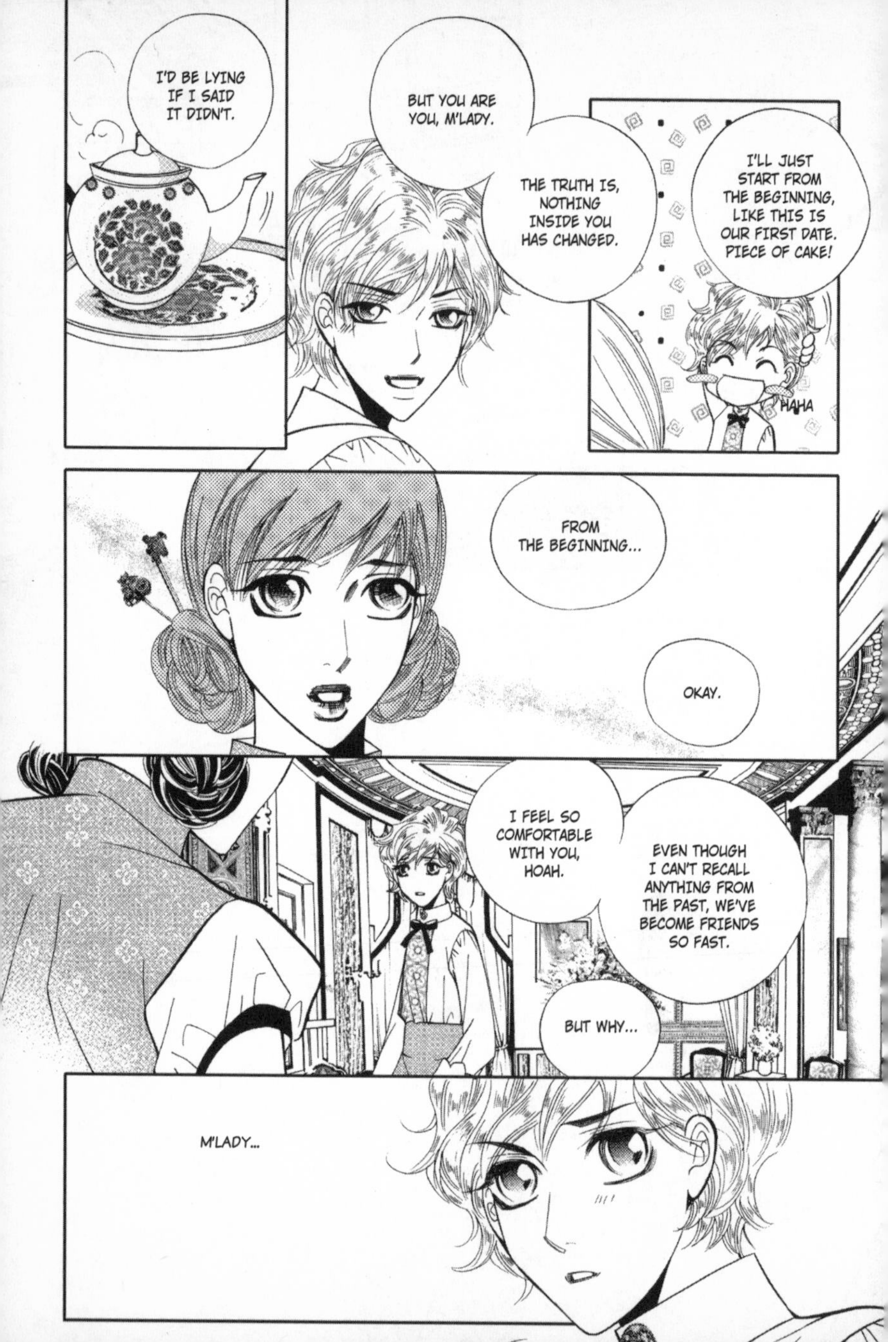
I'D BE LYING IF I SAID IT DIDN'T.
BUT YOU ARE YOU, M'LADY.
THE TRUTH IS, NOTHING INSIDE YOU HAS CHANGED.
I'LL JUST START FROM THE BEGINNING, LIKE THIS IS OUR FIRST DATE. PIECE OF CAKE!
HAHA
FROM THE BEGINNING...
OKAY.
I FEEL SO COMFORTABLE WITH YOU, HOAH.
EVEN THOUGH I CAN'T RECALL ANYTHING FROM THE PAST, WE'VE BECOME FRIENDS SO FAST.
BUT WHY...
M'LADY...

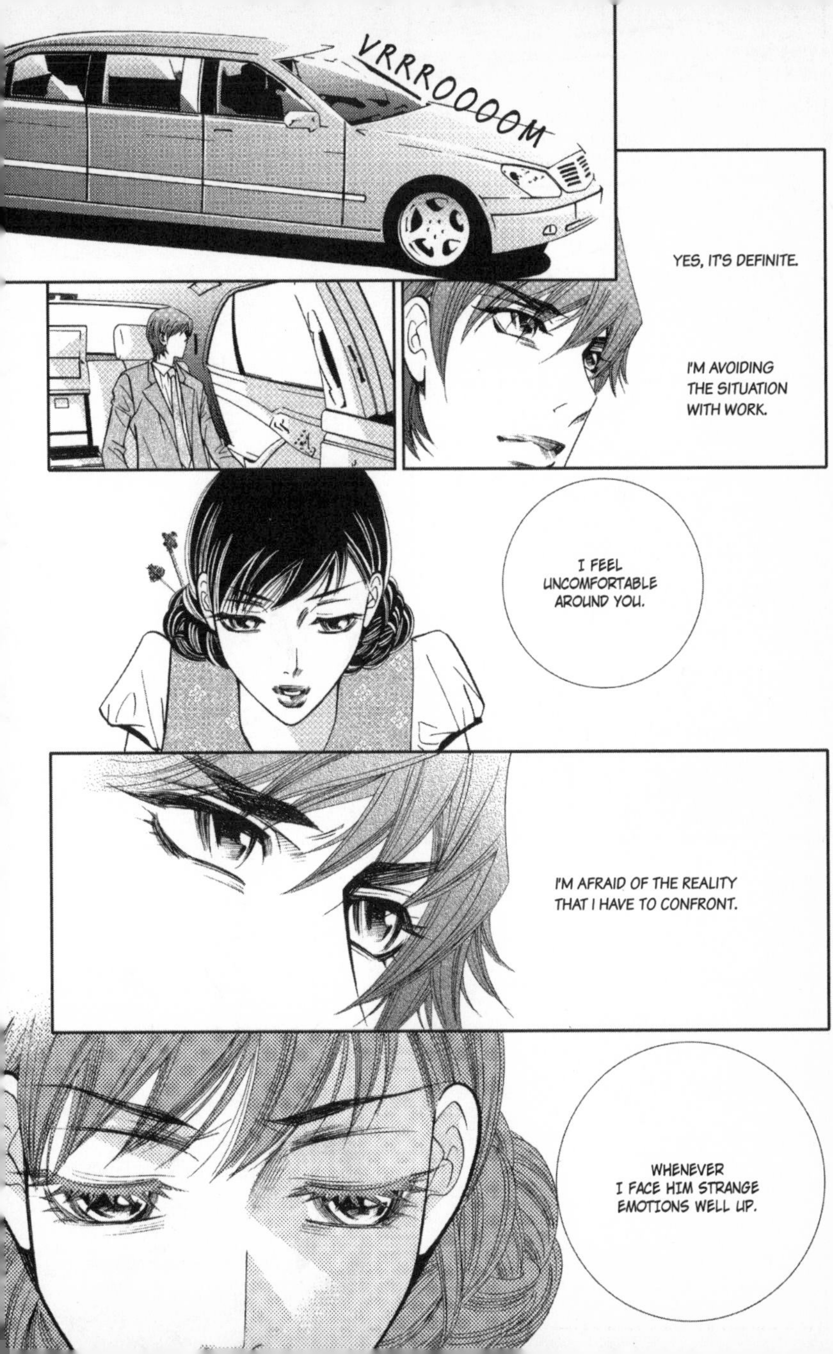
VRRROOOOOM
YES, IT'S DEFINITE.
I'M AVOIDING THE SITUATION WITH WORK.
I FEEL UNCOMFORTABLE AROUND YOU.
I'M AFRAID OF THE REALITY THAT I HAVE TO CONFRONT.
WHENEVER I FACE HIM STRANGE EMOTIONS WELL UP.

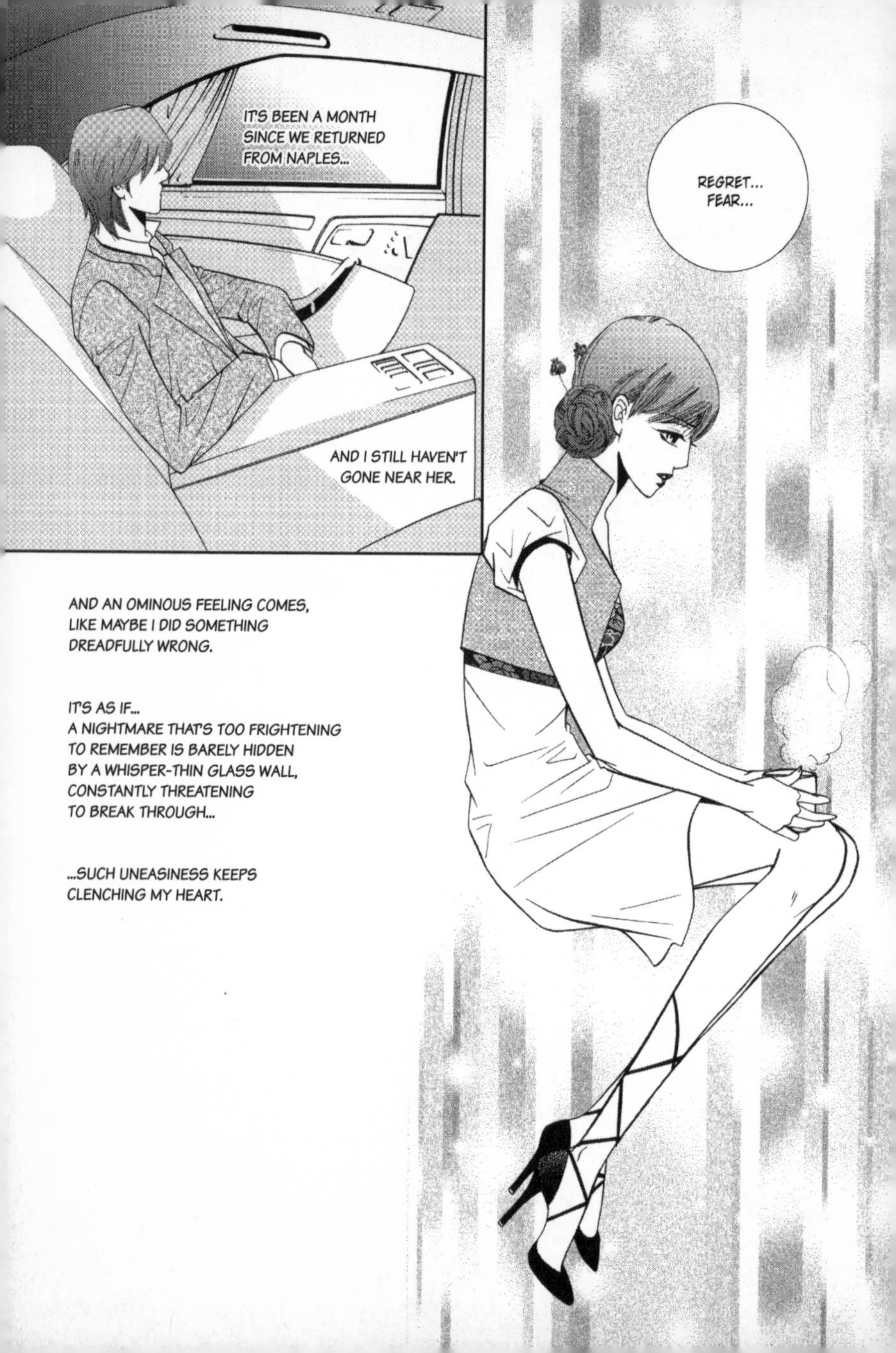
IT'S BEEN A MONTH SINCE WE RETURNED FROM NAPLES...
AND I STILL HAVEN'T GONE NEAR HER.
REGRET... FEAR...
AND AN OMINOUS FEELING COMES, LIKE MAYBE I DID SOMETHING DREADFULLY WRONG.
IT'S AS IF... A NIGHTMARE THAT'S TOO FRIGHTENING TO REMEMBER IS BARELY HIDDEN BY A WHISPER-THIN GLASS WALL, CONSTANTLY THREATENING TO BREAK THROUGH...
...SUCH UNEASINESS KEEPS CLENCHING MY HEART.

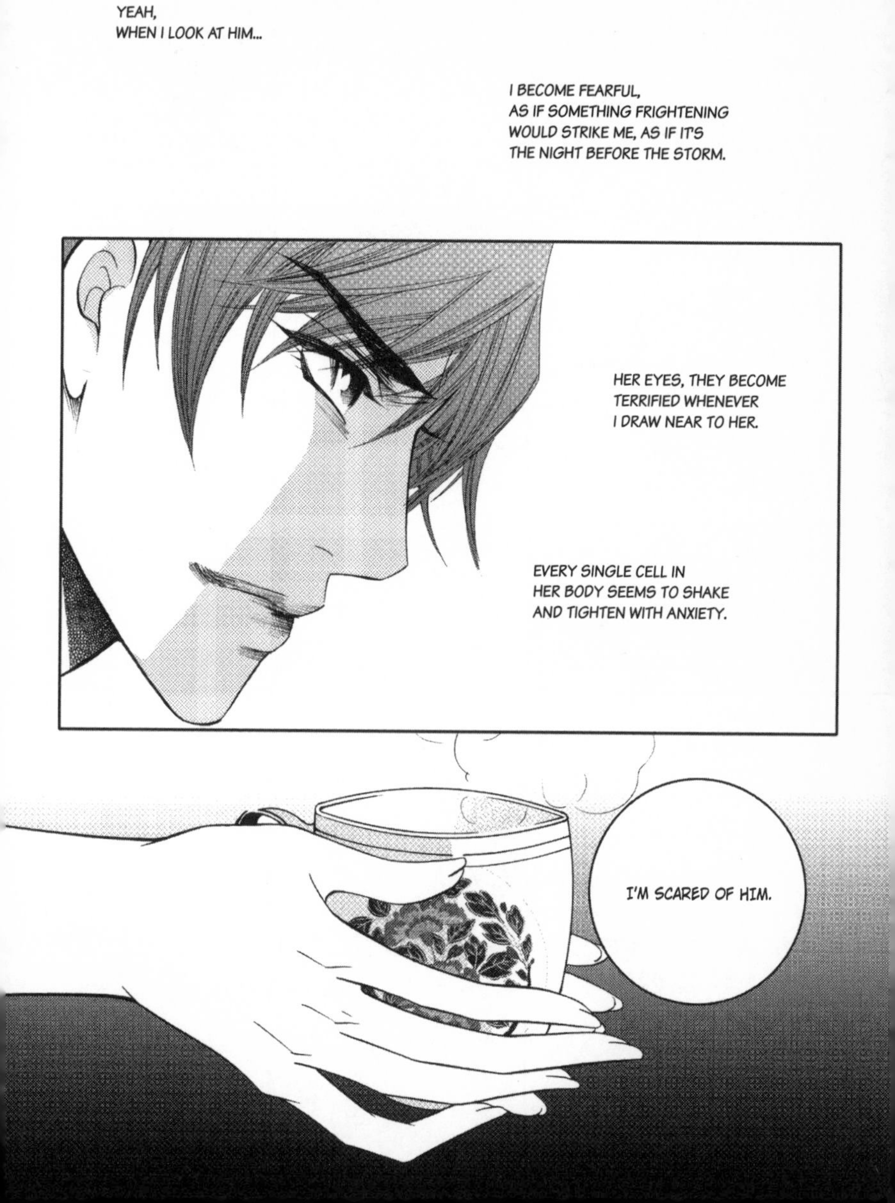
YEAH,
WHEN I LOOK AT HIM...
I BECOME FEARFUL, AS IF SOMETHING FRIGHTENING WOULD STRIKE ME, AS IF IT'S THE NIGHT BEFORE THE STORM.
HER EYES, THEY BECOME TERRIFIED WHENEVER I DRAW NEAR TO HER.
EVERY SINGLE CELL IN HER BODY SEEMS TO SHAKE AND TIGHTEN WITH ANXIETY.
I'M SCARED OF HIM.

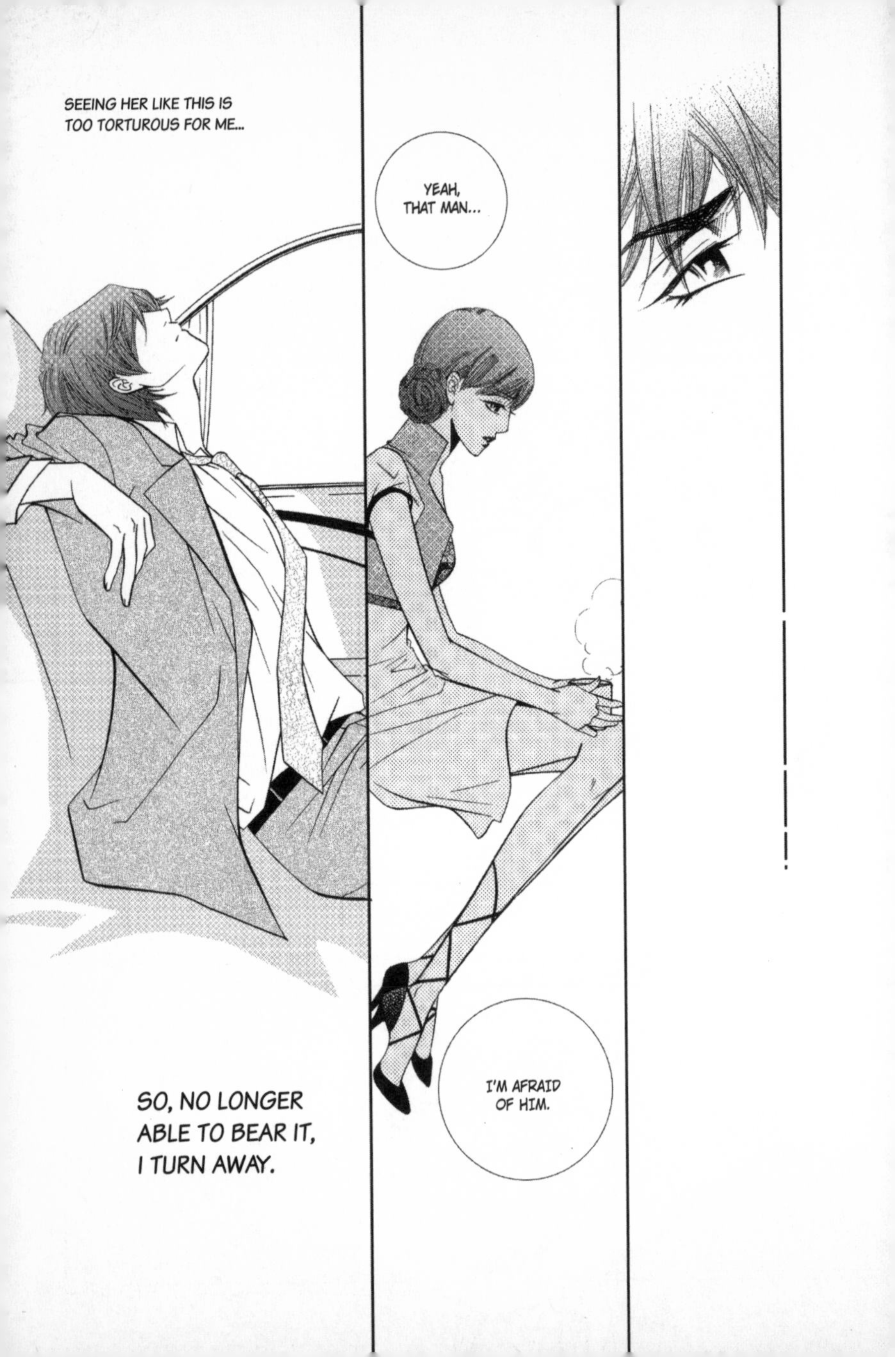
SEEING HER LIKE THIS IS
TOO TORTUROUS FOR ME...
SO, NO LONGER
ABLE TO BEAR IT,
I TURN AWAY.
YEAH,
THAT MAN...
I'M AFRAID
OF HIM.

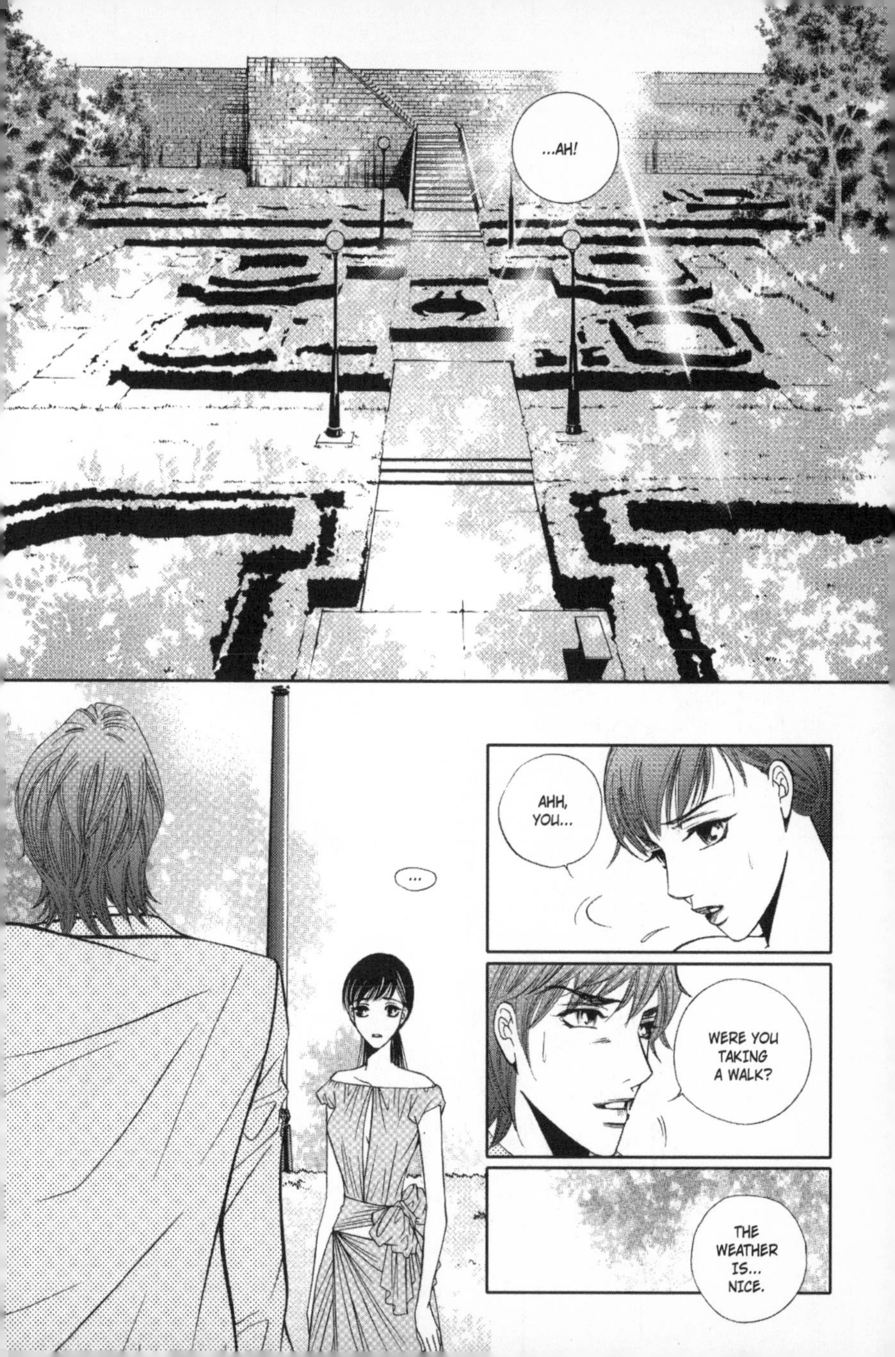
...AH!
...
AHH, YOU...
WERE YOU TAKING A WALK?
THE WEATHER IS... NICE.

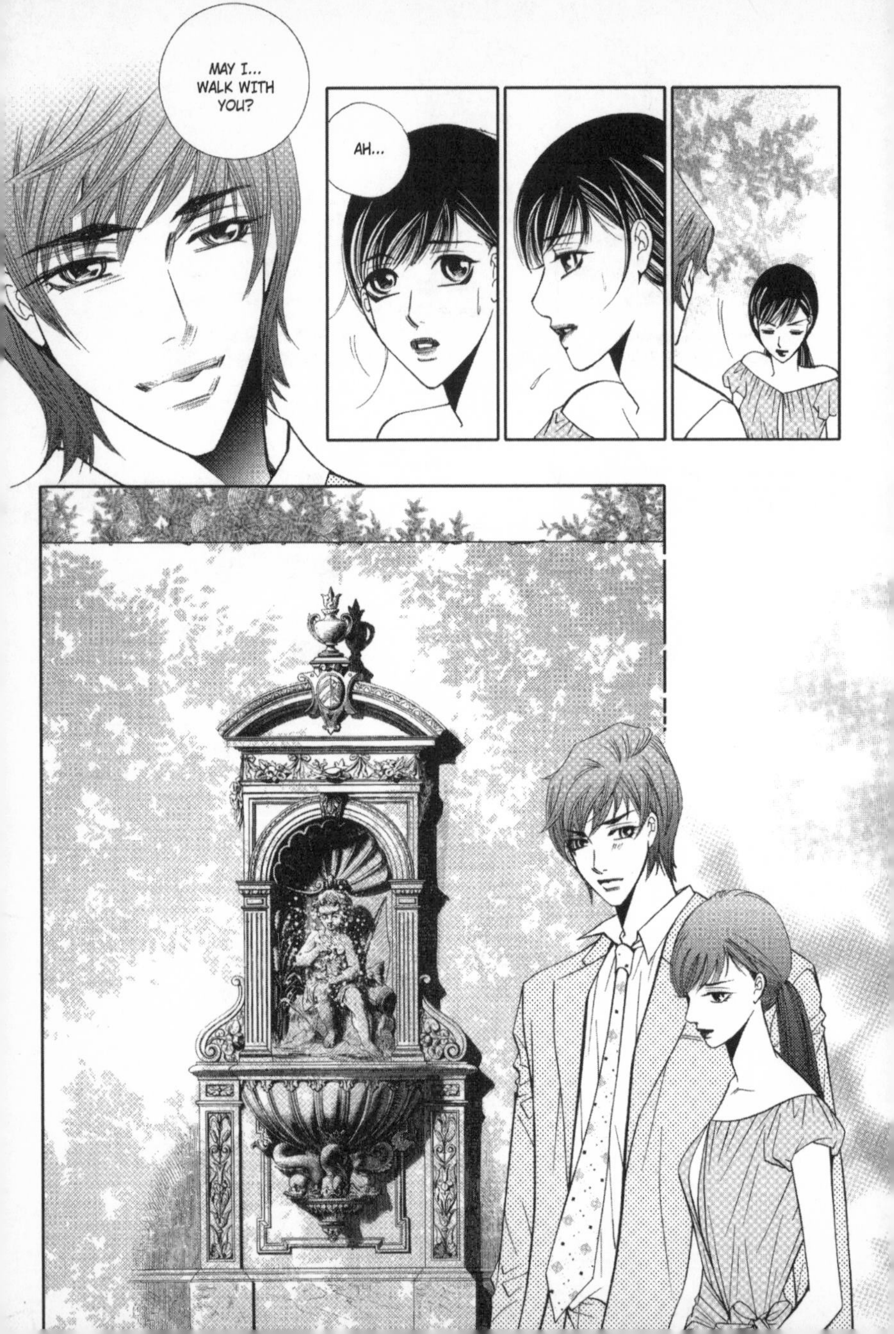
MAY I... WALK WITH YOU?
AH...

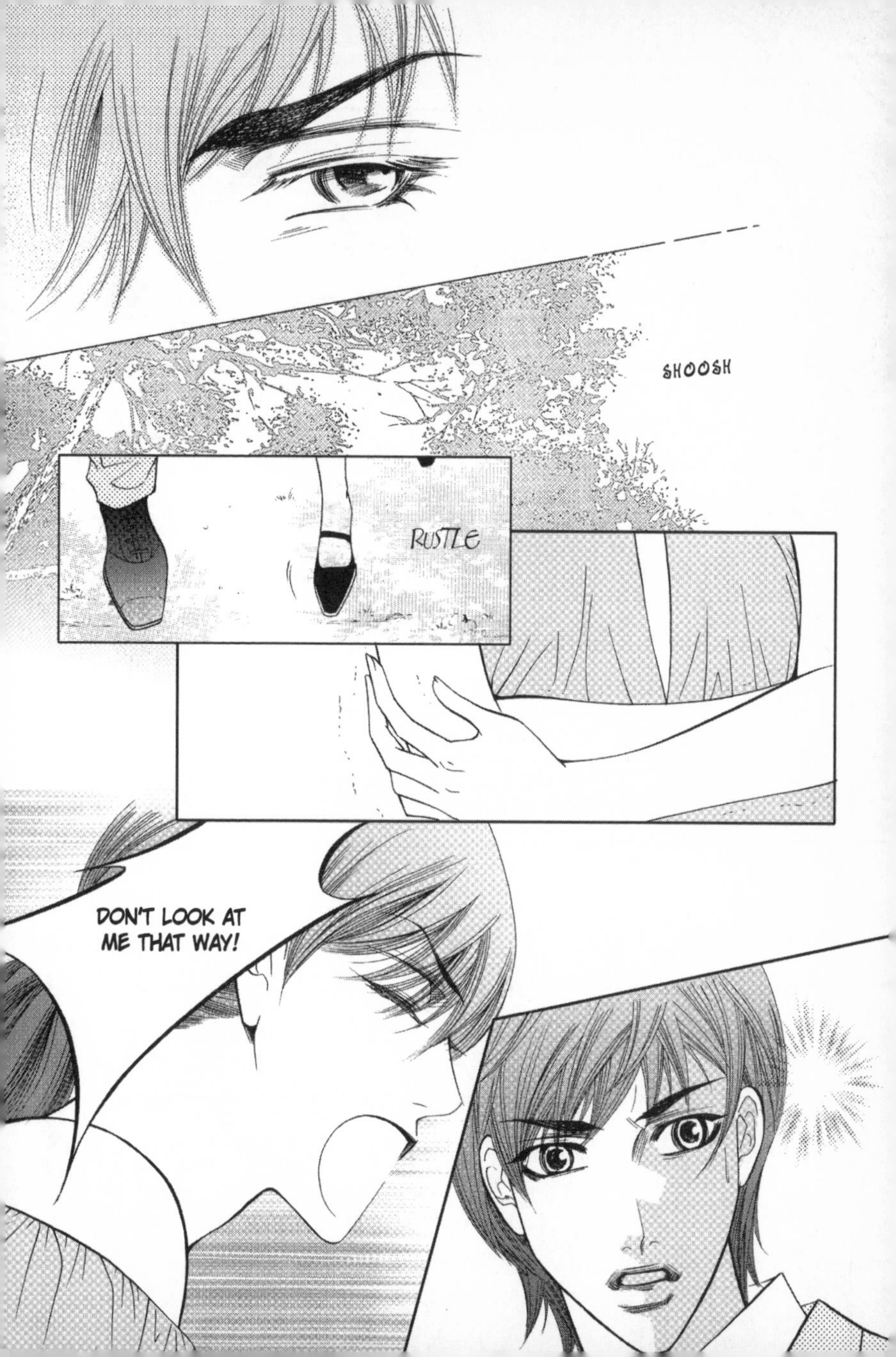
SHOOSH
RUSTLE
DON'T LOOK AT ME THAT WAY!

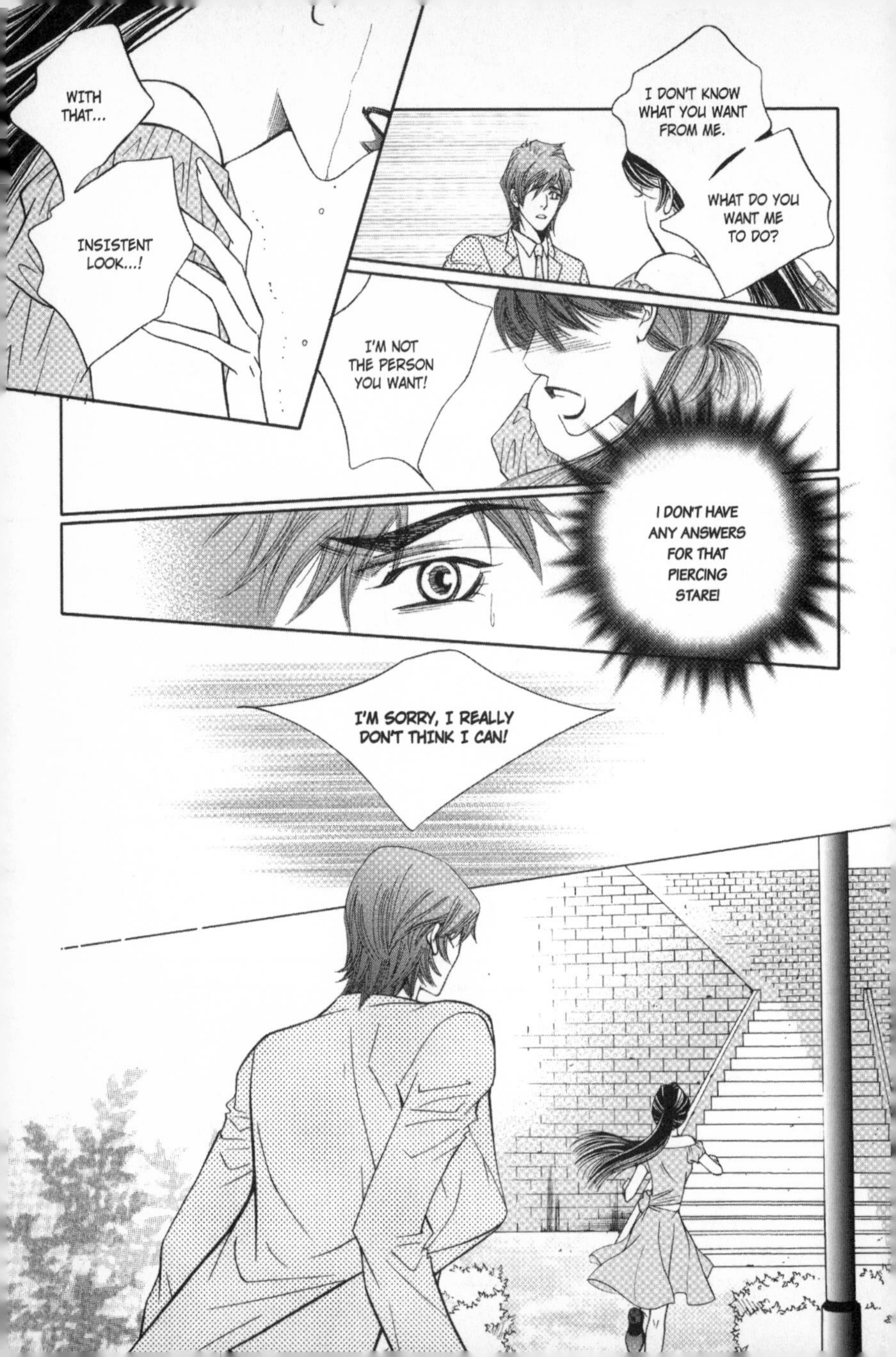
WITH THAT...
INSISTENT LOOK...!
I DON'T KNOW WHAT YOU WANT FROM ME.
WHAT DO YOU WANT ME TO DO?
I'M NOT THE PERSON YOU WANT!
I DON'T HAVE ANY ANSWERS FOR THAT PIERCING STARE!
I'M SORRY, I REALLY DON'T THINK I CAN!

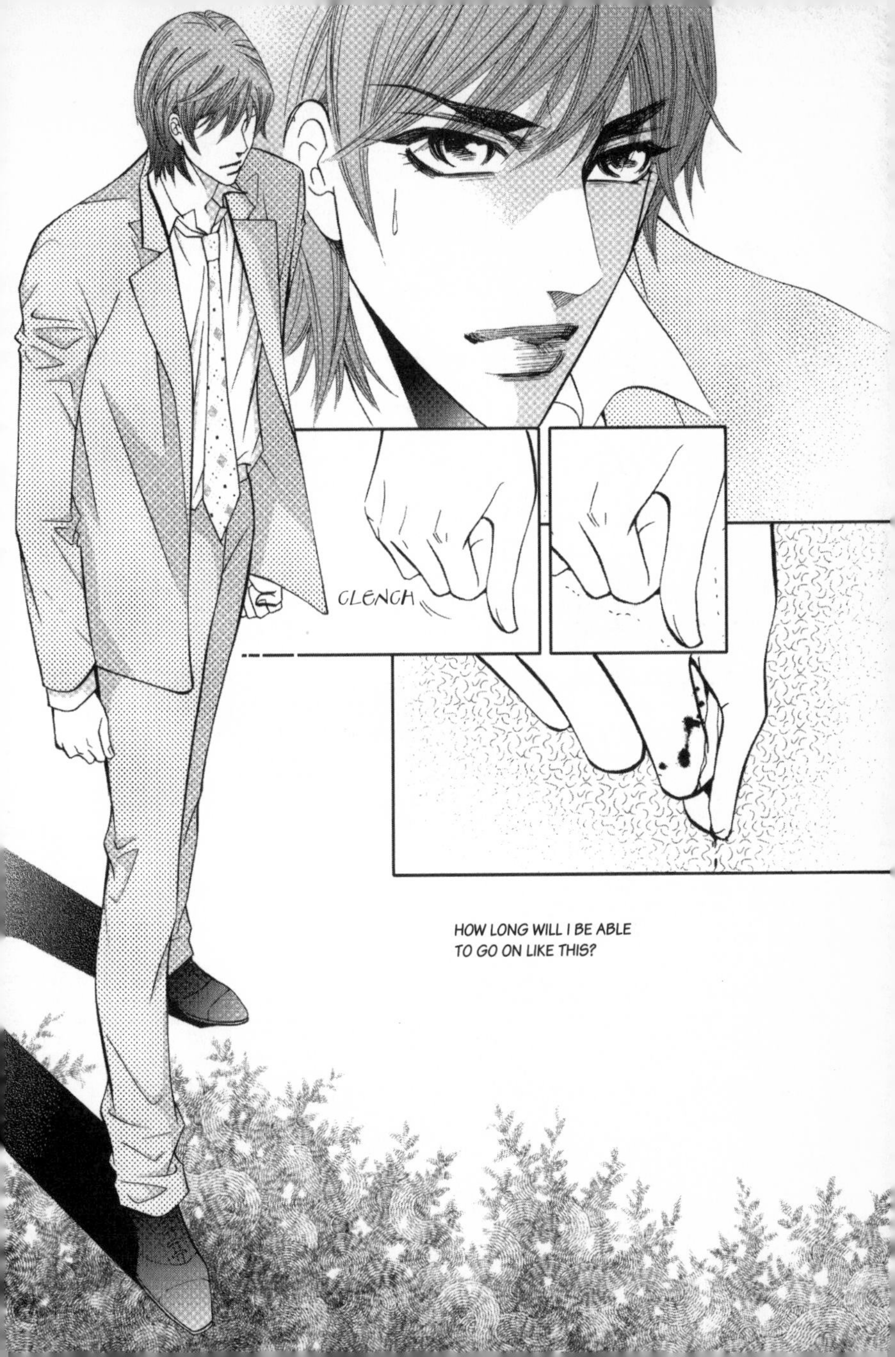
CLENCH
HOW LONG WILL I BE ABLE
TO GO ON LIKE THIS?

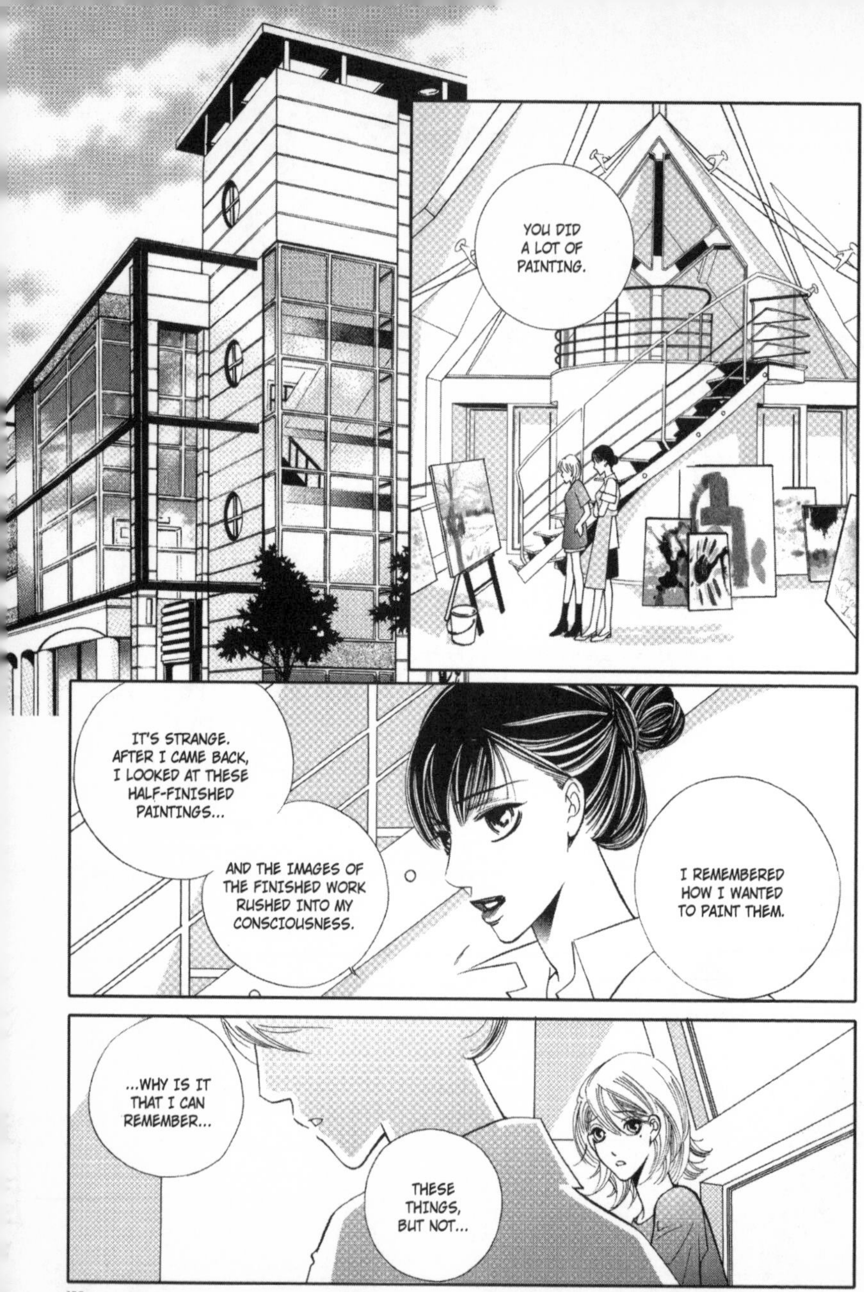
YOU DID A LOT OF PAINTING.
IT'S STRANGE. AFTER I CAME BACK, I LOOKED AT THESE HALF-FINISHED PAINTINGS...
AND THE IMAGES OF THE FINISHED WORK RUSHED INTO MY CONSCIOUSNESS.
I REMEMBERED HOW I WANTED TO PAINT THEM.
...WHY IS IT THAT I CAN REMEMBER...
THESE THINGS, BUT NOT...

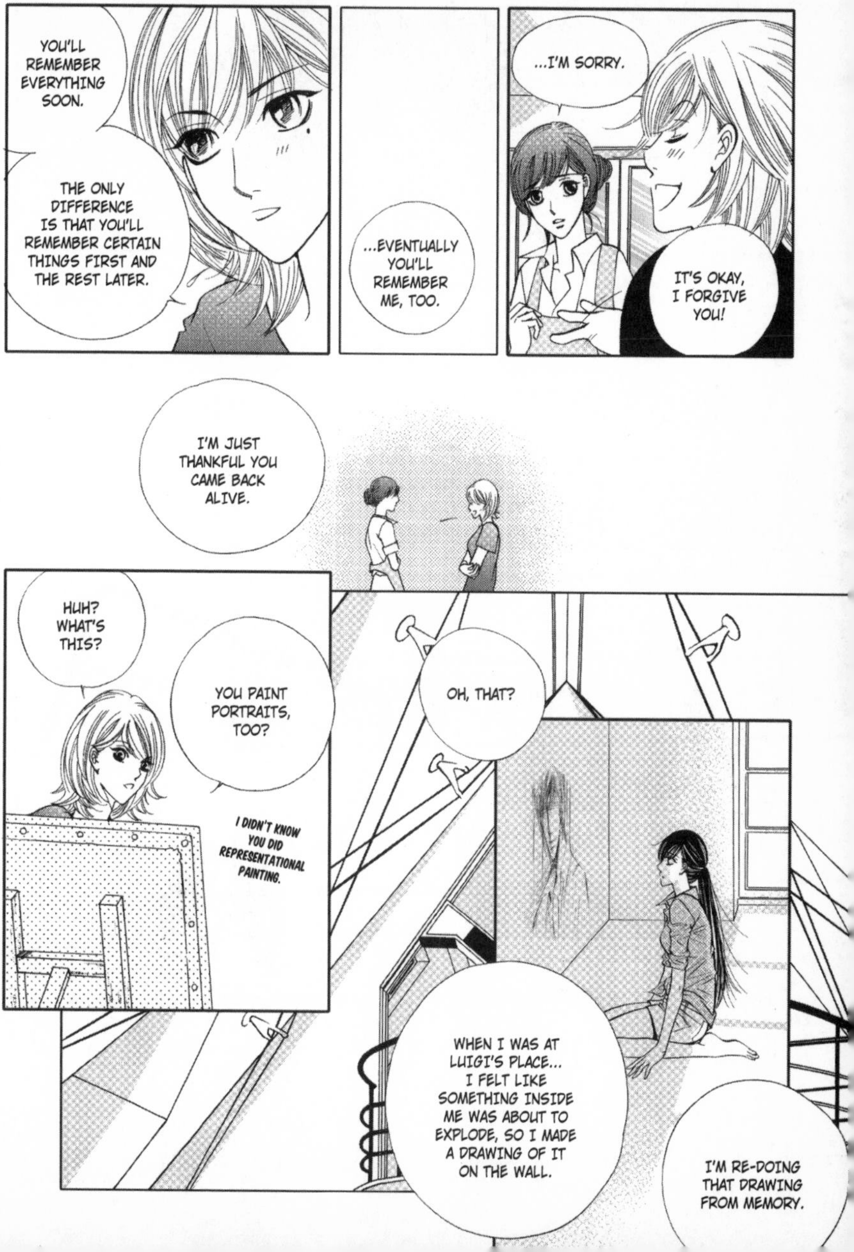
YOU'LL REMEMBER EVERYTHING SOON.
THE ONLY DIFFERENCE IS THAT YOU'LL REMEMBER CERTAIN THINGS FIRST AND THE REST LATER.
...EVENTUALLY YOU'LL REMEMBER ME, TOO.
...I'M SORRY.
IT'S OKAY, I FORGIVE YOU!
I'M JUST THANKFUL YOU CAME BACK ALIVE.
HUH? WHAT'S THIS?
YOU PAINT PORTRAITS, TOO?
I DIDN'T KNOW YOU DID REPRESENTATIONAL PAINTING.
OH, THAT?
WHEN I WAS AT LUIGI'S PLACE... I FELT LIKE SOMETHING INSIDE ME WAS ABOUT TO EXPLODE, SO I MADE A DRAWING OF IT ON THE WALL.
I'M RE-DOING THAT DRAWING FROM MEMORY.

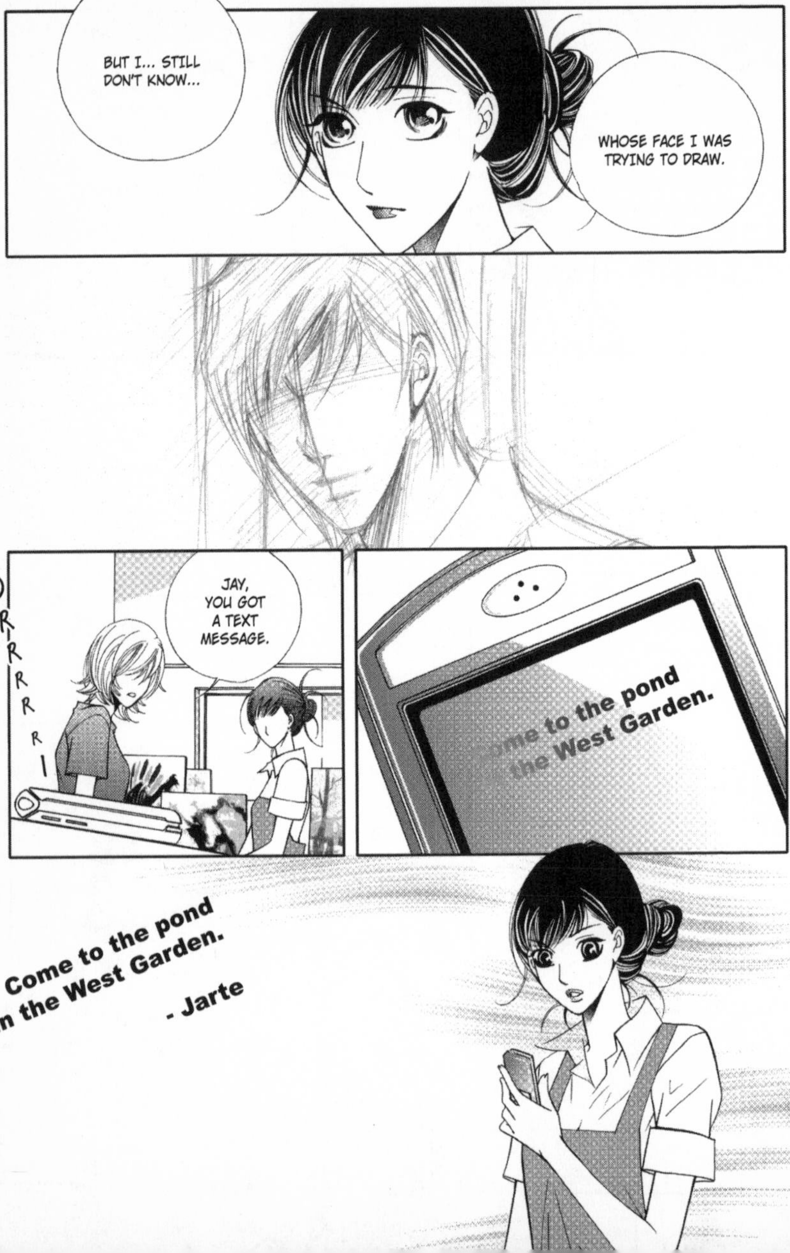

BUT I... STILL DON'T KNOW...
WHOSE FACE I WAS TRYING TO DRAW.
DRRRRRI
JAY, YOU GOT A TEXT MESSAGE.
ome to the pond
the West Garden.
Come to the pond
in the West Garden.
- Jarte

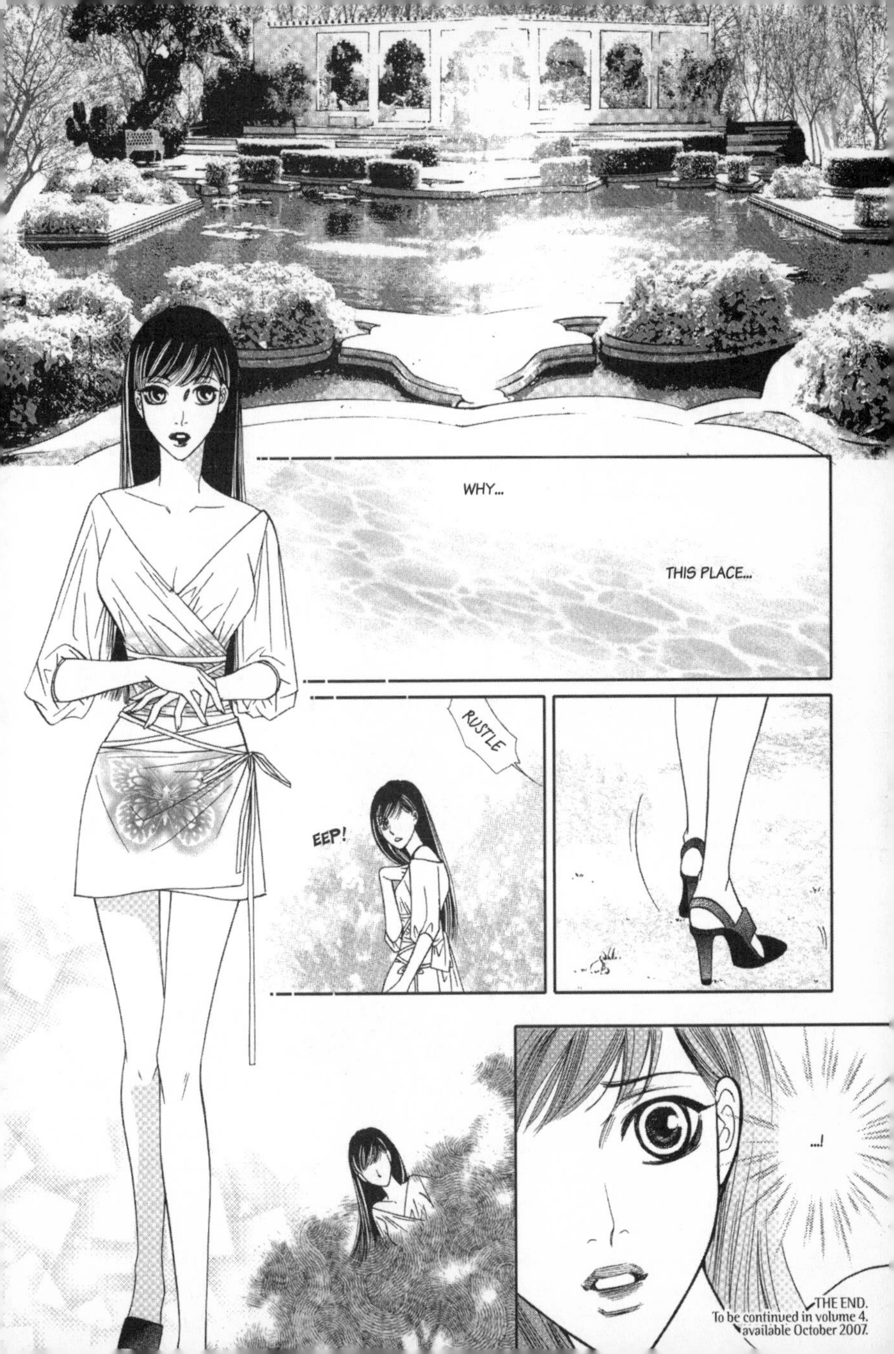
WHY...
THIS PLACE...
RUSTLE
EEP!
...!
THE END.
To be continued in volume 4,
available October 2007.

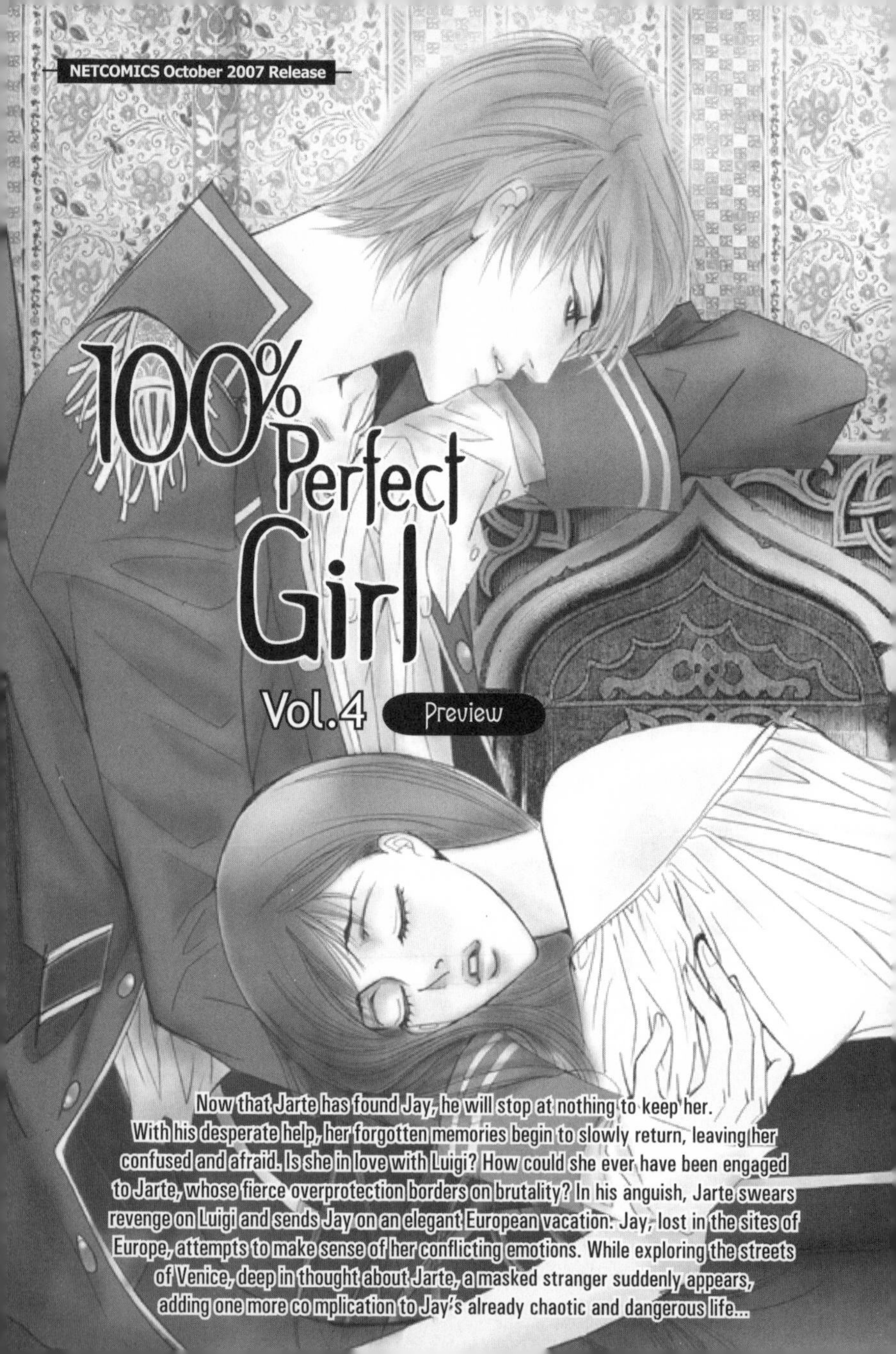
NETCOMICS October 2007 Release
100% Perfect Girl
Vol.4
Preview
Now that Jarte has found Jay, he will stop at nothing to keep her.
With his desperate help, her forgotten memories begin to slowly return, leaving her confused and afraid. Is she in love with Luigi? How could she ever have been engaged to Jarte, whose fierce overprotection borders on brutality? In his anguish, Jarte swears revenge on Luigi and sends Jay on an elegant European vacation. Jay, lost in the sites of Europe, attempts to make sense of her conflicting emotions. While exploring the streets of Venice, deep in thought about Jarte, a masked stranger suddenly appears, adding one more co mplication to Jay's already chaotic and dangerous life...

9 Faces of Love

Manhwa Novella Collection: Vol. 2

Presenting the second volume of NETCOMICS Manhwa Novella Collection --an anthology of the most prominent Korean authors and their works in which every page blazes with uniqueness and originality! Volume 2 of this sensational series contains nine of the most popular shorter works by Wann, the author of *100% Perfect Girl* and *Can't Lose You*. Wann's colorful vignettes depict the most vexing of human emotions, love, in all its guises:

- RETURN OF PRINCESS ROUANA
- BELIEVE YE YOUR EYES?
- A SHORT GAME ABOUT A CHANCE ENCOUNTER
- AUTOMATON
- A COLD
- PURPLE EYES
- LEUCADIAN
- MINT FLAVOR
- A FLYING LESSON

CAN'T LOSE YOU

A whirlwind tale of vanity and conceit, *Can't Lose You* tells the story of two characters who come from opposite worlds, but are united by the most unlikely of circumstances.

Yooi is a desperate girl working day and night to earn pennies in hopes of one day paying off her father's debts and reuniting their family.

Lida lives a life of privilege and excess. She's the heiress to an unbelievable fortune and a betrothed in a marriage she can't wait to fulfill.

Yet, when the two girls meet they discover they share identical faces and their lives take an unexpected turn.

Available now at your favorite bookstores.
Read them online at www.NETCOMICS.com!

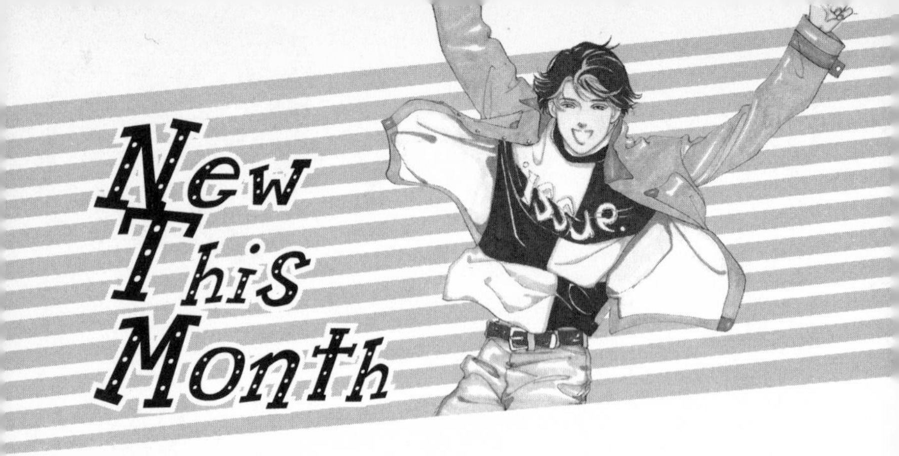
New This Month

Let Dai vol.8

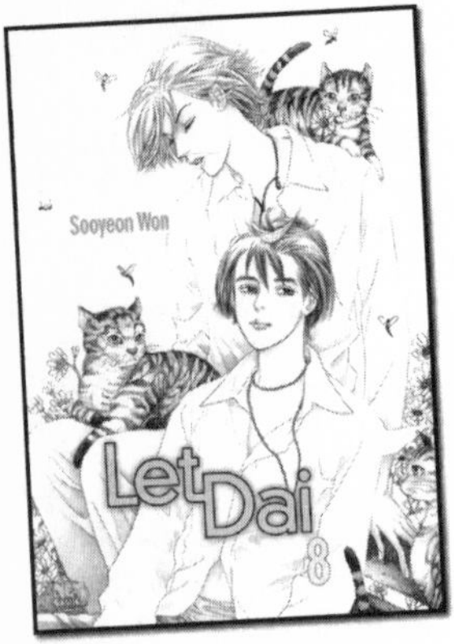
Sooyeon Won
Let Dai
8

by Sooyeon Won

Fate deals a cruel hand to Yooneun as she dares the universe to bring Jaehee to her. It does along with Dai. And Yooneun discovers the depths of a new feeling...fury. Meanwhile, Dai Lee's powerful political family comes together for the first time and Dai has a few words to say to them over their hypocritical treatment of his grandmother. Lying exhausted in the hospital, Jaehee's mother suspects the true reasons for Jaehee's strange behavior. Rival school gangs plot revenge against Dai. The world is closing in on their tragic love affair. Jaehee and Dai rush to the beach to find some peace and relief, but even a simple trip to the beach can become more complicated than anyone could ever imagine.

Boy Princess vol.8

by Seyoung Kim

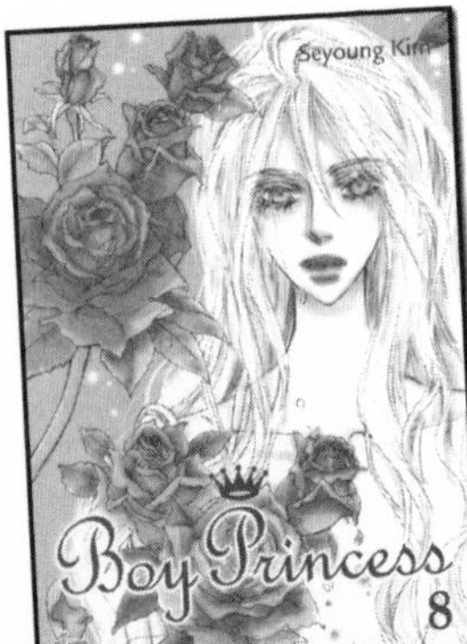
Seyoung Kim
Boy Princess
8

Prince Jed lies imprisoned on charges of treason. Now only a heartbeat away from the throne, Prince Derek wishes to end his bitter conflict with Jed, once and for all. He offers a way to bring back Nicole, but only in exchange for Jed's life. Jed must confess to every dark crime he's falsely accused of and then suffer a death sentence. Glewhin and June discover a horrible treachery amongst their allies and Princess Reiny's life may be at stake. Meanwhile, even as he languishes in prison, Jed commands the loyalty of the army and his soldiers offer him a dreadful choice. Fight the false charges of treason in a trial he's doomed to lose…or overthrow the king and make the treason charges into a reality. The old king observes all the political games with a calculating eye. Soon, he'll make his move and eliminate the game of all its players. And once again, Nicole lies at the center of the plans.

Click vol.3

by Youngran Lee

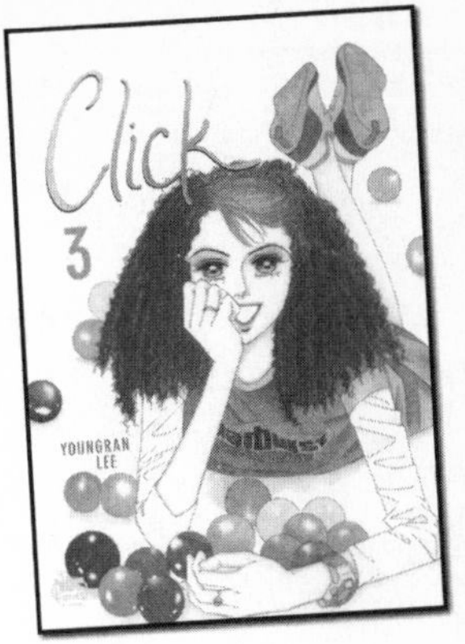

Click
3
YOUNGRAN LEE

Joonha, the transgender head case, and Taehyun, the hotshot rich kid, are actually becoming buddies—so much so that they even team up to take down a card shark at the casino Taehyun's family runs. Is the friendship about to turn into something… more? Meanwhile, figures from Joonha's past keep popping up—and stirring up real trouble. His old friend Jinhoo, now a star piano player, is back in Seoul and not going anywhere. And former nice girl Heewon: is she really as nasty as she acts, or is it all a front? Could she be the reason why brainy Jihan suddenly isn't wearing his glasses anymore? The twists keep coming in the fastest, funniest installment yet of this head-spinning take on young love!

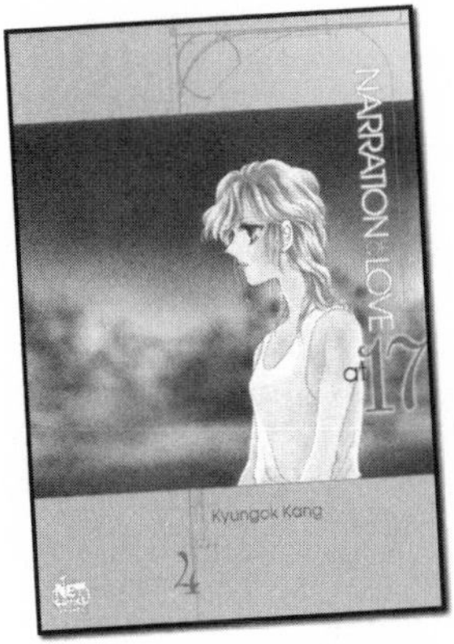

NARRATION OF LOVE at 17
Kyungok Kang
4

Narration of Love at 17 vol.4

by Kyungok Kang

While rehearsing for *The Little Prince*, and nursing a crush for Yunho, Seyoung finds out that he likes her. But her best friend, Hyunjung, likes him, too! For the sake of friendship, should Seyoung tell Yunho to leave her alone? At last the play opens, but will anyone come? A picture of Seyoung is on display in a photography exhibit, but does she look okay? Seyoung has a heart-to-heart with Hyunjung, but is it too late? Though at first reticent to play the fox, Seyoung discovers herself in the part. And as she prepares to bid farewell to 17, Seyoung realizes that, topsy-turvy though it is, life is worth the risk! Finally the dramatic conclusion of *Narration of Love at 17* is here!

Your Lover vol.3

by Seungwon Han

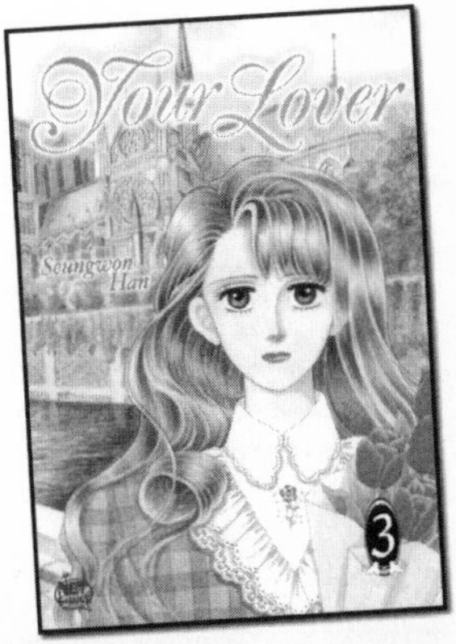

Your Lover
Seungwon Han
3

Despite Gangbin's heartfelt love, Marie struggles to resolve their growing relationship with her past engagement with his deceased brother. Inner and outer obstacles surround them. Joongyoo aggressively courts Marie, while the famous actress Chaeryun dangerously obsesses over Gangbin. Things look up when Marie finally expresses her deepest feelings by telling Gangbin that she loves him, too. However, a single night of passion between them proves to have lifelong ramifications. Suddenly, the question of marriage becomes much more urgent. Pushed into desperation, Chaeryun devises an insidious plan sure to destroy the trust between the two lovers.

Let's be Perverts

Vol. **4**

by Youjung Lee

After hours of watching porn, Perverto and his loser pals have it all figured out: Get a call-girl! Will they know what to do with her when they find her? Hongdan and Mr. Pi keep falling into each other's arms, so Mr. Pi exposes his lusty deeds. Hongdan is impressed! But she can't stop thinking of Perverto, and Perverto can't stop thinking of girls. Nerdy Eunwul struggles to hide her shameful secrets, but school rumors can't be stopped. Is it too late for Perverto to score? Is it too late for Hongdan to graduate?! Will anyone live happily ever after? Hearts, minds, entire identities flip-flop and hop-frog each other in this concluding volume of the inventive, ribald series, *Let's Be Perverts*!

Roureville

Vol. **2**

by E.Hae

Evan Pryce made his name investigating dangerous mysteries, but nothing can prepare him for the small, sleepy town of Roureville. Evan settles in to the quiet life, living with good-natured Jayce and writing his novel. However, when a violent attempt is made on his life, Evan realizes he's very close to uncovering the town's dirty little secret. He renews his investigation and discovers there are as many secrets in Roureville as there are people. Indeed, the biggest secret may have been living with him right under his nose: Jayce.

Dokebi Bride Vol.6

by Marley

Alone and abandoned, Sunbi flees Seoul for the coast in an attempt to reconnect with her past. When she accidentally leaves the train at the wrong stop, she finds herself stranded in a tiny rural village where she encounters a woman full of resentment toward her elderly and decrepit mother. Still plagued by vague, haunting memories of her own mother, Sunbi must find a way to free the woman from the past that torments her—and, in doing so, comes face-to-face with her own demons…

Emperor's Castle Vol.4

by Sungmo Kim

The Emperor now lies bloodied and prone against Ki-Do-Ryu, the Japanese antithesis of the Korean martial art Shi-Nan-Joo. Horribly wounded, Chunhoo is all that lies in between his son Sukgi and the deadly blade of the Japanese master swordsman Matsui. Sukgi barely escapes, bidding the prostitute Semi a melancholy farewell and vowing to come back for her. He flees to the mountains where he meets the secretive and deadly siren Rou. Like him, she's got a history written in blood and a heart turned cold for revenge. One thing's for sure. When vengeance comes, it will come in spades.

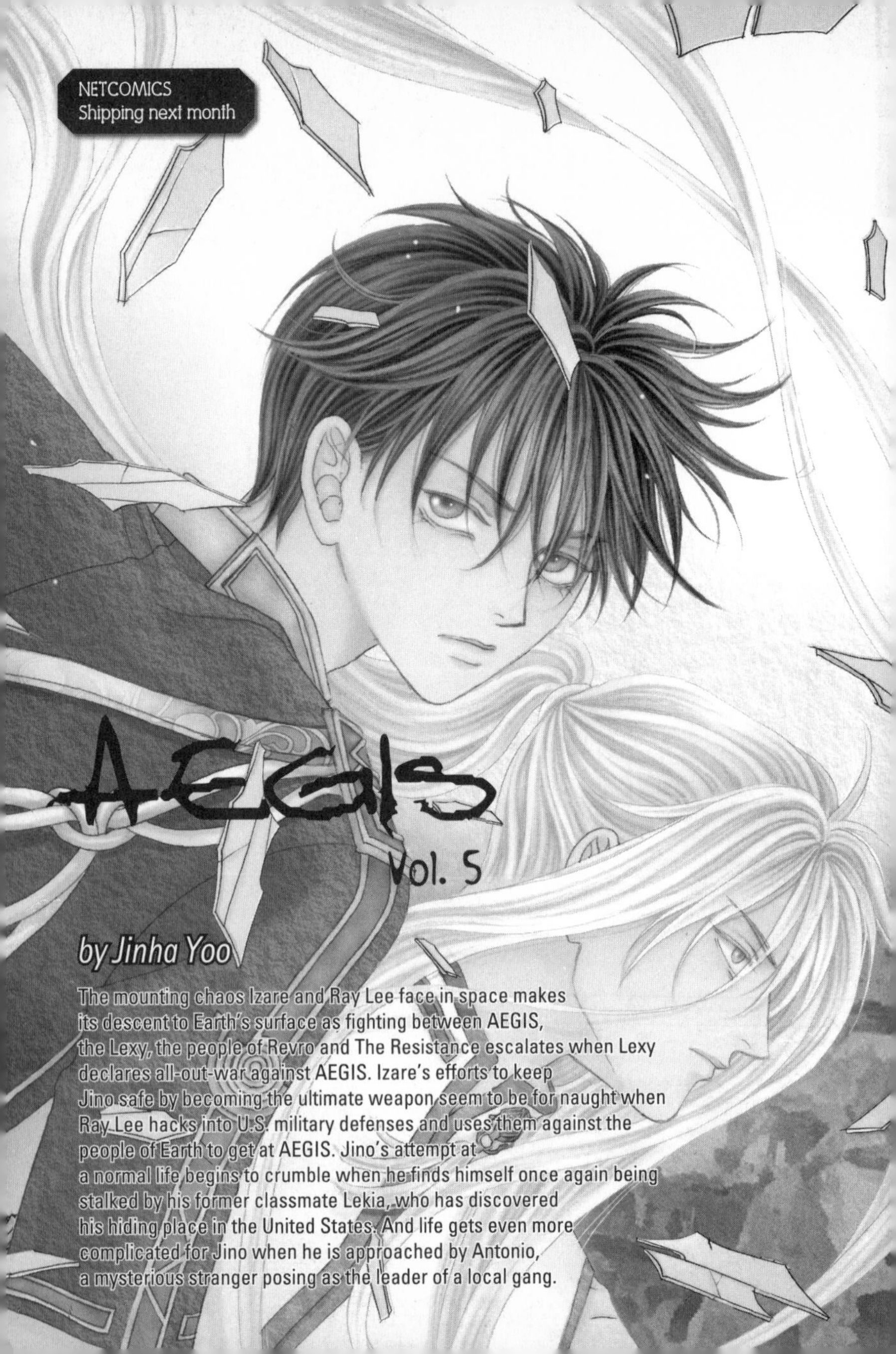
NETCOMICS
Shipping next month
AEGIS
Vol. 5
by Jinha Yoo
The mounting chaos Izare and Ray Lee face in space makes its descent to Earth's surface as fighting between AEGIS, the Lexy, the people of Revro and The Resistance escalates when Lexy declares all-out-war against AEGIS. Izare's efforts to keep Jino safe by becoming the ultimate weapon seem to be for naught when Ray Lee hacks into U.S. military defenses and uses them against the people of Earth to get at AEGIS. Jino's attempt at a normal life begins to crumble when he finds himself once again being stalked by his former classmate Lekia, who has discovered his hiding place in the United States. And life gets even more complicated for Jino when he is approached by Antonio, a mysterious stranger posing as the leader of a local gang.

OPERATION LIBERATE MEN

by Mira Lee

Ashamed of failing her high school entrance exam, a 16-year-old tomboy Sooha just wants to disappear off the face of the Earth. However, when she yells it out loud a mysterious stranger named Ganesha approaches with an offer. He comes from a magical realm called the Para Kingdom ruled by a female military hierarchy that enslaves the male population. Ganesha offers to grant Sooha's wish if she will help liberate the men. Thinking his country sounds like paradise, She instantly agrees. But, when she arrives the men look to her as their new leader and Sooha learns that fate has a funny way of leading people to their destiny.

바람의 나라
KINGDOM OF THE WINDS

by Kimjin

Against the backdrop of the ancient Kingdom of Koguryeo,
the story takes the reader into one of the murkiest periods in Korean history.

Blending fact with fantasy, the drama and mystique of the ancient land
of Koguryeo unfolds around the tragic and romantic entanglements of
the Kingdom's Royal Family.

Koguryeo's ambitious King bravely takes on his powerful neighbors in
this enchanting, poetic and ancient Shakespearean conflict, luring the reader
helplessly into a new realm of love, tragedy, courage and cunning.

Spirits, demons, and imaginary beings lurk within for those daring enough
to open its pages and submerge themselves into the captivating world of
the *Kingdom of the Winds.*